REAPING THE WHIRLWIND

Dominic Etzold

REAPING THE WHIRLWIND

The U-Boat War Off North America During World War I

SCHIFFER MILITARY
4880 Lower Valley Road
Atglen, PA 19310

Other Schiffer books on related subjects

Dönitz's Crews: Germany's U-Boat Sailors in World War II,
French L. MacLean, 978-0-7643-3356-9

The Imperial German Navy of World War I: A Comprehensive Photographic Study of the Kaiser's Naval Forces,
Jeffrey Judge, 978-0-7643-5216-4

Copyright © 2023 by Dominic Etzold

Library of Congress Control Number: 2023931151

All rights reserved. No part of this work may be reproduced or used in any form or by any means—graphic, electronic, or mechanical, including photocopying or information storage and retrieval systems—without written permission from the publisher.

The scanning, uploading, and distribution of this book or any part thereof via the Internet or any other means without the permission of the publisher is illegal and punishable by law. Please purchase only authorized editions and do not participate in or encourage the electronic piracy of copyrighted materials.

"Schiffer Military" and the arrow logo are trademarks of Schiffer Publishing, Ltd.

Designed by Christopher Bower
Cover design by Justin Watkinson
Type set in Times New Roman /Neue Aachen Pro

ISBN: 978-0-7643-6704-5
Printed in China

Published by Schiffer Publishing, Ltd.
4880 Lower Valley Road
Atglen, PA 19310
Phone: (610) 593-1777; Fax: (610) 593-2002
Email: Info@schifferbooks.com
Web: www.schifferbooks.com

For our complete selection of fine books on this and related subjects, please visit our website at www.schifferbooks.com. You may also write for a free catalog.

Schiffer Publishing's titles are available at special discounts for bulk purchases for sales promotions or premiums. Special editions, including personalized covers, corporate imprints, and excerpts, can be created in large quantities for special needs. For more information, contact the publisher.

We are always looking for people to write books on new and related subjects. If you have an idea for a book, please contact us at proposals@schifferbooks.com.

DEDICATION

Dedicated to Edward and Edmund,
who probably told me more than they knew.

Contents

Acknowledgments... 8
Introduction... 10

Chapter 1   America, Meet Deutschland............................ 16
Chapter 2   A Series of Unfortunate Events...................... 31
Chapter 3   The Empire Strikes Back............................. 41
Chapter 4   Changing Tides...................................... 54
Chapter 5   Si Vis Pacem, Para Bellum........................... 66
Chapter 6   They Came to Casablanca for the Waters.............. 85
Chapter 7   My Needle . . . Always Settles between West and South-Southwest . . 93
Chapter 8   A Fisher of Men..................................... 150
Chapter 9   A Tale of Two Cruisers.............................. 195
Chapter 10 An Unending Trail of Destruction, and Oil........... 225
Chapter 11 The Final Voyage of the *U-Deutschland*............. 278
Chapter 12 The Howling Wolves Fell Silent...................... 296
Chapter 13 The End of the Beginning............................ 327

Appendixes
    Appendix A: German Naval Ranks and Their Equivalents
                in the US and Royal Navies...................... 339
    Appendix B: Lists of Sunken or Damaged Vessels.............. 340
    Appendix C: The Sinking of USS *Ticonderoga* from a German Perspective... 348

Endnotes... 356
Bibliography... 390
Index.. 398

Acknowledgments

The COVID-19 coronavirus pandemic would, for most people, appear to be an ideal time for writing a book. Theoretically, the lockdowns would serve as a government-imposed sabbatical where one was presented with swaths of free time to put ideas to paper (or, more likely, a Word document). In my case, nothing could be further from reality.

For one, my full-time job was unimpeded by the virus, and I was not given any pandemic-related time off. In stark contrast, my two children were forced to attend school remotely. This, in turn, transformed my home into a schoolhouse, the kitchen and dining-room tables into classrooms, and my wife into an auxiliary teacher's assistant. It also eliminated many areas in the house that would have otherwise been conducive for research and writing a manuscript, forcing me to lock myself in my bedroom to work at tiny computer desk in my free time (it must be remembered that libraries and other public spaces such as coffee shops were strictly off-limits during this period, at least in New Jersey). During these extraordinary times, I admit I was greatly indebted to my wife, who, besides being a homemaker, mother, and now an amateur teacher, also tried her hardest to provide a quiet environment for me to focus on my work and picked up the slack when I became a hermit. This book would have taken exponentially longer to complete without such an understanding partner.

Additionally, the Deutsches U-Boot-Museum in Altenbruch (Cuxhaven) provided an immeasurable amount of assistance. Despite being closed for the pandemic, Kai Steenbuck was very quick in responding to all my various inquiries and, by making the German war diaries available in a digital format, allowed me to complete my research during a period when both flights to Germany were canceled and the German Marine Archives were closed. Likewise, Kory Penney (marine archivist for the Newfoundland and Labrador Heritage Website) must be given credit for locating a newspaper article (essentially a needle in a haystack) concerning the fates of the SS *Dictator*'s crewmen, a very minor story in a wider narrative, but one essential to providing a comprehensive history of the North American U-boat campaign.

The New Jersey Maritime Museum (particularly Mike Egolf, now retired) also deserves considerable acclaim, not only for helping to provide the catalyst for me writing this book in the form of their various displays from New Jersey coastal shipwrecks, but also because their extensive archives remained open during the pandemic. While the National Archives in Washington, DC, was closed for much of the nearly two years it took to write this book, the New Jersey Maritime Museum opened early and their

Special Subject Notebooks about the sinking of USS *San Diego* allowed me to complete a significant amount of research I would otherwise have had to do when the National Archives eventually reopened to the public.

Finally, I would like to thank my friends Jake Iapicca and S. W. Whelan (both much more talented writers than myself) for not only spurring me back into the daunting task of writing a book, but also providing critical input along throughout the process.

Introduction

The U-boat campaign off North America during the First World War has generally been regarded as a novelty among military historians. As far as naval operations go, it certainly lacked the romance of the cruise of the *Emden* and the drama of the battles of Coronel and the Falklands. In fact, if one were to query the casual "history buff" about their knowledge of U-boat activity during this period, the sinking of the *Lusitania* would be evoked almost universally. More-enlightened individuals would perhaps recall the activities of the Flanders Flotilla and the Dover Patrol or the exploits of *U-35* in the Mediterranean. Very few would realize that the Germans came to the shores of New World; yet, the impact of their arrival was significant, both during and after the Great War.

They first came in peace, with the arrival of the *U-Deutschland* mercantile submarine. This reestablished (at the most marginal level) Atlantic trade, subverting the British blockade by traveling underneath it. The next U-boat off American shores, SM *U-53*,[1] came outfitted as a warship but was nonetheless neutral. It arrived in Rhode Island in October 1916, on what was essentially a public-relations stop before sinking Allied shipping immediately outside American territorial waters. This occurred in full view of US Navy destroyers, who legally could intervene only when it came to the recovery of survivors, much to the chagrin of the British. Finally, the rest of the North American–bound "U-cruisers," whose stories will be fully described in this book, arrived as enemies, whose cargo of mines and torpedoes were now intended for American shipping. This book will not only explain their gradual change in roles but will also analyze the shift of public opinion on both sides of the Atlantic as the relationship between the German Empire and the United States evolved.

The relative lack of erudition surrounding the United States Navy's contribution to the defense of the home front will also be addressed. Like the German submariners who arrived off our shores, the American sailors guarding domestic waters have largely been omitted from the greater narrative of the First World War. Even Adm. William Sowden Sims, president of the Naval War College before becoming the commander of the US naval forces in Europe, almost completely discounts the entire campaign in his 1921 Pulitzer Prize–winning book *The Victory at Sea*. The defense of the continental US was a far-reaching endeavor, achieved using converted yachts, sub chasers, antiquated cruisers, destroyers, defensive sectors, and convoys. The US Navy (including the merchant marine) wasn't merely an ancillary service to the British Royal Navy, as the Anglophile Sims alluded; it has a unique story worth recounting that has mostly been discounted up to this point.

Part of this lies in the fact that only five *Unterseeboote*[2] actually made it across the Atlantic to wage war against the United States, compared to some 370 that operated in the European theater. The obvious result being that there were considerably fewer U-boat attacks on American shores in comparison to the North Sea or the English Channel and thus fewer defensive actions on the part of the US Navy to repel the threat—essentially making the home front appear to be a mere sideshow to the "real action" going on across the ocean. This, however, would be an unfair assessment.

While the American naval force sent to reinforce the British Grand Fleet in Europe certainly found itself in a more U-boat-infested zone of operations, it was in American waters that USS *San Diego* and USS *Minnesota* hit mines laid by German submarines. It was a North American–bound U-cruiser that sank the converted steamer USS *Ticonderoga*, with a massive loss of life, less than 750 miles off Newfoundland. As wooden sub chasers and seaplanes engaged German submarine cruisers off the coast of Cape May, the North Sea–based dreadnoughts USS *New York* and *Texas* were able to fire their massive guns only during war games and target practice (though *New York* was able to sink a submerged U-boat, albeit accidentally).

Moreover, the battleship and destroyer force sent over to Europe had to concentrate their efforts only in specific patrol areas, usually in proximity to a convoy, and in cooperation with British, French, Italian, and Japanese fleets. It was up to the US Navy (and, to a lesser degree, the Royal Canadian Navy) to defend the Eastern Seaboard of North America, an area stretching over 2,000 miles from Nova Scotia to Florida. It is a great disservice that stories concerning these domestic battles occupy a niche in Great War scholarship, existing primarily in local lore or in family scrapbooks. It could, however, be argued that the onus of such a historical omission falls on a lack of widespread scholarship on World War I as a whole.

For nearly a century, the gold standard for referencing the North American U-boat campaign of 1918 has been *When the U-boats Came to America*, by William Bell Clark. This work and the Department of the Navy's publication *German Submarine Activities on the Atlantic Coast of the United States and Canada* have been cited repeatedly by modern historians; however, they truly present only one side of the story and are not without numerous errors. Up to this point, very few historians have attempted to probe any deeper, and those who have largely avoided referencing any German sources. This is perhaps due to lack of access, lack of command of the German language, or, to be cynical, ignorance. To be fair, there are significantly fewer reliable resources available to the modern historian both from Allied and German perspectives in comparison to what exists concerning the Second World War.

World War II has always captured the imagination of history enthusiasts, and for good reason. When the war ended, Allied servicemen returned home with stories that they liberally passed on to their children. Wartime stock footage was plentiful, and movies, television shows, and a multitude of books were written and published with a momentum that has hardly slowed more than half a century later. On a personal note, my grandfather, although too young to serve during World War II, would tell me stories of seeing firsthand the damage the U-boats of that period inflicted on Allied shipping off the New Jersey shore. This certainly piqued the interest of a young boy, which obviously continues to this day. In fact, I often visit some of the places that will be mentioned in this book, and, just as I did when I was a child, still try to imagine the waters off the coastline as my grandfather would have seen them decades ago—littered with wreckage and with U-boats hiding just below the ocean's surface.

This oral tradition most certainly existed after the Great War; however, it was much more subdued—whether it be from the victors or the defeated Central Powers. There wasn't as distinct a line between the protagonists and the villains, and one could argue that every one of the major belligerents (with the exception of the United States) shared the blame for the outbreak of hostilities and ended the war worse off than they were when they initiated it. Generally, the veterans of the First World War returned home and tended not to publicize their experiences, content to stay out of the spotlight and return to a normal civilian life as soon as possible.

In the case of the Germans, even sailors who wished to remain in service found themselves without a navy to serve in, at least not in the traditional capacity they would have imagined prior to the Treaty of Versailles. Many retained their letters and diaries but left them to future generations to dissect and study. Others let their stories live on through dry military records, fantastic newspaper reporting, or propaganda. Even more simply, some let their stories fade away into obscurity.

The problem with this is that many of the stories actually published during, or shortly after, the war reflected the attitudes of the time and are discarded as being propaganda pieces, told through the blur of either a Germanic or Anglocentric lens. Historian Alexander Watson notes in his book *Ring of Steel* that

> [German] private publishers, recognizing that patriotism could be profitable even in the war's third year, exploited and fueled the excitement with hurriedly written, cheap and sensational accounts by submariners of their war experiences. The Berlin publisher Ullstein was the leader in a market that printed no fewer than nine "penny dreadful" U-boat

novels in 1917. They provided a human angle to the submarine campaign, portraying a face of masculine toughness and heroism that neatly complemented the navy's impressive statistics.[3]

One such example was *Kriegstagebuch U-202*, published in 1916 by Kapitänleutnant Edgar von Spiegel von und zu Peckelsheim and subsequently translated into English in the US in 1917 as *The Adventures of U-202: An Actual Narrative* (instead of the literal translation of "War Diary of U-202"). This account, by the author's own admission, features not only liberties taken with the truth but outright fictional accounts—in fact, the submarine he commanded at the time of writing was SM *U-93* (there was no *U-202* in service during the First World War).

While he points out that at least one of the stories in the book was unquestionably a fabrication (chapter VII), it causes the reader to discount what actual facts and experiences were included in the rest of the narrative. Since the implicit intention of his book, and others of the time period, was to improve morale at home and gain sympathy for the German cause abroad (such as in the large German American population within the US), one could consider it to be less a historical work and more of a fable. On the other hand, since these books were said to be transcribed from actual ship logs and diaries, can they not be considered historical resources, worth poring over by historians? What can we actually believe?

If you try to get the truth from any newspaper sources of the period (Central Powers or Entente), you're presented with the same stretching of facts through bias, censorship, or, again, fabrications. The British and American presses were quick to spin yarns about Hun brutality against civilians, and the Germans were equally hasty in justifying their actions as defense of the Fatherland from the British, who were starving women and children through their blockade. Additionally, the Allies often enlarged submarine kill counts and concealed the number of vessels being sunk, while the Germans exaggerated the number of operational U-boats and sunk tonnage.

When the war was brought to the East Coast of the United States, the free American press, rife with yellow journalism, certainly participated in the same methods of propaganda, often aiding in the spread of panic alongside bolstering the fighting spirit of the populace. Freak accidents were often blamed on coastal U-boat attacks or enemy agents, and some newspapers even suggested that there were secret German bases operating within North and Central America.

So prevalent was the U-boat threat, according to US newspapers, that many American servicemen and merchants crossing the Atlantic believed every cresting wave could be shielding a conning tower, and any floating debris observed in the distance had the potential to be a periscope. Sailors detained by U-boat crews often feared being gunned down in the water or poisoned by the provisions offered to them, due to the fantastic stories being circulated during the period. Even today, over a hundred years after the fact, urban legends continue to propagate (such as a U-boat surfacing and shelling the coastal batteries at the entrance of the New York Harbor), primarily due to questionable period reporting that modern reporters and researchers have reiterated without making the effort to adequately check the facts. For English-speaking readers, there have been very few sources up to this point that present a comprehensive picture of the events during this period.

Contributing to this lack of perspective, some U-boat commanders were considered by the British and French to be war criminals. They, like their future generations during the Second World War, were obviously hesitant with sharing their stories and presenting themselves in the public eye. Thus, a counterpoint to the Allied point of view can be difficult to locate. The American reporter and broadcaster Lowell Thomas discovered this firsthand when he went searching for U-boat veterans to interview for his book *Raiders of the Deep*. He noted that (in an extreme example) the British had placed a bounty for the capture of Otto Hersing, commander of SM *U-21*, that followed him into his postwar years of civilian life in occupied Germany, saying,

> The British put a price on his head; and even after the war the French authorities in the occupied German provinces along the Rhine were so eager to snare him that they offered 20,000 marks to anyone who would lure him into territory they controlled. In 1924, a woman in Wilhelmshaven, where Hersing was stationed, thought she might as well reap this little reward [little indeed, since this was the pinnacle year of Weimar hyperinflation]. She asked him to give a talk about his war experiences before a society in Hamburg and told him an automobile would be sent to take him there. Hersing agreed to the seemingly innocent proposal, when, at the last moment, he was tipped off that the plan was to get him into the automobile, hold him, and carry him speeding over into territory under French jurisdiction.[4]

Another U-boat veteran suffering from this stigma, though one that was due to a case of mistaken identity, was Otto Dröscher, commander of SM *U-117* (which will be discussed at length in this book). Dröscher originally commanded the submarine *U-20* and in December 1914 was relieved by Kapitänleutnant Walther Schwieger. During Schwieger's command, the practice of commencing war under the prize rules of previous generations was abandoned by Germany in favor of unrestricted submarine warfare, and *U-20* began sinking civilian ships without warning. The sinking of SS *Ikaria* and SS *Tokumaru* on January 30, 1915, by *U-20* placed Dröscher on the list of war criminals even though he was in command of SM *U-14* at the time (*U-20* also famously sunk the *Lusitania* in May of the same year). The British, not aware of the change of command, placed the onus of that month's sinkings on Dröscher, and the error still appears to be uncorrected in many postwar publications concerning the U-boat war to this day.

The commanders of SM *U-151*, *U-152*, and *U-156*, all featured in this book, also made the list of war criminals. Although none of these officers were prosecuted in the Leipzig War Crimes Trials of 1921, it can't be any surprise that U-boat veterans would be cautious in publicizing their experiences in the immediate postwar years. Instead, they were content with remaining out of the public eye and getting on with the daily struggle of their lives as civilians in a depressed Germany.

This book intends to shed light on the experiences of the U-boat crews, their victims, and the men who fought them to defend the North American coastline, separating fact from fiction and giving a comprehensive account that up to this point hasn't been attained within a single work. It will examine the history of the cross-Atlantic travel of submarines to our shores, both benevolent and belligerent, and examine the gradual change of perception by both sides, from admired friends to abhorred foes. Additionally, although somewhat dry, the development and technical specifications of the U-cruisers and Allied coastal defensive craft will be explored in detail.

At times the stories told in this book may seem fantastic, entertaining, or terrifying, but they will be the truth, or at least as close to reality as can be ascertained by available primary sources. Since this book does not attempt to take any sides, the legacies of both the American and German sailors who served in the Great War can finally rest assured that, after more than a century of disregard, their experiences have been given the thorough and fair study that befits them—presenting them in an equal, unbiased light and restoring their rightful place in Great War scholarship.

CHAPTER 1
America, Meet Deutschland

May 23, 1918, 1900 hours. A U-boat surfaces at the entrance of the Chesapeake Bay while a thunderstorm rages overhead. Korvettenkapitän[1] Heinrich von Nostitz und Jänckendorf opens the hatch of SM *U-151* and takes a moment to reflect on the poetic response of the natural world to his arrival. Looking over to his boarding officer, he remarks, "Well, Körner, do you think this is ominous for the Americans or for us?" As the submarine proceeds northward, deeper into the bay, the weather begins to clear. At midnight the U-boat dives to avoid being detected by surface traffic. Von Nostitz checks with his radio operator: "Any chance we've been spotted?" The response is comforting: "The coastal wireless stations continue to broadcast a message of 'No submarine. No War Warning,' commander." Von Nostitz replies, "We'd better stay down for a while now before we dispense of our gifts to the Americans."

During the day on the twenty-fourth, *U-151* rises to periscope depth and the German commander looks around at the current surface activity. Von Nostitz reels back from the periscope, noticing an armored cruiser appear on the horizon, being trailed by two destroyers. As he is about to give the order to dive deeper, he takes another look and observes a decoy being pulled in tow. "Target practice," he thinks to himself and continues his course toward Cape Henry. At nightfall the order is given to surface, so the submarine can offload some of the mines it carries, courtesy of the Kaiserliche Marine,[2] for the Americans who decided to involve themselves in a European concern.

The sky is clear and the moonlight shines brightly over the raiders. As the crew prepares the mines on the deck of the U-boat, one of them notices a strange light flashing just ahead. Could this be the end of their lucky streak? As this light continues to flash, it reveals the silhouette of a cruiser, now changing its course and heading directly for the U-boat. *"Verdammt!* Get those mines off the deck, quickly!" commands von Nostitz. As the mines are dispensed and *U-151* can finally dive to safety, von Nostitz turns to his chief engineer and remarks, "Quite a different reception than old König got in 1916, *stimmt's?*"

Nearly two and a half years earlier, Paul König, former captain of the *Schleswig* of the Norddeutcher Lloyd Line (NDL), was summoned to Berlin to hear a radical proposal on conquering the British blockade of Germany. He didn't realize at this time, but this was going to be the defining moment of his life. He was to command the largest submarine built to date, and become an overnight hero both in Germany and the United States. This submarine, however, was a mercantile vessel, conceived not in the Imperial Naval Office in Berlin but in the boardrooms of Bremen. A typically German subterfuge that would help break through the blockade and, it was hoped, restore commerce between Germany and the then-still-neutral United States.

The British blockade on the German Empire, the so-called "Starvation War," had begun a little over a year prior, at the outbreak of war in August 1914. This didn't come as a surprise to Germany. As early as 1905, Helmuth von Moltke wrote that the next war would be decided only after a nation's "entire national strength is broken."[3] As an empire built around a vast navy, the British echoed these sentiments and utilized their greatest asset in a way that truly would determine the outcome of the war. Capt. Alfred Carpenter, who commanded the Royal Navy's HMS *Vindictive* during the raid of Zeebrugge, commented after the war that

> war is not merely a struggle between fighting forces, but between opposing "crowds." The destruction of an enemy's Army or Navy are [*sic*] of primary importance as a means to an end, but the ultimate aim of each belligerent is to exert influence on the "crowd," to nourish the will to win amongst their own public and to bring about a feeling of hopeless despair, a complete loss of morale, throughout the enemy's country. It is for that important reason that the sentiments of one's own public must ever be borne in mind by the Higher Command.[4]

This cold rationale of British war doctrine was certainly easy to have from the position of being well supplied. Their control of the seas kept their population nourished, and therefore it shouldn't be any surprise that the Germans, in their position of economic isolation, used the same reasoning for unrestricted submarine warfare and zeppelin raids on London.

As a nation surrounded by enemies, whose only access to the oceans had to pass through the English Channel or around Great Britain through the North Sea, Germany developed a siege economy, ensuring the allocation of raw materials through centralized war departments. By early 1915, however, this was already proving to be insufficient. While the German army was still maintaining a steady supply of food and ammunition at this point in the war, the civilian population was faring far worse. According to historian Robert Massie, in 1914 a Berlin stockyard was slaughtering approximately 25,000 pigs every week for general consumption, and by 1916 that figure dropped down to a scant 350.[5] This was compounded by the German army seizing horses and conscripting the farmers who utilized them, fertilizer shortages (the nitrogen required was being used to make explosives, and the deficit could be acquired only through imports), and, finally, the failure of the German potato and cereal harvest, leading to the infamous "Turnip Winter." The siege economy wasn't working, and the shortages Germany was experiencing could be rectified only through imports, particularly from the United States.

Germany, prior to the Great War, was a significant trading partner with the United States (much as they are to this day), exporting chemicals, pharmaceuticals, and precision instruments and importing raw materials and food stuffs—much of which was vital to the German war effort and the home front. The Norddeutscher Lloyd (NDL), König's employer, had been one of the main arteries of this cross-Atlantic trade and, having seen a dramatic reduction in services to transport such cargo on the surface, decided to make a significant financial commitment to the development of long-distance cargo submarines. They, along with Deutsche Bank, created the Deutsche Ozean-Reederei[6] for this purpose, with Friedrich Krupp Germaniawerft[7] in Kiel (a major manufacturer of U-boats) also being a large stakeholder. Not surprisingly, Germaniawerft, which was to design and manufacture the new cargo submarines, was in particular need of raw materials from the United States; namely, nickel and copper for the fabrication of U-boat hulls and piping.

The British blockade had effectively put a stranglehold on this essential cross-Atlantic trade from the moment it was executed. The following chart clearly illustrates this dramatic decline, beginning with the prewar peak in trade from 1913 to 1916, when German cargo submarines went into operation:[8]

	1913	1914	1915	1916
US exports to Germany	$352	$158	$12	$2
US imports from Germany	$184	$149	$45	$6

Values for goods are given in millions of dollars at their value in 1917.

Concerning the metals required for U-boat production, the prewar level of importing 200,000 tons of copper annually was reduced to just 13,000 tons by 1915, of which Germany could compensate only approximately 40,000 tons through domestic production and confiscation of civilian stocks.[9] By contrast, during this same period the imports to the United States from Great Britain remained relatively unchanged, at a value of approximately $280 million; however, the exports from the US to Britain doubled their 1913 value of $591 million in 1915 and trebled to a total of $1.8 billion in 1916.[10]

Great Britain's ambassador to the US, Sir Cecil Spring-Rice, would perceptively remark that while the United States was getting richer off the British during the war, ultimately the blockade was damaging to American "pride and dignity," since the United States' entire cross-Atlantic trade was under essentially British control.[11] The United States could import or export anything they wanted, as long as Great Britain allowed the ships to get across the ocean.

As Britain was increasingly reliant on the United States for survival, and the Allies were fast becoming exclusive trading partners with the US, the United States still had a need for goods from Germany that Britain and France couldn't offer. Concurrently, by 1916, Germany was already feeling the pangs of starvation, literally and figuratively. It was obvious in both countries that there was a need to resume some means of trade, even at the most marginal level.

Although Germany seemed to have a stopgap solution with the concept of cargo submarines, the problem of who to command these vessels was still looming, since all experienced submariners were involved in combat. Theoretically, due to the NDL being essentially confined to port, there should have been a great surplus of redundant surface ship captains. Indeed, this was precisely the image the German government wanted to present to the world, and they did so with great effect when Paul König's memoir was ghostwritten in 1916.

In reality, most of these captains were naval reservists who went on to perform various roles within the Kaiserliche Marine at the outbreak of war—König being no different. As early as 1894, he held the rank of *Leutnant zur See der Reserve*,[12] going on to achieve the rank of *Kapitänleutnant* in 1904.[13] When he was recalled into active duty in 1914, he went on to serve as a deck officer on the SMS *Brandenburg* in the Baltic. Still, with all his years of naval service, he never once set foot on a submarine. This small detail, however, didn't seem to bother the Deutsche Ozean-Reederei at all. When they narrowed down their search for a potential merchant U-boat commander to König, they needed him for his expertise in a completely different area. König, as the captain of the *Schleswig*, had extensive knowledge of American waterways, specifically in the area of the Chesapeake Bay.

In September 1915, the forty-five-year-old König was summoned to the Hotel Adlon, the most luxurious hotel in Germany at the time, to meet with Alfred Lohmann—an old acquaintance from the North German Lloyd agency and one of the founders of the Deutsche Ozean-Reederei. König would later claim that the questions posed to him during this meeting were rather nebulous. Was he not bored by his dormancy on the Continent? Wouldn't he prefer to set off cruising once again? König's response was equally vague. In his words,

What was an old captain of the merchant marine to say to that? An old captain who had to leave his ship at the outbreak of war, and was drifting about the country like a derelict—while the English cruisers were prowling about the Canal and the Shetlands and taking the American mails from neutral ships at four miles distance from New York? I shrugged my shoulders and was silent.[14]

Alfred Lohmann, founding member of the Deutsche Ozean-Reederei. *Author's collection*

This surprised the man sitting across the table, which led to the topic of discussion becoming much more specific. The questioning quickly evolved: Would König be interested in a nondescript long cruise, to would he be interested in captaining a submersible merchant vessel between Germany and America, with the first trip heading to the Baltimore area? To this, König replied with a resounding yes! Indeed, just two months later König was poring over sketches and blueprints for this new type of submarine, and four months after that he was at the Germania Dockyards in Kiel seeing its steel frame take shape.

The submarine taking shape was the *Unterseeboot Deutschland*, the first of eight merchant U-boats being constructed at Germaniawerft. It had an overall length of 65 m (meters), a width of 8.9 m, and a height of 5.3 m. It was powered by two nonreversible (a critical characteristic), six-cylinder diesel engines (originally intended to be used as generators on battleships) for surface travel and two electric motors for submersed propulsion and reverse. Range was 12,000 nm (nautical miles) (22,224 kilometers [km] / 13,809 miles [mi.]) on the surface, traveling at 5.5 knots and 63 nm at 3 knots submerged—easily covering the nearly 9,000 nm round trip to Baltimore. Its total displacement (submerged) was 2,272 tons.[15] While somewhat shorter in length than the largest combat U-boat of the period, the U-81 class, it was taller and wider, nearly twice the total tonnage, and was capable of traveling more than twice the range on the surface.[16] Its sister ship, the *U-Bremen*, was still being constructed and was to sail at a later date. That was to be commanded by a colleague of König's, Capt. Karl Schwartzkopf, another civilian liner captain recalled into the Imperial Navy.

The *U-Deutschland* "arriving at the mouth of the Weser." *Author's collection*

The *U-Deutschland* was a large vessel to handle, even for a U-boat ace, and in less than three months König and his crew (once again sourced through various units and reserves of the Imperial Navy) would have to become expert submariners. At this point in the war, even experienced U-boat commanders were being sunk trying to break through the British naval defenses and minefields, yet these amateurs would be expected to identify brand-new threats to which they were not accustomed and be able to react to them in an instant.

To improve the prospects of the venture being successful, the officers of the new merchant submarines were given an operational crash course by Kapitänleutnant Hans Rose of the infamous SM *U-53* (his story will be discussed in the next chapter). Additionally, exhaustive trials took place between when the U-boat was launched in March and up to the date of the voyage, to familiarize the crew with submersible travel. However, like their colleagues in the Kaiserliche Marine, much of their essential training would take place "on the job."

The *U-Deutschland* would eventually depart Bremen on June 14, 1916, with a crew of eight officers and twenty-six men. She was loaded with 750 tons of cargo, consisting of dyestuffs and chemicals, pharmaceuticals, gold bullion, and diplomatic mail (which included plans for building a long-range wireless station in Mexico),[17] all with a value of approximately $1 million.[18] Since the cost to build the *U-Deutschland* was 4,135,000 marks,[19] the equivalent of $771,445 in 1916, the value in mercantile submarines was apparent. Crucially, the submarine was completely unarmed. There weren't even small arms on board for the crew to defend themselves with if such a need arose. This stood in contrast to the surface merchant ships of the period, which were equipped with small deck guns, or to the British Q-ships, which were fortified vessels disguised as merchant ships for the sole intention of sinking U-boats.

Given this disparity in armament, it is noteworthy that the Entente considered all submarines to be warships. While this may seem unfair, considering that Allied merchant ships actually were armed, there was some sound reasoning to justify their stance. For one, they realized that any materiel obtained by a mercantile submarine would ultimately be used to facilitate the German war effort, as opposed to being entirely humanitarian in nature. It was extremely unlikely that the *U-Deutschland* would be sailing on a Belgian relief mission. Additionally, due to the clandestine nature of submersible craft, there would be no means for a neutral country's coast guard to inspect the vessel prior to it arriving in port or to ensure that no breaches of neutrality be committed immediately upon departure.

Upon becoming aware of the existence of the *Deutschland* on July 3, 1916, the British diplomat Sir Colville Barclay wrote a rather eloquent message to the US secretary of state Robert Lansing, which outlined the British position concerning mercantile submarines entering neutral ports. In this correspondence he first made a point to emphasize that a U-boat had recently resupplied at a neutral port in Spain and then immediately sank merchant vessels outside those waters, going on to state,

> Now, persistent rumors are current that a German submarine is on its way to a United States port. . . . It is unlikely that a German submarine would cross to an American port except for the purpose of conducting hostile operations on this side of the Atlantic. . . . For these reasons, in the opinion of His Majesty's government, if an enemy submarine attempts to enter a neutral port, permission should be refused by the authorities. If this submarine enters it should be interned unless it has been driven into port by necessity. . . . In no circumstances should it be allowed to obtain supplies. If a submarine should enter a neutral port flying the mercantile flag . . . it is the duty

of the neutral authorities concerned to enquire closely into its right to fly that flag, to inspect the vessel thoroughly and, in the event of torpedoes, torpedo tubes or guns being found on board, to refuse to recognize it as a merchant ship.[20]

This would be a position Britain would continue to argue preceding the arrival of the *Deutschland* and the months afterward, becoming even more fanatical in explaining why underwater craft should never be considered as anything but belligerent in nature. The *U-Deutschland* would indubitably be considered a warship by the British, and therefore it was considered the duty of the Royal Navy to prevent her from ever reaching US shores.

Knowing that the British would be looking to sink the *Deutschland*, by mines or otherwise, Capt. König didn't immediately head westward toward the Atlantic Ocean. Instead, he cruised toward the German naval base on the island of Helgoland. Here he remained for nine days to throw off any British patrols awaiting the submarine, before finally proceeding northward on June 23. He would attempt to circumvent the bulk of the minefields and patrols in the English Channel and the North Sea by instead hugging the Norwegian coastline (the Northern Barrage didn't exist yet) and sailing around the north of Scotland before changing course for the United States. This was a sound strategy, since many U-boat commanders adopted the same course years prior, but it remained not without danger.

König did his best to remain submerged when the surface traffic was substantial, and every effort was made to change course away from steamers observed along the horizon. Nonetheless, just days into his trip an unusual steamer was spotted on a course that wasn't directed at any port. Additionally, it was flying an oversized flag of a neutral country, long after the sun had set for the day. Following protocol, König remained on the surface and continued on his course away from the suspicious vessel; however, once the steamer sighted the U-boat, it then turned sharply toward the submarine and began to swing out its lifeboats. These critical details gave away the true nature of the ship.

Under the Prize Rules initially observed by the Kaiserliche Marine in the war, it was required that U-boats first surface and fire a shell over the bow of a merchant ship, both as a warning and as a signal for the vessel to stop for inspection. The merchant crews would then be ordered onto their ship's lifeboats and would remain there for good if the German commander found the vessel to be carrying contraband, and ultimately decided to sink it. Knowing this practice full well, British Q-ships would often put on a show of panic on the decks of their ships upon sighting a U-boat and then prematurely take to their lifeboats—thus appearing harmless and enticing the submarine closer. During this charade, a skeleton crew would be left on the ship, awaiting the U-boat to get within range of its guns, at which point the ship's colors would be changed to those of the Royal Navy. The vessel's disguises would then be removed, exposing the Q-ship's deck guns, and if all went to plan, the U-boat would be sunk.

König and his crew were able to spot the deception and proceeded to dive, at which point the suspect steamer changed direction at full speed and proceeded away on a zigzag course, believing the *Deutschland* was an armed U-boat preparing to attack. Although a Q-ship was effective against an exposed, surfaced submarine, it was not invulnerable to the torpedoes fired from a submerged one. Although, the *Deutschland* and her crew were able to escape this time, they knew they had been spotted, and their position would certainly be reported to more-confrontational vessels.

Their suspicions were confirmed when the *Deutschland* made contact with a British destroyer immediately upon surfacing at 0200 (2:00 a.m.) the next day; however, a quick return to the depths once again saved the submarine from a premature conclusion to her cruise. Fortunately for the Germans, aside from spotting an auxiliary cruiser in the distance during stormy seas, the remaining trip across the Atlantic would be devoid of any further encounters with the Royal Navy. Still, even after escaping British aggression on the European side of the Atlantic, what sort of reception would await the *U-Deutschland* when she arrived in the United States?

This question almost certainly loomed in König's head throughout the trip. Just over a year prior, on May 7, 1915, the *Lusitania* was sunk by *U-20*, killing 128 American civilians. This was followed by further American deaths in August, when the White Star liner *Arabic* was sunk by *U-24*, and again in November of that year, when the Italian liner *Ancona* was sunk by *U-38* in the Mediterranean. Trade resumption with Germany, particularly through the use of a submarine, may have been fine for American businessmen who cared only for the bottom line, but how would the general American public react to a U-boat arriving on their shores? The Germans wouldn't have to wait very long for an answer.

The first American to meet König and the *U-Deutschland* was the captain of a pilot boat, Fred Cocke, at 0145 on July 9.[21] This rendezvous occurred off Cape Henry at the "3-mile limit," the boundary of American territorial waters. After overcoming the shock of what he saw approaching him at the entrance to the Chesapeake, he boarded the submarine and exclaimed, "I'll be damned; here she is!"[22] He then proceeded to shake the hands of König and his officers and aided the U-boat in finding the NDL tugboat awaiting its arrival. This was just a taste of what was to come for König and his crew.

Three cheers were given for the *Deutschland* and her crew at the quarantine station prior to docking at Locust Point in Baltimore. After this, film crews arrived, vying to get the first shots of the crew stepping onto American soil. When König went to the NDL agency and to customs, he was thronged by crowds asking questions and congratulating him. He later recalled that one woman in particular sympathetically asked if it were true that babies in Germany are starving from a lack of milk.[23] Certainly there were Americans less than enthused about the Hun arriving on their shores, particularly in more-Anglocentric parts of the country such as New England; however, Baltimore had a population of about 94,000 Germans (20 percent of its overall population)[24] at the time, and these crowds were far from hostile.

The *U-Deutschland* arriving in Baltimore. Paul König is pictured in the inset. *Author's collection*

In this chaotic and electrifying atmosphere, König found his only respite from all the attention he was receiving was when he was on board the NDL steamer *Neckar*, which had been in interned in Baltimore since the beginning of the war and would serve as private quarters for the crew. The *Neckar*'s redundant captain, Frederick Hinsch, would serve as a liaison for König (among many other, secret duties, being that he had been recruited as a German agent in 1915[25]) as a representative of the Eastern Forwarding Company—a shell company responsible for the *Deutschland*'s logistics while in the US. To keep away unwanted attention from themselves and the submarine, sentries had to be posted, and the tugboat assigned to the *Deutschland* manned a searchlight every night to observe anything out of the normal. This should not imply that the crew wanted to remain out of sight. The offloading of the *Deutschland*'s cargo would take time, and this trip across the Atlantic was equally as valuable for propaganda as it was in traded goods. As such, when the crew found themselves invited to various German clubs and social parties throughout the city, they were more than happy to oblige—it was, after all, an unofficial part of their job description.

For the duration of the *Deutschland*'s stay in Baltimore, a festival atmosphere prevailed. There were events organized by German American clubs for the benefit of the Red Cross, and it was not uncommon to hear the "Wacht am Rhein" being sung enthusiastically in the streets. The mayor of Baltimore, James Preston, went as far as to host a formal dinner for König and the German ambassador Count von Bernstorff, which was "of an exclusively political nature, and was attended only by politicians and official personages"[26] (whether this was out of genuine goodwill or due to a sense of political opportunism has not been determined). In contrast to the festive mood in the city, however, the mood at the docks was significantly more sober.

Due to the Allies' protest regarding the *Deutschland* arriving in the United States as a potential war-going vessel, the US government was compelled to make a formal inspection of the submarine upon her arrival. This occurred on July 12, lasted about three hours, and concluded that not only were there no armaments on board, but there were also no provisions to mount any— meaning that the submarine could not arm itself when in international waters and then pretend to be defenseless when at port. Interestingly, State Department officials interviewed by the *Washington Times* claimed that even if it were found that the submarine was armed specifically for defensive purposes, it would still be considered to be a merchant ship.[27] Following the inspection, acting secretary of state Frank Polk sent a telegram to the ambassadors in both Great Britain and Germany, stating,

> On July 9, German submarine *Deutschland* arrived in Baltimore bringing cargo dyestuffs. Question as to whether *Deutschland* was war vessel or merchantman was immediately referred to proper authorities, and after careful investigation and consideration, experts reported that they believed it to be a merchantman. This Department announced that in view of the circumstances in this particular case, there was no reason for regarding the *Deutschland* as a war vessel.[28]

This telegram directly responded to British concerns about the possible presence of torpedoes, torpedo tubes, or guns. While the British originally felt that the vessel would be considered mercantile in the absence of those aforementioned items in their earlier correspondence, they seemingly had a change of heart after receiving Polk's telegram, which clearly identified the U-boat as such.

Instead of trying to openly protest the United States allowing the *U-Deutschland* to commence trade, the British ambassador in Washington chastised William Phillips, the third assistant to the secretary of state, and handed him a British internal telegram. The British ambassador also provided Phillips with a photo that allegedly showed the *Deutschland* flying the German naval ensign in Bremen, with the submarine's crew wearing the uniform of the Kaiserliche Marine. Phillips communicated to Polk that the British were not necessarily protesting the State Department's decision on the status of the *Deutschland* but were "merely [trying] to point out the dangers which the decision occasioned."[29] Conveying that accepting some submarines as being mercantile and others as being war vessels would result in the impossibility of defending coastlines in the future and would make espionage simpler through the submarine's ability to land agents on any section of coastline.

What the British telegram actually stated, however, was far more damning and showed a remarkable foresightedness for the fate of German cargo submarines. Sir Edward Grey, the British secretary of state for foreign affairs, was adamant that the United States' decision to allow the *Deutschland* to be considered anything but a war vessel could not stand, and for good reason. Writing to Ambassador Spring-Rice he states that

> it is argued that [the] German commercial submarine carries cargo but no armament and that it should therefore be treated exactly like any other ship. . . . On this it must be observed that [the] most formidable part of a submarine, namely, its submersibility, is one of its inseparable attributes . . . it cannot divest itself of its most dangerous characteristic. If a belligerent were to use for mercantile purposes a vessel which in every respect was designed and armored as a battle cruiser, but which carried no guns, everybody would say: "This is only colorably a merchant ship; nine-tenths of [the] work required to convert her into a completely equipped ship of war of [the] most formidable type has already been put into her and cannot be removed. Clearly it is a ship of war that she should be treated." So, it is with the submarine. It is not torpedoes and torpedo tubes which make her what she is. These are weapons which may equally be possessed by a trawler. What really puts her in a class apart and makes it necessary to treat her under special rules is the indefeasible quality which she possesses of traveling under water. . . . The submersible cargo boat, for all her peaceful appearance, possesses

and must always possess qualities which would enable her at very short notice to be converted into a fighting vessel of the most formidable kind; her case is therefore exceptional and calls for exceptional treatment.[30]

Grey would have to wait less than a year for his fears to be realized, and in 1916 the Allied position was abundantly clear. Even if the United States considered the *U-Deutschland* to be peaceful, in the open Atlantic the British would consider her to be belligerent and aim to sink her.

Before departing Baltimore on August 1, 1916, the *Deutschland* would take on cargo to almost exclusively be used in the war effort—filling her hold with of 802,037 pounds of crude rubber, 752,674 pounds of nickel, and 181,049 pounds of tin for a combined value of $1,053,821.24 (just a little over $25 million in 2020 US dollars).[31] Still, the most-valuable items (at least to the German crew) taken on board prior to departure had the least monetary value.

One was a copy of the London *Morning Post* from July 18, which publicly outlined the British position already conveyed to the American government, openly declaring that

> [the *Deutschland* was] to be regarded as a war vessel and treated as such. The Allies will . . . seek every opportunity to waylay the vessel beyond the American three-mile limit and will sink it without warning.[32]

Another was a German intelligence report, informing König that the British hired fishing vessels to spread antisubmarine nets just off American waters where the *Deutschland* was expected to lay course.

Perhaps to allay some of the concerns of the submarine's crew and the German diplomatic mission about hostile British vessels lying in wait, the *Deutschland* was provided with an escort out of the harbor in the form of a Baltimore police boat and a revenue cutter. This, however, did not extend to the American 3-mile limit, and once outside the harbor the Germans would essentially be left on their own. Indeed, when the *U-Deutschland* finally departed to rousing cheers throughout the Baltimore harbor, König could take little comfort in the well-wishing of his newfound admirers. He knew, more than anyone else, what he would likely be facing once he made it to international waters.

When the *U-Deutschland* left behind the entrance to the Chesapeake Bay, she did so at dusk, with König hoping that nightfall would aid in their breakthrough back to Germany. Traveling on the surface as he approached the 3-mile limit, König claimed that he and his crew were temporarily blinded by two searchlights coming from unidentified fishing trawlers. These lights, upon spotting the submarine, then went into a vertical position, sending a beam into the heavens that was visible for miles. Rightly believing this to be a signal to warn British cruisers lying in wait for the submarine, König then gave the order to dive and proceeded on a course parallel to the coast. Interestingly, this signal also allegedly attracted the attention of an American armored cruiser, which König later suggested was present to enforce American sovereignty within its waters. After spotting additional British flagged ships in the distance, using their own searchlights to locate the *Deutschland*, König then proceeded eastward toward home at periscope depth, surfacing only hours later only when the threat of being sunk had subsided.

This rather dramatic incident would prove to be concerning for the US government, since it was feared that such actions, were they actually carried out by American fishing boats, would violate the United States' declared neutrality. As such, an inquest was launched a month later by the State Department, which found that although fishing boats from Virginia were present in the area, the boats observed by König were in fact registered to Halifax, Nova Scotia.[33] While the Canadian fishing boats had a commercial alibi for being in the area, they also had an obvious motive for assisting the British in their hunt for the *Deutschland*. In the end, Germany found the State Department's findings to be satisfactory, and no onus was placed on the US for any violations of neutrality.

Remarkably, considering the drama right outside the American 3-mile limit and the encounters with British vessels on the inbound voyage, the rest of the *Deutschland*'s journey home went without incident. Upon her arrival back in Bremen on August 25, König and his crew were once again given a well-deserved heroes' reception. The foundation had now been laid—mercantile submarines could effectively be utilized to break the English blockade. Indeed, prior to his departure from the United States, König confirmed that another U-boat, the *U-Bremen*, would be forthcoming, declaring,

> It may arrive within eight weeks or less. . . . We have proved that their [the submarines'] range is practically unlimited, that the British blockade, so called, cannot hinder them, and that they are economically feasible.[34]

What he didn't tell the American press was that more than just cargo submarines would be arriving in the future. König had suggested to his superiors that it would be beneficial for the U-boats of the Kaiserliche Marine to also make the trip and focus their attacks on the Royal Navy on the other side of the Atlantic. Since the smaller, war-outfitted U-boats were believed to have been incapable of making such a long journey, their attacks would be completely unanticipated and would thus have a greater chance for success. Additionally, such attacks could also clear the routes for the cargo submarines so other captains wouldn't have to dive to avoid Q-ships and destroyers as König had.

The Admiralstab[35] agreed, even if they weren't quite sure how such a task could be accomplished. When the *Deutschland*'s sister submarine, the *U-Bremen*, would make her journey to the New World, she would be doing so with a friend.

CHAPTER 2
A Series of Unfortunate Events

On Sunday, September 3, 1916, Kapitänleutnant Hans Rose finds himself in Wilhelmshaven overseeing the refitting of his latest command, SM *U-53*. He had been the commander of this new vessel for just over four months, having served his time as an instructor in the U-Boot Schule,[1] first training cadets with the submarine *U-2* and later preparing his cadre of commercial U-boat captains for their mercantile campaigns[2]. His command seemed to be plagued by bad luck from the onset. In July, after spending eight uneventful days on patrol, he was finally able to sink the British steamer *Calypso*[3] off the coast of Norway. He had believed it was a British auxiliary cruiser and sank it without warning, making this the first merchant vessel ever sunk by torpedo by a surfaced U-boat.[4] Rose was rewarded with a damaged steering gear for all his efforts during that patrol.

Perhaps this wasn't the worst trade-off. Just under 3,000 tons of cargo went to the bottom of the North Sea, and his U-boat was able to return home to fight another day, albeit barely. On the way to Wilhelmshaven from the Imperial Navy base in Helgoland, *U-53* rendezvoused with SM *U-51*, commanded by Kapitänleutnant Walter Rumpel, and proceeded to the dockyards together, since both required repairs. Although the trip was less than 50 nautical miles, and deep within German territorial waters, *U-51* wouldn't complete the short journey. She was torpedoed by the British submarine *H 5*, commanded by Lt. Cromwell Varley, at the mouth of the Ems River—within 5 miles of Borkum's coastal lightship.[5] Although Rose and his crew escaped, Rumpel and thirty-three other officers and crew perished in the incident.[6] The fact that this occurred well within the protective range of the German High Seas Fleet and German minefields was not lost on Rose. He could only wonder what the outcome could have been if he were off the coast of England, or farther into the Atlantic—the dominion of the Royal Navy.

More bad luck was to accompany Rose during his third mission, on August 18, 1916. *U-53* was given a scouting role to shadow the British Grand Fleet and report on their positions during Adm. Scheer's second attempt at bringing the High Seas Fleet into battle with the Royal Navy. Upon making contact with the Grand Fleet, an attempt was made at sinking one of the British destroyers; however, a miscalculation in the heading angle of the torpedo caused it to miss wide.[7] This was followed by Rose continually reporting the correct strength of the British fleet, but due to busy wavelengths (the U-boats on the mission were also competing with airships

31

and the other ships of the High Seas Fleet), there were significant delays in receiving the information at the High Command. These were compounded by numerous other reports of varying accuracy from the eight naval zeppelins taking part in the operation, whose vistas were constantly obscured by heavy cloud cover. Upon finally getting his last message through in time, Rose suffered the indignity of having his report ignored in favor of an erroneous report made by Kapitänleutnant Prölss in zeppelin *L-13*.[8] The High Seas Fleet retreated, and another great opportunity was squandered.

Hans Rose. *NH 92860, courtesy of the Naval History & Heritage Command*

Having completed another uneventful fourth mission, Rose returned to Wilhelmshaven for a scheduled refit of his boat. With his crew on leave during the repair work, and it being a Sunday, Rose was perturbed by the summons to meet with his boss, the North Sea *Führer der Unterseeboote* (FdU, leader of the U-boats), Fregattenkapitän Hermann Bauer.[9] Certainly, his lackluster record made it unlikely that this was a celebratory social call from his superior.

Fregattenkapitän Hermann Bauer, like his colleague in the airship wing of the Imperial Navy, Führer der Luftschiffe Peter Strasser, was a hands-on commander. He was intimately familiar with the construction and operation of U-boats, with Adm. Scheer noting that "he himself took part in the fighting expeditions of the U-boats in the blockaded area around England, in order to be able to form his own opinion of the circumstances in which the U-boats under his command had to operate."[10] He was a man who not only couldn't be fooled by his subordinates but also couldn't expect them to do the impossible; yet it seemed that that was precisely what he was going to ask of Rose.

Upon receiving Rose aboard the SMS *Hamburg*,[11] he asked the commander, "Do you trust yourself and your boat to sail to America?"[12] Although he wouldn't admit it, it is likely that Rose thought Bauer was making some kind of practical joke. The Admiralstab, taking König's advice, wanted Rose and *U-53* to trail the mercantile submarine *U-Bremen* to the United States and attack any enemy ships lying in wait to sink the defenseless U-boat on its return trip. Having completed the first leg of the mission, *U-53* was then to proceed to the US naval base in Newport, Rhode Island, and pay a courtesy visit. As if this wasn't enough, she was then to return home, sinking any British ships in international waters along the US coast that she happened to come across.

U-53, being a U-51-class submarine, had a theoretical range of 9,400 nm (17,400 km / 10,800 mi. at a moderate speed, in ideal conditions),[13] about three-quarters of the range of the *U-Deutschland*. Assuming a direct route from Wilhelmshaven to Newport, such a trip would be just under 8,000 nm. This being wartime, a direct route was out of the question, and the trip would not be simply a quick jaunt to the United States and back. Bauer was seemingly asking the unachievable of his commander, or was he?

In Rose's autobiography, *Auftauchen! Kriegsfahrten von U-53*, he claims that he requested thirty hours from Bauer to think over the plan and then implies that it was up to himself to gather the minds and develop a means of converting *U-53* to a cross-ocean submersible, given an additional two weeks to physically convert the vessel. In reality, this was likely an intentional aggrandizement designed to fortify the myth of Hans Rose during the Third Reich era, when his book was published. His mission was conceived in the Admiralty, approved by the High Command, German political leaders, and was even given the blessing from the kaiser.[14] To emphasize the significance of his mission, Rose personally received his orders from the chief of staff of the High Seas Fleet, Adolf von Trotha, aboard Adm. Scheer's flagship SMS *Friedrich der Große* in Helgoland. His specific orders were as follows:

1. After the arrival of the submarine *Bremen*, which is to be expected in New London on around September 15th, enemy naval forces are expected to guard the eastern approaches of the Long Island Sound. You are to seek out and attack these forces if they are outside of

the US territorial waters (3-mile limit) and also outside a line running from Montauk Point Lighthouse ... to Gay Head Lighthouse, which the Americans consider sovereign, inland waters.

2. After completing this task, you should make call at Newport, Rhode Island[,] in order to give the American Naval authorities an opportunity to visit the boat. ... Newport must be left after a few hours at the latest, so the authorities do not have time to hold the boat under legal pretexts. Do not replenish any supplies with the possible exception of fresh provisions.

3. If you do not encounter any enemy forces, or they are within the limits specified under 1, you should still approach Newport as specified under 2, while observing necessary caution toward the enemy[,] whom it cannot be assumed with certainty that they will respect American neutrality.

4. After completing these tasks, or if they have to be abandoned, trade wars may be waged in accordance with Prize Rules, provided this would be possible without endangering the boat.

5. Messages are to be transmitted via Nauen according to the attached order.

6. For the journey home, a pick-up point will be planned south of the Faroe Islands. Information will be provided about this by the FdU.

7. In the event that the boat needs to lay up in a neutral port, the regulations ... number 65 will apply.

8. Enclosed is an excerpt from this order which you can provide to American authorities if required to show that the boat has the necessary supplies on board for the return home.

At the highest Order
Admiral von Holtzendorff[15]

Given the specifics of these orders, there certainly must have been more preparation in place prior to Rose accepting his mission in order to guarantee its success.

Further evidence of this can be seen in the slight disparity between the modifications that Rose describes, first in his autobiography and later in 1966, compared with those described by Scheer and other sources. *U-53* was armed with four torpedo tubes (two at the bow and two at the stern) and carried eight torpedoes on board, with six stored forward and two aft.[16] Rose would go on to claim that six torpedoes were loaded, which were "two more than the design called for," with one of the extra torpedoes being "stowed under his bunk."[17] In reality, the submarine was carrying only forward torpedoes (since the rear tubes were going to be used for other purposes, described below), and six would have been the normal complement. The means in which they were stored on board, along with the extra supplies for this unconventional journey, could be debated, but in all likelihood they were loaded as per design of the U-boat. Rose's son Christian, when interviewed about the conversion of the submarine by Markus and Gertrude Robinson for their biography of the U-boat ace, remarked that "my father knew how to spin a good yarn."[18] Using Scheer's description, the changes to the U-boat were as follows:

> The supplies of the boat had to be increased so as to make the voyage possible. Four ballast tanks were altered for use as fuel tanks, so that the oil supply was increased from 90 cubic meters to 150 cubic meters; the supply of lubricating oil of 14.5 cubic meters was considered sufficient for the voyage. Added to this, there was the increase of fresh water and food supplies, so that the boat's draught was increased by 40 centimeters. So far as her sea-going qualities were concerned, her commander reported that the boat rode very steadily on the whole, but that every sea went over her upper deck.... Consequently, for those on duty on the bridge, the voyage, especially at first, was a tremendous strain.[19]

The additional water supply mentioned above was accommodated by filling two of the four trim tanks, usually filled with seawater, with fresh water, as well as the two rear torpedo tubes, in order to increase available drinking water to 7,000 liters (still barely adequate for such a journey). Despite any variations in the description of the submarine, it is no embellishment in stating that *U-53* and her crew were going to pushed to their absolute limit on the journey.

U-53 was slated to depart from Helgoland on September 15 to clear the return route for the *U-Bremen*, which should have arrived in her second port of call within the United States just a day prior. Perhaps spinning another yarn (but one of significance concerning the timetable of events), Rose remarks in his autobiography that he personally observed the *Bremen* departing from Helgoland in late August, wherein he hailed her captain, Karl Schwartzkopf, who then responded by thanking Rose for the training.[20] If this were true, it would indicate that, following the example of the *Deutschland*, she left port in Bremerhaven and then proceeded eastward to throw belligerent parties off her scent.

Like the *Deutschland* that preceded her, the *Bremen* was traveling with a cargo of German exports, but it also was bringing something special. The *Bremen* was traveling with capital intended for the American submarine designer Simon Lake to begin the construction of German cargo submarines within the United States. Lake actually wanted to tour the *U-Deutschland* while she was in Baltimore but was refused entry by König. The Norddeutscher Lloyd was averse to having any visitors other than those required by the State Department, but was especially opposed to Lake inspecting the submarine since, amazingly, he threatened to sue the NDL for infringing on his own patents concerning the creation of underwater cargo fleets.

This is perhaps not as far-fetched as it sounds, since Lake spent years in Europe designing submarines for the German, Austro-Hungarian, and Russian navies before returning to the United States in 1912. He was familiar with the requirements of the Kaiserliche Marine and certainly had the necessary political connections to make such a venture fruitful. To prevent this lawsuit going forward, an impromptu meeting was held with members of the NDL and König, and instead of discussing lawsuits, a joint enterprise was agreed upon, with the NDL supplying an initial start-up capital of $100,000,000—the aforementioned cargo to be delivered by the *Bremen*.[21] The establishment of a cargo submarine plant within the United States could have had dramatic implications for Germany during the First World War, if only the *U-Bremen* actually made it to its destination. Instead, she was sunk just over a week into her voyage.

The cause of the *U-Bremen*'s demise remains a mystery to this day, and the theories behind her sinking also make one question whether the intentions of *U-53* were really to protect it first and then make a political statement later. Perhaps the most likely and least dramatic explanation was that the submarine suffered from an internal accident during her journey and went down with all hands. This is what Paul König would claim during the second arrival of the *Deutschland* on November 2, 1916.[22] It was initially believed that confirmation of such an incident was found in the report that a life vest washed up on the shore of Portland, Maine, marked "Bremen, Shutzmarke [*sic*], 5 Eppinghaven, Wilhelmshafen."[23] The misspelling of *Schutzmarke*, the anglicized spelling of Wilhelmshaven, and the fact that the letters were painted instead of stenciled, however, gave this away as a poor hoax. Another possible, yet unsubstantiated, cause could have been the result of the *Bremen* hitting a mine, just as many other U-boats had during both world wars; however, other scenarios do exist.

The first is sourced from the 1931 book *The German Submarine War, 1914–1918*, which claims that the *Bremen* was sighted south of Iceland on a course toward Baltimore. The Royal Navy's 10th Cruiser Squadron, responsible for patrolling the waters between Britain and Iceland, was dispatched to intercept her. Upon reaching the area, the HMS *Mantua* was alleged to have rammed a "heavy, submerged object"[24] that was believed to have been the U-boat. However, this could easily be written off, since the incident does not appear on the ship's log, nor did the captain make any claim for the sinking.

Another scenario that could be given a bit more credence was that the *Bremen* was sunk by a British submarine off the Shetland Islands. In this account, by Edwyn Gray in *A Damned Un-English Weapon*, the British submarine *G-13* was patrolling along the known U-boat routes out of the North Sea off the coast of Scotland when a submarine identified as the *Bremen* was spotted. The British submarine fired her two starboard forward torpedoes, which missed (being significantly out of range), circled around and fired her portside torpedo and missed, and then finally turned to fire one more torpedo from her aft tube and heard an explosion, which was believed to be a hit on the *U-Bremen*.[25] This was likely the route that the *Bremen* took toward the United States (as opposed to the shorter, mine-laden English Channel route), and the alleged distance from the *G-13* to the *Bremen* was 7,000 yards, or nearly 4 miles. The *G-13* would have been armed with four 18-inch Mk. VIII in the forward tubes, which had a maximum range of 4,000 yards, and one 21-inch Mk. IV torpedo in the stern, with a range of 8,000–13,500 yards,[26] making the hit on an enemy submarine from the single rear tube plausible. *G-13* was also given credit for sinking the minelayer *UC-43* in the same area half a year later, so sinking a U-boat was certainly within the capabilities of her commander, Lt. Cmdr. George Bradshaw. The British Admiralty, however, did not credit the submarine with the kill, since there was insufficient evidence to confirm the sinking. This source also mistakenly claims that the *Bremen* survived the attack and returned to Germany, being converted to a surface vessel in 1918.[27]

It is the last two scenarios that makes one question the outlined priorities of the Admiralstab concerning *U-53*'s stated mission. If the first priority was to protect the merchant submarine, it would have been far more logical that Rose would have departed just ahead of the *Bremen*, while maintaining contact with her throughout the voyage instead of taking on this role only for the *U-Bremen*'s return voyage. In this role, *U-53* would have been able to spot enemy vessels and report their positions via encoded wireless transmissions back to the *Bremen*, advising her to dive or attacking the hostile craft, thus avoiding the uncomfortable situations König found himself in with the Q-Ship and the destroyer on his trip to the US. Certainly, König feared being sunk on his departure from US waters, but the bulk of the British naval defenses that he encountered were located in European waters.

Instead, Rose would discover that the *Bremen* never made it to port. On October 3, sixteen days into his trip and on the American side of the Atlantic, *U-53* intercepted a message transmitted from "the President of an unknown station,"[28] claiming that *Bremen* had been captured. While he wasn't sure whether or not she had actually been captured, Rose concluded that *Bremen* was definitely not in New London.

An additional clue to the true mission of the *U-53* lies in oral instructions given to Rose by von Trotha back in Helgoland:

> The Admiralty does not want you to arrive [in Newport, Rhode Island] before October 5th. Your appearance off the American coast and the eventual attack on British warships should coincide with the entry of our troops in Romania, which is scheduled for the beginning of October.[29]

In personally telling this to Rose instead of putting it in writing, there allowed for deniability should something go wrong during the cruise, masking the true intentions of his mission.

By appearing so far from base and attacking merchant shipping, the illusion of the strength of the current combat-outfitted U-boats could possibly dissuade the United States from entering the war, along with Romania and the other latecomers hoping to improve their geopolitical standings. Had *U-53* and the *U-Bremen* traveled as a pair, it would be more likely that they would be spotted together and sunk, resulting in disaster for both of their missions. In this regard, the first instructions given to Rose should have been considered ancillary to his other assignments, which the German government obviously considered to have greater long-term ramifications for the war than a modest resumption in cross-Atlantic trade. The fact that the *U-Deutschland* went unescorted in her second cruise (which will be discussed in a subsequent chapter) further reinforces this concept.

SM *U-53* departed Helgoland on September 17, 1916, having been delayed two days due to poor weather. Rose would be taking the northern route, circumnavigating the British Isles, just as the *Deutschland* and *Bremen* had done previously. Ironically, given Rose's previous experience with airships, naval zeppelin *L-17* was provided as an escort out to sea until bad weather forced the zeppelin to retire to base.[30] Once again, Rose's string of bad luck appeared unremitting. The next day brought increasingly bad weather, and the fact that the U-boat was so heavily laden caused water to continuously pour into the conning tower and the air intakes for the diesel engines. The submarine's antenna mast was also damaged and required repairs on an almost daily basis for the remainder of the journey. Conditions did not improve on the nineteenth; in fact, they nearly caused a premature ending of the cruise.

While approaching the Shetland Islands, the port engine failed due to a seized piston. Rather than push ahead in the storm on only one diesel engine, Rose decided to dive to prevent further damage to the boat and allow time for his crew to repair the engine—a task that would take two days, a spare piston, and three attempts at mending the damaged cylinder wall.[31]

U-53 would eventually escape the blockade and by the twenty-first was in the Atlantic, heading westward; however, this would not be the end of Rose and *U-53*'s troubles. He had had repairs made on his starboard diesel engine on the twenty-third, and the boat was found to be leaking fuel, resulting not only in a waste of a precious commodity, but also an oil slick outlining the submarine's course. This too was repaired, but only after two members of *U-53*'s spent an hour in 12°C (54°F) water working on the submarine's exterior.[32] The next malady arrived with the ship's compasses on the twenty-fourth, being 30° off and causing the U-boat to nearly run aground, and yet another on the twenty-seventh, when two intake valve springs broke in the port engine.[33] Both issues were rectified quickly; however, this was enough to make the officers of the boat hold a vote to decide whether or not to continue onward. Not surprisingly, the vote was unanimous to complete their mission.

On the twenty-eighth, although the weather didn't improve, *U-53* was at least spared more mechanical failures. This was fortuitous since the submarine now was approaching commercial shipping lanes and would have to dive to avoid being detected. It was also this day that Rose would learn the fate of the *U-Bremen* by intercepting a broadcast from Long Island, New York (at this point in his cruise, the German radio signal from Nauen was no longer reliable). With part 1 of his orders now negated, it was time to proceed with what could be argued was *U-53*'s true mission—showing the imperial war ensign in US waters and sinking enemy ships.

Prior to arriving in Newport, Rhode Island, on October 7, *U-53* dropped anchor off the coast of Massachusetts, and the entire crew set about making themselves and their submarine presentable. They were, after all, in the United States partly to impress the US naval authorities. In what was likely another example of Hans Rose taking poetic license, he recalls that one of his crew members (Obermatrose Noorman), who previously cared little about dental hygiene, went to great lengths polishing his teeth during this period. When questioned by the captain about this, he replied that the whole purpose of the trip had been "to show the Americans our fangs so they should experience something too."[34]

At dawn, *U-53* dove to periscope depth and sailed westward along New England's southern coastline toward Rhode Island, making sure to remain just outside the 3-mile limit. Though the *U-Bremen* wasn't going to need protection, Rose still had orders to seek out and sink and British warships that might still be present in the area. Despite the sun shining brightly and visibility being perfect, the British were nowhere to be seen. The Royal Navy, believing that the *Bremen* was the only submarine expected in the US that week, felt that their mission was complete, and retired back to their base in Halifax, Nova Scotia. With no available targets, *U-53* surfaced and by noon had entered American waters.

As the afternoon hours drew near, *U-53* proceeded on the surface toward Newport, unsure of the reception she would receive. Perhaps like many other Europeans arriving in the New World at the beginning of the twentieth century, Hans Rose's luck would finally begin to improve. After all, the storms that followed *U-53* all the way from Germany had finally disappeared, and not a cloud could be observed in the sky; it was a beautiful day to make a social call.

CHAPTER 3
The Empire Strikes Back

On October 7, 1916, approaching 1400 hours, the submarine USS *D-2*, commanded by Lt. G. C. Fulker, is making her usual patrol outside Naval Station Newport. Things have quieted down significantly since the presidential review of the fleet back in May 1915. Back then, *D-2* was just a small component in the fifty-ship menagerie stretching nearly 4 miles in length down New York City's harbor, displaying the might of the modern US Navy. The American sailors certainly felt some eagerness to prove their mettle and extend the Navy's undefeated record. The Spanish-American War being essentially a turkey shoot for the USN, it had been nearly a century since the US faced a maritime opponent (excluding the Civil War) it could consider a peer.

Some must certainly have also felt a bit restless. Here they were at home while the two most powerful navies in the world were battling each other across the seven seas. This perhaps rang even truer for American submariners. The last time an American submarine saw action against a foreign ship was in 1775,[1] and yet American civilians were now being killed at the hands of German U-boats at an alarming frequency.

The American submarines were nothing to scoff at; although underdeveloped compared to their German counterparts, they were still capable craft. In the case of the "D" class of submarines, although being powered by two modest 600-horsepower (hp) gasoline engines and having a diminutive total displacement of 337 tons, they were still armed with four 18-inch torpedo

The diminutive USS *D-2* on the surface. *Author's collection*

tubes.² During the presidential review in 1915, a sailor aboard the presidential yacht, the *Mayflower*, remarked, "Did you see [the submarines] today? Weren't they cute—like little whale pups setting on the water—yes? They say they've got them where they can turn somersaults now. Great, yes—but terrible too, when you think they're liable to come your way some fine day."³

The fanfare of nearly a year and a half prior must have seemed like ages ago for Lt. Fulker. Routine had set in, and aside from the occasional fishing vessel or tug coming a little too close to the naval base's perimeter, *D-2* wasn't seeing much excitement by the fall of 1916. Although there were reports of a U-boat in the vicinity of Newport, these were felt to be false alarms. Typically, submarines prefer attacks at night or in conditions that would limit their chances of a periscope being spotted. They don't show themselves on beautiful autumn days, particularly on the surface, yet that's exactly what Fulker saw through his periscope that afternoon sailing directly into Narragansett Bay. "I don't believe it; it really is a U-boat!" he thought to himself. Overcoming his astonishment, he orders out, "Surface, and have someone raise our colors immediately!" Lt. Fulker may have been itching for action, but he did not want to be the commander responsible for bringing the United States into a world war in 1916.

Meanwhile, Kapitänleutnant Rose in SM *U-53* is equally astounded, but for entirely different reasons. "The damned English are going to sink me right here within American territorial waters,"⁴ he thought as he cursed himself and his situation. All the while, part 3 of his orders was being recounted over and over in his mind—approach Newport "observing necessary caution toward the enemy[,] whom it cannot be assumed with certainty that they will respect American neutrality." To save his boat and his crew, he ordered the U-boat turned hard to port to make it as small of a target as possible while he considered his next move. To his relief, just as his turn was completed, the unidentified submarine surfaced and he saw the stars and stripes raised above her stern. Rose picked up his megaphone and hailed over to his American colleague, "I greet my American comrades and follow in your wake!"⁵ Fulker, less dramatically, responded simply with an "Okay,"⁶ and *U-53* closely followed *D-2* into port. Fulker, perhaps not wanting to give the wrong impression to the destroyer force anchored at the base, wisely wired ahead to advise of the situation. By 1500, *U-53* was anchored among the American destroyers in the Newport Naval Station, and Rose and his crew got ready to put on their best diplomatic faces.

Upon arriving into port, *U-53* was met by a duty officer, who asked if Rose's intentions were to intern the submarine, to which he just laughed and replied with the negative. Rose, recalling his instructions to remain only a few hours, met with the harbormaster and the port doctor and requested that the health inspection be waived due to time restraints and the fact that his crew would not disembark from the boat. No chances were going to be taken with the U-boat overstaying its visit and being detained on legal contexts. Fortunately for *U-53*, this was granted, and Rose proceeded to make his first call to the station chief, RAdm. Austin M. Knight. The encounter between the two was recalled by Rose:

> I went ashore at once to visit the Station Chief. Admiral Knight received me in his office in the spacious station building. He started the conversation with the words: "Where is *U-Bremen*?" I shrugged my shoulders and thought: Well, poor *U-Bremen* hasn't arrived. Where can she be? The conversation was formal:
>
> "Do you want to be interned?"
> "No."
> "Do you want to disembark any sick crew members?"
> "No, my crew is perfectly healthy."
> "Then you would like to carry out repairs on your boat?"
> "No, the boat is in flawless shape."
> "So, what are you actually doing here?"
> "I just wanted to pay you a formal visit, Herr Admiral."
> —Long pause—
> "Do you want water, food, or fuel?"
> "No, thank you, I am well supplied with all of those things."
> "Ah, that's good because I wouldn't have given you them anyway."
> "Why not, Herr Admiral? According to international law, you would be obliged to do so if I asked for them."
> —Embarrassed silence—
> I made my bow and left. Apparently, Admiral Knight was unsure what to do with me and shied away from any responsibility.[7]

Writing about this conversation in 1918, the American writer Lawrence Perry does not deny that it happened, but he believed that Rose was stretching the truth a little, and he makes an attempt at softening Knight's perceived demeanor. He claimed,

> Subsequent testimony of that German commander was that the American naval officers appeared somewhat embarrassed at the visit, suggesting men who were confronted by a situation which they were not certain

how to handle. The statement of the German officer had a humorous sound and may have been humorously intended. In any event, Admiral Knight . . . [was] very polite, and in due course paid the Germans the courtesy of a return visit.[8]

It is plausible, yet somewhat difficult, to imagine that Knight wasn't dumbstruck by an imperial German submarine paying him a social call in the midst of a world war, but all sides of a story must be considered. Hans Rose would deny that Knight returned his visit in his version of that day's events, which will be forthcoming in this chapter. Nonetheless, the remainder of Rose's visits were more cordial and reported as such by all sources.

RAdm. Gleaves, the commander of the Atlantic Fleet's destroyer force, was aboard the cruiser USS *Birmingham* and, having received Fulker's earlier transmission, was eager to meet the German commander. When Rose paid him a visit, he wanted to know all the details about the trip and if Rose had any news about friends the admiral had in the German navy. Rose was happy to oblige, and more. He exaggerated the length of his trip to imply that his class of submarine had a much-greater range than was actually possible in a single trip. He also overstated the number of supplies that were on board, to indicate that he would be capable of operating for months instead of what in reality was just barely adequate for this single excursion. So far, this part of *U-53*'s mission was going perfectly.

The crew of *U-53* taking on American visitors in Newport. The destroyer USS *Birmingham* is pictured in the background. *NH 50090, courtesy of the Naval History & Heritage Command*

When Rose made it back to *U-53*, he found the submarine surrounded not only by curious US Navy officers, but also by a group of the officers' wives who were eager to see this German spectacle. Adm. Gleaves, repaying the courtesy, arrived shortly thereafter with his wife and daughter, and visitors were then allowed on board for a tour. Champagne and cake stowed specifically for the occasion were served, phonographs were played, and both naval personnel and civilians were given almost complete access to the boat. Both the American and German sailors appeared to let their guards down, and conversations, given the circumstances, were unusually casual—at least superficially. It was reported that the crew was willing to tell all they knew about the U-boat, with the exception of their names, and when one of the German officers was asked if he spoke English, he replied that he doesn't speak "English," but "American."[9]

One of the visitors to the U-boat was an American naval intelligence officer who was busy noting the details of the boat to prepare a future report, while German sailors followed the lead of their commander in exaggerating the capabilities of their vessel. While the estimation of the surface range of *U-53* was just slightly overstated to the Americans, the traveling radius of 450 miles under battery power given by Chief Engineer Möller[10] was an outright lie. *U-53*'s actual submerged range was a modest 55 nautical miles.[11] The modifications made to the vessel and its subsequent seaworthiness on the trip across the Atlantic were conveniently omitted from their descriptions. Nonetheless, the American officers appeared to be taking the bait and were left awed by the U-boat's technological superiority. Rose's mission appeared to be moving along swimmingly until RAdm. Knight appeared to have second thoughts about the German presence at the naval station.

The relaxed crew of *U-53* during their visit to Newport. *NH 85128-A, courtesy of the Naval History & Heritage Command*

CHAPTER 3 | The Empire Strikes Back

Perhaps still embarrassed by his awkward conversation with Rose, Knight declined to make a personal visit to the U-boat and instead sent the harbormaster to deliver his bad news. Claiming that because the port doctor hadn't approved the travel of Americans onto the submarine, the call had to come to an abrupt end. When Rose rebutted that the quarantine was waived by the port doctor upon his arrival, awkward silence followed before the officer admitted that the station chief insisted on ending the visit. To Rose, this was an indication that Knight had been in contact with Washington after receiving Rose in his office, and that the true colors of American neutrality in the war were coming to light. Knight *had* been in touch with Washington, but contrary to Rose's perception of Americans not being entirely neutral, it seemed that the US government anticipated the diplomatic conflagration that would ensue, and didn't want to be caught in the crossfire. Rose would learn just how genuinely unbiased the United States wanted to remain in this war the very next day.

Deciding against pressing the issue any further and realizing he had accomplished what the Admiralty set out for him to do, Rose elected to weigh anchor and depart American waters immediately. Cleverly, while Rose was onshore earlier that day, he picked up some American newspapers to bring back to the U-boat.[12] What may have seemed like an innocent gesture disguised diabolical intentions. Since the United States was still neutral at this point, local newspapers carried uncensored shipping lists; Rose had procured essential intelligence to commence the fourth part of his orders. Laurence Perry, again writing in 1918, hypothesized that this single act was the sole reason for *U-53*'s call to Newport. How much of this was saving face, since the US was still engaged in the Great War at the time of publishing, is left for the reader to determine. He wrote,

> Did our naval officers think this was the last of her? Possibly, but probably not. They knew enough of the Germans to realize, or to suspect, that their minds held little thought those days of social amenities and that such calls as were made upon neutrals contained motives which, while hidden, were none the less definite.[13]

At 1730, *U-53* set out from Newport with her crew assembled on the deck, saluting the American ships they passed and receiving waved caps and cheers in return. To rid himself of the prying eyes of curious surface vessels and reporters, Rose gave the order to dive, and *U-53* disappeared just as suddenly as she arrived. *U-53*'s next destination was the North Atlantic shipping lanes in international waters just beyond the Nantucket lightship. The remainder of the night was spent resting and returning the submarine to combat readiness—the trade war against Great Britain and her allies was going to resume the next day at dawn.

Under the terms of the Sussex Pledge of May 1916, Germany had promised the United States that its U-boats would give ample time for passengers and crew to board lifeboats prior to their ships being sunk. This was a direct result of Germany sinking the French passenger ship *Sussex* without warning. Although no Americans were lost in the sinking, President Woodrow Wilson threatened to break diplomatic relations with Germany should they continue the practice of unrestricted submarine warfare. Hans Rose would follow this pledge to the letter.

At approximately 0535 on Sunday, October 8, the American freighter *Kansan* would be the first vessel to catch up with the surreptitious U-boat. After a shot was fired across her bow, the *Kansan* received a message via Morse code from *U-53* instructing her to halt and to send over a crew with the ship's papers. According to the papers provided to Rose, the *Kansan*'s cargo consisted of soda bound for Genoa, Italy. Hans Rose himself claimed this as true in his war diary,[14] as well as in 1937[15] and 1939,[16] expressly stating that no contraband was present on the ship. Rose's biographers, Markus and Gertrude Robinson, posit that the *Kansan* was actually loaded with horses, iron, and steel bound for St. Nazaire, France, followed by Genoa, Italy[17]—cargo that would certainly be used by the Allies in waging war against Germany.

If this were true, the freighter legally could have been sunk then and there, but Rose allowed the ship to proceed. Assuming the Robinsons' account as reality, Rose must surely have felt that there were better pickings in the area and that sinking an American ship so close to the US coast was unlikely to improve the United States' tenuous relationship with Germany. One could also speculate that Rose was given additional verbal orders not to sink any American ships whatsoever, since Capt. Smith of the *Kansan* claimed that he was permitted to proceed only after convincing Rose of the nationality of his ship.[18] The next ships to come into *U-53*'s path weren't as fortunate.

At 0653, *U-53* spotted the British steamer *Strathdene* 2 miles off the Nantucket lightship. *Strathdene* was owned by Burrell & Sons in Glasgow, was 4,321 gross registered tons (GRT), and was bound from New York to Bordeaux.[19] Rose signaled the ship to stop and bring over the ship's papers, but the captain ignored the request. It was not until *U-53* fired a shot across the ship's bow that the captain finally stopped and complied with Rose's next signal to abandon the ship. Although the nature of the cargo was undetermined, the fact that this was a British ship meant that it didn't need to be carrying contraband to be sunk. A single torpedo from *U-53* fired at *Strathdene*'s cargo hold was unable to sink the ship, but the continuation of the attack had to be abandoned temporarily as another vessel arrived on the scene.[20]

The next ship to enter Rose's sights was the Norwegian tanker *Christian Knudsen*, 3,878 GRT. At 0803 the tanker stopped as per *U-53*'s signals, and the captain, Petter Grotness,[21] took to a boat to bring over the ship's papers. Although Norway was a neutral country, the ship's cargo consisted of gasoline destined for London.[22] This was considered contraband, thus making her a viable target. When her captain arrived on *U-53*, Rose instructed him to return to his ship and follow *U-53* back to the *Strathdene* so he could finish off that ship before sinking the *Christian Knudsen*. Grotness willingly complied. As *U-53* proceeded to sink the *Strathdene* with the submarine's deck guns, the *Christian Knudsen* waited her turn just a few miles away—her crew making use of the delay by packing up their belongings and taking to lifeboats. At 0953, *U-53* returned and fired a torpedo at the waiting tanker. Yet again, a single torpedo proved ineffective, and *U-53* once again resorted to her two 8.8 cm deck guns, but these too couldn't sink the ship. Rose noted in his war diary that "success is completely negative as the ... oil leaks out of every shell hole, the steamer gains buoyancy."[23] Finally, at 1054, *U-53* fired yet another precious torpedo to finally sink the resilient, unarmed merchant as a new victim was observed approaching from the east.

This new target was the British steamer *West Point*, 3,847 GRT, on a course from London to Newport News in ballast. Unlike the previous two ships sunk by *U-53*, the *West Point* sent out a distress signal after warning shots were fired across her bow. This signal was picked up by the *Kansan*, which then headed back toward the danger zone to assist in picking up survivors, as well as by the Newport Naval Station. Rose ordered two shots to be fired in the back of the ship, which immediately silenced the radio transmissions, and the ship was quickly abandoned. A few more shots were fired into the hull to ensure that this wasn't a Q-ship and that there weren't any hidden defenses on board.[24] Once Rose was confident that the ship was abandoned, a demolition party was sent over to sink the ship with explosive charges instead of wasting further shells or torpedoes. At 1140, the *West Point* went down.

Rose, perhaps expressing concern over *West Point*'s distress signals, ordered a test dive at 1235 and informed his crew that once the steamer crews reached the safety of the Nantucket lightship, *U-53* would begin the journey home.[25] Unbeknown to Rose, at 1255, Adm. Gleaves dispatched all available destroyers at the Newport Naval Station to proceed to the area to aid in the rescuing of survivors. No instructions were given to the destroyers regarding what to do should the U-boat be found to be in American territorial waters; the order merely said,

> Destroyers are ordered to assist steamer reported fired on by German submarine. Be ready for action. Communicate Light ship. On completion [of] duty return.[26]

Four hours after the *West Point* had been sunk, Rose noted that her crew was still about 4 nm from the safety of the lightship and that other Atlantic-bound ships that were approaching the area began turning back toward American waters.[27] Nonetheless, *U-53* remained in position to ensure that all stricken crews were rescued, and it was still able to find inbound targets.

At 1540 the Norwegian steamer *Kapana* was stopped by *U-53*, but, finding that her cargo consisted mainly of grain for the American market, she was allowed to proceed.[28] Just an hour later, the Dutch steamer *Blommersdijk* was spotted, and Hans Rose would get his chance to gauge the American neutrality he derided the previous day.

The *Blommersdijk*, 4,850 GRT, was officially en route from New York to Rotterdam.[29] Although the Dutch were neutral, her cargo could still consist of contraband and thus required inspection. Immediately after Rose finished signaling the ship to halt and bring over her papers, he spotted a destroyer approaching in the direction of the Nantucket lightship. Fearing that the destroyer was British, Rose ordered *U-53* to dive; however, further scrutiny through the safety of the periscope indicated that the destroyer was flying the stars and stripes and that a large number of American destroyers were approaching at "irregular intervals."[30] Rose was now presented with a quandary.

Having previously doubted American neutrality when he was asked to leave Newport, Rose could assume the destroyers were hostile, and break off the attack. In doing so, he would avoid the dangers posed by a superior naval force but would also lose the intimidating effect of his prior call in Newport. He could also choose to continue his assault at periscope depth, but the U-boat's slow speed would put it at a significant disadvantage to a potentially hostile destroyer squadron—all but ensuring that he and his crew would likely perish in the attempt. Finally, he could put his faith in American neutrality and trust that he would be unmolested in his attacks, since *U-53* was outside the American 3-mile limit and hadn't violated any of Germany's promises in the Sussex Pledge.

Rose's war diary, as was typical of military logbooks, cites only the facts of the circumstances and does little to convey emotions; however, while reflecting on this event in 1926, he stated,

> Years have passed since all this happened, but my heart still skips a beat when I think of the terrible risks that we ran. I understood that I was responsible for whatever happened. I had to decide one way or another, and when I think the matter over today, I still believe that in similar circumstances I should again do just as I did at the time. The most difficult decision was whether we should remain submerged when the American

destroyers first approached us. Had we stayed under water we should have run less risk of immediate conflict with the United States, but we should also have surrendered the whole purpose of our journey.[31]

Notwithstanding the gravity of such options, the time notations on his war diary indicate that he came to his conclusion in less than fifteen minutes. The decision was made to surface, and the die was cast. Upon surfacing, the *Blommersdijk* sent out a boat to *U-53* with the ship's papers and also begin transmitting distress signals. *U-53* put an end to that by firing a warning shot across her bow. Additional warning shots were directed at an approaching steamer of unknown origin, which promptly turned and halted. Rose noted that once this steamer turned, it was found to be unarmed and carrying passengers.[32] Fortunately for Rose, the American destroyers headed toward the lifeboats already in the water instead of his submarine and proceeded with their rescue mission. Although they remained in the vicinity of *U-53*, the destroyers did not take any hostile actions toward the U-boat.

Upon inspecting the *Blommersdijk*'s papers, Rose learned that she was fully laden with cargo, some of which was contraband. He also made the discovery that while the official destination of the ship was given as Rotterdam, it also carried American health certificates indicating that it was to make a stop in Kirkwall—the largest harbor in the Orkney Islands and near the base of the British Grand Fleet.[33] Adm. Gleaves, in his report, noted the contraband as being specifically wheat and automobiles, with an actual destination being Liverpool.[34] This secret destination wasn't in the ship's papers and wasn't volunteered by any of the ship's officers who were sent from the *Blommersdijk*, leaving Rose to make another crucial choice.

By now, sixteen American destroyers had arrived to the area, and Rose found himself controlling the fates of both a neutral steamer carrying contraband and a halted passenger liner full of civilians, including women and children. Although the American destroyers were at this point only observing and providing humanitarian aid to the stranded sailors, there was no guarantee what they would do next if they sensed that they were being provoked or if they felt harm was going to come to any American civilians. Rose is particularly descriptive of this dilemma in his war diary, writing,

Under normal circumstances, I would have decided on a milder course. Here, however, the situation was such that, in order to spare American feelings, I wanted to let the passenger steamer, whose nationality I had not even been able to secure because of the increasing darkness, proceed on its way after looking at its papers. I now had to seriously worry about giving everyone involved the impression that the presence of the

> American destroyers caused me to give in and to renounce my rights. I therefore decided to shoot [the *Blommersdijk*] and, lying about 500 m from *Blommersdijk*, gave her the signal "leave the ship." The preparations for this had already been largely made on *Blommersdijk*, apparently in anticipation of this decision.[35]

In this entry, Rose makes it clear that he made the decision to sink the *Blommersdijk* in an effort to save face, not because of her cargo of contraband. He also, perhaps in an effort to avoid another public-relations disaster like the *Lusitania*, decided to allow the unidentified passenger steamer to go along on her way. The actual events that followed would not proceed as Rose anticipated—in fact, they would border on farce.

The first kink in Rose's plan came about while *U-53* towed back the *Blommersdijk*'s officers on her lifeboat. With so many destroyers present in the area, Rose noted that

> maneuvering had to be carried out with great care. When the boat of the *Blommersdijk*, which had been used by the officer with the papers, was towed back to the steamer by me, *U-53* came so close to the American destroyer number 53 [USS *Winslow*, DD-53] that I had [to] reverse both engines to avoid colliding with it. We managed to clear about 50 m from each other. As I reversed, I threw off the tow rope, so that its crew didn't stop at *Blommersdijk*, but continued directly to the destroyer. . . . I told the officer I would give the crew 25 minutes to abandon ship . . . but to ensure no one is injured, he should lower the flag as a sign that everyone has left the ship.[36]

That didn't happen. Instead, *Blommersdijk*'s crew abandoned ship but neglected to lower their flag. This forced Rose to approach the ship and call over his megaphone to confirm there was no one really left on board. Additionally, an American destroyer was found to be too close to the *Blommersdijk* to sink her with a torpedo, so the destroyer had to be warned via Morse code to move out of the way.[37] The destroyer complied and, once again, the US Navy allowed *U-53* to carry on her business unimpeded.

The second glitch in Rose's designs occurred when the unidentified passenger liner stopped in response to *U-53*'s warning shots. This steamer was the British SS *Stephano*, 3,449 GRT,[38] captained by the Canadian Clifton Smith[39] and carrying a cargo of codfish oil and passengers, of whom forty-seven were American.[40] Unaware that Rose intended to let the ship proceed unhindered, Smith gave the orders to launch the lifeboats before *U-53* even arrived to check his papers, stating,

After the warning shots, I stopped my engines right there. My radio operator began to send out the S.O.S. and, for the benefit of the American destroyers in the area, he kept repeating that we have American citizens aboard. Two of those destroyers [USS *Ericsson* and *Balch*] came racing toward us, until they were near enough to see all that was happening. The sub fired three more shots at intervals. None took effect, but it was enough for me. I issued orders to abandon ship.[41]

Neither American feelings nor the *Stephano* would be spared that evening. Despite Rose's best intentions, all passengers were discharged from the *Stephano* while *U-53* was preoccupied in sinking the *Blommersdijk*.

U-53's limited supply of torpedoes was not to be spared either. Returning to the scene of the *Blommersdijk* at 1950, Rose made an attempt at sinking her with a single torpedo fired at her fourth hold. Following the trend of that day, this torpedo caused the ship to list but was unable to sink her. Realizing that British destroyers would surely have been dispatched from their base in Halifax by this point, Rose decided not to waste any time in shelling the ship and fired his penultimate torpedo at her third hold. This second torpedo finally sank the *Blommersdijk* at 2020, and *U-53* headed toward the *Stephano* to inspect her papers—Rose would find an empty ship waiting for him.

As *U-53* approached the unmanned liner, most of the American destroyers headed back to their base in Newport; only *Ericsson* and *Balch* remained, since they were still in the process of taking on passengers from the *Stephano*'s lifeboats. With no additional ships in sight, Rose sent over a prize crew to scour the ship for additional supplies and then to sink her with explosive charges. Unfortunately, both tasks resulted in failure. The tender sent from *U-53* leaked badly, and the extra weight of the supplies caused her to start sinking. To keep the boat afloat, all the newfound provisions were cast off into the Atlantic. The explosive charges set by the demolition crew were unsuccessful in sinking the liner, so Rose once again resorted to his two deck guns. These also had no visible effect toward bringing down the liner. Ultimately, the decision was made to fire the last torpedo on board at the *Stephano*, resulting in the ship finally sinking at 2230 that evening.

Observing the two remaining destroyers departing westward back to base, Rose gave the order to begin *U-53*'s homeward journey. Overnight three British destroyers arrived in the area to search for the German marauder; however, no signs of the day's events remained, and they opted to retire to their base instead of continuing to sweep for any U-boats. In just under seventeen hours, *U-53* was able to sink five ships completely unhindered by the Royal Navy and in total compliance with the Sussex Pledge—the trip had proven to be a great success. While there was nothing to be done in respect to protecting the *U-Bremen*, *U-53* sent a very clear message to the British and the Americans. Germany can subvert the blockade and strike you, even on the other side of the Atlantic.

To further emphasize German submarine strength on his return trip, Rose would have *U-53*'s identification number on the conning tower repainted to give the appearance that there were more U-boats in operation off the United States than his lone boat. *U-53* first changed to *U-48* and then to *U-61*—the number the submarine would arrive back in Germany with on November 1.[42]

The crew of *U-53* was overjoyed at the day's accomplishments, but they seemed to weigh heavily on her commander. Rose noted in his war diary that immediately after sinking the *Stephano*, he tried in vain to contact Ambassador von Bernstorff in Washington to report on the day's proceedings.[43] Reading between the lines of Rose's entry, this is indicative that he was probably less concerned with reporting his successes and was instead anxious for reports from the German embassy concerning the political ramifications of his trip. He would later write,

> The crew were all delighted, and I too was relieved, to feel that we had seen the shackles fall from the German submarine campaign. But I was greatly worried during the next few days, wondering whether I had done right, and whether war with the United States could be averted.[44]

His apprehension was indubitably warranted, since the intimidating message Germany intended to send to the United States was beginning to have the opposite effect. As Rose's crew sang their cheerful "pirate songs" on their voyage home, the tune back in the United States was beginning to change to a more bellicose tenor.

CHAPTER 4
Changing Tides

On October 10, 1916, Frank Lyon Polk, the acting American secretary of state, sent a telegram to the US chargé d'affaires in Berlin, advising on the events of the eighth. It was very brief and carried the warning that it was for informational purposes only and not for communication to the Foreign Office. The State Department knew the diplomatic firestorm was about to begin, and wanted to have all their ducks lined up in a row in preparation for it. Polk noted that while no loss of life occurred in *U-53*'s attacks, the "feeling throughout the country [is] much aroused."[1] This "arousal" was most clearly observed in the American newspaper headlines, where the laudatory tone of the previous German submarine visit to the American coast had completely vanished. They were replaced by headlines of derision and resentment.

The *New York Tribune* dedicated an entire page to photos of the *Stephano*'s passengers arriving onshore, under the headline "The U-boat Terror Crawls to Our Doorstep." The photos and their captions were published to inflame the emotions of the American reader. This included a photo of a couple and their two infants, described as "a pity-impelling group." Another photo depicted women and children "wearing and carrying clothing hastily gathered before they took to the lifeboats on the torpedoed liner." There was even a picture of a young woman who, despite supposedly having "left $8,000 in cash in the hulk of the *Stephano*," still made an effort to smile for the photographer.[2] The newspaper failed to mention that the liner was evacuated voluntarily, preempting any prompting from the U-boat's commander, who had no intentions of even sinking her.

Understandably, the British government and public were also particularly piqued by the events of October 8; however, their ire was directed more toward the Americans than the Germans. Much of this was relayed by American ambassador Walter Page in Britain back to the State Department on October 18, 1916:

> Lord Grey in a purely private conversation informs me that his speech last night in the House of Lords was an effort to hold back the almost fierce public feeling here against our Government till we shall officially make known the facts about the German submarine *U-53*. . . . The newspapers here have reported that the submarine was given an opportunity at Newport to ascertain the movements and whereabouts of British and neutral ships and went forth at once and sunk them.[3]

The British were actually already well aware of the facts. To his credit, Sir Edward Grey did well in allaying the wrath of the British public and political class. In this speech he elucidated on the legalities involved with the United States' neutrality, noting that the US Navy had no legal right to intervene in *U-53*'s attacks since they occurred in international waters. This would be his public, tactful face. Privately, however, Lord Grey was far from supportive of the US stance on the matter and posed a question to Page that was, in reality, a thinly veiled threat. He said,

> I do not know whether that [Rose being given the opportunity to obtain a newspaper with shipping lists] to be true or not, but if it be true let me put this question to you. Suppose a British cruiser had gone into Newport and got similar information and had gone out and stopped neutral ships and searched them for contraband in these same waters, would we not have received a protest immediately. . . . If a German submarine be allowed by the American Government to sink neutral ships so near American waters, [the] British Prime Minister will push the British Government to search neutral ships for contraband in the same waters.[4]

Ambassador Page went on to explain that the British public reserved most of their indignation for the fact that an American destroyer obeyed Hans Rose's request to move out of the way so *U-53* could sink a neutral ship. This British disgust was further compounded by the perceived silence of the United States concerning apparent German violations of the Sussex Pledge in the North Sea and the Mediterranean. Page ends his telegram with the ominous statement that the "British public are disposed to construe our longer silence as an unwillingness even to protest to Germany about the exploits of the *U-53*."[5] The British, like Rose back in Newport, were of the opinion that the United States wasn't entirely neutral in the war and should start acting like the ally they were understood to be.

Despite the British diplomatic pressure on Washington, the State Department responded to Page's telegram in a defiant manner—echoing Wilson's reelection platform of keeping the US out of the war. Responding on October 22, 1916, acting secretary of state Polk was quick to point out British hypocrisy in the *U-53* affair. He noted that the State Department made no reports to Germany concerning Allied warships being stationed at the entrances to major American harbors at the beginning of the war, nor did they report the fact that these warships often made calls to US ports for the purpose of gathering intelligence. Cuttingly, he further emphasized that the United States didn't even make a formal statement to

Germany when British ships operated within Filipino waters (the Philippines were still a US territory in 1916) searching for German civilians.[6] Directly responding to Sir Edward Grey's warning, Polk stated,

> It is a matter of common knowledge that Allied ships can be found patrolling off the North Atlantic coast at all times. We protested against the hovering of these cruisers so close to territorial waters, but the British Government replied that they could not abandon any of their belligerent rights, adding, however, that instructions had been given to British ships not to approach Ambrose Light nearer than six miles. According to our advices, Allied ships are still examining neutral ships off our coasts.[7]

This correspondence clearly illustrates the United States' impartial diplomatic position while also pointing out that it was the British who historically benefited from this neutrality up to that point in the war—not the Germans. In October 1916, a month prior to the election, this was not necessarily a safe position for the incumbent Democrats to take.

On October 28, 1916, the United States had to accept the fact that the Germans weren't entirely honoring the spirit of the Sussex Pledge, as the British press had alluded to earlier. The SS *Marina*, an armed British cargo ship, was sunk off the coast of Ireland by SM *U-55*—torpedoed without any warning. Of her total crew of eighty-three, fifty-three were Americans, of whom seven perished. Affidavits by the surviving crew members stated not only that the steamer was attacked without warning, but also that the submarine did not offer any assistance in aiding the survivors.[8]

This directly contradicted German chancellor Bethmann-Hollweg's assurance to the American ambassador in Berlin, James Gerard, that U-boats "may exercise the right of visit and search, [but] must not torpedo or sink vessels without warning, and must not sink any vessel unless the passengers and crew are put in a place of safety."[9] The State Department, although not discussing the details of the event with the press, claimed that "the outlook [was] more disturbing than it [had] been at any time since the sinking of the Channel steamer *Sussex*."[10]

Diplomatic ties were once again in danger of being severed, and American newspapers actively reported on the new U-boat crisis. A formal investigation by the United States and Germany would reveal that the U-boat commander confused the ship for a "transport in the British admiralty service,"[11] and full reparations were provided, but this wouldn't be determined until December of that year. In the meantime, the press would report on conjecture, all the while reporting additional U-boat attacks, often carrying American-consigned cargo.

The next month's election results would exemplify the changing mood of the American populace. Woodrow Wilson, campaigning on peace and neutrality, barely edged the Republican challenger, Charles Evan Hughes, who favored mobilization for an eventual American involvement in the war. Although Wilson carried 62 percent of the states, he was able to win only about 49 percent of the popular vote. The voting was so close that Hughes was assumed to be the winner on the evening of election day—only to be upset by the late results from California in favor of Wilson (by less than half a percent of the state's popular vote).

Most of Wilson's electorate were in the less populated South and Southwest. Here there was a strong desire to let the Europeans kill each other off without any American interference, and certainly not at the cost of any American lives. Hughes secured the more densely populated, industrial states in the Northeast and Midwest, where there was much-greater support for the Allied cause. Here, there were stronger ties to England, both culturally, historically, and (more significantly) economically. These were the parts of the country that were getting rich off the European war, with their populations having a huge, vested interest in the "military-industrial complex."

Correlating with this booming economy, it was also the harbors of the Northeast that experienced firsthand the effects both of the U-boats and German saboteurs on cross-Atlantic trade. The explosion at Black Tom Island had occurred only three months prior to the election, and a German agent, Capt. Franz von Rintelen, had been actively sabotaging American industry and shipping (through direct methods such as pencil bombs or more-nebulous means such as organizing labor strikes) since as early as 1915. Not surprisingly, it was these areas where the major US newspapers, the social influencers of the period, were based.

So precarious was Wilson's position of neutrality in the United States that just two days prior to Election Day, he, growing more and more uncertain about his election prospects, penned a letter to Secretary of State Lansing informing him of his intention to resign should Hughes win the election. This wasn't a case of being a sore loser. His missive indicated that given the state of world affairs at time, he didn't want the lame-duck period to prevent necessary foreign-policy measures from being taken. He formulated a plan in which, pending his election loss, he would appoint Charles Evan Hughes as secretary of state and then he and Vice President Thomas Marshall would resign, allowing Hughes to ascend to the presidency prior to the formal inauguration.[12] A president Hughes could then begin implementing his policies immediately, and the turbulence of a four-month lame-duck period could be avoided.[13] It was into this contentious political climate that the *U-Deutschland* once again set out for American waters.

On October 8, just as Hans Rose and *U-53* were preparing for their busy day outside the American 3-mile limit, Paul König and the *U-Deutschland* departed Wilhelmshaven bound for New London, Connecticut. The *Deutschland*'s cargo was similar to that of her first trip, consisting of chemicals, dyestuffs, pharmaceuticals, and securities; however, a new code book was also loaded on board the submarine. Hidden within the diplomatic mail, this book was to be delivered to Ambassador von Bernstorff at the German embassy in Washington, DC.[14]

The fact that just a single code book was provided and considered sufficient for secret diplomatic communication during wartime was both peculiar and perilous. It was an oversight that would have devastating implications in the months to come, since this cipher, having not been replicated and distributed to other imperial embassies, would be useful only in communicating from Washington to Berlin. Radio transmissions with the German embassy in Mexico, for example, would still rely on using the old set of codes, long since cracked by British intelligence.

Arriving on November 1, the *U-Deutschland* would encounter a completely different atmosphere than she had in Baltimore, mostly due to the recent appearance of *U-53* in nearby Newport. Now fully aware that *U-53*'s visit was intended to coincide with the departure of the *U-Bremen* from American waters, the United States was now leery as to whether the *Deutschland* was fully a commercial venture or if another trap was being laid by the Kaiserliche Marine. Capt. König did little to dispel such thinking.

During a press conference on the afternoon of his arrival, he was asked if he could expect any difficulty in returning to Germany. Instead of using his charm to sidestep the question, he replied that he "would not be surprised if the *U-57* met him off the coast to provide an escort through the blockade."[15] Whether it was König's intention to scare off potential British threats or simply prolong Rose's intimidation campaign with this outlandish statement is unknown. What is known is that this was a terrific tactical blunder, given the United States' evolving opinion of Germany.

König's gaffe had two significant factors working against it. The first was that *U-57* had not received orders for such a mission (*U-57* was busy patrolling the North Sea shipping lanes at the time), nor were any modifications, such as those required by *U-53*, made for such an endeavor. The second was that König now essentially gave the United States a novel reason for reassessing the nature of the *Deutschland*, despite having done so extensively on her first trip. Fearing that König would be communicating with hostile vessels off the coast, the State Department ordered the *Deutschland* to disable her radio during her time at port. Additionally, a formal inspection by Yates Stirling Jr., the commander of the Atlantic Fleet's Submarine Flotilla, was scheduled for the next day.

In a total departure from the State Department's previous inspection of the *Deutschland*, Cmdr. Stirling's new assessment arrived at conclusions that completely aligned with those stated by the British secretary of state for foreign affairs, Edward Grey, back in July. Stirling noted that while the *U-Deutschland* was currently an unarmed cargo submarine,

> the vessel could be quickly converted into a commerce raiding submarine by the mounting of several guns on the non-watertight superstructure housing within the superstructure; a certain amount of stiffening would be required. The vessel could also be readily converted into a mine-laying submarine, launching the mines from the superstructure deck; the watertight hatches are large enough to pass a mine sufficiently large to do considerable damage.[16]

He would go even further by positing that the *Deutschland*, in taking on fuel and supplies in the United States, could act as a mother ship for the smaller, combat-outfitted submarines, drastically extending their ranges and the lengths of their patrols. If this role was taken on by the *Deutschland*, the submarine would cease to be a merchant vessel and would legally become a tender for the imperial German navy. Nonetheless, König was allowed to remain at port and proceed with his commercial activities, albeit under intense scrutiny.

For their part, the Germans did little to allay any uncertainties surrounding her nature. The Norddeutscher Lloyd, to the displeasure of the local, white dockworkers, insisted on using the same handpicked, African American stevedores who were hired back in Baltimore. This was a precaution taken by the NDL, since they believed that African Americans were less likely to

The *U-Deutschland* offloading in New London, Connecticut. *Courtesy of Library of Congress*

CHAPTER 4 | Changing Tides

commit sabotage or engage in espionage for the British (the actual press statement concerning this measure was worded rather more repugnantly). Nonetheless, the Germans must have felt that they weren't completely trustworthy, since they were strip-searched prior to beginning their shifts.[17] Reporters were once again refused access to the submarine, and just as on the first trip, the *Deutschland* was kept well away from the inquisitive eyes of the public. Rumors abounded, and the lack of openness from the Germans allowed them to spread like wildfire.

Deepening the mistrust between the Americans and the Germans, local reporters were finally able to get a firsthand story on the *Deutschland* when a drunken member of her crew accosted a local woman at a bar and then pulled a knife on the barman who tried to intervene on the woman's behalf. The issue was settled with a bribe of $50,[18] but this did little in repairing the image the *Deutschland* was painting of herself and the barbaric "Huns."

This shouldn't imply that the *Deutschland* received entirely negative coverage while in New London. The *Deutschland* would reestablish a mail route between the US and Germany through a monthly contract negotiated earlier that October. This was beneficial to both countries, since British warships intercepted all mail being transported between the United States and northern Europe and submitted it to a thorough search, often resulting in seizures. Likewise, just as in Baltimore, the mayor of New London and local German American societies held banquets for König and his crew. These, however, were far more muted than they had been in July and were scarcely reported on by the major newspapers.

Instead, the dominant news stories concerning U-boats that week revolved around the ongoing investigation of the SS *Marina* sinking, and further British losses, such as the *Arabia*, *Bogota*, and *Gulf of Suez*, at the hand of U-boats. The *New York Tribune* was quick to point out that the *Gulf of Suez* was the "third steamer with cotton consigned to American importers that has been sunk in the last ten days."[19] *U-Deutschland* no longer made headlines and instead occupied mere footnotes well beyond the front page. The American love affair with German submarines was clearly over. If Germany wanted to repair the increasingly negative public perception of U-boats, the *Deutschland* would have one final attempt as she prepared to depart Connecticut.

Upon receiving customs clearance on November 16, 1916, König and his crew planned to sail from New London shortly after 0100 the next day. The submarine's hold contained 1,000 tons of cargo worth about $2 million (in 1916 dollars) and consisted of rubber, copper, nickel,[20] and 6.2 tons of silver transported from California on horse-drawn wagons.[21] This departure, differing from the first voyage from Baltimore, only continued to fuel American antipathy for the German U-boats.

While a festival atmosphere surrounded his departure from Baltimore, König now, suspiciously, wanted to slip away in the middle of the night, despite assuring the press that "when the *Deutschland* left, he would go in daylight, so that those from whom she had been hidden by the warehouses, the floating screen, and the tarpaulins might have at least a parting look at her."[22] König went so far as to go see a motion picture show, announcing that afterward he would spend the evening with friends at the Mohican Hotel, and then, midshow, excused himself and rushed to the pier to depart.[23]

This was probably due to the fact that wireless reports from incoming steamers indicated that British warships were observed patrolling off the American northeastern coast. König, knowing that *U-57* wasn't really awaiting him, likely wanted to avoid his cruise back to Germany becoming a public spectacle, and, in avoiding publicity, also evade being attacked and sunk by the awaiting Royal Navy. Nonetheless, the limited press on hand was perturbed by this sudden change of plans and set off in a launch to shadow the departing submarine. They would be especially fastidious in noting what they observed that night.

The first act scrutinized by reporters concerned the *Willehad*, another Norddeutscher Lloyd steamer docked in New London to be utilized by the *Deutschland*—just as they had with the *Neckar* in Baltimore. As König was beginning to leave the dock, the *Willehad* was seen beaming its searchlight down the Thames River instead of toward the water in front of the departing submarine. Additionally, the *Deutschland* and her supporting tugs, *T. A. Scott Jr.* and *Cassie*, were running with their navigation lights on—directly contrasting König's implicit intention of secretly slipping away from New London in darkness. At least one member of the press observing this light show concluded that its only logical explanation would be to signal an awaiting *U-57* somewhere in the Long Island Sound.[24]

Next, König refused to take a pilot on board, instead relying on Capt. John Gurney in the *T. A. Scott Jr.* to guide him out of the Long Island Sound. This also seemed suspicious to the newspapermen but was actually in line with US regulations, which specified that in the absence of having a pilot on board, an escorting tug (whose master was by default a pilot) could be utilized for that purpose. König boasted to reporters earlier that week about not requiring a pilot, instead relying on his skill and the seaworthiness of the *Deutschland* to get to sea. In reality, he didn't want to have to stop and allow a pilot to disembark from the submarine, putting himself in a vulnerable position in the open water should British warships suddenly turn up. This pretentious crowing would soon force König to have to eat his words.

For all of König's confidence in himself and his submarine, he was still inexperienced with the local waters, particularly "the Race" approaching Race Rock Light, where the tidal currents are extremely treacherous. It was here, at approximately 0230, that the *T. A. Scott Jr.* ran into a shifting current and swung to port, directly in front of the approaching *Deutschland*. Aware of the predicament the ship was in, Capt. Frederick Hinsch (once again present as a representative of the Eastern Forwarding Company) yelled over to Capt. Gurney to bring the ship up to full speed; however, Gurney misinterpreted the command and instead signaled to stop the tug's engine.

König, realizing he wouldn't have time to steer clear of the tug, attempted to stop, but it was too late—the *Deutschland*'s bow rammed the port side of the *T. A. Scott Jr.*, rolling it over and causing it to sink quickly (it should be remembered that the *Deutschland*'s diesel engines were not capable of going in reverse; to do so the crew would have to switch to the electric motors, a process nearly impossible to perform quickly in an emergency). Capt. Hinsch was thrown from the ship upon the collision and would be rescued from the water by the *Cassie*. Unfortunately, Capt. Gurney and his crew of four would perish in the incident, not being able to escape the stricken tug, while the *Deutschland* was able to return back to port on her own power.[25] The *Deutschland* was about to make headlines again, but for all the wrong reasons.

The next day a federal inquiry, along with a libel suit on behalf of the tug company and the five victims of the sinking, had already been set in motion—all of which now made front-page news. The federal steamboat inspector, Capt. W. E. Withey, was speculated to have a particular interest in why Frederick Hinsch, a German, was the sole survivor on the *T. A. Scott Jr.*, as well as why he was purported to be the one giving commands to Capt. Gurney. As the investigation and lawsuit went forward, König and his crew were barred from going aboard the *Deutschland* for any extended period of time, and repairs to the submarine were strictly forbidden. It wasn't until a bond of $97,500[26] was posted by the Eastern Forwarding Company (just under half the value of the writ of libel against the submarine) that repairs could be made to the bow of the *Deutschland* and she could once again prepare to head back across the Atlantic.

On November 21, 1916, König once again departed New London, but this time he chose another tactic. Since no British warships were reported to be in the area since the *Deutschland*'s first attempt at leaving, König sailed from New London unannounced, but in broad daylight and with more-favorable tidal conditions. This time, his single accompanying tug, the ironically named *Alert* (once again with Capt. Hinsch on board), trailed half a mile behind the submarine and returned to her pier shortly after the

Deutschland passed "the Race" safely.²⁷ Although a crowd of thousands of locals lined the Thames to watch the submarine depart, it was reported that König left so suddenly that the crowds, assembling twice along the riverbanks that day, went home disappointed.

Ultimately, the federal investigation into the accident would confirm that the collision was caused by an error in the bell signals given by Capt. Gurney, but this did nothing to lessen the rapid decline of Germany's standing within the United States. The civil case against the *Deutschland* still went forward and was settled out of court, with restitution being paid to the families of *T. A. Scott Jr.*'s deceased crew months later. All the propaganda benefits gained by the *Deutschland* in her first trip had been washed away in rapid succession both by her return to American waters and by the arrival of *U-53*. By late 1916, however, Germany was putting less faith on winning over the hearts and minds of neutrals and was instead beginning to favor a more direct approach at winning the war.

The desperate situation of the Central Powers in 1916 was forcing Germany's hand into a dramatic final effort at crippling the Allied supply system—the resumption of unrestricted submarine warfare. Although the campaign had been abandoned following the United States' ultimatum and Sussex Pledge in April that year, and the fact that Chancellor Bethmann-Hollweg remained against it (fearing of further alienating neutrals), German military command saw no other option. VAdm. Scheer, at this time commander in chief of the High Seas Fleet, gave up on trying to appease American sentiments, remarking,

> For ever so long America had systematically prevented us from using our most effective weapon. Our attitude gave our people the false impression that, despite America's objections, we were still going to use our U-boat weapon with all our might. The people did not know that we, pledged to the nation by our big-talking, were only pretending to carry on the U-boat campaign, and America laughed because she knew that it lay with her to determine how far we might go. She would not let us win the war by it. We did not wield our U-boat weapon as a sword which was certain to bring us victory, but . . . we used it as a soporific for the feelings of the nation and presented the blunt edge to the enemy.²⁸

He goes on to state that while the United States may not have desired to enter the world war against Germany, America certainly did not want Germany to emerge victorious from it.

Adm. von Holtzendorff, the chief of the naval staff, had originally supported Bethmann-Hollweg and the Sussex Pledge but, due to the insistence of Scheer and Gen. Ludendorff, eventually came to the agreement that a "half and half" campaign would be ineffective in changing the course of the war. If Germany wanted to win and win quickly, the unrestricted U-boat campaign must be waged ruthlessly and immediately. Now a disciple of the Scheer and von Tirpitz school of U-boat warfare, he prepared a memorandum for the German general staff that December, outlining how the war could be won by the U-boats in five months.

If a truly unrestricted submarine warfare campaign went into effect, the von Holtzendorff memorandum calculated that German submarines would be able to sink at least 600,000 tons of per month and subsequently scare off another 1.2 million tons of neutral cargo. Britain's wartime requirement of 10.75 million tons of food and supplies would effectively be cut by just under 40 percent.[29] This ambitious plan was made knowing full well that, if it were implemented, the United States would surely enter the war on the side of the Allies. Von Holtzendorff parried this concern, noting that even though all possible steps should be taken to avoid a break with the United States, "the fear of such a break should not overawe us at the crucial moment to the extent of causing us to renounce the use of the weapon which promises us victory."[30]

The German general staff, headed by Generals Hindenburg and Ludendorff, were unafraid of the Americans. They believed that the United States wouldn't be able to raise an army in time to make an impact on the war, even if the conflict was not concluded in the anticipated five-month period. Popular opinion was also beginning to swing to their side, since ordinary Germans exceedingly wanted to strike at the Americans, who they felt were directly contributing to their demise.

Up to this point, many Germans had looked toward the United States and Wilson as the means by which peace could finally be achieved, but as more and more German soldiers were being killed at the hands of American-manufactured munitions, it became nearly impossible to continue to look toward America for their salvation. A popular German trench book of the period, titled "American Neutrality," made the claim that since 1898, Germany "gazed with astonishment upon the Americans as the 'people of the future' in the 'land of unlimited possibilities' until we felt the hellish effects of American shells."[31] Wilson, for all of his talk against the barbarity of war, declined to entertain an embargo on these shells, or other weapons exported to the Allies, despite being pressured to do so by German American groups.

His justification was that his administration "could not interfere with free trade."[32] This hypocrisy did not go unnoticed, particularly by the German military leaders. Ambassador Gerard poignantly observed that the military, of course, absolutely despised America and claimed that America could do no more harm by declaring war than it was doing then to Germany; and that possibly the war preparations of America might cut down the amount of the munitions available for export to the enemies of the Empire.[33]

The problem for Chancellor Bethmann-Hollweg was that this was also the opinion of the general public. An American newspaper correspondent in Germany noted that, in 1916,

throughout Germany today the hatred for America is bitter and deep. It is palpable and weighs you down. All the resentment, all the blind fury, Germany once reserved for England alone have been expanded to include us, and have been accentuated in the expansion. . . . The Germans have an outlet for their feelings against England. They express themselves on the battlefields and through the Zeppelins and submarines; but against America they lack a method of registering their enmity.[34]

The drive toward resuming unrestricted submarine warfare was unrelenting, even better if it enraged the United States. With such a public change in disposition, the chancellor's own party, like all good politicians, was beginning to turn against him. Nonetheless, Bethmann-Hollweg still managed to hold on as chancellor for the time being. Both he and the kaiser would still need to sign off on the plan, and by the end of 1916 this had not yet occurred.

Ominously, in the United States, alongside the newspaper articles concerning the *Deutschland* in November 1916, there were also stories about the hasty expansion of the US Navy. Readers were assured that steps were being implemented to counter the U-boat threat, if and when it arrived on American shores. Though Wilson had just been reelected on an antiwar platform, the United States was not going to share the fate of Capt. Gurney—caught unawares by a suddenly shifting tide.

CHAPTER 5
Si Vis Pacem, Para Bellum

January 6, 1917, Berlin. The American Association of Commerce and Trade is giving a dinner for the American ambassador to Germany, James W. Gerard, at the opulent Hotel Adlon—incidentally, the same hotel König was summoned to back in 1915. With the exception of the kaiser, all the big names in Berlin are present, from the state secretary for foreign affairs, Arthur Zimmermann, to the managing director of Deutsche Bank, Arthur von Gwinner. Even literary notables such as Hans Delbrück and Ludwig Fulda are in attendance. Representing the Americans are various newspaper correspondents and the brewers George Ehret and Gottfried Krueger, of New York City and Newark, respectively, both visiting their country of birth. Reflecting on the night in 1917, Gerard described it as a "German American love feast"[1] but also noted a sense of desperation about it, as if this were a final gesture to preserve peace between the two countries.

Shortly after Vice Chancellor Karl Hellferich finished extolling Gerard for being one of the few diplomats who truly understood the German psyche, Herbert Bayard Swope, of *New York World* fame, approached the ambassador's table. "Say, Jim, quite a party, isn't it? Still think what you told me back in October is true, that the Germans are set on resuming unrestricted submarine warfare?"[2] Gerard, gazing at Zimmermann lighting an Upmann on the other side of the room, responds without looking up, "I do, Herb. The Germans think that with Wilson reelected, he'll keep the US out of war at any cost; they can insult, flout, and humiliate us with impunity.[3] I wouldn't be surprised if they decided on that path already." Swope interjects, "So this means war then?" Gerard doesn't respond and instead rises from his seat. He's being motioned to the podium. "We'll talk about it after I finish my speech."

After thanking his hosts and greeting the guests in the room, Gerard begins his address. He comments about his recent trip back to the United States in October—choosing to leave out the part of his voyage where his liner had to change course to avoid Hans Rose's foray outside Nantucket. Instead, he speaks of the financial aid he brought back with him, intended for German war widows and orphans. He also doubles down on the well-wishing that pervaded the speeches that night, saying that "so long as my personal friends like Zimmermann . . . were in office, I was sure that the good relations between the two countries would be maintained."[4] Acknowledging the applause and once again thanking his hosts, Gerard returns to his table and the anxious Swope. "To answer your earlier question, with the current political climate in Germany, I don't think the prospects for going to war have ever been better."

Twenty-six days after this dinner, German ambassador von Bernstorff notified American secretary of state Lansing of Germany's intentions to resume unrestricted submarine warfare. Although a memorandum in the note outlined a zone of operations that excluded the North American coast, and ensured that if certain criteria were met, the "sailing of regular American passenger steamers may continue undisturbed,"[5] this was too much for the United States to tolerate. On February 3, President Wilson announced to Congress that diplomatic relations with Germany would be severed. Shortly after the contents of the Zimmermann telegram to Mexico (also sent in January 1917) were revealed to the US by Great Britain, the United States declared war on April 6, 1917.

Considering the relatively short period of time that elapsed between the breaking off of diplomatic relations and the declaration of war, one would assume that preparations had been made to begin naval operations against Germany well in advance. In reality, the US Navy had been preparing for a different type of war with Germany up to late 1916 and, by the time of the declaration of war was issued, was in a state of rapid flux.

The US Navy developed "War Plan Black," preparing for a future war with Germany, as far back as 1913, but its focus was on a Germany seeking to expand its colonial empire to the Western Hemisphere—namely, the Caribbean. In this plan, the Navy would allow the Kaiserliche Marine to enter the Caribbean and overextend its supply lines, at which point the United States would send a concentrated force of vessels to seek out the Germans and destroy them. Coastal defense would be left to the Army, who had been in the process of developing and improving coastal fortifications since 1886. No tactics whatsoever were developed around the US Navy being engaged with Germany along domestic coastlines or within European waters.

When the Great War broke out, no one could fathom that the much-vaunted German High Seas Fleet would be bottled up in German coastal waters for the war's duration, or that they would place such a great offensive emphasis on submarines. The American naval preparations, therefore, were overly reliant on battleships and armored cruisers at the cost of destroyers or other antisubmarine craft. Adapting to the changes in warfare being observed in the Atlantic was, due to politics, proving to be exceptionally slow.

Since August 1914, Admirals Bradley Fiske and William Benson (as well as the assistant secretary of the navy, Franklin Roosevelt) had been pressing the secretary of the navy, Josephus Daniels, to place the Navy on a war footing and expand it. At this time, the idea was to build up a force adequate for defense of the North American continent instead of for the purposes of intervening in the conflict in Europe. Nonetheless, such requests fell on deaf ears.

Daniels, having been appointed to the position of secretary of the navy by Wilson (a newspaperman by trade, his only qualifications for the job being, perhaps, that his late father was once a shipbuilder), was intent on following his policy of neutrality. As long as the United States wasn't in an immediate danger of being attacked, the Wilson administration felt that any steps toward naval war readiness could be construed as being provocative and going against the American neutral position. Nonetheless, certain small steps were being taken toward preparedness in the years 1914–15.

The first was in January 1915, when Congress passed the Coast Guard Act, creating the modern US Coast Guard by essentially merging the Revenue Cutter Service with the US Life-Saving Service. The Coast Guard was modeled around the Navy; however, it was under the command of the Department of the Treasury instead of the Department of Defense. Although theoretically charged with the protection of the American coastline and territorial waters, there was little the Coast Guard could do in standing in the way of a threat from the imperial German navy. This certainly would not be considered an incitement by any major European naval powers.

The next step was quite a bit more significant: the establishment of the position of chief of naval operations in May 1915. This was a direct response to grievances by Adm. Fiske, who felt that Daniels wasn't doing enough to prepare the United States for a war he felt was inevitable. Writing in 1919 about the early situation in the war, he stated,

I could see the German machine smashing its way across the mineral-bearing part of France, crushing the comparatively improvised machines of England and France, and threatening the very existence of the United States—and we watching the spectacle as a child watches a fire spreading.[6]

Fiske wanted the Department of the Navy completely reformed to include a general staff as well as an independent office of the chief of naval operations that would operate beyond the control of politicians and, correspondingly, the variable whims of public opinion.

Naturally, he viewed himself as being the ideal candidate for such a position. This, however, was unacceptable to the Wilson administration, which rightfully countered that the Navy did not set foreign policy; elected officials did. Instead, a more diluted chief of naval operations (CNO) position was created, wherein the chief would act as an advisor to the secretary of the navy, helping to guide policy rather than independently set it. It would also consolidate the loose assemblage of various bureaus and departments composing the current Navy under a centralized command structure. As an obvious slight to Fiske, Adm. Benson was appointed to the position, and he immediately began building on some of Fiske's ideas, albeit in a more diplomatic fashion. The loss of American life on the SS *Lusitania* the month of his appointment certainly helped him get his point across.

The sinking of the *Lusitania* on May 7, 1915, was the catalyst for moving Wilson and Daniels toward a state of readiness for an eventual war with a major naval power. Wilson, horrified by the incident, authorized his emissary, Col. Edward House, to meet with British foreign secretary Sir Edward Grey to discuss having Britain end the classification of foodstuffs as contraband, in an effort to pacify the Germans into ceasing U-boat attacks.[7] This was a fruitless endeavor that caused Wilson to reevaluate American naval strength in comparison with other contemporary naval powers. If America lacked the diplomatic power to influence Britain, whom she was keeping afloat with funding and supplies, how would the US Navy be able to deal with another emboldened power emerging victorious from the Great War? Wilson's solution was to "let us build a Navy bigger than hers [Britain's] and do what we please."[8]

When Benson, in June 1915, proposed the creation of an advisory council, the reestablishment of the Joint Army and Navy Board, the creation of an Atlantic Submarine Flotilla, and moving naval aviation within the office of the chief of naval operations, all his requests now met with approval from Daniels.[9] The importance of the CNO was even more apparent in October that year, when Secretary Daniels charged the Navy General Board with creating a five-year naval program to realize Wilson's aims. CNO Benson now found himself having to explain to Daniels "what various ships were for and how newer ones differed from older models."[10] For all of the administration's discounting of Adm. Fiske's earlier suggestions about naval expansion, the United States seemed to be buying in wholesale under Adm. Benson.

These prewar efforts to expand the Navy culminated in the Naval Act of August 29, 1916. Through this bill, Congress authorized greater importance to be given to the role of the chief of naval operations, making it a position more akin to a deputy of the secretary of the navy instead of merely an advisor. More importantly for Wilson's goal of becoming the strongest naval power, the bill authorized the construction of

> ten first-class battleships, carrying as heavy armor and as powerful armament as any vessel in their class . . . Six battle cruisers . . . Ten scout cruisers . . . Fifty torpedo-boat destroyers to have the highest practicable speed and greatest desirable range of action . . . Nine fleet submarines . . . Fifty-eight coast submarines of which number three to have a surface displacement of about 800 tons . . . and twenty-seven,

which shall be the best and most desirable and useful type . . . One submarine, equipped with the Neff system[11] of submarine propulsion . . . Three fuel ships . . . One repair ship . . . One transport . . . One hospital ship . . . Two destroyer tenders . . . One fleet submarine tender . . . Two ammunition ships . . . [and] Two gunboats.[12]

The heavy emphasis on battleships and cruisers was indicative of the naval philosophy of the period—the Battle of Jutland had occurred just a few months prior, putting a dent in the myth of British naval invincibility, and Hans Rose had not yet made an appearance off Rhode Island. However, coastal defense on a smaller scale wasn't entirely ignored.

A clause in the Naval Act provided for the creation of a Naval Coastal Defense Reserve to be included in the existing reserves. It allowed for current Navy reservists (formerly naval militiamen transformed into a Naval Reserve through the act) to enroll in classes relevant to coastal protection, such as with torpedo boats and minelayers, or as radio operators, but more importantly,

provided, that the Secretary of the Navy may be permitted the enrollment in this class of owners and operators of yachts and motor boats suitable for naval purposes in the naval defense of the coast; and is hereby authorized to enter into contract with the owners of such power boats and other craft suitable for war purposes to take over the same in time of war or national emergency upon payment of a reasonable indemnity.[13]

This would essentially lay the groundwork for the American sub chaser and coastal patrol fleets that would be hurriedly assembled less than a year later. Correspondingly, the act also appropriated an "Emergency Naval Fund," which provided the US president with $115,000,000 to be distributed at his discretion to "secure the more expeditious construction of authorized and for the purchase of construction of such additional torpedo destroyers, submarine chasers, and such other naval small craft."[14]

In November 1916, following *U-53*'s foray off the northeastern coast, the US recognized that the emphasis of the Naval Appropriations Act may have been wrongly placed. Realizing that war with Germany was growing more and more likely, and that U-boats would be the most probable opposing vessels, an update program began for American destroyers. The Cassin class, which included nine of the seventeen destroyers that responded to Rose's attacks, were originally equipped with four 4-inch deck guns and eight 18-inch torpedo tubes. Beginning with DD-51 (*O'Brien*), destroyers were upgraded to 21-inch torpedoes, a standard that would continue through World War II.

At the time, the public was told that this change to "giant torpedoes" would make the US "among the most powerful in the world," since the new torpedoes had an effective range more than 4,000 yards greater than the previous type, besides being faster and more powerful.[15] In truth, the Cassin and Tucker classes, despite the upgraded armament, were obsolete in comparison to the British and German destroyers of the period. The fact that there were only sixty-seven total destroyers (including the early Bainbridge class, produced at the turn of the century) in service in November 1916 also made them essentially useless in a cross-ocean war—potentially being stretched far too thinly in such a vast operational zone.

This shortage was partially addressed on March 4, 1917, when a supplemental Naval Appropriation Bill was passed, increasing the number of destroyers and coastal antisubmarine vessels to be built—including the new, flush-decked Wickes and Clemson classes, of which some 273 would eventually be produced by 1920. Bills, however, can provide only for the means to construct new destroyers and antisubmarine craft. The matter of actually getting the necessary vessels built and manned quickly was something else entirely. For the time being, the upgrade program for existing destroyers, in lieu of putting new classes into service, would have to suffice.

Additional urgency was placed on the creation of a larger destroyer fleet when Adm. William Sims was dispatched to London on March 31, 1917. Here he learned of the true situation facing the British concerning the U-boats, and pressed for the "maximum number of destroyers to be sent [to Ireland], accompanied by small anti-submarine craft."[16] He further noted that "at present our battleships can serve no useful purpose in this area, except . . . for moral effect against anticipated raids by heavy enemy ships in the channel out of reach of the British main fleet."[17]

CNO Benson and Secretary Daniels were less than enthused about the concept of making the USN an auxiliary of the Royal Navy. They both worried that dispatching their limited destroyer force across the Atlantic would leave home waters inadequately protected. Concerning how to actually prepare for the modern war with Germany, they were being pulled in entirely different directions, depending on who was giving them the advice. Benson's materials deputy, Adm. McKean, noted,

> Had we listened only to Sims, and we did listen to him hardest, it would have been all destroyers. Had we listened only to Gleaves, it would have been cruisers and transports. Had we listened only to Cone, the whole Navy and Navy Department would have been in the air. Had we listened to Fullam only, the navy yards and appropriations would have been devoted to his old armored cruisers. Had we listened to Grant only, it would have been subs at one time and old battleships at another.[18]

CNO Benson would, ultimately, dispatch a small destroyer force to England to placate Adm. Sims (along with battleships and sub chasers), but his first concern remained with the home front. He would later state that his "first thought at the beginning, during, and always was to see that our coasts and our vessels and our own interests were safeguarded."[19] This sentiment was reinforced by his order that no additional US destroyers be sent overseas until the new ones being constructed became available. He went on to state to Sims that "no destroyers can be diverted from [the] present occupation . . . for the purpose of acting as screening vessels of capital ships of [the] Grand Fleet."[20]

The Bainbridge-class destroyer USS *Paul Jones* (DD-10) on a "U-boat hunt" off the Virginia coast. She has an impressive "dazzle" camouflage paint job. *Author's collection*

Although the United States had not formally declared war in March 1917, Benson concentrated the Atlantic Fleet within the Chesapeake Bay and pressed ahead with plans to build up a fleet of coastal defense vessels. Additionally, on March 27 the Department of the Navy issued a warning to all domestic naval stations and ships to keep a "special bright outlook"[21] for the presence of German submarines along the US coast.

Just a day prior to the formal declaration of war against the Central Powers, President Wilson gave an executive order (#2584) to establish defensive areas along twenty-nine major American maritime hubs (including Manila in the Philippines). This established regulated entrances to each named harbor and required authorization from the harbor-entrance patrol for any entry or exit. If any vessel attempted to enter a harbor without authorization, the harbor patrols were sanctioned to fire upon and sink it. Furthermore, access to these areas was denied to any foreign vessels between sunset and sunrise. If any U-boats were lurking off American shores, foreign vessels would be at their mercy should they arrive at a defensive area in the darkness.

This executive order turned the coastal waters of the United States and its territories into a war zone. It did not, however, specify how these areas would be manned or what vessels would be used to patrol them. This was left to Secretary Daniels to figure out, and, utilizing the Coast Defense Reserve clause of the Naval Appropriations Act, he had the Navy begin commissioning private yachts and small craft for this purpose.

Capt. Alexander Moffat (USNR), in his memoir *Maverick Navy*, describes the rather haphazard and casual nature of how some of these vessels were sourced. A wealthy childhood acquaintance of his, given the pseudonym Len Breed, proposed that he should lease his small yawl to the Navy for a dollar a year so that he and "a bunch of good fellows as a crew"[22] could cruise around New York Harbor all day on patrol and then go ashore every night. When Moffat informed his friend that his craft wouldn't be suitable for the Navy, the conversation went as follows:

"Could you get a good one for say $35,000?" he asked quickly.
"Probably."
"Good. You see what you can buy for $35,000 and then we'll get a couple of friends of mine and enlist on it. I'll tell them you are to be captain. Can you buy the boat tomorrow?"
"Wait a minute, Len. This afternoon I passed an examination for machinist's mate. Tomorrow I've got to take the physical and sign up."
"Don't do it. Get the yacht first. Then we'll find out what rating you have to hold to be captain and then sign you up as that."[23]

Moffat did find a yacht, and he and Breed were able to lease it to the Navy, with the Navy agreeing to all of Breed's conditions concerning the crew. After a brief oral examination at the naval personnel office, Moffat entered the US Naval Reserve as a chief boatswain's mate, fourth class. When it was discovered that only a commissioned officer could command the yacht, Cmdr. Taintor, of the personnel office, simply promoted him to ensign, swearing him in on the spot. Moffat would later go on to command sub chaser *SC-77*, sailing across the Atlantic despite having no navigational skills whatsoever. Although Moffat's story borders on the fantastic, the fact that nearly five hundred similar vessels were leased from April 1917 through the end of the war makes it likely that Moffat's experiences likely weren't exceptional.

The private vessels leased by the Navy were of various types and size and were suitable solely for intraharbor patrolling, not antisubmarine warfare. This role would have been ideally filled by destroyers; however, there simply weren't enough produced to accommodate Sims in Europe and the home front. Lt. William Washburn Nutting, who would go on to command a European theater–bound sub chaser, summarized the issue:

> Then all at once we became uncomfortably conscious of our long and unprotected coastline, the vulnerability of which already had been forcefully demonstrated by the arrival of the "Deutschland" and the escapade of the "U-53." Our venerable confidence in our ability to take down the old musket from its peg on the wall, if the occasion actually demanded it, and walk out and chasten the world, depending rather on American nerve than on any equipment or preparation in particular, was suffering a rude awakening. We thought of our destroyers. They were few. We ordered many more of them. When would they be completed? In two years at the earliest.[24]

The immediate solution for the shortage of defensive vessels was wooden, 110-foot, American-designed sub chasers that had gone into production back in March.

The United States already had a head start in the fabrication of these vessels, since the American shipbuilder ELCO (the Electric Launch Company in Bayonne, New Jersey) had developed and built 80-foot motor launch (ML) boats for the British Royal Navy as early as April 1915. The power behind these boats was also sourced in the United States, since they were equipped with two 220 hp gasoline engines built by Standard Motor Company in Jersey City, New Jersey.[25] The MLs numbered about five hundred in service by November 1916 and had already been serving in a sub chaser role, as well as launch duties in the infamous Zeebrugge and Ostend raids. While it would have been possible to simply begin producing these for domestic use, the Navy desired more-powerful boats with better oceangoing qualities.

The design for a new type of sub chaser was left to the naval architect Albert Loring Swasey in cooperation with the Naval Bureau of Construction and Repair. Unlike the ML boats in British service, where speed and maneuverability were of the essence, the USN favored range, armament, and durability at a cost of overall speed. Like their British cousins, they were constructed of wood, utilized a 3-inch Poole deck gun, and had a very shallow draft, as to be "immune from torpedo attack."[26] Unlike the British ML boats, they were 110 feet in length, utilized three of the 220 hp Standard Motor Company engines, were equipped with two machine guns (either Lewis guns or Colt M1895/14 types, depending on the boat), and carried eighteen Mk. II 300-pound depth charges instead of the British late-war maximum of ten.

Of these eighteen depth charges, two were loaded into the Y-gun located just behind the pilothouse, and twelve were loaded into the launching racks at the stern of the boat (the remaining four were in ready racks).[27] The crews were also armed with small arms, consisting of M1917 or M1903 rifles for the men and Colt M1911 pistols for the officers.

Also differing from the British ML, the American sub chasers were equipped with wireless telephones and, more importantly, hydrophones to detect submerged U-boats. Since the sub chaser's maximum speed of 17 knots was barely able to surpass that of a surfaced U-boat, the best tactic for a sub chaser was to force the submarine underwater and then attack it.

Most sub chasers were equipped with S.C., M.B., and K hydrophones. Both the S.C. and M.B. tubes were shaped like a "T" with listening "ears" located on its extremities. One end of the "T" would transmit sound to the operator's right ear, and the other to the operator's left ear. In order to utilize these hydrophones, the sub chaser would have to be stopped and the operator would turn the tubes until the detected sound was of equal intensity in both ears. When this was achieved, the location of the submerged object and its direction could be determined in relation to the sub chaser. The S.C. tube was installed on the port side of the keel and suffered from the sounds it picked up being obscured by water washing against its ears. The M.B. tube was located directly opposite to the S.C. tube on the starboard side, and although it was less susceptible to environmental interference, it was more complicated and often leaked.[28]

The third hydrophone, the K type, was of triangular shape, with ears located at its three corners. This was the most sensitive device on the chaser and was used to detect surfaced submarines before they had time to submerge. Theoretically, the K hydrophone had an operational radius of about 30 miles and could completely eliminate water noise; however, due to the fact that it too could be used only when the sub chaser was stopped, most of its advantages were negated. A final M.V. hydrophone type was equipped on some sub chasers produced very late in the war, but because of its late appearance it was never actually used during the conflict.

Various shipbuilders (thirty-eight in total) throughout the United States were awarded contracts to manufacture these sub chasers, to accelerate the pace that they would be ready for service. Although they leaked, required constant repairs, and had the profile of a surfaced submarine (a cause for future operational incidents), they were cheap and easy to manufacture quickly. As long as they could get a submarine below the surface and keep it there while an endangered vessel escaped, their battle was half won.

A small group of anchored, 110-foot sub chasers. *Author's collection*

An additional sub chaser / destroyer hybrid was developed by the Ford Motor Company, proposing to take advantage of their mass-production facilities. Intended to address the leaks and poor fuel economy of the wooden sub chasers, these ships were constructed of flat steel panels and were powered by steam-powered turbines. Dubbed "Eagle Boats," one hundred were ordered, but they were produced so late in the war that none saw any wartime service, and many boats were canceled before they could be produced.

A Ford Eagle Boat and her crew in 1919. This vessel was launched too late to serve during World War I. *Author's collection*

By the time the Naval Act of 1916 was altogether put on hold on July 27, 1917—with Daniels ordering a stop on battleship and cruiser construction in favor of destroyers,[29] deliveries of sub chasers had already begun. When Adm. Sims wrote to Secretary Daniels earlier that month, on July 16, 1917, he reiterated the need for a US naval presence in Europe, stating,

> The submarine campaign [in Europe] has become so intensive, and the available submarine craft have been so inadequate to meet it, that the necessity for increasing the anti-submarine forces in the war area to the maximum possible extent has become imperative.[30]

He further insisted that as long as the German capital ships could be kept at bay, there wouldn't be any risk of "disintegration" of the American fleet by sending small craft ahead of the battleships and cruisers he had previously requested.

Although surface vessels were the primary concern of the Navy following the declaration of war against the Central Powers, the Navy also began to put significant emphasis on naval air power, both for patrolling and antisubmarine purposes. Prior to April 1917, the US had just a single base in Pensacola, Florida, and, due to the relatively new concept of using airplanes and dirigibles in wartime, had taken advantage of this revolutionary technology only on a reconnaissance mission over Mexico in 1914. With a potential German coastal threat now looming, the Navy hastily began construction of naval air stations, with the primary focus being the US East Coast.

Ground was broken for these stations during the spring of 1917, and most were fully operational by the late summer and early fall of the same year, with twenty-seven being constructed in the continental United States. Of these (including the original station at Pensacola), twenty-one were located on the East Coast. Naturally, the naval airmen would need something to fly, and while the US Army Air Service favored French-built planes, the Navy would opt for domestically sourced Curtiss aircraft.

The Curtiss Aeroplane and Motor Company had been producing seaplanes for the Royal Navy as early as 1915, in the forms of the Model R (namely, the R-2, a conventional, multipurpose biplane that could have floatplanes adapted to it) and the H (mostly the H-12, a flying-boat design to be solely used for naval purposes), and thus no time was lost in research and development when the Navy began placing orders. In 1917, the two primary R models purchased by the Navy were the R-6 and the R-9—both two-seater floatplanes, with the latter being specifically developed as a bomber. The Navy would take delivery of only a scant 190 varying Model R planes—not from a shortage of production, but because more of an emphasis would be placed on the Model HS seaplanes.

These HS planes were upgraded forms of the earlier Model H and were to be used primarily for antisubmarine patrols. Approximately 1,090 HS-1/HS-1L[31] and HS-2/HS-2L seaplanes would be ordered. Their primary armament would consist of a single, flexibly mounted .30-caliber Lewis gun on the front of the aircraft (the seaplane was a pusher-type aircraft, meaning the engine was behind the pilot, and the observer was seated within the front nose of the plane), which would later be accompanied by a Davis gun (essentially an artillery gun that could fire 6-pound shells) and either two bombs (the Mk. IV type with a 120-pound charge) or two depth charges (the Navy utilized two different sizes, one with a 117-pound charge and the other with a 217-pound charge), depending on the mission. It was this type of plane that would be the first aircraft to engage a U-boat off the American coast in 1918.

HS-2L seaplanes at Cape May Naval Air Station, New Jersey, in 1918. *NH 2678, courtesy of the Naval History & Heritage Command*

Secretary Daniels must have felt confident with the pace of the Navy's coastal defense program, since, despite his earlier objections, he now felt comfortable with sending not only the best American destroyers to Europe and the Mediterranean, but also a contingent of sub chasers. He may have also been assuaged by Sims's dismissal of the U-boats as a domestic threat in the same letter. Sims wrote,

> The difficulties experienced by enemy submarines en route and in operating as far from their bases as they now do are prodigious. Operations on our coast without a base are impracticable, except by very limited numbers for brief periods, purely as diversions. In view of our distance

from enemy home bases, the extent of our coastline, and the distances between our principal ports, it is a safe assumption that if we could induce the enemy to shift the submarine war area to our coasts his defeat would be assured, and his present success would be diminished more than in proportion to the number of submarines he diverted from the more accessible area where commerce necessarily focuses.[32]

The Germans were certainly willing to test his theory, as evidenced by cruises of the *Deutschland* and the *U-53*. After the United States declared war in April 1917, the question looming on American naval minds was "Where are the German U-boats?"

The simple answer to this question was in the North Sea and the waters around Great Britain and France. Here they were making a concentrated effort at achieving the desired minimum of 600,000 monthly tons sunk to force Britain into submission with all their available operational U-boats. However, just like their colleagues in the American navy, the Kaiserliche Marine was also making changes as early as the summer of 1916 in preparation for an eventual cross-Atlantic war.

In May 1916, less than a month before the *U-Deutschland* made her first trip to the United States, Grand Admiral Prince Heinrich of Prussia made a proposal for the development of an *Unterseeboot Kreuzer*,[33] with the capability of waging a trade war throughout the expanses of the Atlantic. His specifications for the new submarine were as follows:

Displacement: approximately 10,000 tons

Operational range: 20,000 nautical miles

Speed: a maximum surface speed of 30 knots and a submerged maximum of 15 knots

Machines: diesel motors, whose number would be determined by the state of current technology to meet the prescribed speed requirements

Armament:

   (a) Artillery: four 15 cm or 21 cm deck guns to be installed on the midship line, an additional four 10.5 cm deck guns for the purpose of defense against torpedo boats or aircraft

   (b) Torpedoes: four bow torpedo tubes, two stern torpedo tubes, and two above-water broadside tubes

Armor: 300 mm deck armor, no side armor

Boats: in niches on the deck[34]

The state secretary for the navy, Adm. Eduard von Capelle, held a conference to discuss this tall order on May 27, 1916. During this meeting, concerns were brought up about the size of the engines required to meet the desired maximum speeds, maneuverability, total displacement, and even the size of the crew and their accommodations. It was decided that compromises would have to be made, and due to the submarine cruiser likely being of only a moderate maximum speed, its primary weapon would ultimately be artillery, followed by torpedoes, and finally mines. Adm. von Capelle concluded the conference with the opinion that technology being developed would ultimately solve some of the concerns of the session, but that "it remains to be seen whether their [the U-Kreuzer's] military usefulness will actually fulfill all the desired hopes placed on it. In any case, their military use will not be easy."[35]

Development of the U-Kreuzer began in earnest in June 1916 at Germaniawerft in Kiel, for U-cruisers SM *U-139*, *U-140*, and *U-141* (an additional thirty-one U-boats of this class would be ordered through the end of the war). Differing from the specifications proposed by Prince Heinrich, these submarines had a total submerged displacement of 3,050 tons and a significantly reduced armament. The broadside torpedo tubes were eliminated entirely, as were half the suggested deck guns. Instead, the submarines were designed to use two 15 cm (5.9") L/45 deck guns as the primary form of artillery (with a firing range of 15,860 yds. / 14,500 m) and two additional 8.8 cm (3.46") guns for the purpose of firing warning shots and flare grenades and for antiaircraft use (these smaller-caliber guns were never actually installed). The six 50 cm (19.7") below-deck torpedo tubes were retained in the four bow / two stern configuration, and a maximum of twenty-four G6AV[*36] torpedoes could be stowed on board.

Detail of the L/45 15 cm deck gun as seen on *U-155* after the war.
USN Historical Section

In lieu of the broadside tubes, the intended space now contained one MAN-Brown six-cylinder, four-stroke diesel generator.[37] Propulsion was achieved through two MAN ten-cylinder, four-stroke diesel engines (with *U-139* being equipped with two additional Germania two-stroke diesels and *U-140/141* with two additional MAN six-cylinder, four-stroke diesels).[38] Speed was nearly half what Prince Heinrich desired, at just under 16 knots on the surface and 7.6 knots submerged. Range for these initial U-cruisers approached the proposed 20,000 nautical miles but ultimately fell short at 17,750 nm (32,873 km / 20,426 mi.) on the surface at 8 knots (the 20,000 nm range would be achieved in future U-139-class submarines). The new *U-Kreuzer* would have a crew of six officers and fifty-six sailors, plus an additional prize crew consisting of one officer and twenty men—a significant increase over the four officers and thirty-two sailors aboard Hans Rose's *U-53*.

A cruiser minelaying submarine was also put into development at about the same time as *U-139–141*—the type UE II, or the U-117-class (Project 45) submarine. Although the specifications of the UE II weren't remarkable compared to those of the U-139 class, being a rather diminutive 1,880 total tons in displacement, they were a dramatic improvement over the earlier type UE I / U-71-class minelayers.[39]

Intended for minelaying operations to the Azores (and beyond), the new cruiser minelayer was equipped with two MAN six-cylinder, four-stroke diesels, making a total of 2,400 hp (over 2.5 times the power of the earlier type) and a maximum speed of 14.7 knots on the surface and 7 knots submerged. The range was nearly double that of the earlier type, at 13,900 nm (25,743 km / 15,996 mi.) on the surface at 8 knots and 35.5 nm submerged.

Armament consisted of four 50 cm bow torpedo tubes (with twenty G6AV* torpedoes being stowed on board), two 100 cm mine-launching tubes at the stern (intended for forty-two 200 kg charge UC 200 mines and an additional thirty 100 kg charge TK "*Torpedo Kaliber*" 50 cm diameter mines), and two deck guns (one 15 cm and the other 8.8 cm).[40] The minelayer would be crewed by four officers and thirty-six enlisted men and would not employ a supplementary prize crew.

Akin to the American issue of having fantastic plans that wouldn't be realized in time for an immediate, potential conflict, these cruiser submarines would be constructed in late 1917 / early 1918 and wouldn't actually be commissioned until early to mid-1918. If the Germans wanted a chance at striking America quickly, another means of doing so would have to be found. A possible solution to this problem lay with the merchant submarines of the Deutsche Ozean-Reederei.

German UC-200 mine pictured on the deck of a captured U-boat. *Author's collection*

The American declaration of war against Germany now made the *U-Deutschland* (and the six other merchant submarines being developed) redundant. Prophetically, the Kaiserliche Marine didn't wait for a formal declaration of war with the United States to begin work on converting these submarines for combat use. On September 2, 1916, the imperial navy had proposed modifying the *Deutschland* and subsequently commissioning the remaining commercial U-boats under construction as war vessels.

The application for these vessels was undecided at this point, but the imperial navy narrowed the scope down to three possibilities: (1) converted to be used as fuel transports or as submarine escorts, (2) converted to large minelayers, or (3) converted into a U-cruiser, with an emphasis on strong artillery capabilities.[41] Interestingly, FdU Hermann Bauer preferred a refashioned version of the first option, with a role more closely aligned with how the British perceived the *Deutschland* to be used on her first voyage. Bauer envisioned a U-boat acting as a mobile submarine command center, tracking enemy vessels and coordinating U-boat attacks via its wireless transmitter.[42]

This new type of strategy could have had a dramatic effect on the *Handelskrieg* against the Allies, perhaps even winning the war for Germany, and would be a precursor to how U-boats operated in the Second World War. This mode of operating, however, was not to be in 1916. Instead, the Kaiserliche Marine decided on the third option, with support from Germaniawerft, who believed that the U-cruiser was the most viable option given the current state of merchant submarine construction. In the case of the *Deutschland*, being the only completed U-boat of this type in service, plans for conversion were hastily drawn up in five days, and the submarine was commissioned into the imperial navy on February 19, 1917.

In a process that lasted under two months, the *Deutschland*, now SM *U-155*, received enlarged, 1.65 m diameter propellers that increased her surface speed by a meager 2.4 knots to 12.4 knots (submerged speed was actually decreased by 1.5 knots to 5.2 knots); additional fuel bunkers, which more than doubled her range to 25,000 nm; two heavy, high-muzzle-velocity, 15 cm deck guns appropriated from the battleship SMS *Zähringen* (ending service in late 1916 to become a training ship); an enlarged and reinforced deck to accommodate the guns; and six externally mounted, 50 cm "lattice" torpedo tubes.[43] These external tubes were arranged in a four-bow, two-stern configuration and were set at an angle of 15° to the sides of the U-boat. Obviously, with these tubes being externally mounted, the torpedoes could be loaded into them only when the vessel was surfaced, and, once loaded, were constantly exposed to seawater, dramatically affecting their durability. This would be a problem that would plague *U-155* in the cruises to come.

An additional, less exciting, but extremely practical part of the conversion (and one that Hans Rose would've benefited greatly from on his long cruise) was the addition of a water production system. This was developed for the creation of potable water, thus eliminating the need to use up valuable space on board for storing fresh water. This system was already designed into the aforementioned U-139- and U-117-class submarines.

The other six mercantile submarines would differ slightly from *U-155* both in design and equipment once they were completed. Since they were still in the process of being built when the decision was made to convert them to combat duty, modifications could be made during fabrication that weren't possible on the *Deutschland* and could be made with a minimal impact to their prescheduled launch dates.

U-155 after being fully converted to a U-Kreuzer in late 1917. Her earlier external torpedo tubes are obviously missing in this photo. *Author's collection*

CHAPTER 5 | Si Vis Pacem, Para Bellum

What was to become the *U-Oldenburg* became SM *U-151* and was launched on April 4, 1917. This was followed by *U-156* (launched April 14), *U-152* (May 20), *U-157* (May 23), *U-153* (July 19), and *U-154* (September 10). These cruiser submarines were identical to *U-155* in power, range, and handling but differed in armament. Two conventional 50 cm torpedo tubes were built into the hull at the bow of the submarine (none were located at the stern), eighteen torpedoes could be stowed on board, and the artillery consisted of twin 15 cm L/45 (initially 10.5 cm) guns and two 8.8 cm anti-aircraft guns. Due to the extensive cargo space provided for the U-boats' original role, these U-cruisers also had the option to carry mines that could be offloaded from their decks. Ultimately, *U-155* would be properly converted to these specifications in December 1917.

With three U-cruisers now available for use within months of the United States declaring war on Germany, it appeared that the Kaiserliche Marine was slightly more prepared to face the US Navy on the other side of the Atlantic than the Americans were to defend themselves—at least on paper. In reality, *U-155* wouldn't begin her first war patrol until May 23, followed by *U-151* in July and *U-156* in August. Neither would be heading toward the Eastern Seaboard of the United States, nor would their missions go exactly as planned. Instead, their first patrols would head toward the Azores and the West Coast of Africa, attempting to sink vessels along the trade routes off Spain and into the Mediterranean Sea. Here they would continue the blockade of England, in a place where the convoy system had not yet taken full effect.

CHAPTER 6
They Came to Casablanca for the Waters

When the *Deutschland* entered the war as the SM *U-155*, she did so without Capt. König, who had now returned to the imperial navy as commander of the SMS *Rio Negro*.[1] He was replaced by Kapitänleutnant Karl Meusel—*U-155* being his first submarine assignment. To ease the transition into commanding such a unique submarine, much of the former crew of the *Deutschland* remained on board, including two of the officers. They were, after all, sailors in the Kaiserliche Marine from the get-go, and this was merely an extension of their current service. These experienced submariners would be instrumental in training the significantly increased wartime crew complement of the *Deutschland* in its new role as a U-Kreuzer—which had more than doubled to six officers and fifty enlisted men (plus one officer and nineteen sailors to be used as a prize crew), from the original mercantile crew size of eight officers and twenty-six men. Their first patrol began on May 23, 1917, and would take them to the Azores and back—it would prove to be 104 days of misery for the new commander and his crew.

Mechanical faults with the hurriedly converted submarine began the very first day at sea. The first malfunction involved the main compressor motor breaking, which in turn revealed a flaw in the U-boat's cooling system as the auxiliary compressors running off the diesel engines caused them to overheat. Although just a day out from port and with a justifiable cause for returning for repairs, Meusel pressed on with his mission, opting to mend the submarine at sea.

Three days later and in the midst of a pursuit, water entered one of the diesel engines, resulting in a destroyed exhaust valve and reducing the U-boat to single-engine power. The cause of this incident was discovered to lie in the means by which the submarine was sealed off during a dive. The complex mechanical controls simply operated too slowly during a dive to ensure that the U-boat was watertight. Regrettably, this issue had actually been reported by Kapitänleutnant Meusel when *U-155* was still in port, but was overlooked during the haste to get the submarine put into operation.[2]

More issues were found with shoddy workmanship when a pipe passing between the outer and pressure hulls collapsed, once again causing water to flood the engine room when the main intake valve for the single functioning diesel engine was opened. Now, if Meusel wanted to run on diesel, the only means of getting oxygen to the engine was through an open conning tower hatch or an air vent located aft of the engine room. Eventually, the second diesel engine was repaired at sea, but this corrected only one issue on a quickly growing list.

The starboard engine would break another valve two weeks later, and just over two weeks after that the electric motor responsible for operating the rear horizontal planes would also fail. Although the engine was once again repaired, the electric motor could not be rebuilt or replaced with a spare. The decision was made to swap it with the rudder motor, forcing the latter to be operated by mechanical controls and significantly reducing the submarine's turning radius. More electric motors would fail in the weeks ahead, including the drive motor for the periscope, which again forced the crew to operate devices by hand. If the submarine had to act quickly in the midst of combat, these manual operations would be serious handicaps.

In the middle of July, yet another hot exhaust valve fell victim to contact with cold water, and the starboard diesel was once again put out of commission for the second time in as many weeks. This patrol was quickly becoming a cycle of pursuing and attacking targets and then spending days repairing everything that broke during the attempt. Eventually both engines had to be completely rebuilt at sea—a task made possible through the presence of a small machine shop within the U-boat, but even this did not prevent a blown cylinder head on the port engine days later.

U-155, now being pushed to its limits, was no longer the reliable, well-performing, cross-Atlantic vessel that the *Deutschland* had been. Certainly, the engines intended for use as generators on battleships didn't appear to be up to the task of combat patrols. While these mechanical breakdowns were trying enough on the green *Kapitänleutnant* and his crew, they were further compounded with issues in the U-boat's armament.

The first concerns originated with the externally mounted torpedo tubes. Not only did these put strain on their mounting struts when *U-155* was sailing, but they also dramatically slowed the submarine and decreased its fuel economy and, correspondingly, its range—cutting it into less than half what it had been designed for. Because the torpedoes had been loaded prior to setting sail from Kiel, they required periodic service from within the tubes when the U-boat was on the surface.

Ideally, inspection and maintenance would be performed as much as possible; however, this being a task that was tedious, time consuming, and dangerous for *U-155*'s crew, it was performed less often than the designers at Germaniawerft may have envisioned. By the time the first service occurred, less than a month into the patrol on June 15, all the torpedoes were found to be in poor condition (three were noted to be certain duds), with all being inoperative just a few weeks later. Though some were able to be repaired and put back into service, the same could not be said of Meusel's confidence in them. While Meusel did find success with his torpedoes on future occasions, his first attempt at firing a torpedo on July 7 resulted in the projectile sinking to the bottom of the ocean.

Meusel had far more success with *U-155*'s 15 cm deck guns, opting to fire them at long range out of concern for the U-boat's large surface silhouette and slow speed. These, however, were not immune to his incessant criticism, which seemed to encompass *U-155* in its entirety. The slow speed and decreased range, caused in part by the external torpedo tubes, were further compounded by the added mounts for the large deck guns, which protruded from the hull perpendicularly. Since the bulkheads were permanently positioned at a right angle to the rest of the submarine, they essentially acted as an obstruction to the otherwise streamlined shape of the vessel. Additionally, the recoil from the 15 cm guns sent shock waves through the hull of the submarine—loosening the lids on the ammunition cases and the mounts for the deck guns themselves, making them unsteady and thus inaccurate when firing.

Despite having his crew retighten the guns' mounting bolts, as well as place metal shims between the mounts, Meusel sullenly recorded in his war diary that after repeated use of the deck guns they "ceased to be precision weapons."[3] Perhaps attempting to find a solution with a smaller-caliber cannon, the crew would actually dismantle a 7.6 cm deck gun from the British collier *Snowdonian* and bring it on board. Ultimately, however, the crew had to throw it, and its weighty ammunition supply, overboard, so as "to not question the boat's readiness for diving."[4] Notwithstanding the unceasing mechanical failures and the unremitting grievances from her commander, *U-155*'s maiden patrol was an indisputable success. Meusel managed to sink nineteen merchant vessels totaling 53,503 gross registered tons,[5] and his submarine covered a distance of 10,220 nautical miles (18,927 km / 11,761 mi.), of which 620 nm were submerged[6]—easily exceeding the 7,550 nautical miles traveled by Rose in *U-53*, as well as more than doubling the tonnage sunk by him.

Although the hurriedly converted *U-155* was initially found to be slow, vulnerable, and painfully unreliable, its superior range had proven that the submarine could wreak havoc on patrols well beyond the trade routes defended by the Allies. With Adm. Sims campaigning for a strong American presence in the North Sea, a German submarine cruiser, if able to escape the Northern Barrage, could potentially repeat the same successes in the Western Hemisphere, where the length of coastlines was wider and defenses were more sparsely distributed.

Ideally, the time to strike the United States was at this point in 1917, before the United States could meet the destroyer and submarine chaser quotas set by the Navy. The Germans, however, weren't completely done trialing their new submersible cruisers in an operational area on their side of the Atlantic.

Shortly after *U-155* had returned from her maiden patrol, on September 3, 1917, Korvettenkapitän Waldemar Kophamel (former FdU of the Pola Flotilla in the Mediterranean) departed with his new command—SM *U-151*. He too wouldn't be heading west toward the Americas, but south—beyond the Azores and off the coast of West Africa as far as the French colony of Senegal. Since *U-151* had been converted to combat service while still under construction, theoretically it would have been a superior vessel, with fewer operational hiccups than its sister submarine, *U-155*. It did not have the externally mounted torpedo tubes that plagued the former *Deutschland*, and since the transformation from the *U-Oldenburg* to the *U-151* occurred with less haste in the factory, it also ought to have been devoid of any issues surrounding workmanship and reliability. Ultimately, Kophamel would experience some minor mechanical faults akin to Meusel on *U-155*, but his war diary otherwise describes a resilient submarine more than capable of withstanding not only mechanical issues, but enemy fire.

Like with Meusel on *U-155*, mechanical issues first began with his submarine within the first week of his cruise. Fortunately, this would be about as bad as things would get concerning issues resulting from poor workmanship with the U-boat. In stormy weather west of Ireland, he noted that

> the shape of the ship and the resulting movements favor undercutting the cruiser, so that the engines have to be stopped several times. Some of the ammunition stored on the upper deck is released, and there are also losses due to [ammunition] rolling overboard. Minor damage to the upper deck and loss of items inadequately secured. A temporary accident involving the rudder motor forces the prolonged rudder operation by hand. Use of weapons from ocean swell strength 4 impossible.[7]

The "temporary accident" involving the rudder motor isn't described any further in the mission's abstract or in the war diary itself, where its operation is described as being simply "unclear." Nonetheless, Kophamel proceeded onward and did not shy away from engaging the enemy—testing the durability of the submarine under more-extreme combat conditions than *U-155*.

The first test occurred on September 17, when *U-151* sighted what Kophamel believed to be the British steamer *Winona* (2,084 GRT) about 200 nm southwest of Ireland. In reality, *Winona* was just one of the aliases of the British Q-ship *Stonecrop* (the other being *Glenfoyle*). After opening fire on the steamer and receiving small-caliber return fire, the *Winona* appeared to catch fire (an intentional ruse by the Q-ship's commander, Blackwood, through the use of the ship's smoke apparatus specifically for that purpose), and lifeboats were sent out.

Kophamel, already familiar with Q-ship practices, ordered the U-boat to periscope depth and approached the apparently stricken steamer for a better look. He believed that there was nothing suspicious other than the now-unmanned 4.7 cm deck gun aboard, and *U-151* surfaced and was met with fire from hidden 10.2 cm deck guns at a range of about 600 yards. As Kophamel ordered the submarine back below the surface, he noted that it was hit numerous times by shells and explosives. Although the U-boat was damaged, he still attempted an underwater attack against the steamer—giving up only when he found that the submarine was too slow to make a successful forward torpedo shot at the *Winona*'s bow. Kophamel wryly noted in his war diary that the steamer "could have been destroyed with an angled or a rear [torpedo] shot,"[8] but alas, his submarine was equipped with only two forward tubes.

Lt. Cmdr. E. Keble Chatterton recounts this incident in his book *Q-ships and Their Story*—based solely on the report of the Q-ship's commander, Captain Maurice Blackwood.[9] Apparently failing to cross-check his sources, he repeats Blackwood's misidentification both of the submarine and her commander as being *U-88*, with Walter Schwieger (of *Lusitania* notoriety) at the helm. Despite this blatant factual lapse, he does correctly state the location, time of the encounter, and initial sequence of events, going on to say that the Q-ship encountered one of the "biggest [U-boat] types, over 200 feet long."[10] His story starts to deviate at the point when the *Winona* begins firing at the U-boat, with Chatterton asserting that the fire from the Q-ship was so effective that one shot "split the conning tower in two"[11] and that subsequent shells ultimately caused the U-boat to sink.

For their part in "sinking" the nefarious Walther Schwieger and his crew of "barbarians," the commander of the ship received the Distinguished Service Order, and three of his officers received Distinguished Service Crosses. In reality, *U-88* hit a mine off the Frisian Islands in the North Sea ten days prior to this skirmish, not southwest of Ireland. Luckily for Korvettenkapitän Kophamel and the crew of *U-151*, their reality was quite a departure from the stories in British mythology.

Kophamel noted in his war diary that the next day, ammunition boxes on the deck were replenished from below-deck storage and the boat was repaired. There were three registered hits from the 10.2 cm shells noted on the damage report, and their resulting damage was as follows:

The first hit punched through the ammunition elevator, damaged the port bridge, fresh[-]air mast, and the conning tower, [and] the rear edge was slightly dented. The ammunition elevator fails for the duration of the operation; tower leaks out of some rivets.

The second hit tore off the sight on the front 15 cm deck gun and penetrated the starboard front net deflector. Gun remains ready for use with the aiming devices on the right side.

The third hit was port front into the superstructure deck and smashed several rounds in the front 15 cm stack of shells.[12]

U-151 was far from being sunk, and the very same day the U-boat was repaired, Kophamel once again went on the offensive against merchant shipping.

In the month that followed the repairs to the submarine, *U-151* sank four merchant ships totaling just under 12,000 GRT; however, another test of the durability of the U-Kreuzer arrived on October 12. Here, Kophamel came upon an unknown British vessel believed to be a small cruiser or a destroyer off the Strait of Gibraltar. Sighting the ship from about 10 km away, Kophamel ordered *U-151* to a depth of 25 m and steered toward the vessel, eventually rising to a depth of 15 m. Upon raising the periscope to get his bearings in relation to the mystery ship, Kophamel was shocked to see that it was already on top of the submarine, ramming the U-boat aft. Kophamel's war diary insists that this ramming must have been an accident, since it was "impossible that the submarine was seen beforehand."[13] He then ordered the submarine back to a depth of 25 m and recorded that fifteen seconds after the collision, an explosion was heard that he believed to be a depth charge—resulting in water leaks through the compass bushing and some rivets.

After a half hour elapsed, and propeller noises could no longer be heard from the U-boat, Kophamel again rose to periscope depth and found the horizon to be devoid of any enemy craft. Upon surfacing, he took inventory of the damage, noting,

The destroyer tore open the superstructure deck to a length of about 7 m, broke off the magnetic compass . . . and took the net deflector antenna with it. Six blows from each of the screws can be seen on the deck; pieces of the propeller blades also present on the deck.[14]

Once again the crew of *U-151* repaired the damage the best they could for the remainder of the day and continued with their patrol.[15]

While Meusel's war diary was a litany of mechanical faults with his command, Kophamel, although not dealing with any serious mechanical faults, repeatedly described being too slow for attacks to be successful. In the dissection of his war diary extracts, he is often criticized for opting for slower, submerged attacks instead of surfacing and attacking at a faster speed with his deck guns when conditions allowed. One extraordinary instance of this was on October 28, 1917, when *U-151*, after allowing the French steamer *Malte* (8,222 GRT) to escape toward Dakar (*U-151* losing a surface pursuit against this ship), sighted an unidentified 10,000 GRT, four-masted British steamer. Kophamel once again opted for an underwater attack, and once again the prize escaped, thanks to her superior surface speed. The officer inspecting his war diary uncharacteristically gave him the benefit of the doubt in this instance but emphasized that

> here it may have been one of the large English auxiliary cruisers and a surface attack could be questionable. Otherwise, however, the rule for the slow U-cruisers must be that every un-escorted steamer must be attacked immediately on the surface under normal circumstances—during the day with artillery, at night with torpedo or artillery. The submerged attack during the day using torpedo tactics is to be limited to particularly favorable prospects; otherwise, missed opportunities will greatly increase.[16]

Nonetheless, *U-151*, despite being slightly less aggressive than the imperial navy may have desired, traveled 11,719.5 nautical miles (21,704.5 km / 13,486.5 mi.), of which 338.7 were submerged, over the course of 114 days—sinking fifteen ships (if the "destroyer" is included) for a total of approximately 45,000 GRT and further damaging another seventeen. Once again, a Deutschland-class U-Kreuzer had had an unequivocally successful patrol, this time not only traveling extreme distances but surviving damage from two separate attacks.

Perhaps even more important toward the resumption of the U-Kreuzer war against merchant shipping were the lessons learned from *U-151*'s journey. The conclusion of the FdU's review of the voyage reads as follows:

> The result [of the patrol] is generally in line with expectations. Even if there are consistently no precise details about the attack conditions that have occurred, it seems as if too much favoring of submerged attacks has occasionally had a detrimental effect on the possible successes. In particular, it is to be regretted that a successful attack could not be carried out against any of the convoys encountered. In the future, the specification of more precise data about the individual attack conditions is to be demanded.

Particularly noteworthy is the question of the radius of action. The trip table, in approximate agreement with the design data, looks to be, in good weather and cruising at an average speed of 5.4 knots, 22,140 nautical miles. This ship was fully equipped with supplies to last 104 days and for traveling 17,149 nm. In actuality, the ship has consumed almost all the operating material with an average speed of 4.3 knots in 114 days and has covered only 11,719.5 nm.

The great loss of travel due to the sea and wind naturally plays the biggest role in this difference; nevertheless, it is so large that it is necessary to check the details carefully. [The] result will determine the actual use of the U-cruisers of the Deutschland type in relation to the radius of action.

The efficiency of the U-cruiser, on the basis of the days of operation . . . will probably not be possible to be increased very much in the future, since the long traveling distance to the operational area cannot be avoided. After all, it should be made as short as possible in the future. Also, the simultaneous appearance of several U-cruisers in the restricted area will make it more difficult for the enemy to patrol the trade routes effectively, and thus, through the occasional tactical cooperation of two or more U-cruisers, operational efficiency can be increased.[17]

In December 1917 and the initial months of 1918, the Admiralstab would send three more Deutschland-class submarine cruisers (SM *U-156*, *U-157*, and *U-152*) back to the operational zone between the Azores and the northwestern African coast. The intention was to replace *U-151* and, due to the slower speed of the U-Kreuzer submarines, continue to prey on the less defended Mediterranean and African merchant traffic. Since the goals set in the von Holtzendorff memorandum had not been realized, and the war was far from being over in five months, there were other plans in store for *U-151*. Now under the command of Korvettenkapitän Heinrich von Nostitz und Jänckendorf, SM *U-151* would finally head westward and bring the war to the shores of the United States.

CHAPTER 7
My Needle . . . Always Settles between West and South-Southwest

London, April 30, 1918. VAdm. William Sowden Sims is sitting at his desk poring over clippings from the *Army and Navy Register*, the *New York Tribune*, and the *Washington Post*—all of which are critical not only of himself, but also the relationship between the American and British navies. Although he vented about these articles (and lamented the lack of American censorship concerning the pieces) in the form of a letter to the assistant CNO, Capt. Pratt, the previous day,[1] they remain stewing in the back of his mind. "That damn Irishman Connolly . . . ," he thinks to himself. "As if we didn't have enough enemies to deal with over here with the Germans, we have to import some American ones to muck things up." A knock on the door interrupts him from bemoaning any further, and British rear admiral William Reginald Hall, the head of the Admiralty's cryptanalysis section, enters.

"A little early for our daily briefing, isn't it, Reggie?" remarks Sims. Adm. Hall, with his eyes characteristically blinking away, responds, "Well Old Bean, if you knew what information I had for you today, you would be more enthusiastic for my untimely arrival. I couldn't trouble you for a tipple to mark the occasion, could I?" Sims, a far less cordial fellow than his English counterpart, deprecatorily responds, "You know I never touch the stuff, Reggie. Sit down and impart upon me this pressing intelligence."

"Always straight to business, eh, Sims? Well, it seems our friend Kaiser Bill finally set his sights on the new world." Sims barely reacts to this news. For months he had downplayed the threat of U-boats coming to America, believing that they, in their small numbers, could achieve, at the very best, only propaganda victories for the German public. According to Sims, "If the enemy voluntarily assists us by transferring his operations to the Atlantic Seaboard, his defeat will come the sooner."[2]

"So, what are we dealing with here, one of the new submarine cruiser types you've been keeping track of in Kiel, or the merchant type we've already encountered off the Azores?" Hall responds, "In this case, the latter, a Deutschland-class-type submarine. Our agents confirm that none of the new U-cruisers are currently in service and that just one of the converted merchant subs began heading westward around April 19. The Germans know which ports your troop transports depart from and also that your material transports leave Newport News toward Bermuda. It can be assumed with confidence those will be the likely targets. As always, we'll report any progress she's making across the Atlantic once better information becomes available."

93

"I see," replies Sims. "I'll cable this over to Benson as soon as possible. Thanks again for your exceptional intelligence reports, Reggie; we truly have a valued partner in the Royal Navy. Any chance some of my American intelligence officers could return the favor and offer your team any assistance, maybe cooperate in cracking some ciphers?"

Hall smirks. "I'm sorry, old chap; I haven't the foggiest notion what team you're referring to. Just a bit of luck that we happened to pick up that signal, I suppose. Besides, it would seem that you have plenty of wireless traffic to monitor on your side of the Atlantic. After all, we wouldn't want Mexico to get any more enterprising ideas . . ."

The gibe wasn't lost on Sims, but rather than react, he posits one final question to his colleague. "It is my firm belief the Germans will fail in any attempt at making any strides toward naval victory, but as it is our current policy to retain only 'the older and less effective destroyers, together with a number of submarine chasers'[3] along the Eastern Seaboard, do you think the Germans will have a chance at surprising us?" Hall rises from his seat and, as he begins to gather his papers, leaves Sims with one final quip: "I'm sure you're quite correct that they will fail, but this sort of cross-Atlantic cruise is certainly a daring act on the part of the Boche. Regretfully, their pluck has already proven ruinous for any ships that dare sail outside of convoy protection. Whatever measures you Americans decide upon to counter this threat, just remember that 'mistakes may be forgiven, but even God himself cannot forgive the hanger back.'[4] Good day, William; I look forward to our meeting tomorrow."

Following the briefing that day, Adm. Sims cabled a message to Secretary Daniels, indicating that it was likely that a submarine of the cruiser type would arrive on the Atlantic coast. He stressed that these should not be feared, since they historically have sunk "only" between 30,000 and 40,000 GRT (perhaps an intentional underestimation of the actual figures) on their four-month cruises, and that the smaller U-boat types, incapable of making it across the Atlantic, were far more dangerous. He emphasized that no change to naval policy should take effect, since any losses from these U-cruisers "must be accepted . . . they will be small, and will not, for many reasons, be regularly carried on."[5]

The next day, Sims sent an additional message, this time to CNO Benson, sparing any mention of current naval defensive policy or any of the downplaying of the U-boat threat he had expressed to Daniels. Instead, he gave the specifics on when the submarine could be expected on the Eastern Seaboard, and its typical method of attacking vessels (through the use of its deck guns), and then laid out a strategy for defeating the U-boat, oddly suggesting that although the U-cruiser is particularly vulnerable to depth charges, the most effective defense against the invader would be an American submarine.⁶ It would seem that while he exuded supreme confidence to Daniels, he wanted Benson to ensure that he wouldn't have to eat his words if things went awry.

The submarine in question was, in fact, SM *U-151*, and, as British Intelligence in "Room 40" predicted, it would be traveling alone. What the British and Americans were not aware of was that *U-151* received a series of upgrades, as well as a new commander, during a refit in the preceding four months before departing westward. It would not be the same U-boat they were familiar with off the Azores, and would have an entirely new bag of tricks to use against Allied shipping.

U-151. Author's collection

Following *U-151*'s patrol off northwestern Africa, in December 1917 the U-boat received a much-needed overhaul. It seemed that the numerous engine failures experienced by Meusel on the well-sailed former *Deutschland*, but largely eluded by Kophamel on *U-151*'s first patrol, finally caught up with the converted *Oldenburg*. A statement by the commander of the Unterseekreuzer Flotilla, Fregattenkapitän von Koch (at the conclusion of the submarine's war diary from December 27, 1917, through April 18, 1918), noted that although the new commander and crew progressed quickly through training at the U-boat school and the artillery training ship, significant delays were experienced due to problems with the diesel engines' rebuild—specifically that the replacement pistons were a modified older type and appeared not to have been tested enough prior to being ordered into service.⁷

Korvettenkapitän Heinrich von Nostitz und Jänckendorf. *NH 65860, courtesy of the Naval History & Heritage Command*

U-151's new commander, Korvettenkapitän Heinrich von Nostitz und Jänckendorf, although beginning his career in the Kaiserliche Marine as far back as 1898, would (like Meusel) be cutting his teeth with U-boats in this exceptional patrol. The aforementioned delays, resulting in the nearly four months that elapsed between the beginning of repairs to the submarine and its eventual mission toward the United States, proved to be extremely providential for the new commander. Not only was he able to acclimate himself to his new command through test dives and shooting exercises, he was also able learn his crew's capabilities and fashion them into his own mold.

The fact that he was green seemed to elude the crew or at least was not a concern of theirs, on the basis of the perspective of the submarine's boarding officer, Oberleutnant zur See Fredrick Körner. He would later recall in Lowell Thomas's *Raiders of the Deep* that:

> Korvettenkapitän Heinrich von Nostitz und Jänckendorf received orders to pick a crew of daredevils and equip and provision our giant under-sea boat for a five months' voyage. Nor were we told where we were headed for. Apparently, however, it was to be something on the Jules Verne order. Fine! We were ready for anything in those days . . . at that time we all felt certain of victory.[8]

While Körner's embellished yarns did well in conveying his excitement for the voyage and building an entertaining narrative for Thomas to publish, he omitted the specifics of the boat's overhaul, his training, or the changes made to the U-boat, instead opting to skip straight ahead to his cruise. These overlooked particulars, although perhaps dry, included both significant technological developments that affected the U-boat's capabilities, as well as the lessons for the commander and crew that were imparted from Kophamel's prior excursion. These advances greatly improved the tactics of the Deutschland-class submarines, ultimately bringing them closer to Prince Heinrich's visualization of a U-Kreuzer two years earlier.

The first was the development of the T-K or "Teka" mines. These torpedo-caliber (*Torpedo **K**aliber*) mines were the same diameter, although roughly half the length, of the standard U-boat 50 cm G6AV* torpedoes and were designed to be released from conventional torpedo tubes or from the deck of the submarine. Egg shaped in appearance, they had an anchor attached by a chain that after being dropped from the deck on the surface or launched while submerged would sink to the seabed and subsequently release and arm the mine. On the top of them were hollow, lead contact horns (Hertz horns) that, when depressed, would break glass tubes filled with an electrolyte (usually sulfuric acid) held within. The released electrolytes would then flow into the mine and close the circuit of the galvanic element (essentially a lead-acid battery), which would then energize and detonate the 100 kg of nitrotoluene contained within the mine, causing a massive explosion. They could be adjusted both for the ocean depth as well as how far below the surface they would float. These had originally been intended for the Project 45 (U-117 class) minelaying submarines, but while the mines were ready for service in April 1918, the minelayers were not.

Since the Admiralstab noted that the large, slow, Deutschland-type submarines were rarely successful with torpedo attacks or engaging convoys during their patrols around the Azores (the commanders preferred attacking solitary vessels, using the deck guns or sending boarding parties armed with explosive charges), it was decided to trial the new mines with *U-151* along the major harbors of the American East Coast. Since they were smaller in length, every one torpedo that could be stowed on board the submarine could instead be replaced with two mines. For *U-151*'s cruise to the United States, six Teka mines were available for releasing from the deck of the submarine, and eight were loaded to be released from the torpedo tubes.

Additionally, a smokescreen system (*Nebel-U-Boots-Anlage* or *N.U.A.*) was developed whereby two smoke bombs located on the aft of the submarine could be activated to provide cover for a duration of four minutes. Now the large surface silhouette of the U-Kreuzer, which was so often griped about in the preceding war diaries, could be hidden during a surface attack. It also had the obvious benefit of enabling the submarine to escape should it find itself facing superior firepower from an armed merchant or naval vessel.

Finally, cable cutters were equipped to the submarine for the purpose of severing the undersea telegraph cables from New York City to both Nova Scotia and Panama. Although this was not necessarily new technology (one of the first acts of the Royal Navy in the Great War was to cut German cross-Atlantic telegraph lines), this would be the first time a submarine would make the attempt.

SM *U-151*, now fully refitted and equipped, departed Kiel on April 18, 1918, escorted by the torpedo boats *T-130* and *T-158*. Von Nostitz's mission would be to sail westward undetected, lay mines in the Chesapeake and Delaware Bays, cut the aforementioned telegraph cables, and sink any other targets of opportunity in American waters. Like the *Deutschland* that preceded her, SM *U-151* set a course northward across the North Sea and then westward, with an initial destination of the Chesapeake Bay. Two years earlier, *U-53*, with its comparatively small range of operation and armament, had proven that a trip across the Atlantic could be fruitful attacking only Allied or neutral vessels carrying contraband. Now that the United States was at war with Germany, concerns about violating neutrality no longer existed, and U-boat commanders would no longer have to be discriminating in their pursuits. There would certainly be ample targets presenting themselves on the vast, sparsely defended American coastline.

While Adm. Sims had merely warned of the likelihood of a German submarine approaching the Eastern Seaboard of the United States on May 1, 1918, the very next day concrete evidence of the U-boat's presence was ascertained through a signal from an American steamer, about 400 nm north of the Azores. The message, received by a British naval station in Kingston, Jamaica, and forwarded to the Office of Naval Operations in Washington, DC, simply stated that the ship had engaged an enemy submarine, and gave the location of latitude 46° N, longitude 28° W.[9] Fortunately, German records provide a better description of the encounter, including the identity of the vessel—the *Port Said*. Korvettenkapitän von Nostitz described it in his war diary:

> Steamer with two stacks, promenade decks, about 8,000–9,000 gross tons in sight. Came up to about 110 hundred meters; submerged; Danger of attacking not forthcoming. Surfaced 60 hundred meters in its wake and the artillery battle began. Steamer returned fire from 4–6 cannons and quickly escaped our range of fire through an intense zig-zag course and a speed of 13–14 knots. The steamer reported its location at latitude 46°25' N, longitude 28°10' W.[10]

Oberleutnant Körner goes on to state (although erroneously claiming a torpedo was fired) that

> on the second of May the shout arose, "Steamer ahoy!" She proved to be a big armed ship and our Admiralty orders were not to attack any ship until we had reached the American coast, so that our trans-Atlantic

submarine raid might remain a secret until we were in our main field of operations. However, the steamer was too great a temptation, and there are times when order should not be carried out too strictly. Even if our position were broadcasted now, it could do very little harm. . . . We attacked. Our torpedo missed. Then we tried our guns. She got away. Then we caught her wireless warning: "The *Port Said*. We have encountered an enemy submarine." She concluded her message by giving the latitude and longitude.[11]

The fact that this steamer escaped von Nostitz must have nagged on him, since shortly after he broke off contact with the American ship, he stopped a Danish schooner (*Poseidon*) in ballast. Upon halting the sailing ship and checking her papers, the *Poseidon* was allowed to proceed solely because it happened to be located "outside the restricted zone." Von Nostitz also noted that the Danes had spotted the American steamer that eluded *U-151*, continuing on a course for Baltimore, and also observed a hospital ship on an easterly course. After making the decision to press on with his patrol toward the US East Coast, he radioed his location back to the German naval station in Rügen.

It is telling that von Nostitz recorded that the hospital ship was sighted on an easterly course just prior to radioing his location back to base. Körner, in his interview with Lowell Thomas, describes the commander and crew as being extremely humane to their victims, and in many ways (which will be discussed later) they were, but obviously one would always present themselves and their comrades in the best of light—in fact, he neglected to mention the entire encounter with the *Poseidon* in his narrative. Since von Nostitz chose not to turn eastward and search for it, one could only speculate what his intentions were in reporting its presence in his grid, but in all likelihood, he was doing so in order for other U-boats closer to Europe to pursue it.

Hospital ships were considered to be viable targets by the Germans during the First World War, and it appeared that von Nostitz was fully committed to his duties. His release of the empty Danish sailing ship solely on the grounds that it was spotted outside the restricted zone indicates that he had very few qualms about sending an unladen vessel to the bottom of the Atlantic, with a crew stranded on lifeboats some 400 miles from land, had only it been in his sanctioned area of operations.

Just a few weeks after encountering the elusive American steamer and the *Poseidon*, *U-151* would make contact with the British steamer *Huntress* at latitude 34°26' N, longitude 55°28' W (about 1,000 miles off the Outer Banks of North Carolina, or just over half the distance across

In a photo of a U-cruiser often mistaken for *U-151*, this is *U-157* stopping the Spanish steamer *Infanta Isabel de Borbon* off Cádiz. Both being converted merchant U-boats, they were identical. *Author's collection*

the Atlantic toward Baltimore). Upon observing two deck guns located on the ship's stern, von Nostitz opted to submerge and attack the vessel by using a torpedo. The torpedo would miss, and yet again another merchant would evade the U-cruiser through superior speed and a zigzag course. Abandoning any further attempts to attack the ship, *U-151* returned to the surface and picked up a radio transmission from the *Huntress* to a British station in Bermuda, identifying herself and reporting that she had sighted the submarine's torpedo wake.[12]

This transmission was received by the British, who, once again, forwarded it to the US Navy. This resulted in the Navy Department sending out a broadcast on May 16, advising of the possibility of an inbound German submarine. It read,

> "Most Secret"—From information gained by contact with [an] enemy submarine, one may be encountered anywhere west of 40 degrees west. No lights should be carried, except as may be necessary to avoid collision[,] and paravanes should be used when practicable and feasible. Acknowledge, Commander in Chief Atlantic Fleet, Commander Cruiser Force, Commander Patrol Squadron, Flag "San Domingo," Governor Virgin Islands, Commandants 1st to 8th, inclusive, and 15th Naval Districts.[13]

Additionally, the domestically based sub chasers were ordered, during their normal coastal patrols, to proceed to the locations reported by any ships transmitting SOS signals.

Interestingly, the Department of the Navy's 1920 publication *German Submarine Activities on the Atlantic Coast of the United States and Canada* (and the 1929 book *When the U-boats Came to America*, which almost exclusively cited the earlier Navy publication as a source) notes that the reports from the *Huntress* and the *Port Said* "were considered authentic," but did not feel that definite evidence of the submarine existed until May 19, when an SOS was received from the American steamer *Nyanza* about 300 miles off the coast of Maryland—claiming that she was being shelled by the sub. These were followed by similar reports from the American steamer *Jonancy*, again claiming being shelled, and then a U-boat sighting report from the British steamer *Crenella*—all of which occurred within 150 miles of the American eastern coastline. Here, the American records begin to significantly deviate from German accounts.

Following his engagement with the *Huntress* to the point that *U-151* actually entered Cape Henry, von Nostitz's war diary records sighting no fewer than twenty vessels, including a five-masted schooner, a large tanker, and a four-stacked armored cruiser of the Charleston class.[14] All were observed from a distance and then evaded (the German word *ausgewichen*, meaning "dodged," predominantly appearing in the logs during this time frame) by means of submerging or steering away on the surface. This is confirmed by the diaries of the ship's boarding officer, Fredrick Körner, including the act of submerging to the ocean floor for a few hours to await the evening darkness prior to entering Cape Henry, since surface traffic was far too busy. Further proof of not engaging these ships exists in the *Artillerie-Munitionsnachweisung* (essentially a log of the amount of shells dispensed and their caliber) of von Nostitz's war diary, in which no shells are listed as being fired from May 2 through May 25.

Given that the submarine made an effort to avoid such prime targets so close to the American coast, it is unlikely that von Nostitz willingly gave away his position by shelling smaller targets of less consequence, once again violating his orders from the Admiralstab to remain out of sight. It is far more probable that the submarine was indeed spotted by these vessels prior to diving or speeding away, and their captains instead merely imagined they were being shelled out of excitement or hysteria.

This hysteria appeared to be exactly what the US Navy wanted to prevent from occurring within American waters. Although the broadcast from May 16 warned of the possibility of a U-boat operating west of 40° W, on May 17, a confidential memorandum endorsing caution in reporting U-boats was sent from the office of the CNO to the naval forces located in American coastal waters. It advised,

In view of the possibility of hostile submarine operations off our coast, it is necessary to indicate a general method of procedure with regard to war, with assistance of and handling of merchant ships in order that same motive and same general system may prevail throughout.

The following instructions will be observed.

War warning first.

It is most important that the public and that ships be not falsely alarmed nor that a state of mind be aroused which would produce a situation more dangerous than the presence of submarines themselves. It is also to the advantage of the enemy that many and false warnings should be disseminated for the purpose of confusing and holding back the natural flow of ships. To prevent this, the promiscuous broadcasting by District Commandants of warnings, verified and unverified, will cease.[15]

The memorandum ultimately ended on the note that it was up to local station commanders to decide the best way to act, and indeed the 4th and 5th Naval Districts, headquartered in Philadelphia and Norfolk, respectively, canceled all leave and prepared their minesweeper and sub chaser fleets for readiness. Nonetheless, since these districts were essentially in the dark concerning the actual location of *U-151*, it seemed that they preferred to toe the line of restraint, no warnings were issued, and the patrol craft did not engage in any offensive operations.

It is therefore not surprising that von Nostitz neglected to mention receiving any further warnings of *U-151*'s location in his war diary following his encounter with the *Huntress*, with Körner more descriptively stating (following the same incident with the British steamer) this:

With our presence thus announced, we could no longer hope for our approach to the American coast to remain unheralded. You can bet that we kicked ourselves for our own stupidity. . . . Later on, we caught a radio news dispatch from the American coast. To our great joy it ended with the usual: "No submarine, no war warning . . ." Day after day we caught that same reassuring close of the wireless news. . . . We had been luckier than we deserved.[16]

The Germans had believed that a lack of communication between the British and the Americans caused the news of *U-151* attacking the *Huntress* not to reach Washington—they couldn't envision that it was instead due to the Americans' fear of arousing panic by broadcasting potentially false alarms. Incredibly, even on May 25 there was still speculation about whether or not German submarines would actually reach the United States, and defense plans were being developed in the likelihood that the Germans would focus their efforts on the Florida Straits.[17]

To his credit, RAdm. Edwin Anderson (commander of Squadron One in the Atlantic Fleet Patrol Force) outlined very formidable defensive strategies for the straits. He suggested three potential systems and planned to utilize every craft available in his district for protective purposes, including submarine chasers, scout patrols, converted yachts, gunboats, submarines, seaplanes, blimps, and kite balloons.[18] Unfortunately, this was too late and focused on an entirely incorrect area (though other districts could have adopted the strategy). By this point, von Nostitz was already deep within American waters, well north of Florida, bringing the war in Europe to the shores of America.

On the evening of May 23, 1918, von Nostitz found himself at the entrance of the Chesapeake Bay, observing Cape Charles to the north and Cape Henry to the south—the maritime traffic was remarkable. Despite the abundance of targets, he decided on a course of action whereby *U-151* would submerge to the seabed during the daylight hours and then proceed deeper into the bay under the cover of darkness; his mission of sneaking in undetected and then laying mines took top priority.

During the daytime of the twenty-fourth, von Nostitz ordered *U-151* to periscope depth to safely reassess his situation—it did not improve. In the northeast, he observed a cruiser and two destroyers on a northerly course. In the east, another cruiser was observed (likely USS *Charleston* again) towing a 6-by-60-meter (about 20 by 200 feet) target, along with an 8,000-ton, armed steamer, and some smaller coastal steamships.[19] The decision was made to resubmerge and attempt to lay mines after dusk. Surely with such congestion on the surface, these waters would be an ideal location for minelaying. Von Nostitz set his sights on the area near the light buoy 2 CB;[20] here, he felt, the six deck Teka mines would be certain to find a valuable prey.

Despite it being a clear night, von Nostitz commanded *U-151* to the surface at 1840 that evening. Steering toward the light buoy, his crew casually prepared the mines on the U-boat's deck, preparing to launch all six at intervals of 100 m. Fortunately for the Germans, the blackout orders for navy vessels were still being ignored, and an unidentified "incoming warship"[21] was quickly spotted traveling toward the surfaced submarine. Von Nostitz ordered his now-frantic crew to immediately discard the mines before crash diving, accomplishing the task before the unidentified cruiser could close within half the distance to the submarine.

Once again, fortune seemed to favor the Germans, since the warship apparently didn't notice the U-boat and was traveling in its direction by mere coincidence. Just a half hour later, *U-151* came back to the surface to find the warship completely out of view, and the previously dispensed mines already lying below the bay's surface. As the Germans anxiously monitored radio news broadcasts from Arlington, Virginia, that night, they were once again greeted by the words "no submarine, no war warning." Still undetected, von Nostitz now turned north, toward the direction of the Delaware Bay.

U-151's war diary notes that the depth of the mined area of the Chesapeake on May 24, 1918, was about 11–14 m deep (35–45 ft.), and the mines were set at a depth of just 5 m (about 16 ft.). It also cites the location of the mines, noting the first being thrown at 36°53'5" N latitude and 75°49'5" W longitude, and the last at 36°50' N and 75°50'5" W.[22] This translates to approximately 9 miles off the coast of Virginia Beach, and about 11 miles southeast from the midpoint between Cape Henry and Cape Charles. This was certainly a prime area for laying mines; however, it proved to be ineffective.

Eberhard Rössler claims in his book *Die Deutschen U-Kreuzer und Transport-U-Boote* that the mines were unsuccessful since a mine detached from its anchor on May 25, and the rest were soon discovered afterward.[23] This isn't corroborated in any American naval reports or newspapers, which were, at the time, mostly reporting that the U-boat peril (across the Atlantic) was all but over. At this point in May, no war warning was issued, and the Navy was still hypothesizing that a U-boat would strike around the Florida Straits on the twenty-fifth.

In actuality, the mines remained in place without contacting any vessels, only to be discovered by the Navy months later. According to a US Navy report on minesweeping operations, the first of von Nostitz's six mines would be located and destroyed on June 22, 1918, and the final one on September 9. Nonetheless, a poorly handwritten note exists in *U-151*'s war diary that alludes to the 353 GRT tugboat *Waltham* being sunk by these mines. Rössler (quoting Arno Spindler's *Der Krieg zur See 1914–1918: Der Handelskrieg mit U-Booten*) also states this tug as possibly being sunk, but erroneously names it as the *Walthan* and locates the sinking as occurring in the Delaware Bay.[24]

The sinking of the *Waltham* by mines off Virginia was, in fact, reported by the *New York Times* as being true (along with two coal barges) on June 6, 1918,[25] but was retracted on June 9, after the owner of the tug and barges, Staple Transportation Co., confirmed that they were very much afloat.[26] The Germans would have to hope for better luck as they made their way farther north along the East Coast. As it happened, they wouldn't have to venture very far.

On the morning of May 25, about 20 mi. / 32 km off the Virginia coast (and just 50 mi. / 80 km from the mined area in the Chesapeake), von Nostitz sighted a three-masted schooner directly ahead of him. He first approached the vessel submerged, and, finding it unarmed, came to the surface, fired a warning shot at a distance of 5,000 m, and signaled for the crew to abandon ship immediately. The German commander noted that the ship apparently didn't understand what was happening, since she showed no flag and turned and stopped only after additional warning shots were fired. This sequence of events was confirmed in the testimony of the schooner's captain, C. E. Holbrook, who attested that he believed the U-boat was an American vessel, not fully realizing his true state of affairs until von Nostitz came alongside and asked, "Do you want me to kill you?"[27] The Navy's plan to avoid panic among American merchantmen was apparently working too well.

After sending over a prize crew, the schooner was identified as the *Hattie Dunn* (435 GRT), in ballast and bound for Charleston from New York City. With nothing to salvage from the ship, the boarding party was ordered to sink her with explosive charges and to take her crew back as prisoners. Since von Nostitz did not want news of his presence to be confirmed by survivors showing up on the shore, it appeared that American crews would be taken on board as unwilling guests of the Kaiserliche Marine for the immediate future. Before the sinking and taking on of prisoners could be accomplished, however, another target presented itself on the horizon about 10 km away. Instructing his crew to proceed with sinking the *Hattie Dunn* and to follow the U-boat with the ship's lifeboats, von Nostitz proceeded toward the next pursuit, a somewhat larger, four-masted schooner.

Believing that the new craft had observed *U-151* in the process of sinking the *Hattie Dunn* and was now heading toward the shore, von Nostitz sped toward it and once again fired a warning shot from a distance of about 8,000 m. In an almost identical scene as earlier, the captain of this new vessel, the *Hauppauge*, also did not seem to grasp the situation, and more warning shots (some registering hits on the vessel above the waterline) were required before the ship turned toward the U-boat and stopped. According to von Nostitz the ship appeared to be "brand new," was 1,446.5 GRT, and was also in ballast en route from Norfolk, Virginia, to Portland, Maine (with a stopover in New York City).[28] Capt. Sweeney, of the *Hauppauge*, was ordered to present his papers to the U-boat commander, and, as they were being checked over, the prize crew and prisoners from the *Hattie Dunn* caught back up with the submarine.

Oberleutnant Körner and his team were immediately sent back into action to take prisoners and provisions and to sink the new prize, once again, with explosives. While von Nostitz's log recorded that supplies were taken on board, Körner noted that these were specifically hydrographical charts, books, and, most importantly, fresh food that would spare the crew from their current diet of canned meals.[29] By now, seventeen prisoners were on board *U-151* accompanying the submarine on her way to lay the remaining eight Teka mines throughout Delaware Bay. Since luck was seemingly on von Nostitz's side this cruise, one more ship would fall prey to *U-151* that day, sailing directly into the U-boat's path.

Despite hearing deck guns firing in the distance earlier in the day, Capt. C. W. Gilmore of the *Edna* continued on his course from Philadelphia toward Santiago, Cuba. He was headed directly toward the area where the *Hauppauge* was sunk. The *Edna*, like the other ships sunk on the twenty-fifth, was a small schooner of just 325 GRT and was loaded with six thousand cases of motor oil and four thousand cases of gasoline.[30] Unlike the other two captains that day, upon hearing a single warning shot and then sighting a second shot that landed just 50 feet off the ship a minute later, Gilmore stopped and immediately raised the American flag. To his surprise, the German war ensign was raised from the opposing submarine, being observed about 5 miles northwest. For the third and final time that day, a prize crew from *U-151* was sent over to take prisoners and sink the vessel. Gilmore described the incident in more detail, as well as the charges used, as follows:

> Two German officers and four men came over to the *Edna*'s railing; they shook hands with us and greeted us just the same as they would have done men on one of their own naval vessels. They ordered us to lower our boat and gave us 10 minutes to abandon ship, saying they were going to blow her up. They asked me where I was from, where I was bound, and what my cargo consisted of. The officer in charge took me into the cabin and said he wanted me to come below and that he wanted my papers. When we got below, he said to me:
>
> "Now don't get excited; if you want to change your clothes and get everything of value to you, we are going to be around here an hour."
>
> He took possession of all my official papers, which I had encased in an envelope. When I came from below, I noticed that they had placed some little black tubes about 10 inches long and one-half inch in diameter, which looked like sticks of dynamite, and which were tied to ropes extended over the side of the vessel abreast of the main hatch.
>
> Twenty minutes after the German officer and his crew had boarded the schooner, and after I had had time to have everything of value placed in the lifeboat; he ordered us to proceed over to the submarine, and laughingly said:

"You will find some of your friends over there."

Upon being ordered below I found Capt. Sweeney of the *Hauppauge* and Capt. Holbrook of the *Hattie Dunn* . . .[31]

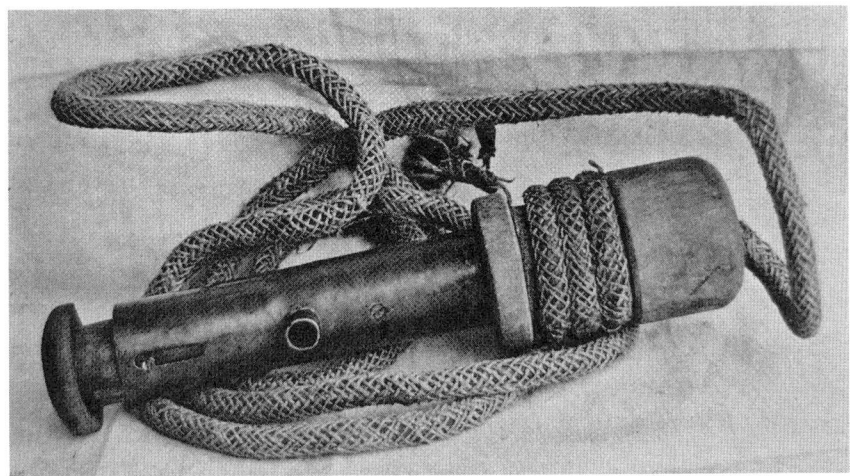

An unexploded explosive charge found aboard the *Edna*. USN Historical Section

Gilmore did indeed find friends aboard. Oberleutnant Körner would later recall that Gilmore and Sweeney had been old friends who, although still living in the same town in Maine, hadn't seen each other in nearly thirty years due to constantly being at sea—it took a German submarine to finally reunite the two off the Virginia coast.[32]

Ultimately, the *Hauppauge* and *Edna* would not completely sink and would be discovered by a passing ship, hours after encountering *U-151*. Von Nostitz observed this ship and her searchlight but opted to sail away from it on the surface, unaware that unexploded charges would be discovered on the wrecks, affirming the presence of the U-boat. Providence, however, as will be seen in the forthcoming paragraphs, still favored the Germans. For the time being, twenty-three prisoners were aboard *U-151*, and receipts were written out to the captains of the three sunken ships, indicating their vessels' names, the coordinates where they were sunk, the date, and the name of the U-boat commander.

Postwar analysis of the attempted sinking of these ships by the Navy claims that *U-151* intentionally targeted these ships because they were of the slow, sailing type and were not equipped with radios—making them easy targets that lacked the ability to report that they were being attacked. It is more likely that these were just targets of opportunity that would supply von Nostitz with desirable provisions and valuable intelligence. Certainly, their sunken tonnage was negligible, and taking aboard so many prisoners on an already crowded U-boat was likely more trouble than it was worth otherwise. Supporting this theory, von Nostitz's war diary indicates that the crews were interrogated, critically revealing that *U-151*'s presence remained completely unreported:

> The captains of the three sunken sailing ships unanimously stated that they did not yet know anything about our stay on the American coast. It wasn't expected that German submarines would actually come over. Since the American [radio] station is still broadcasting "no war warning," our presence actually seems not to be known yet. In order to avoid our presence being disclosed by the crews of the sunken sailing ships, it has been decided to keep them on board for as long as possible. For a later disembarkation, two boats were taken along and lashed to the deck.[33]

Adding additional credence to the theory of von Nostitz gathering important intelligence, Capt. Sweeney of the *Hauppauge* later remarked that the captive crews were allowed on the deck periodically (to smoke and socialize) in the days to come, where they were further questioned about certain vessels observed along the coastline. Of particular interest to the Germans were "the little kite boats"[34] that they sighted on May 27, which the Americans identified as the new sub chasers, as well as the coastal barges that littered the coastline. On the basis of Sweeney's statement, it appeared that not only was the Navy not aware of *U-151*'s existence, but the sub chasers were making no attempt at locating the submarine through their many listening devices or patrols. At this time, it appeared that the US Navy was actively working against sounding any alarms.

A 110-foot sub chaser (*SC-121*) viewed from a distance. Their small size makes it obvious why the Germans described them as being "kite boats." *Author's collection*

Contrary to helping the situation by raising attention to the U-boat threat, the official stance from the Department of the Navy at this time was one of silence. Censorship of the facts began with the original sightings of *U-151* by the *Nyanza*, *Jonancy*, and *Crenella* on May 19, as the Navy completely quashed any facts from these observations from reaching the public. Unfortunately, as more of the crews from these vessels spoke to the press upon reaching port, the Department of the Navy was forced to suppress the leaks more publicly. On May 27, as *U-151* traveled on the surface spotting sub chasers in the distance, the Navy released a statement to local newspapers declaring that not only was there no evidence to indicate the presence of any German submarines on the American East Coast, but reports of a British vessel firing on a U-boat off the Virginia Capes could likely be attributed to mistaking wreckage "or some other floating object" for a submarine.[35]

Von Nostitz, completely unaware of the American vow of silence, proceeded northward toward Delaware Bay, once again dodging any lucrative targets he came across. Such examples included a 10,000-ton steamer, a sailing ship, and a large, "brightly lit steamer"[36] near the Overfalls Shoals lightship off Cape May, New Jersey, on May 26. Using the lightship as a bearing that same evening, he ordered his submarine to periscope depth and steered toward it. Once *U-151* came within 600 m of the lightship, the crew prepared to begin launching the eight remaining Teka mines on board. This would not resemble the cakewalk they had experienced off Cape Henry.

As the mines were being prepared, strong currents at the entrance of the bay would cause *U-151* to uncontrollably rise and fall between 10 and 20 m in depth. The German crew would fight these currents for just over an hour before finally getting their opportunity to complete their minelaying mission—launching them from the torpedo tubes at periscope depth. Körner's recollection of this event to Lowell Thomas describes a scene of panic, with equipment breaking and the U-boat being forced to the surface, where some mines were thrown overboard, and the remainder were launched through the torpedo tubes. While this is a suspenseful story (he also claimed that *U-151* laid hundreds of mines during her American cruise), it is not corroborated in the ship's logs, which state on May 27, beginning at 0050, the following:

0050: After the boat has calmed down again, the first 4 mines are launched. After throwing mines 1 and 2, bearings from the *Overfalls* [lightship] can still be taken; from then on there are no more fires [from the lightship] to be seen in the periscope. After launching the 4 mines [we] grounded the submarine to prepare the next 4 mines.

> 0151: Detached from the seabed, went to periscope depth, can't make out any fires. Launched the last four mines according to [the U-boat's] course, journey, and time.
>
> 0310: Surfaced. Thick fog close to the boat, heard fog signals from a steamship.
>
> Submerged. Boat laid aground.
>
> 0657: Surfaced. While running on the surface, the frequency and type of fog signals heard indicate that there is very lively traffic from smaller coastal steamers in front of the entrance of the bay. Such steamers are repeatedly avoided without being able to see them.
>
> 1000: As a large steamer came into view on the starboard side, it was necessary to dive, the boat was laid aground in 46 m of water to wait for things to clear.
>
> 1200: Latitude 38°50' N, Longitude 74°6' W. About 88 nautical miles.
>
> 1210: Surfaced. Proceeded onward to complete the cable cutting assignment outside New York.[37]

Given the maritime traffic noted by von Nostitz in his war diary, it appeared that he chose the location of his minefield wisely. Despite his best efforts, however, only one of these mines found a target (this incident will be discussed later in the chapter). Continuing northward toward New York City, von Nostitz reverted back to his usual pattern of avoiding contact with any surface vessels.

On May 28, 1918, about 61 nm off Asbury Park, New Jersey, and 71 nm south of the New York City harbor (specifically 40°5' N, 72°51' W), *U-151* began the first leg of her cable-cutting mission—her target being the Western Union line from Coney Island to Nova Scotia, laid in 1889. The new cable-cutting device to be deployed was described by Körner as being "something like a glorified angling tackle,"[38] and the American crews on board claimed that although they weren't allowed to approach the unknown apparatus, they understood its intended purpose. Traveling on the surface that day, von Nostitz described its operation in his war diary:

> 1015: Cable device deployed, with course 210° and towed utilizing both electric and diesel motors. Length of the towline 260 m; Water depth 50–70 m.
>
> 1110: The force on the dynamometer rises to 3 t and then falls back to normal. . . . It can be assumed that the southern cable laid by Western Union in 1889 was cut.

1227: With the device still in use, submerged under water and dodged a tanker that steers 110°. In spite of the deployed cable device, the boat dives normally and can be kept at periscope depth very well.

1307: Submerged [apparently a mistake in the log and should be "surfaced"]. Swing on the dynamometer to 3 t. The pointer slowly went to 3 t, stopped for a few seconds, and then suddenly fell back to 0.2. It can be assumed that the southern German cable is cut.

Rotated slowly from 10° to 40°. The dynamometer swings to 4 tons and back to 0.3 tons.[39]

This operation would continue for the entire next day through the morning of the thirtieth, when the cutting device was finally reeled back in.

The Germans would succeed in severing the lines to Canso, Nova Scotia, and Colon, Panama, although this was only of a minor benefit to them since the cables were of marginal significance and were repaired on June 25 and July 4, respectively.[40] At this point *U-151* set a course east-northeast, toward Nantucket, once again continuously avoiding contact with surface vessels, including what was believed to be an unlit destroyer. Auspiciously for the Germans, thick fog accompanied them for the duration of this trip, and the crew was able to service and prepare their torpedoes for the next part of their mission without haste—even getting some help from the crew of the *Hauppauge* in moving them about the submarine.

On May 31, von Nostitz recorded that the fog, which was once a benefit for the submarine, now became a nuisance, and his intentions to observe maritime traffic between Nantucket and Fire Island had to be canceled. Searching for better conditions, he ordered *U-151* farther south from Nantucket, where he felt he would find targets along the routes of the coastal ships into the Gulf of Maine. It was at this point that he made the decision to finally free his captives, confiding in a mate of the *Hauppauge* that if a suitable vessel was spotted, the crews would be released to it.

Unfortunately for the imprisoned American crews, they would have to wait a little while longer to be freed, since weather reports indicated the fog would last another eight days in the area. As such, von Nostitz made the decision on June 1 to abandon the undertaking to the Gulf of Maine and instead to steer even farther south, back toward the New Jersey shore, where the weather would likely be better.[41]

Unbeknown to the German commander, nearly 280 mi. / 450 km southeast of *U-151*'s position that day, the American battleships USS *Ohio*, *New Hampshire*, and *Louisiana* thought they were being attacked by a U-boat in the waters of Hampton Roads, Virginia. Here, after returning to their base upon completion of a target practice session, a crew member of USS *Ohio* believed he had spotted a periscope, and the submarine alarm was signaled. Interestingly, the commander and some other crew members of USS *New Hampshire* claimed that they not only sighted the periscope but also observed a torpedo wake across the stern of the ship. The three battleships increased their speed, spread out, and began zigzagging, all the while firing their cannons and torpedo batteries at anything appearing suspicious. Two sub chasers would subsequently be dispatched to the location of the phantom engagement and, not surprisingly, found no signs of an enemy submarine.

Once again, the US Navy was paying for their reluctance to immediately issue a war warning back on May 17. Had they erred on the side of caution from the very beginning, it was possible that *U-151*'s position could have been tracked more accurately, or, at the very least, aggressive patrolling would have prevented her from traveling on the surface so often and observing American merchants and warships without being spotted. As the situation now stood, a German submarine was believed to be off the Virginia coast, while in actuality an onslaught off the Jersey shore was just about to begin.

U-151 began the morning of Sunday, June 2, 1918, about 62 mi. / 100 km off the coast from Atlantic City, New Jersey—it was going to be a very busy day for von Nostitz and his crew. At 0620, *U-151* sighted the American three-masted schooner *Isabel B. Wiley* (776 GRT), out of Philadelphia. Almost immediately after *U-151* stopped the sailing ship with a warning shot, an 1,869 GRT steamer, the *Winneconne*, bound for Rhode Island from Norfolk laden with 1,819 tons of coal, was also spotted by the raider. Interestingly, Capt. Waldemar Knudsen of the *Winneconne* noted that his chief and third mate had also spotted *U-151* in the distance at this point, but (just as earlier ships encountering the German raider did) believed the "dark object" alongside the *Wiley* was an American patrol boat.[42]

Prioritizing the larger prize, von Nostitz fired a warning shot at the steamer, and, upon halting the ship, a boarding party was sent over. Surprisingly, just as the *Christian Knudsen* did with *U-53* back in 1916, the *Isabel B. Wiley* remained in place (perhaps fearful of the U-cruiser's long-range deck guns) awaiting her fate, with her crew taking advantage of their borrowed time by gathering their belongings and taking to the ship's lifeboats at their own pace.

In a typical fashion, once the crew of the *Winneconne* took to their boats, the steamer was dispatched using explosive charges. At this point, von Nostitz hailed over to the *Wiley*'s now-evacuated crew, instructing them to row alongside the U-boat. Here, somewhat breaking his promise to his captured American crews on board, von Nostitz distributed his prisoners among the life rafts of his new victims—he would not be sparing one of his newly acquired targets to allow his former prisoners to return home in comfort. Providing the stricken crews with fresh water and provisions, he sent them on their way while the German prize crew boarded the *Isabel B. Wiley*, stripped her of supplies, and sunk her with their small bombs.

The crews of the five vessels would eventually be picked up by passing steamers nearly twenty-four hours later—too late to warn any other ships that day of the dangers lurking within the waters. Unfortunately, as they spent the day lying helpless in their lifeboats, they could only listen to the gunfire and explosions in the distance as *U-151* continued to claim more victims.

The next ship to cross *U-151* was the *Jacob M. Haskell*, a four-masted schooner of 1,778 GRT, carrying coal from Norfolk to Boston. She was spotted at 1125 that morning just under 20 miles southeast from the *Isabel B. Wiley* engagement. Following the pattern of the day, *U-151* signaled her to abandon ship and then sent a boarding party over to sink the vessel with explosives. Capt. W. H. Davis of the doomed schooner gave a description of the *Sprengpatronen* and how Oberleutnant Körner and his party placed them, stating:

> During this time, the bombing party had placed four bombs over the ship's side—two forward, one on each side, and two aft, one on either side. The bombs were about 6 inches in diameter and 14 inches in length. They were hung so that the bombs themselves rested about 2 feet under the surface of the water and alongside the schooner's hull. The men went about their work in a business-like manner; the officer was so polite that he almost got on our nerves. Each seaman was armed with two automatic revolvers [Luger P04 pistols] and a long vicious-looking knife.[43]

This time Körner's team chose not to take on any further provisions (despite the insistence of the *Haskell*'s cook), opting to blow up the vessel and get on their way. It would appear that the Germans had gotten quite efficient at this operation, since only twenty-five minutes elapsed between sighting the schooner and sinking it. Before sailing away from the wreckage at 1150 that day, Körner called over to the lifeboats and advised them to head toward New Jersey, since it was only about 40 miles west—von Nostitz too would be changing his course to a more westerly direction.

At 1450 that day, now just 13 miles southwest from the *Wiley* and about 70 miles from Atlantic City, New Jersey, *U-151* came across the *Edward H. Cole*, another coal-laden, four-masted schooner of just under 1,800 GRT. She would be sunk in a nearly identical manner as the *Jacob M. Haskell* and would hardly be worth mentioning except to once again illustrate the relaxed attitude of the American mariners, who believed that it was impossible for Germans to be in the area.

Of the three main accounts of the encounter between *U-151* and the schooner, two concur that the captain was asleep at the time, but all indicate that the schooner was surprised by the U-boat's presence. Körner's account took one extreme, going as far as to describe happening upon a ghost ship, which he and his team boarded, ultimately surprising the crew, located below deck.[44] The ship's captain, H. G. Newcombe, took the opposite extreme, claiming that he was off the main shipping route due to having to follow "God's good winds," but spotted the German submarine 2,000 yards away before ultimately abandoning ship.[45] It is hard to believe that the sailing ship was caught so unawares, considering that the chief officer of the *Winneconne*, stranded on a lifeboat nearly 20 miles north of the area, testified that he began hearing shots fired beginning at 1130 that day and continuing through the night (to say nothing about the explosions from the German bombs). Certainly, this commotion must also have been heard by the crew of the *Edward H. Cole*, located even closer to the action.

Reality can likely be ascertained by reading into what is perhaps the most credible account—the one that took the middle road in explaining the encounter. Robert Lathigee, the ship's mate, confirming that the captain had taken a nap, claimed that he and another sailor on deck didn't react upon sighting *U-151*, since they both believed she was a US naval vessel with reservists "trying to have fun with us sailors of the merchant marine."[46] Not realizing the true situation until the German war ensign was observed on the approaching U-boat, nothing was done to avoid *U-151* until it was too late—a familiar story from earlier sailors falling victim to the raider.

It is probable, just as with the *Hattie Dunn*, *Hauppauge*, and *Edna*, that the sailors on the *Edward H. Cole* did in fact hear firing in the distance that day but merely assumed it to be American in origin. Unfortunately for the remaining ships in von Nostitz's sights that day, the US Navy wasn't in the area and wouldn't be coming any time soon.

Just an hour and a half after dispatching the *Edward H. Cole* (and only about 10 miles distant), von Nostitz sighted a 3,210 GRT steamer, the *Texel*, loaded with sugar bound from Puerto Rico for New York City. Although a warning shot was fired from *U-151* at a distance approaching 2,000 m to get the steamship to stop, this time the potential prey rushed to get away. Instead of panicking, her captain, K. B. Lowry, ordered his engines to full speed and initiated a zigzag course (later excusing himself of responsibility in giving up the ship by noting that he was specifically following the method of evasion prescribed by the United States Navy Department[47]), causing the U-boat's second warning shot to also miss. The third shot from *U-151*, however, found its target, with von Nostitz stating it was only after "the third hit close to the starboard side and covered the bridge with explosives"[48] that the ship finally came to a stop.

Capt. Lowry, still needlessly trying to justify the loss of his vessel, claimed that it was only after sighting a second U-boat and realizing escape was hopeless that he stopped, at which point *U-151* fired upon his motionless ship, scoring a hit. Lowry wasted no time in evacuating his vessel, with him and his crew taking to lifeboats before the German *Prisenkommando* (prize crew) even arrived with their favored *Sprengpatronen*. The Germans would make quick work of sending all the sugar to the bottom of the Atlantic, with Körner later quipping that it went down to "sweeten Davy Jones's coffee." Unbeknown to the Germans, their sinking of the *Texel* stopped more than just sweeteners from reaching their destination, since the *Texel* was scheduled to transport an American railroad gun for use on the western front on her very next voyage.[49]

The entire engagement, from sighting to sinking, lasted the whole of an hour and twenty minutes. The fact that the prize crew was so efficient with boarding and sinking vessel was auspicious for the Germans, since, shortly after observing their next victim, *U-151* intercepted a wireless message from an unknown station broadcasting that the schooner *Wiley* was sunk by an armed German submarine.[50]

Apparently, some of the crew members from the *Wiley* had been picked up and were reporting *U-151*'s presence. This caused von Nostitz to think twice about approaching the newly spotted steamer, and, instead of advancing on the surface as he was able to do so often on the American East Coast up to this point, he opted to first submerge and observe the new target at periscope depth for nearly twenty minutes. This was to be his most sensational encounter of the day.

The new vessel being hunted by *U-151* was the *Carolina*, a 5,093 GRT American passenger steamship sailing from San Juan, Puerto Rico, to New York with more than two hundred passengers on board and 6,000 tons of sugar. The liner's assistant wireless operator, H. W. Werner, had also received the same warning advising of the sinking of the *Wiley* by a U-boat and, figuring that the *Carolina* was only about 13 miles away from the reported position, calculated that the U-boat was likely still in their immediate proximity. He quickly notified the chief operator, E. W. Vogel, who then summoned the ship's captain, T. R. D. Barbour.

Without alerting the passengers, the liner's captain ordered the ship to full speed and changed course, zigzagging all the while. He also ordered lookouts to keep their eyes on the sea and advise him if anything suspicious was sighted. Ironically, it was one of the ship's passengers who was the first to spot the submarine but, believing it to be an American vessel, failed to notify anyone other than a nearby passenger that it was there. Luckily, a forward lookout would spot the submarine, but by then it was already too late, and shells from the U-boat's deck gun would soon be forthcoming.

Finding the vessel to be unarmed, von Nostitz ordered the U-boat back to the surface and fired a warning shot at the *Carolina* while raising a flag signal notifying the steamer to stop. This only caused the vessel to turn away at speed and for her radio operator to begin transmitting SOS calls. Vogel, the *Carolina*'s radio operator, recalled that his messages were received by a wireless station at Cape May, New Jersey, which then requested the ship's position. Before being able to transmit the ship's coordinates, however, Vogel claimed that he received another signal, this time from the U-boat's wireless operator, saying, "You don't wireless—we don't shoot,"[51] going on to note that the signal's frequency was so faint it was obvious that the Germans didn't want it to be picked up any farther than the immediate vicinity.

Despite being notified by the *Carolina*'s captain that his intentions were to give up the ship, Vogel ignored the Germans' ultimatum and sent one more additional SOS. At this point, von Nostitz ordered two more warning shots to be fired closer to the ship, which finally caused it to halt and begin offloading the passengers into lifeboats. Unlike prior incidents that day, this was not a smooth operation. Although most of the passengers were orderly while they evacuated, some panicked and attempted to jump into boats already loaded with women and children. This fright manifested itself somewhat differently in the case of lifeboat number 5, which would be lowered into the water too quickly, causing its passengers to be thrown off the launch and into the ocean. As all of this was occurring, *U-151* circled the ship, not only observing the spectacle but ensuring that all the passengers in the water made it back onto their lifeboats.

Once Capt. Barbour, who was believed to be the last person to depart the vessel, boarded his launch, von Nostitz called over to him to confirm that no one was left on board, and received the affirmative. The German commander, now believing that the more than three hundred passengers and crew were safely in lifeboats, then focused his attention on his own current situation and the fact that the US Navy was now fully aware of his presence. Abandoning the use of the U-boat's favored explosive charges, he instead chose to make haste in sinking the vessel, opting for a torpedo (which failed) and eventually his large deck guns. He wrote,

> Since visibility is decreasing and wireless traffic from warships can be heard in the vicinity, it is decided to sink the steamer with a torpedo. On the surface, launched torpedo from port tube. Torpedo turned immediately after leaving tube 4, stroked to starboard, then to port, then again to starboard, came up and sank. The steamer was then sunk by artillery.[52]

His war diary, however, omits an interesting detail about this episode that reflects favorably on the character of himself and his crew. Prior to the order being given to sink the steamer, members of the German boarding party noticed that one of the *Carolina*'s crew members was still aboard the ship, and he ordered the lifeboats back to retrieve the forsaken sailor. According to an unnamed survivor,

> Ten boats were lowered, and everybody got in. There was little or no confusion [the survivor apparently wasn't near lifeboat 5]. All the time the submarine lay as close as possible, members of her crew standing on her deck watching us or busying themselves about the boat.
>
> After all the lifeboats had swung away from the *Carolina* [one of] the German officers aboard the abandoned steamer hailed one of the lifeboats and ordered her to return.
>
> This frightened many in the other lifeboats [other accounts indicate that the passengers believed the Germans were going to shell or machine-gun them as they lay helplessly], but after a time we found out the reason for the German's action. In going through the steamer, he found a fireman who had been left behind and he had ordered the lifeboat to return for him.
>
> When this last boat was cleared of the ship again, the Germans left the *Carolina*. In a few minutes the submarine fired seven shells into her, and the steamer burst into flames.[53]

Shortly after sinking the passenger ship, von Nostitz recorded that another unidentified steamer in the area radioed her position and began sending signals for the *Carolina*. Rather than press his luck pursuing an additional target that night, he sailed away, heading back down the American coast toward Cape Hatteras—it had been a good day for *U-151*.

The total tonnage sunk on June 2, 1918, amounted to 14,517 tons, but unfortunately this day would also add human life to the *U-151*'s tally. Despite the best efforts of the Germans to avoid creating casualties in the sinking, this attack would not be victimless, and the reality of the U-boat war would once again shock the American public. At the time the lifeboats were launched from the *Carolina*, the weather was clear, the temperature was warm, and the sea was calm. The launches remained together that Sunday evening as they headed toward the shore; however, a storm formed and came upon them quickly, causing them to separate and, ultimately, one of the boats to capsize.

The boat would be righted and capsized repeatedly throughout the duration of the storm and the pitch-black night. Unfortunately, once both had passed, it was found that only nineteen of the thirty-five survivors who were originally on the launch still remained on board. A young woman, Elena Donato Virola, was one of these missing passengers and would luckily later be located by the lifeboat and recovered from the water alive. She was able to survive the ordeal by clinging to two dead bodies that still had their life vests on (she did not have hers) for nearly ten hours—one of which was, tragically, her now-deceased fiancé.[54] This news, however, wouldn't become public until June 4, and in the meantime, *U-151* continued to claim more victims.

On June 3, 1918, long after *U-151* had originally laid mines the area of Delaware Bay, von Nostitz continued his cruise southward. Coincidentally, a mock U-boat hunt involving every destroyer, sub chaser, and naval seaplane was initiated by RAdm. Stephen McRae Winslow of the US 4th Naval District in Delaware Bay that morning. Adm. Winslow and his staff, observing the drill, "were fully convinced, after a two-hour demonstration, that there was no danger of a submarine attack."[55] The Americans had no idea that their drill would become reality just hours later. The Germans too would be surprised by the news they intercepted.

On the same morning of the third, the wireless operator on *U-151* (now located about 100 mi. / 160 km from the Delaware Bay minefield) began picking up wireless signals of particular interest. Not only was *U-151*'s presence being reported, it was being claimed that she was traveling with friends. According to von Nostitz's war diary entry that day,

> 1530: In the morning the first wireless warning was received from Cape May about a German submarine that had been unequivocally located between Cape Hatteras and Block Island. At noon, the same station radioed the location of a sighted submarine 25 nautical miles south-east of Barnegat. In the evening, the Arlington wireless station warns of several submarines.
>
> At 2:40 PM the wireless call for help was heard from a steamer that had run into our mines near the Overfalls lightship. Steamer is apparently called "Herbert L. Pratt." Name was not correct. Steamer must have sunk very quickly.
>
> 1740: In 170° sighted sailing ship.
>
> 1830: It is the American 4[-]mast schooner "Sam C. Mengel" Pensacola (925t) from Seconndé (Gold Coast) [Accra, Ghana] to New York, cargo palm kernels.
>
> 1935: Crew in the boat released, sailing ship sunk by explosive cartridges.[56]

While the *Samuel C. Mengel* was sunk quickly and without incident, with her entire crew making it back to shore, the steamer radioing distress signals earlier that day would not go unnoticed and would be the catalyst for finally spurring the US Navy into action.

The steamer in question, despite von Nostitz's feeling it was incorrectly named, was in fact the *Herbert L. Pratt* (7,145 GRT), a tanker transporting crude oil from Tuxpan, Mexico, to Philadelphia. She had struck one of *U-151*'s Teka mines in Delaware Bay but ultimately did not sink. Despite the mine putting a nearly 10-by-7-foot hole in the bow of the ship, and the crude oil igniting, only the very forward section of the ship was submerged and, as the rest remained afloat, was able to be salvaged and repaired (the tanker would subsequently become USS *Herbert L. Pratt* and would make two cross-Atlantic trips transporting fuel for Navy warships stationed in European waters). Although it was originally believed that a torpedo struck the tanker (a Navy airman, Ens. Allyn Ryerson Jennings, actually claimed that he dropped depth charges on a U-boat after spotting its periscope near *Herbert L. Pratt*'s lifeboats[57]), the truth would quickly be established, and, on June 4, the remaining mines were discovered and swept up.

The *New York Tribune* reported that while "destroyers, submarine chasers, and hydro-aeroplanes were seeking the German submarines off the mouth of the Delaware Bay, the government discovered that the raiders had sprinkled mines off the [bay's] entrance."[58] One mine was scooped up by a minesweeper, and the remaining mines were easy to locate since they had already broken loose from their anchors and were either floating on the surface or were beached due to a flaw in the mines' underdeveloped fastening system.[59] The proverbial cat was out of the bag now, and this news, combined with more accounts from survivors of *U-151*'s attacks being published in the newspapers, led to a U-boat frenzy sweeping over the American public.

Secretary Daniels assured citizens that there was nothing to worry about. He claimed that the domestic naval districts were more than adequate to handle the U-boat threat and would be dispatching all their resources to hunt for the marauding U-boats operating off the East Coast. Indeed, on June 3, the office of the CNO made a request for all available antisubmarine craft from the 1st through 7th Naval Districts to report for duty immediately, with an additional call for any destroyers currently being repaired in the Norfolk and New York Navy Yards to be prepared for service as soon as possible. Both Daniels and CNO Benson firmly believed that the entire purpose of the Kaiserliche Marine sending U-boats to the American coast was to scare the American public into demanding that the Navy call back all of its current forces based abroad, and, like Adm. Sims, refused to fall into this trap. The problem was that the American public did in fact seem to be scared and now believed U-boats to be everywhere.

The Navy, which wanted to avoid hysteria just weeks prior, was now fanning the flames. Rear Admirals Fechteler and McLean (commandants of the Norfolk Navy Yard and 5th Naval District, respectively) made statements to newspapers that there were currently as many as five U-boats in American waters, which had been simultaneously spotted off the Virginia capes and the coasts of New Jersey and North Carolina. Not surprisingly, neither these alleged submarines nor American warships had yet to engage each other.[60]

With so many reported U-boats potentially hunting along the entirety of the Eastern Seaboard, the major ports of New York, Philadelphia, Baltimore, Boston, and Norfolk were ordered to be closed on the evening of June 3. Although Boston Harbor was closed for only about an hour, Norfolk refused to allow any vessels to sail outbound, and New York and Philadelphia were closed to all traffic until a proper handle could be gotten on the situation. Since this holding period was seemingly indeterminate at the time, some ships whose cargo was considered essential (for example, foodstuffs, coal, or metals) transferred their shipments onto trains—a longer and more costly alternative.

Meanwhile, marine insurance rates skyrocketed. By June 4, there were already increases between 700 and 2,300 percent under the assumption that heavy losses of tonnage would be imminent in the coming weeks. Some marine underwriters simply ceased to insure any ships or cargo "pending developments" in U-boat activities and the government's policy in stopping them.[61]

One of the most dramatic "developments" concerning merchant shipping came from Washington in the form of the Coastwise Routing Office. Coming into effect during the port closures on June 3, this new department within the Office of Naval Operations placed all commercial shipping in the hands of a Navy district commandant. The local district commander would be responsible for routing shipping and organizing convoys. This was a crucial strategic change that was to have the greatest effect on the U-boat scourge (particularly in the Second World War), but it still did little to quell the immediate alarm of the greater public.

Rumors now abounded about the existence of secret U-boat bases in North and Central America. There was even talk that the *Deutschland*, after departing from Baltimore on her maiden voyage, first traveled south to map routes and establish German supply bases before returning back to Germany. These usually focused on areas with large German settlements, primarily in Mexico and the Caribbean, and revolved solely around hearsay. Regardless, by June 19, Secretary Daniels would actually authorize a $1,000 reward for any person who could provide authentic information about such facilities, leading one to question whether monetary gain helped spread such fabrications. One report, however, speculating on the presence of a base located in the Yucatán Peninsula, was taken seriously enough by the government that US Secret Service agents were sent to investigate[62]—much to the chagrin of Mexican diplomats. Naturally, no bases were found, although true to some suspicions, Latin America was indeed found to be teeming with German agents.

The American public also began to imagine spies among the populace, reporting anyone believed to have any German sympathies to the authorities. Even a survivor of the recent attack on the *Carolina* (Belmont Joseph von Jenny, a Hungarian by birth, but now a wealthy US citizen living in Queens, New York) was detained upon reaching shore after other passengers reported him as being suspicious. He would go on to claim that he lost $17,000 worth of gold and $8,000 worth of jewels when the *Carolina* went down, a significantly large sum of money to squander if he were actually a spy. He would further elaborate that "that damn German name of mine was what caused the trouble down there. I said and did nothing that could be construed as having the slightest tinge of disloyalty . . . I am happy that I escaped with my life and will soon see my family."[63] Indeed, in just under two weeks, a single U-boat had Americans in complete disarray, and without any tangible evidence that adequate defense measures were being put into place.

In New York City, Police Commissioner Enright took matters into his own hands and ordered the city to go to blackout conditions in the evening hours, out of fear of German airplane raids or naval coastal bombardment—an act unique to New York City in World War I.[64] This event is somewhat humorous when viewing it from a twenty-first-century lens, but when one considers the confusion and dread surrounding a more recent event such as September 11, 2001, one could hardly fault the metropolitan authorities from overreacting.

What was happening in the United States in that first week of June was exactly what von Holtzendorff desired in his now-infamous memorandum. Allied tonnage was being reduced not just by physically sinking vessels, but by scaring them into remaining at port. By the time *Herbert L. Pratt* struck the mine in Delaware Bay, *U-151* had already caused a property loss of $4.5 million (over $80 million in 2021),[65] with countless other goods now sitting idly in closed harbors. Although von Nostitz had already exhausted his supply of Teka mines, his patrol was far from over. As he continued the hunt, all the American naval districts could do was continue to search for the invader, and they would now be out in numbers.

On the morning of June 4, 1918, *U-151* was now far from the relentless American combing in Delaware Bay, and once again off the coast of Virginia, about 130 miles east-northeast of Norfolk, at 37°25' N, 73°44' W. It appeared it would be another turkey shoot for the German submarine, since ample targets were already presenting themselves on the horizon; however, von

Nostitz was about to encounter the newly heightened US naval presence in the area. At 0605, just forty-five minutes after abandoning the pursuit of a distant steamer, he stopped the *Edward R. Baird Jr.*, a small, three-masted sailing ship carrying lumber from Jacksonville, Florida, to New York.

Although his boarding party placed explosive charges on the ship, von Nostitz did not wait about to observe the sinking, since a more lucrative target was sighted, as he recorded in his war diary:

> 0705: During the sinking [of the *Baird*], a tanker with a colorfully painted side wall [von Nostitz means camouflaged in the "dazzle" pattern of the period] comes into view at 250°. Opened fire at 1.3 km. Steamer runs strong zigzag courses and returns fire with a stern gun. Volleys are close to the boat. At the same time, the steamer issues an "Allo" message [an Allied code indicating the sighting of a submarine, followed by its location and the time it was spotted], with the signature "Poléna."
>
> 0755: Ceased fire and turned away, as a cloud of smoke comes into view to the left of the steamer and soon it is identified as a destroyer coming at us at high speed. Submerged. Went on a course of 160° at 40 m depth.
>
> [AM hour, time illegible:] To periscope depth. Destroyer near the sinking ship, at the same time 2 sailing ships and a fully rigged ship in sight, which is circled by the destroyer. After some time, the destroyer comes out of view on a zigzag course of approximately 260°.
>
> [AM hour, time illegible:] Surfaced.
>
> In 275° a destroyer is sighted at a high speed and because the distance [from the U-boat] is very large, it can be avoided on the surface.
>
> Received wireless warning from Arlington to all vessels: Enemy submarine may be encountered between latitudes of Charleston and Nantucket shoals.[66]

The steamer being pursued by *U-151* was not the *Poléna*, but instead the French tanker *Radeoleine*. Interestingly, Oberleutnant Körner, even years after the war, also was confused as to the actual identity of the ship, believing that it was likely British since it was painted with dazzle camouflage and, given its zigzag course and effective use of its deck guns, must have encountered other U-boats in the past.

The initial American destroyer mentioned by von Nostitz was USS *Hull* (DD-7), a slow, outdated Bainbridge-class destroyer launched in 1902 and commanded by R. S. Haggart. Although obsolete, the importance of her presence in the waters off Virginia that morning could not be overstated. Of foremost significance was the fact that even an obsolescent destroyer (actually one of the first ever "torpedo-boat" destroyers built for the US Navy) was capable of scaring off a U-Kreuzer. Although the submarine was slower, it was significantly better armed and had the ability to attack beneath the surface; however, it still opted to evade the American warship. This was an initial test of Adm. Sims's theory that the outdated destroyer fleet would be adequate in defense of the American coastline and that the newer types would be better suited for use in numbers in European waters—so far, it seemed to be working.

Additional importance of USS *Hull* can be ascribed to her remaining in the area to warn and protect other vessels. Although Haggart never actually located the U-boat, he approached the tall ship *Doon*, the "fully-rigged ship" described by von Nostitz as being circled by the destroyer, and then remained in the area until 1300 continuing to search for the enemy.[67] Without firing a shot or launching a single depth charge, USS *Hull* had halted the attack on a major Allied target and prevented the sinkings of at least three others.

This incident, followed by the arrival of the second destroyer that finally forced *U-151* out of the area, clearly illustrated the effect that destroyers and sub chasers may have had if they were dispatched in numbers to the major American shipping routes upon the initial notice of a U-boat approaching the US coast. Their subsequent absence in the area for the remainder of the day instead allowed *U-151* to return to the offensive and exemplified the cost of momentarily letting their guard down.

At 1615 that evening, with the US Navy apparently retiring from their U-boat hunt, von Nostitz spotted his final victim of the day just 30 mi. / 50 km from the attack of the *Edward R Baird Jr*. Here the *Eidsvold*, a 1,570-ton Norwegian steamer carrying sugar from Guantánamo, Cuba, to New York, was stopped and then sunk with *U-151*'s deck gun—but not before von Nostitz approached the vessel submerged to confirm that it wasn't armed.

The captain of the steamer, Johannes Johansen (referred to as J. Johnson in American sources), initially described the benevolence of the German boarding party to authorities. He recalled that they first apologized for having to sink the vessel and then allowed him as much time as he needed to calm down his wife (also on board) and gather her belongings prior to boarding the lifeboats. Curiously, considering the amity he just encountered, he then commented that this could have been a ruse and the Germans may have had underlying devious intentions, stating,

> The submarine remained in view till dusk. She seemed to follow us slowly waiting for some vessel to come along and try to pick us up, when she would become very easy prey for the submarine.[68]

It is possible that von Nostitz was trailing the submarine for exactly the purpose of entrapping another merchant; *U-151* would in fact adopt that strategy later in the patrol, but on the basis of the circumstances of the day, this is likely not probable.

Shortly after sinking the *Eidsvold*, *U-151*'s wireless picked up the war warning being sent from Arlington, advising all ships that a U-boat had been sighted at 0900 that morning and giving its location as 37°38' N, 73°44' W. Von Nostitz noted in his war diary that American news broadcasts warned that even more submarines were expected along the coastline. Due to this unwanted attention, he recorded that he "intended to lie in wait for the steamship traffic going to and from Baltimore for a few days here at the mouth of the Chesapeake Bay about 100 miles from land, also outside of the night patrols."[69]

In stating this course, he made it clear that he did not want to follow the lifeboats deeper toward the coast, where in all likelihood he would run into more American warships. Von Nostitz and his crew would instead take the night off, opting to resume their strike against American shipping early the next morning.

At dawn on the fifth, *U-151* returned to the offensive, spotting an old 100-ton, two-masted whaling boat, the *Nicholson*. Von Nostitz, now exercising extreme caution, approached the shabby vessel submerged, before surfacing close to it and firing a warning shot across her bow. Oberleutnant Körner, in what could otherwise be construed as another tall tale to Lowell Thomas had it not been confirmed by the US Navy (which erroneously records it as happening later that day), described a pitiful scene that provides some insight into the character of the German officers aboard *U-151*:

> We ran south all night and at daybreak sighted a sail. An old craft lumbered up. There was a shout, a kind of long howl, as the lookout, a negro, saw a submarine pop suddenly out of the water and fire a shot across the ship's bows. A score of black men and several whites swarmed the deck, tumbled into boats, and rowed frantically toward us.
>
> "You will be sunk in ten minutes," I said to them.
>
> "Well, ain't that the dickens," twanged an old white man, the captain. "What'll we do now?"
>
> He seemed so genuinely downcast that I asked where the craft was from, and what she was doing.
>
> "We're from Mississippi," he replied sorrowfully, "and we're whalin'—leastwise we intended to. We was on our way up around Greenland to do a bit of harpoonin', but now it looks like we ain't goin' to. It sure is tough."

He continued that the ship was owned by several poverty-stricken families in a town on the Mississippi coast. It was all they had in the world. They lived scantily on the proceeds of the whaling. The old skipper plucked up courage as he told his tale.

"You don't have to sink us, Cap'n, do you?" he protested in his slow voice. "If you do it'll certainly be tough on us."[70]

Körner goes on to explain how sinking this vessel would have had very little impact on the outcome of the war and that the Germans could only smile at each other seeing the released crew rejoice at their good fortune, cuttingly going on to question what would have happened to a German whaling boat had it happened upon the British blockade.

The release of the *Nicholson* is peculiar since, on the basis of its potential impact on the war, it did not deviate much from prior (or future) ships sunk by *U-151*; namely, the *Edward R. Baird Jr.*, the *Edna*, or the *Poseidon* (released only because it was located out of the restricted zone). There could be no other reason for sparing the ship other than commiseration on the part of the Germans for the plight of the poor whalers, perhaps knowing that their mercy, when reported, could make headway toward winning over hearts and minds for the German cause. In this case von Nostitz didn't attempt to make any excuses. His entry in the submarine's diary notes the contact but simply states, "Sailing ship released."[71] This brief moment of warmheartedness would be contrasted with the cold reality of submarine warfare just hours later.

At 0900 that day, at 36°39' N, 74°3' W (about 25 mi. / 40 km southwest of where the *Eidsvold* was sunk and about 100 mi. / 160 km from the Virginia coastline), *U-151* spotted smoke clouds on the horizon. Once again, von Nostitz ordered the submarine to submerge to better observe the vessel from periscope depth.

This was a prudent decision since the ship was identified as the British steamer *Harpathian* and, being a British merchant, was armed with a deck gun located on the stern. Von Nostitz's war diary entry reads as follows:

Smoke clouds in sight at 110°

Submerged. Initiated under water attack. Steamer has a gun at the stern.

Launched starboard torpedo. Distance 800 m, angle 70°, steamship course 290°. Hit. Immediately after the shot, turned to starboard for 35 m. Went to periscope depth. The steamer lies with her aft section completely in the water.

Surfaced. Steamer has already sunk.

3 lifeboats are floating on the water. . . . It was the English steamer *Harpathian* from London (4,588 t) in ballast from Plymouth to Newport News. The steamer had a 10 cm gun, 2 artillerymen as operators, 40 men all Chinese as crew. Drinking water was given to the boats, a lightly wounded person was bandaged, boats released.[72]

Capt. Owens, of the *Harpathian*, would go on to explain to the commander of the Division Transport Force at Newport News that his ship sank in about seven minutes and that von Nostitz called the lifeboats alongside the U-boat to inquire if all crew members were accounted for or hurt.

Owens went on to explain that the "lightly wounded person" was in fact taken aboard the submarine for treatment and then returned to the lifeboat, where Owens was given a course to the nearest landfall. His crew described von Nostitz as "a gentlemanly murderer," who "did all he could to make the survivors feel comfortable,"[73] including supplying them with American tobacco (likely taken from a previous victim that cruise).

At approximately the same time that *U-151* was sinking the *Harpathian*, the US Navy was still busy at the mouth of Delaware Bay, nearly 150 mi. / 240 km north, sweeping for mines and hunting for additional U-boats. They were put on high alert after eleven mines had been located, with eight of them being towed back to the naval base at Cape Henlopen, Delaware, and the remainder being detonated by rifle fire. Embarrassingly, the mines discovered were American, with the *New York Tribune* calling out the folly and noting that

> the naval authorities refused to state if the mines were American or German. Opinion as to their origin differs among seagoing men. Displayed here [Lewes, Delaware] are signs warning all to beware of floating mines. As this was posted some time ago, many believed that the mines discovered were among those planted by American forces and which had broken from their moorings.[74]

Even more humiliating was this discovery of American mines being the impetus for additional minesweeper, sub chaser, and naval aviation patrols in an area now completely devoid of U-boats.

These sorties resulted in one "hydro-aeroplane" dropping depth charges on a phantom submarine, one rumor that a submarine was captured by sub chasers near the Overfalls lightship, and, finally, two reported U-boat sinkings by sub chasers. In all this commotion, one American sub chaser (*SC-132*) would actually be lost when it struck the protected cruiser *Tacoma* (C-18) and sank off Barnegat Light, New Jersey. The Navy noted in 1920, with the clarity of hindsight, that *U-151* "would have been obliged to cruise 100 knots in two hours to have been in the position given the object fired upon by the chasers."[75] In domestic waters it seemed that the local naval districts were adamant that more than one U-boat was present, despite insistence from Adm. Sims that only one had made the journey across the Atlantic.

Amusingly, von Nostitz had been listening in to the radio transmissions from Cape May and believed his mines had found more victims. At noon that day he noted in his diary, "Wireless transmission from Cape May: 'Evidences [of] enemy submarine one mile off Cape Henlopen' (Apparently another vessel hit one of our mines again)."[76] Although another victory by Teka mine that day was in reality just wishful thinking, von Nostitz could be excused for making that assumption on the basis of the commotion over the radio. He would, however, add one more genuine sinking to his tally that evening.

Despite the war warnings being broadcast from Arlington, and the feverish activity farther north that day, *U-151* approached and stopped the Norwegian steamer *Vinland* (1,144 GRT) just 50 miles (106 km) from Cape Henry, on the surface and unopposed. The *Vinland* was transporting sugar from Guantánamo, Cuba, to New York and her master, Capt. Bratland, recounted to Oberleutnant Körner and the German boarding party that he had read the warnings about German submarines off the United States before departing Cuba but ultimately "dismissed them as merely another of those Anglo-Saxon war rumors."[77] He also seemed to be confused by the abnormally large size of the U-Kreuzer, as future testimony indicated that he believed the submarine resembled a cargo ship in deep draft, both from a distance and when his lifeboat approached the submarine.

Due to the absence of any threat, and the fact that the *Vinland* didn't transmit any SOS messages, the Germans allowed the Norwegian crew as much time as they needed to gather their belongings and helped themselves to two bags of sugar before dispatching the vessel with explosives. The entire encounter lasted the whole of twenty minutes. Meanwhile, more warnings were being broadcast from Arlington, now indicating the location where the *Eidsvold* sank, and, according to *U-151*'s war diary,

> The wireless warning from Arlington indicates that the Americans are expecting the presence of several submarines, at least one of them close to Delaware Bay, the second further out at sea. Every now and then a destroyer can be heard via wireless in approximately 30–40 nautical miles distance.[78]

The location of this unknown destroyer so close to the entrance of Chesapeake Bay indicates that the US Navy was still placing emphasis on harbor protection in lieu of offensive patrols deeper into the coastal shipping lanes. As it was, the lifeboats from the *Vinland*, although rowing westward from about 50 miles from the shore, wouldn't be picked up until June 7, by the destroyer USS *Rathburne* (DD-113)—which only happened to be in the area as it was making a precommission trial run southward from the Cramp Shipyards in Philadelphia. Since various U-boat sightings along the coast were pulling naval resources in all directions, it is perhaps justifiable that the Navy continued to place its warships in the areas most concentrated with commercial shipping.

In the early-morning hours of the next day, June 6, *U-151* sighted three vessels in the approximate area of the previous night's sinking. These included a several-decked, two-stacked steamship of approximately 11,000 tons leaving Baltimore, and two tankers, one outbound and the other inbound. All engagements had to be broken off since the U-Kreuzer couldn't manage to keep up with the high speeds of the vessels. Apparently, the first two ships did not spot the submarine, but the third one pursued by von Nostitz, the British tanker *Mantilla* (5,660 GRT), sent out an "allo" message at 1000 pinpointing the submarine at 36°02' N, 73°31' W.

Unfortunately for the American coastal defenses, *U-151* was actually nearly 65 miles north of the coordinates reported by the *Mantilla* (about 130 mi. / 210 km east of Cape Henry and off the Virginian coast at 36°57' N, 73°33' W)—a discrepancy that von Nostitz made a point of logging in his war diary. Further complicating matters for the Navy was another reported sighting at 1400 that day by the American steamer *Cacique*, claiming a U-boat was spotted at 31°05' N, 75°35' W, off the coast of Savannah, Georgia, and nearly 425 mi. / 684 km south of *U-151*'s actual position. As von Nostitz laid his submarine on the seabed that night, his radio operator picked up another broadcast from Arlington stating,

> Enemy submarines may be encountered anywhere between Nantucket and Cape Hatteras. Steamer torpedoed and sunk 9 a.m. June 5th 36°16' N, 74°0' W [again, the *Eidsvold*].[79]

Reports like this were pushing American naval districts into exhaustion—now hunting phantom submarines in an operational zone encompassing nearly the entire US East Coast. All the while, more fallacious U-boat sightings continued to direct their coastal defenses away from *U-151*'s actual location.

On June 7, von Nostitz once again gave his crew a break, and spent much of the morning lying on the ocean floor before surfacing and performing test dives in the evening—*U-151*'s location now at 37°7' N, 73°2' W, or now nearly 160 mi. / 258 km from Cape Henry. Although no surface vessels were spotted by *U-151* that day, US Coast Guard Station 115 (on Long Beach Island, New Jersey) and a British ship, the SS *Huntsend*, claimed to have spotted the U-boat at 39°41' N, 74°5' W, and at 39°45' N, 73°2' W, respectively—placing the Germans in an area off New Jersey that they had already vacated over a week prior.[80] Regrettably for the Americans, it would take the events of the next day to refocus their efforts on finding the lone submarine.

At dawn on the morning of June 8, von Nostitz spotted what would be one of the most valuable targets of his entire cruise—the Norwegian steamer *Vindeggen* (3,179 GRT). After a brief chase and two warning shots, the vessel was halted at about 0530, and her captain, Edvard Ballestad, approached the submarine on a launch with the ship's papers. Upon the discovery that the *Vindeggen* was carrying a cargo of 2,100 tons of copper and a thousand balls of wool (essential materials for the German war effort) from Antofagasta, Chile, to New York City, von Nostitz made the decision to offload the cargo into the U-boat before sinking her (à la the modus operandi of Korvettenkapitän Karl von Müller on the SMS *Emden*).

There were also two other pieces of precious cargo present on the ship that required special treatment—the wife and two-year-old daughter of a deadhead captain with the surname Ugland (no first name is given in any sources). Once again, the paradoxical nature of the Germans was to be displayed over the next day and a half, swinging from callousness to an abundance of benevolence.

Since the sea was particularly rough, and the danger of an attack by an American destroyer was ever present so close to the coastline, von Nostitz sent the captain back to his ship and signaled him to follow the U-boat farther offshore. This would take them away from the main shipping routes and American patrols, where the exchange of cargo would take place undisturbed in relatively calm seas. Both vessels left the area together at 0730. Contrary to the account of the *Vindeggen*'s captain, who believed he was following the U-boat in pursuit of another target, it wasn't until both vessels were already sailing eastward that von Nostitz spotted another steamer, which he erroneously identified as the *Villareal*. At this point the Norwegians were told to wait for the U-boat to return as it submerged and proceeded to the new contact, and were warned not to try to escape, since the large deck guns of the U-Kreuzer were exceptionally good.

This new victim was, in actuality, the American steamship the *Pinar del Rio* (2,504 GRT, formerly the SS *Saba*, not the *Villareal* as even Körner suggested in the postwar years), laden with sugar bound for Boston from Cuba. Upon sighting *U-151* coming to the surface in proximity to the steamship, her crew immediately began taking to the ship's boats. Körner (since his accounts always seemingly skim over the questionable acts of the German sailors while aggrandizing others who project heroism and goodwill) does little to describe this event, but von Nostitz makes a point in his diary of further communicating the roughness of the sea, which he alluded to when he stopped the *Vindeggen*.

Instead of helping the merchant crew, he, rather coldly, commented only on the difficulty of shooting in rough seas, while also extolling the efficiency of his deck guns, noting,

> When approaching the steamer and leeward, a heavy sea washes 4 men of the crew overboard. All the people could be fished out again despite the very heavy swells. The operation of both guns in this heavy swell which kept people under water is worthy of note. *Villareal* is sunk by 2 shots. Released crew in the lifeboats.[81]

This coldness exhibited by von Nostitz was echoed by the *Pinar del Rio*'s captain, John Mackenzie, in his interview with the *New York World* newspaper. He claimed that after evacuating his ship,

> We rowed over to the U-boat and asked, "What will we do next?" The Commander of the submarine asked us if we had all our papers and other property and I said[,] "Yes," although I had left about $300 worth of clothes and personal effects on board. "All right, goodbye," the commander said, and the U-boat got underway and sank the *Rio* with shell fire.[82]

Indeed, just as quickly as *U-151* came upon and sank the *Pinar del Rio*, von Nostitz abandoned her crew in tempestuous waters and returned his attention to the awaiting *Vindeggen* and her valuable booty—instructing the Norwegians to continue following the U-boat eastward through the night.

The accounts of the survivors of the *Pinar del Rio* are interesting, since all claim that *U-151* sank another vessel (some claim two) shortly after their ship went down. Aside from American newspaper reports from the survivors, the additional sinkings are not corroborated in any other sources. What is perhaps more significant than the alleged other sinkings in the published reports from the crew members is their explanation of why they felt the *Vindeggen* was following *U-151* farther out to sea.

Although the *Pinar del Rio*'s survivors correctly saw a "follow me" signal sent from the U-boat to the *Vindeggen*, they believed that the future victim of von Nostitz was actually a German "mother ship," sailing in support of the submarine in waters so far from Europe.[83] This supposition, now being spread through the articles of major newspapers, continued to stoke American fears of German ubiquity within the waters of North America. While the *Vindeggen* was certainly not a fully fledged German collaborator, her crew would cooperate with the men of *U-151* over the coming days and would fare far better than the survivors of the *Pinar del Rio*.

After traveling eastward through the night, *U-151* began the transfer of cargo at 0900 the next day in an area 250 mi. / 400 km off the coast of Norfolk, Virginia. To expedite the process, the crew of the *Vindeggen* were utilized as laborers, with some even being taken aboard *U-151* to help with the offloading of the copper cargo. All the while the German prize crew remained aboard the steamer supervising the transfer, keeping a lookout for any patrol ships and tending to the needs of Mrs. Ugland and her daughter, Eva.

In sharp contrast to the way the *Pinar del Rio*'s crew were treated by the German sailors, Mrs. Ugland and her daughter were offered accommodation in Oberleutnant Körner's quarters to make her wait more comfortable. While Mrs. Ugland was frightened by the thought of going into the belly of the submarine (her husband would instead bring some wicker furniture onto the ship's deck for her to rest on), Eva was given tours and treated to a variety of sweets by the U-boat's cook.

The process of transporting the copper cargo was slow going and laborious. Part of the *Vindeggen*'s crew was sent to the hold of the ship, where they would begin passing the copper ingots onto the deck, where some sailors from the German boarding party would then move them toward the side of the ship, where the remaining Norwegian crew would finally take them aboard three of the ship's lifeboats and row them over to the submarine and then transfer them into the U-boat. During this process, which continued until 2000 that night and then into the following morning, *U-151* remained moored to the *Vindeggen* in a rather helpless position should American warships suddenly approach.

Fortunately for the Germans, once again American coastal patrols were focusing their efforts on phantom submarines, far away from the vulnerable *U-151*. The 5th Naval District, based in Norfolk and responsible for the zone in which von Nostitz was currently operating, found itself engaged within the coastal waters of Cape Henry, nearly 250 miles west of *U-151*. Here, the dreadnought battleship USS *South Carolina* (BB-26), which had been assigned to East Coast patrols since war was declared on Germany, and the sub chaser *SC-234* believed they had spotted a periscope. In response, the battleship began firing her guns at the alleged submarine, and the sub chaser dropped depth charges throughout the area. Not surprisingly, no evidence of a sunken U-boat was found, and the Germans, so far eastward, appeared to be oblivious to all the action closer to the shore.

Despite there being no mention of intercepting any radio transmissions alluding to the engagement in *U-151*'s war diary, von Nostitz was still remaining cautious. Upon completing that day's transfer of copper at 2000 (which amounted to 40 tons), von Nostitz noted that his submarine remained moored to the *Vindeggen*, and the ship's crew, along with the German boarding party, stayed on board the steamer—which, due to already having bombs placed aboard, was "ready to be blown up immediately."[84] Luckily for all parties involved, this drastic action did not need to be taken, and the offloading of copper would resume the next morning.

Between the hours of 0500 and 1100 on June 10, an additional 30 tons of "pure, 100% electrolytic copper" was transferred over to *U-151*, making for a total of 70 captured tons. In order to accommodate the additional weight, water and iron that were already on the submarine as ballast and trim weights had to be dumped overboard. Apparently, this first attempt at regulating the U-boat's trim was unsuccessful, since a day later the war diary records that an additional 16 tons of iron were dumped and the means by which ammunition was stowed had to be adjusted—but that was a problem for a later date. Of immediate concern was what to do with the *Vindeggen*'s crew and additional passengers once the steamer was finally blown up with the *Sprengpatronen*.

Given that a woman and a child were on board the lifeboats, von Nostitz opted not to merely just say "goodbye" and send them on their way. Instead, the lifeboats were tied off to the submarine and were taken in tow toward the main shipping lanes, where the German commander intended to hand them off to another ship closer to the coast. After traveling just over 35 miles (56 km) westward, and still nearly 100 miles from the coastal shipping lanes (and over 200 miles from the coastline), smoke clouds were spotted on the horizon. This, however, was not to be the promised salvation for the *Vindeggen*'s survivors.

After sighting the distant steamer, the Germans untied the towing lines from the U-boat to the lifeboats and instructed their crews to row toward the distant steamer—von Nostitz was about to employ the tactic described by Capt. Johansen of the *Eidsvold*. Once the lifeboats were off and rowing away from the U-boat, von Nostitz gave the command to submerge and follow closely behind them toward the unidentified vessel. Precisely as planned, once the steamer sighted the lifeboats and approached them to pick up the survivors, *U-151* surfaced and fired a warning shot at the Good Samaritan—it got the message.

The new prize for *U-151* was the *Henrik-Lund*, a Norwegian steamer of 4,322 tons carrying a cargo of coal, copper, and engine parts from Norfolk to Rio de Janeiro. Her crew immediately began taking to their boats upon the first warning shot, and once again von Nostitz sent over his prize crew to sink the ship with explosives. Unfortunately, now there was no more room aboard the submarine to take on any more vital war materiel. This, however, did not mean that nothing was removed from the doomed steamer. Her captain, Axel Kaltenborn, had asked Oberleutnant Körner if he could have permission to retrieve some of his belongings before his ship was blown up. Permission was granted, and Kaltenborn returned not only with his belongings, but also with beer, champagne, and local newspapers for the German crew; he was then brought on board *U-151*.

While *U-151*'s crew relished in the high-quality libations from the New World, von Nostitz was more interested in what the Norwegian captain could tell him in the form of intelligence. He recorded this in his war diary:

The captain explains that he met some patrols (steam trawlers) 2–3 hours ago. Upon departure from port, he was told by a responsible authority that he had nothing to fear anymore, the German submarines had already left again. He was given an eastward sailing course up to 100 nautical miles, after which he could maneuver freely. All of our sinkings were published in the newspapers. So far, 16 ships are listed by name. Of those, 2 vessels must have already run into our mines, as the sinking of the "Villareal" [once again he misidentifies the *Pinar del Rio*] and "Vindeggen" in America cannot yet be known, and we have only sunk 14 vessels excluding these two.[85]

Incidentally, this was the first time the German crew was able to read about themselves from the point of view of their victims. Not surprisingly, they were insulted by the terms "Hun" and "gentlemanly murderer" that the newspapers liked to use, but otherwise found the stories to be fairly accurate and fair in their portrayal, with most referring to them as being polite and considerate. They were about to give the newspapers more-positive survivor stories to write about.

Instead of leaving the now sixty-eight survivors of the *Vindeggen* and *Henrik-Lund* in their lifeboats to fend for themselves so far from land, von Nostitz ordered them to be tied to the submarine and towed yet again to find a suitable rescue ship. Heading westward, von Nostitz finally found his ship at 2150 that evening in the SS *Brosund*, a Danish steamship en route from Oporto, Portugal, to New York City. Steering toward the vessel and letting loose the tow lines so the lifeboats would coast in the direction of the steamer's bow, von Nostitz stopped and waited to ensure that the stricken crews were safely rescued. The passengers, not surprisingly, believed they were being used as decoys yet again, and the crew of the *Brosund* also appeared to be a little leery of the situation, with *U-151*'s war diary noting that once the lifeboats came alongside the *Brosund*, the steamer immediately switched off all its lights.

While von Nostitz says nothing further about this incident other than that the crews were rescued and the steamer sped away, Körner recounted that the survivors were instructed to make as much noise as possible and fire off rockets to get the ship's attention, and if the ship refused to take them on board, they were to tell the captain that a U-boat was in the area and would torpedo him.[86] He then goes on to claim that it appeared that the *Brosund* was indeed going to flee, at which point the gun crews aboard *U-151* trained their deck guns on the ship, and once the Danes spotted the U-boat in the distance prepared to fire upon them, they finally rescued the crews from the lifeboats. Regardless of how the incident actually unfolded, it is certain that the Germans stayed in the area to confirm that all the survivors were taken to safety—they would reach New York City two days later.

As von Nostitz observed the *Brosund* sail away on a course of 20°, his radio operator picked up a signal over 100 miles southeast of their location, stating, "SOS SOS. Submarine firing on *Walter d'Noyes* 3417 7053 N W."[87] Interestingly, von Nostitz made a comment about this signal in his war diary, which stated that this submarine could possibly be *U-117* or *U-140*. This is the first time he mentions any other U-boats in his logs, and although he was mistaken about the actual presence of another submarine (neither submarine had been in the area at that point in time), this indicates that he was aware of the submarine minelayer and U-Kreuzer and that their future patrols would take them to the United States (radio logs indicate that an actual confirmation of their upcoming departure, via a wireless broadcast from Nauen, would not reach von Nostitz until June 27). Not contemplating any further on the mysterious wireless message, the German commander ordered a test dive and proceeded northward, back toward Delaware Bay.

During these evening hours of June 10, the US Navy once again found themselves preoccupied investigating possible U-boat sightings well north of *U-151*'s actual location. At 1840, Coast Guard Station 82 (Point O'Woods, a hamlet on Fire Island, New York) had reported spotting a periscope heading in an eastbound direction, which was echoed by a nearly identical sighting from neighboring Coast Guard Station 83, also on Fire Island. Just under an hour after the New York sightings, the American submarine USS *L-5* (one of four oceangoing submarines designed by the Lake Torpedo Boat company of Simon Lake) not only believed she had observed a submarine on the surface at 37°32' N, 73°49' W (just under 90 mi. / 145 km southeast of Ocean City, Maryland), but claimed that a torpedo was fired at her that missed just ahead in front of her bow.[88]

In all likelihood, *L-5*, not a German U-boat, was the cause of another erroneous submarine detection earlier that day. This time by both a fishing boat and naval patrol plane that reported the presence of an enemy submarine, just under 10 miles northeast of Winter Quarter Shoals (or just off the coast of Maryland)—well within the American submarine's patrol area. Four additional false alarms would be sounded that day, but all were far too distant from *U-151*'s actual location to be considered credible. It is therefore no surprise that von Nostitz intercepted a wireless broadcast from Arlington the next day, yet again warning all vessels that "enemy submarines may be encountered between Nantucket and Hatteras, to the eastward and southward of Nantucket and to northward of Bermuda."

With so much reported action in so large of an area, even he began to buy into the myth of more U-boats operating off the American coast. After assuming that *U-117* or *U-140* was the cause of the SOS transmission the prior day, additional intercepted "allo" messages led him to send out his own wireless signal, attempting to reach his potential comrades. Since the call went unanswered, *U-151* was ordered to dive and continue her northward course. Ultimately, he would make another fruitless (and final) attempt at contacting the additional U-boats he believed were operating off the American coast on June 13. Coincidentally, his actions later (and even more so on the fourteenth) would allow American naval authorities to hone their search for the elusive raider.

On the evening of June 13, about 130 mi. / 210 km southeast of Delaware Bay, *U-151* encountered two exceptional vessels that could have greatly increased the Germans' total sunken tonnage if they were successful in sinking them—the *Llanstephan Castle* (11,293 GRT from London) and the *Keemun* (9,074 GRT from Liverpool). *U-151*'s war diary reads as follows:

> In 110° large steamer [the *Llanstephan Castle*] with a course for Baltimore in sight. Steamer is brightly painted, but still easy to see. Tried to advance on the surface as the boat [the U-boat] is in the setting sun. Steamer still sees the boat . . . turns away and gives an "allo" signal.
>
> In 140° [second] steamer in sight [the *Keemun*], the course was about 290°. Steamer turns away right after the sighting . . . maybe due to the "allo" signal. After coming up to about 1200 m on the surface, steamer completely turns away. Opened fire, steamer replies, sails out of range. Abandoned pursuit.
>
> The second steamer sends the wireless transmission, "SOS SOS 3758 7247 NW 'Keemun' gunned."[89]

The SOS message recorded in von Nostitz's war diary was only the first of many sent by the *Keemun*. Between the hours of 2000 and 2143, American naval radio operators at Cape May and the Philadelphia Navy Yard picked up no fewer than eight SOS messages giving the *Keemun*'s location and course and that she was being shelled.

Upon receipt of the initial call for help, the 4th Naval District out of Philadelphia dispatched a contingent of destroyers and sub chasers to the area to hunt for the U-boat and pick up any survivors. Unfortunately, due to the delay in receiving the messages and the time it took to travel to the area, the American warships found neither the *U-151* nor the *Keemun*, with the former changing course back to the southeast and the latter well on her way to port. Although they came up empty-handed, the US Navy coastal defenses were no longer looking for a needle in a haystack, and their attention was now confined to a much-smaller operational zone. Unfortunately, at this point *U-151* was already beginning to steer eastward on her return voyage to Germany.

When the *Llanstephan Castle* reached her destination of New York City, Capt. Chope reported to authorities that he and the other officers on his ship initially believed that *U-151* was a British S-class destroyer (Chope referred to it as a "T" type, likely due to the fact that many of these destroyers had names beginning with "T"), since the U-boat's periscopes resembled funnels and the deck guns were of an unusually large caliber. This confirms other testimonies, namely from the captains of the *Hattie Dunn* and the *Winneconne*, that the U-cruiser looked more like an Allied destroyer when surfaced and should have immediately put into question the other varying reports of mysterious floating objects and periscopes—it can only be wondered how many vessels actually already spotted the U-boat but assumed it was an American surface ship.

If there were any doubts about *U-151*'s actual location, the sinkings of the *Samoa* and the *Kringsjaa* on June 14 finally put them to rest. At 0500 that day, about 60 mi. / 96 km southeast from where *U-151* engaged the *Keemun*, von Nostitz observed the 1,138 GRT, three-masted, Norwegian barque *Samoa*, bound for Perth Amboy, New Jersey, from Walvis Bay, South Africa (now in Namibia), with a cargo of copper and wool.

Her captain, Harold Grostock, recounted to naval authorities that the U-boat did not approach the merchant for nearly an hour before firing a warning shot and having the crew abandon ship, ultimately going on to sink the barque with shellfire. Interestingly, the captain's account mentions nothing about the presence of any other ships in the area (perhaps due to Navy censors), while German sources indicate that an American destroyer incredulously passed them by. Von Nostitz's war diary, very concisely, noted that "in 290° smoke clouds in sight, an American warship, whose back and bridge are clearly visible, with southerly course, steers away without seeing us."[90] Körner's account is much more descriptive:

> She [the *Samoa*] had just trimmed her sails and we were making ready to board her when a destroyer appeared, keeping a course that would take her past us a few miles off. We had launched our small boat and could not submerge right away. The destroyer must certainly see us, or, at any rate, notice the schooner lying there with furled sails. A frantic harum-scarum scene as all hands scurried aboard and below. The destroyer did not change her course. Surely, they must have a better lookout than that! She kept straight on her way and vanished on the horizon, leaving us quite free to deal with our prize.[91]

The identity of this American ship is unknown, but it was likely one of the older destroyers based in the 5th Naval District at Norfolk, Virginia—possibly even USS *Paul Jones* (DD-10), which took on the survivors of the *Samoa* from the schooner *George W. Truitt Jr.*, which had originally rescued them on June 15. Given that its presence put a scare into the Germans, their next course of action seems almost suicidal.

After von Nostitz wrote Capt. Grostock a receipt for his vessel and subsequently sank her with *U-151*'s deck guns, he took pity on the crew, which was now stranded on lifeboats just under 200 mi. / 320 km from the nearest landfall. Realizing that they wouldn't get far on their lifeboats, which were solely powered by oars, von Nostitz sent a wireless message to all the nearest American stations, giving the location of the stricken sailors. His log notes at 0750 that morning:

> Wireless transmission from us to all: "Two boats of sunken vessel 3730 7210 NW adrift please pick up." To accommodate the crew of the "Samoa."
> An unnamed, onboard station answers our signal: "What was the latitude?"[92]

This was eventually confirmed, and a reply of thanks was sent to the U-boat, though it did not appear to raise any particular alarms at the local naval districts. Instead of sending any potential wireless messages to the destroyer (or coastal sub chasers, for that matter) to have it turn around and aid survivors, the only additional wireless broadcasts received by *U-151* from that morning into the afternoon were from Arlington and consisted of outdated war warnings from U-boat sinkings on the ninth through the thirteenth. This must have emboldened von Nostitz a bit, since he would repeat nearly the same sequence of events later that day when he engaged the *Kringsjaa*.

At 1300, *U-151* began a chase that would last over three hours with the 1,750-ton, four-masted, Norwegian barque *Kringsjaa*, en route to New York City with a cargo of linseed oil from Buenos Aires, Argentina. It is a testament both to the quick speed of sailing ships when the wind was in their favor and the relatively slow surface speed of the U-cruiser that the Norwegians nearly escaped—giving up only after panicking and dropping their sails when *U-151* fired two desperate shots from an impossible distance.

After giving themselves up, the same process from the morning's sinking repeated itself, again with the Germans sending out a radio transmission advising that two boats from a sunken vessel were adrift, now at the coordinates 38°2' N, 71°40' W[93] (about 46 mi. / 75 km northeast of where the *Samoa* sank, and about 188 mi. / 302 km from the nearest landfall at Ocean City, Maryland). Shockingly, *U-151* still did not pick up any wireless traffic from the US Navy about the latest victims, and it wouldn't be until the next day that the crew of the *Kringsjaa* was picked up by USS *Patterson* (DD-36), depositing them in Lewes, Delaware, on the seventeenth. Meanwhile, *U-151* was able to continue her east-northeasterly course back home unhindered.

In the following days, *U-151* found little in the way of contacts; however, on the sixteenth, now about 270 mi. / 437 km from the coast of the Delaware, von Nostitz spotted two steamers, both of which were able to evade the U-boat. The second of the sighted ships gave an "allo" message identifying itself as the 4,408-ton *Gordon Castle* and giving its location as 3813 6833 NW. This would be picked up by the Royal Navy station in Bermuda, which, in turn, quickly rebroadcast a warning that was accurate both in time and location.

Unfortunately for the US Navy, this message was competing with more-outdated warnings from the Cape May station and four additional false U-boat sightings, all placing *U-151* much closer to the American East Coast. As a result of the Navy focusing their efforts within domestic waters, the first major encounter between *U-151* and an American warship would not occur in support of the *Gordon Castle*, but instead by mere chance two days later.

Continuing his cruise eastward, and now just under 690 mi. / 1,100 km from the New Jersey shore, von Nostitz began what would be the most dramatic day of his patrol by spotting a large British steamer shortly after 0800 on June 18. According to von Nostitz's war diary:

0820: Straight ahead of us steamer is in sight with a course of 265°.

0822: Submerged. Attacked underwater.

0902: Launched torpedo from starboard tube. Hit. Range 700 m; angle 80°, enemy's course 265°, enemy's heading estimated 12 nm. Steamer listed port side and sagged aft.

0921: Surfaced. Steamer is abandoned. Crew drifts in 7 boats. Approached boats, towed one with the captain on board and drove to the steamer. It is the English, former Russian, steamer "Dwinsk" out of Liverpool (Cunard Line), 8,173 tons, on the voyage from Brest to Newport News to collect troops and ammunition. Steamer had a 12 cm gun and countless lifeboats and rafts on the deck, and was painted gray, white, and black in stripes. Torpedo hit the engine room; ship could not transmit wireless message.

1050: The sinking of the steamer was accelerated by artillery. Crew in boats released.[94]

The steamer would finally sink below the surface at noon, with twenty-four of her fifty-one crew members perishing in the encounter and *U-151* remaining in the area to observe it going down. The hunter, however, would become the prey just fifteen minutes later with the appearance of another vessel on the horizon.

Neither von Nostitz's war diary nor Körner's account gives any justification for the nearly hour and a half that elapsed between releasing the crew of the *Dwinsk* and engaging their next target at 1215 that day—the American auxiliary cruiser / troop transport USS *Von Steuben* (ID-3017, and former SMS *Kronprinz Wilhelm*).[95] The mostly likely explanation, and one supported by testimonies of both the captain of the *Dwinsk*, Henry Nelson, and the commander of the *Von Steuben*, Capt. Yates Stirling Jr. (who had inspected the *Deutschland* on her second cruise), is that the Germans were waiting in the area to trap another troop transport, using the lifeboats as bait as they had with the *Vindeggen*.

Regardless of the ambiguity regarding the time lapse, the German sources are quite clear that upon sighting another potential victim, they quickly submerged and positioned themselves to attack. Von Nostitz's war diary noted that just five minutes after observing a large, four-stacked steamer, he gave the order to dive and initiate the hunt. After waiting for the *Von Steuben* (although the Germans wouldn't know the identity of the ship until after the encounter) to turn toward the lifeboats of the *Dwinsk*, he fired his portside torpedo at 1259. These American sailors, however, were not amateurs and quickly turned the tables on their attackers.

Capt. Stirling, obviously already familiar with U-boat attacks and potential traps, approached the boats of the *Dwinsk* on a zigzag course and, as they came nearer his lookouts, not only detected the incoming torpedo early but was also able to spot *U-151*'s periscope. In response, Stirling commanded his gun crews to their stations to begin firing at the torpedo while he initiated an evasive maneuver—steering his ship to the starboard and ordering his engines to full astern. After successfully dodging the German projectile, the *Von Steuben* then proceeded toward *U-151*'s last known location to drop depth charges. Von Nostitz, experiencing his first encounter with *Wasserbomben*, describes the barrage:

> 1301: Heard detonation, probably depth charges. Immediately went to a depth of 40 m. Detonations, now certainly made out to be depth charges, are getting closer. We go to a greater depth. At 65 m strong detonation close to the boat. Assuming that it is a depth charge, we go even deeper to 82 m. The boat holds very tight. As it turned out after surfacing, the strong detonation was caused by the bursting of the fresh air mast. Gyro compass is switched off, also, if possible, all command panels.
>
> A total of 15 detonations are heard, 8–10 of which were depth charges.
>
> 1400: Surfaced. As there is no sign of the steamer, we headed towards the boats of the "Dwinsk" sailing northwest.
>
> According to the boats, the 4-stacked steamer was an American whose name could not be determined. It could only have been the former German steamer "Kronprinz Wilhelm."
>
> 1600: Apart from the air supply mast, due to the water pressure of 82 on the hull, the receptacle and the telephone buoy are depressed. Wireless warning from Arlington indicates that "Kronprinz Wilhelm" reported our location.[96]

Fredrick Körner described the same event as one of intense dread and with far more, perhaps fantastic, details.

While von Nostitz noted changes of depth as if they were intentional, Körner described an uncontrollable plummeting, which, he correctly stated, far exceeded the shipyard's rated depth of 50 m. He also claimed that his commander decided it was better to die fighting it out with the cruiser than dying in the deep, and had to blow all tanks in order to get the submarine to the surface—an emergency maneuver that not only would give away his true position (from the burst of air escaping to the surface) but would leave the U-boat momentarily helpless. Reading between the lines of the war diary entry, there is one primary reason to believe Körner's version of the events to be correct.

Following the incident with the *Von Steuben*, unlike previous encounters *U-151* had with American warships, von Nostitz does not mention first going to periscope depth to inspect the surface traffic and then, finding it to be safe, coming to the surface. Instead, it was only *after* the U-boat surfaced that he discovered the *Von Steuben* had disappeared—receiving final confirmation of this from the *Dwinsk*'s lifeboats still present in the area. Had the American cruiser/transport been sailing only with a destroyer escort, had it been better armed, or had it simply not been afraid of additional U-boats in the area, the situation may have ended much worse for the German sailors.

As it happened, the lone USS *Von Steuben* had expended all the depth charges on board in a single pass over *U-151*, and, after doing so, Capt. Stirling then ordered the ship full ahead and proceeded out of the area—electing not to stop to take on any of the survivors of the *Dwinsk*. Believing that he was indeed in a trap and there were additional U-boats in the area, his decision was a logical one. Stopping to save the men in the lifeboats would have certainly endangered his own crew and, in sinking, would have reduced the chances of survival for the British sailors already in the water. Although no rescue attempt was made, Stirling did promise Capt. Nelson that he would radio their location so that another ship could come to their aid in safer conditions. The wireless transmission intercepted by *U-151* at 1600 that day was the American captain making good on his pledge. While Stirling would be awarded both the Navy Cross and the Légion d'Honneur for his actions that day, hindsight reveals just how much of an opportunity for sinking a U-boat he had squandered in retiring from the engagement.

As Capt. Stirling and USS *Von Steuben* proceeded westward at full speed, the fortunate Germans, surviving their first major brush with death, left the area and continued back on their course toward home. Although this was the point at which Fredrick Körner's tale to Lowell Thomas concluded, it would not be the end of the story for *U-151*, which was not shying away from any potential targets that came in her way.

On June 19, now over 600 mi. / 965 km from the nearest American coastline, the German raiders spotted a 5,000-ton armed and camouflaged steamer. This was followed by a 6,000-ton large freighter the next day. Attempts were made at attacking both the vessels, though rough seas and heavy storms prevented Korvettenkapitän von Nostitz from adding to his tonnage count. In both cases he ends his logs with the term *Waffengebrauch ausgeschlossen*—use of weapons out of the question. Success would come with better weather on the twenty-second, when *U-151* encountered the 2,966-ton Belgian steamship *Chilier*, en route from Barry, Wales, to Sandy Hook, New Jersey, in ballast.

Finding the Belgians armed with "a 1916 manufactured 9 cm cannon capable of shooting up to 110 hm"[97] on the stern, a first attempt at sinking was made with a torpedo, which missed when the steamer suddenly changed course. Following the torpedo's failure to impact, *U-151* came to the surface and overwhelmed the single Belgian gun crew with superior firepower from the U-boat's twin deck guns at a range of 600–700 m—forcing the Belgian crew to take to their boats. At this point, von Nostitz's prize crew was once again dispatched to the ship to sink her with explosives.

Interestingly, it appeared that von Nostitz's compassion for his victims had dried up at this point, opting not to send out a signal giving the location of lifeboats despite the afflicted sailors being about 675 mi. / 1,085 km from the nearest landfall at Nova Scotia (specifically 39°13' N, 53°31' W). Almost mockingly, shortly after departing the area, *U-151* picked up the latest submarine warning from Arlington advising of the sinking of the *Dwinsk* and warning all vessels that U-boats may be encountered "west" of longitude 50°, following the inbound steamer routes into the United States. The crew of the *Chilier* would ultimately be rescued just over five days later; however, they would be six sailors fewer in number, since part of the crew drowned after their boat capsized in rough seas.

Continuing on his course back to Germany, von Nostitz would be able secure yet another victory for his patrol. This occurred on June 23, when *U-151* encountered the Norwegian steamer *Augvald* (incorrectly identified in German sources as the *Answald*), now nearly 925 mi. / 1,490 km from the closest American port (39°3' N, 52°47' W). The entry to *U-151*'s war diary is both very descriptive and also somewhat vague in what actually occurred during the sinking:

> Submerged. Let steamer pass while under water. It is painted uniformly gray, the insignia on the smokestack is also painted over, but the name is white. Whether it is armed cannot be determined exactly, a trestle observed at the stern could possibly be a masked cannon.
>
> Surfaced. At 60 hm, stopped steamer with artillery shots. Steamer raises a flag that cannot yet be made out, apparently stops, but after a short time turns towards the boat. Fire about to be reopened until it is noticed that the steamer stops again, and boats are launched. Gave signal: "Send a boat!" After waiting for 2 hours lee of the steamer about 40 meters away, it is assumed that the steamer is either a trap or completely abandoned. Artillery fire is opened again, with the first shots aimed far away from the steamer in order to give the people aboard the opportunity to show some signs of life, then with a slow approach, effective shooting at the ship. Steamer burns and slowly sinks.

From a closer distance it is found that it is the Norwegian steamer "Answald" from Hangesund (3,406 tons). It has been abandoned by the crew, and despite searching, nothing can be seen of the boats. Steamer is not armed but painted a warlike black and gray without any neutral markings.

Submerged because of bad weather.[98]

The *Augvald*'s captain, Hans Høie (Hoye in American sources), and chief engineer, Alfred Petersen, both gave accounts of the sinking upon being rescued that help fill in some of the missing details, but their testimonies also beg further questions.

They both confirmed that the only two lifeboats on the *Augvald* were launched after *U-151* fired a second round of warning shots, one with Høie and twelve crew members, and the other with Petersen and thirteen others. Apparently, they did not understand von Nostitz's signal to send a boat, and immediately started sailing away from the ship, going on to claim that *U-151* did not approach until they left the immediate proximity of the *Augvald*. While it is obvious the Germans believed they were encountering a Q-ship (or at the very least, some kind of armed transport, since the paint scheme was very similar to that of the *Dwinsk*), it is unclear how they could have lost sight of the lifeboats during the two hours they took to determine their next course of action—particularly with von Nostitz and his officers keeping such a close eye on the vessel.

During this period, up to the point the *Augvald* was sunk, both Høie and Petersen claimed that they observed *U-151* lying in wait and then ultimately coming closer to the steamer to sink her. This meant that their boats must have been quite close to *U-151* the entire duration of the engagement. They further elaborated that (just as von Nostitz logged in his war diary) upon dispatching their steamer, the German U-boat submerged and departed, evidently paying no attention to their lifeboats. Although von Nostitz recorded that the weather was poor and there were large ocean swells, one would assume that even a casual search would have yielded a lifeboat sighting, especially with other officers on the bridge also seeking the Norwegian sailors. In all likelihood, the colder side of the Germans' demeanor once again presented itself, and they simply didn't care.

Although the *Augvald* would be the last steamship sunk by *U-151* on this particular patrol, it was not due to a lack of trying on the part of the Germans. Due to Adm. Sims' and Secretary Daniels' insistence on keeping their main complement of their fleet across the Atlantic or on convoy duty, as *U-151* continued on her course back to base, she began to encounter significantly more American warships closer to European waters than she had on the American East Coast—all of which were going to put up a fight.

On June 24, now halfway across the Atlantic, strong seas and poor weather prevented von Nostitz from attacking an 8,000 GRT, camouflaged steamer similar in appearance to the *Dwinsk*; however, on the morning of the twenty-fifth, he began to encounter scattered vessels from a France-bound convoy escorted by USS *Columbia* (C-12). Despite the conditions not improving from the previous day, the German commander must have found these targets irresistible, since he chose to pursue them even though "torpedo firing [was] ruled out and use of artillery [was] very difficult."[99] Shortly after being outrun by a tanker and a potential escort and then choosing not to pursue a steamship headed in the opposite direction, von Nostitz set his sights on a steamer approaching him from the rear. According to *U-151*'s war diary:

> [time illegible:] Submerged. Let the steamer pass as the ocean swells ruled out torpedo shots. Steamer has a powerful stern gun.
> 0700: Surfaced. Opened fire on steamer at 100 hm. Steamer returns fire with well-positioned shots from its 12 cm stern gun. Steamer runs at high speed and course about 60°.
> 0745: Ceased fire and abandoned pursuit.
> [time illegible:] Allo report from the shelled steamship. "Glenlee" (5,200 tons) [in reality 4,915 GRT], Glasgow, chased and shelled steering north 55° east SOS lat. 40 long. 49 NW.[100]

Nearly twelve hours later, *U-151* would intercept another straggler from the same convoy—the *Dochra* (ID 1758), a British-built cargo ship commissioned by the US Navy and carrying seaplanes.

This time, as *U-151* sped toward the ship on the surface to get within artillery range, the Americans saw the approaching Germans and then initiated a preemptive barrage from all her deck guns. Although no reason for breaking off the battle was given by von Nostitz in his war diary, one can assume that he likely found himself outgunned and completely lacking the element of surprise.

Von Nostitz would have a similar experience two days later when he encountered another American ship, USS *Lake Forest* (ID 2991), returning in ballast after offloading her cargo of coal in Scotland. This vessel of the Naval Overseas Transport Service appeared to confuse the German commander, who, after observing it from periscope depth, noted that it was "a relatively small steamer, with an unusually large gun at the stern, a structure on the forecastle, and a framework that looks like an extendable spotlight."[101] Although the Germans were the first to open fire during the engagement, the Americans were quick to respond with "vigorous" return fire that, despite falling short and wide, was enough to stop *U-151* from proceeding with the attack. Von Nostitz commented that even after the chances of striking the U-boat were hopeless, *Lake Forest* continued to fire, before setting a smoke screen and speeding away.

Shortly after breaking off contact with *Lake Forest*, the German commander would try and fail to engage two additional vessels. Although he had believed these ships to be commercial steamers, in reality these were the US Army transport ship *McClellan* and the cruiser USS *Minneapolis* (C-13)—a pair that could have potentially finished the job *Von Steuben* had started. Both the warships had spotted the submarine, with the latter reporting its location and course, but luckily for the Germans, none of the escorts took up the search.

It was perhaps due to being frustrated by this lack of success that von Nostitz would end the twenty-eighth of June by making what could be considered a relatively insignificant vessel the final victory of his cruise. Now just over 1,500 mi. / 2,535 km from the coast of Ireland, *U-151* stopped the 124-ton Canadian schooner SS *Dictator* with a warning shot and demanded to see her papers. While the Germans had previously allowed the diminutive, 100-ton *Nicholson* go on her way on the American East Coast, they did not extend the same courtesy to this equally small sailing ship, opting to sink her and her cargo of salt from Cádiz, Spain, bound for English Harbour, Newfoundland. Interestingly, the *Dictator*'s Canadian merchant mariner crew were taken aboard the U-boat as prisoners of war, in lieu of being abandoned in the middle of the Atlantic. They would remain in various prison camps within Germany (where two of the six crew members would perish, one through pneumonia and the other being crushed by a shunting train) until the conclusion of the Great War.[102]

In the week that followed the sinking of the *Dictator*, *U-151* remained on the hunt, spotting no fewer than seven vessels, but all these targets would elude the Germans for one reason or another. After allowing a well-lit hospital ship to sail onward unmolested on July 1, von Nostitz was forced to concede four additional steamers, including a 6,000-ton large troopship, to bad weather. This fruitless streak would culminate with a brief firefight with the *Nevasa* (9,071 GRT) on the third, with the British vessel also being able to break away from the German attackers through her superior surface speed and the combination of her smoke clouds and the heavy fog above the water's surface. No additional steamers would be sighted for the remaining two weeks of *U-151*'s patrol.

It was during this unproductive week that attempts were made at contacting SM *U-156*, which departed Germany on June 15 for the United States but would have been near to *U-151*'s current location at that point in her cruise (about 500 mi. / 815 km north of the Azores). *U-151*'s radio logs indicate that on June 20, U-boat headquarters notified von Nostitz that *U-156* had already sailed past the Shetland Islands and that "apart from important news about the minefield situation, report the location . . . every 2 days."[103] Although *U-156* was precisely in the proximity of *U-151* at the time, repeated wireless transmissions from *U-151* went unanswered. It is unclear why no response was received from the other U-Kreuzer, since all signals broadcast both from Nauen and Rügen (for both U-boats) appear to have been received by von Nostitz for the remainder of his journey.

This lack of communication between U-boat commanders would cause von Nostitz to have to reenter the "English Restricted Zone" without any current intelligence on Allied minefields or hostile contacts in the North Sea. As the Germans proceeded on the final leg of their return voyage, the next two weeks' watches would yield nothing in the way of commercial shipping or other outbound U-boats; they would, however, produce plenty in the way of heat coming their way.

As the Germans made their way around the northern tip of the British Isles, *U-151* barely escaped a torpedo attack from an unidentified submarine. This encounter occurred at 60°22' N, 6°29' W (now just 130 mi. / 210 km north of Scotland), with von Nostitz noting,

> Shot at by a submarine with 2 torpedoes. Turned away for a short time, then continued onward with both diesels. Shots were noticed in good time and both motors were immediately stopped, so both torpedoes passed the front.[104]

This was followed by a periscope sighting on the fifteenth, and then another two attacks by enemy submarines on the seventeenth as *U-151* hugged the Norwegian coast to avoid the British blockade. After nearly four months of being at sea, it seemed that the Allies' best attempts at locating and attacking *U-151* (using Adm. Sims' favored method of sinking U-boats) came when she was just days from arriving back in Kiel.

When von Nostitz finally returned home on the twentieth of July, he had cruised for just under 11,000 nautical miles (12,561 mi. / 20,215 km) and was responsible for sinking or damaging 59,925 gross tons of shipping (see appendix B), a monetary loss exceeding $25 million (in 1918 dollars)[105]—far surpassing the 30,000–40,000 tons that Adm. Sims estimated in his initial cable to Secretary Daniels. While this would appear to be a German triumph, from the standpoint of the US Navy, the patrol was a total failure.

Despite the high overall tonnage sunk or damaged and the fact that forty-seven lives were lost during the raid, the Navy would not be sending any of the warships currently in service in Europe and the Mediterranean back to

American waters. To them, the most-vital ships for the Allied war effort were the troop transports, which had, during the month of June, set a new record for the transfer of American soldiers, and of which *U-151* was able to sink only one—which was empty on its return voyage. The vessels sunk by von Nostitz had been largely smaller, antiquated types that were not carrying, and could not hold, an abundance of war material and were thus expendable to the US Navy when considering the larger picture.

This should not, however, imply that American Navy leadership was completely apathetic about the U-boat threat at home. In the midst of *U-151*'s onslaught, Adm. Sims, who had initially completely discounted the military value of a lone U-cruiser, was beginning to have doubts about the effectiveness of existing domestic defenses and looked to the British for help. Given that there were currently no vessels in American waters outfitted like Q-Ships (although there were decoy schooners towing American submarines as U-boat traps; see chapter 10), he sent a secret message to Sir Oswyn Murray, the secretary of the British Admiralty, requesting that either one or two spare British ones be sent to the American East Coast, or, barring that, that the British lend the United States an officer to impart his experiences with Q-ship development so that the Navy could develop their own.[106]

When Sims subsequently asked for approval from the CNO for this request, he also made the suggestion to begin arming coastal sailing ships with a 4-inch deck gun as a "temporary expedient." Not surprisingly, CNO Benson was not on board with this plan and stated his reservations in a cable sent to Adm. Sims on June 12:

> Department does not deem it advisable to begin the operation of Q boats on this side of the Atlantic.
>
> (First) In the operations this far conducted by *U-151* considerable precaution has been taken to safeguard life, the result has been very few casualties. The military value with ships sunk has been very small.
>
> (Second) The success of Q boats would be entirely in the initial stages, later their value as taken from your own report would be very small and their use would be met by reprisal in some form. The great danger of reprisal lies in its effect on the public mind and the pressure it might bring to bear to hold force here which should be dispatched abroad.
>
> (Third) Department feels that in a short time through its routing and arming of ships and with the proper distribution of its available forces, it will have the situation well in hand without materially decreasing its output across Atlantic.[107]

Once again, Adm. Benson had affirmed the Navy's view of *U-151* having little impact on the war effort, and he assured the commander in European waters that the situation at home would soon be well under control. The Germans, however, did not share the American perspective.

In his report to the U-Kreuzer command following the patrol, von Nostitz pointed out that the lack of American coastal defenses was advantageous for the U-cruisers, and precedent should be placed on the transport of raw materials instead of just human cargo (although he still believed that the Navy would be forced to recall many of their better ships and crews to counter the U-boat threat). Sections 2 and 3 of his analysis are particularly telling:

> 2. According to Americans, American coastal shipping has increased significantly in size and importance for economic life. As a result of great transport difficulties, there is a strain on the railways which currently only handle the transport of war materiel. Everything else, especially the very important coal supplies, has to be transported by water if possible. The whole fleet of sailing ships only deals with coal transport. The traffic from West Africa, South America, and the West Indies is also very important for the supply of raw materials (copper, wool, rubber). From now on all this traffic will probably be kept close under the coast and either convoyed or heavily guarded. Patrolling is very easy on the relatively short stretches, so nothing can be done against this traffic in the future without a restricted area declaration. Its damage would mean a radical disruption of American economic life.
>
> 3. The patrol ships and countermeasures were weak for the time being. They existed solely on the main routes, and were carried out by destroyers, submarine hunters, and submarines. According to statements by Americans, there are only a few and older vehicles with untrained personnel available for them. All good material and personnel would have been sent to Europe; their recall would be necessary if submarines continued to operate on the coast.
>
> No convoys or securing of individual steamers were observed anywhere, nor was there any aircraft or airship surveillance.
>
> The port entrances are guarded and partially closed by nets and mine barriers. Due to the fact that none of the sunken ships showed the slightest reference to defensive measures of a similar kind in writing or map material, it can be concluded that outside of the [harbor] entrances with pilotage there is no such thing.[108]

His superiors agreed and concluded that besides the American coastline, which was ripe with essential war resources, the approaching routes from Africa, South America, and the Caribbean should also be included in future operational areas, where shipping was most likely to be unsecured.

An editorial published in the *Kölnische Volkszeitung* (concerning *U-151*'s expedition to the United States) noted German these sentiments more colorfully, stating,

> The North Americans may now feel the fist of the warlord. They need not be surprised. He who sows the wind reaps the whirlwind, even when he sits on the other side of the great herring pond, where he is under the delusion that his is safe from the storm.[109]

Indeed, more U-boats would be forthcoming, albeit not the hurricane force that German propaganda had suggested. The American coastal defenses, also gaining valuable experience through *U-151*'s raid, would be waiting.

CHAPTER 8
A Fisher of Men

On July 21, 1918, on the southeastern tip of Cape Cod, Lt. Elijah Williams is sitting back at his desk on this hot, hazy Sunday morning. Typically, he wouldn't find himself in charge of the Chatham Naval Air Station, but today his commander, Capt. Phillip Eaton, was in the air with most of the station's pilots in search of a Navy dirigible that had somehow gone missing days prior. Looking down at the hot cup of coffee sitting in front of him, he thinks to himself, "I swanny . . . only a Yankee could drink hot coffee on a morning like this. What I would give to be cooling down with some nice Cheerwine from back home right now." He leans back and peers at the clock on the wall, almost 1030.

Returning to the coffee in front of him, he notices a slight ripple on the liquid's surface, proceeded by a dull thunderclap in the distance. "Huh . . . I don't recall any storms in the forecast today." The subsequent rumbles rouse him to his senses. "That ain't thunder, that's shellfire!" Immediately, Lt. Williams rises to his feet and runs toward the hangar, eager to get his planes in the air and seek out the enemy. Once inside, he finds only a skeleton crew of mechanics and naval airmen. "Where in tarnation is everyone?" asks the panting officer. One of the mechanics begins to answer, "Well, sir, Captain Eaton . . ." Williams immediately cuts him off. "I know Eaton and his group are in the air; I mean everybody else!" The response is disconcerting: "Playing baseball against the minesweeper squad in Provincetown, sir."

Making due with the resources available, Williams is able to assemble a crew and get a Curtiss HS-1L loaded with a Mk. IV bomb and ready to fly. Unfortunately, fouled spark plugs render the seaplane dead in the water. Flabbergasted, Williams surveys the hangar to see what else he could get in the sky. "What about that Curtiss, number 1695?" A mechanic responds, "Sir, that one is having crankshaft issues; pilots have reported an odd knocking and vibration; we were just about to break down the engine." Looking nearly defeated, Williams makes a plea to the pilots surrounding him. "Look, men. The Germans are here; we need to get something in the air and put an end to this bombardment. For the time being this is all we have left. Anyone willing to take their chances with 1695?"

Ens. Eric Lingard steps forward: "I'll fly her, sir." Lingard was a native Massachusettsan who had previously worked at the Fore River Shipyard in Quincy, building sub chasers to counter the German U-boats. He had enlisted in the Navy because he "wanted more direct action"[1] and had envisioned himself flying for the Navy off the coast of France—where he would be certain to encounter U-boats. Unfortunately, his extensive knowledge of local waters made him invaluable to the home front for coastal patrol duties. After flying seemingly endless exhibitions for various loan drives and fruitless local patrols, Lingard felt his chances of encountering a German submarine would never be realized. Today, he'd finally be getting his chance to engage the enemy. HS-1L number 1695 was quickly prepped for flight, and Lingard and his crew, consisting of a copilot and observer, sped down the water runway and took to the sky. The time was 1054, and their destination was Orleans.

The U-boat intended for Lingard's bomb was SM *U-156*, another converted submarine of the Deutschland class that had previously completed a dramatic patrol off the northwest coast of Africa months prior. While that patrol had been under the leadership of Kapitänleutnant Konrad Gansser, an experienced U-boat ace who began his career in 1915 with SM *U-33*, the cruise to the United States would be commanded by Kapitänleutnant Richard Feldt,[2] also a veteran officer with a career dating back to 1900, albeit never in the U-boat service. Like von Nostitz, he would be gaining his first experience with submersibles on a patrol that would take him an extraordinary distance but would, ideally, be less perilous than engaging the well-protected shipping in European waters.

U-156 would depart Kiel on June 16, 1918, with orders to, just as with *U-151*, plant mines within the major North American shipping lanes; sever a transatlantic telegraph line between Orleans, Massachusetts, and France; and subsequently resume the trade war on Allied shipping along the American East Coast—with a particular emphasis on the fishing fleets off New England. On the basis of the tactics Feldt adopted on his patrol, it would appear that he was influenced more by the exploits of Korvettenkapitän Karl von Müller and the crew of the SMS *Emden* than any of FdU Hermann Bauer's lectures. Under Feldt's command, *U-156* would go on to resemble more of an East Asian commerce raider than a U-Kreuzer, employing visual subterfuges, commandeering a merchant ship, and bringing the war not only to American mariners but to coastal townspeople. Unfortunately, we can ascertain what Feldt's true motivations were only from sources other than the man himself, since his war diary remains with him and his crew, in the bottom of the North Sea—a fate that will be elaborated on later in this chapter.

The first indication of *U-156* leaving port for the United States came on June 29, once again originating from British Intelligence in Room 40. *U-156* had torpedoed an armed British merchant steamship in ballast, the SS *Tortuguero* (4,175 GRT), three days prior and 205 miles northwest of Ireland, with twelve sailors being lost in the sinking. This resulted in Admiral Sims sending out a rather ambiguous cable advising the following:

Second cruiser submarine at sea. At present off west coast of Ireland. Her field of operations not yet known. Cannot reach longitude of Nantucket before July fifteenth. Shall keep department informed.[3]

Although the operational zone and estimated time of arrival mentioned by Sims were certainly nebulous, this time the Navy would not refrain from passing on the warning to the American public, which had been reeling from *U-151*'s recent raid.

In the time that elapsed between *U-151* first arriving in the United States and the time it took *U-156* to arrive, the Navy had been bombarded with criticism from newspaper editorials and government officials not only for the lack of any initial warning, but also for the sense that there was inadequate protection for American harbors and waterways. After all, none of the warships in service in Europe were being recalled, and coastal defense remained largely in the hands of reservists operating obsolete vessels. While Secretary Daniels would not budge on his position of keeping the bulk (and the best) of American vessels overseas, steps were being taken to improve the protection of domestic waters.

First, resources including sub chasers and smaller coastal patrol craft from less threatened naval districts were transferred to the 1st through the 5th Naval Districts, where enemy submarine activity was more likely to take place. Second, the lack of aerial patrols described by von Nostitz in his postpatrol analysis was being addressed, despite the Navy not having any knowledge of the German commander's report. Twelve new naval aviation units had been created for the purpose of flying regular patrols over the American coastline and could be armed with either bombs or depth charges in order to attack a U-boat if and when the opportunity presented itself. Last, submarine hunter squadrons consisting of destroyers, sub chasers, and a limited number of submarines would be making regular patrols of the shipping lanes outside the major harbors. In the event that a definite U-boat sighting was reported, these vessels would then concentrate themselves at the naval base nearest to the U-boat's location and sail to the reported area to collectively engage the enemy submarine.

In an effort to prevent district commandants from being shy in issuing war warnings (as they initially had with *U-151*) and getting complacent with the lack of recent sinkings, a dispatch from the office of the CNO was sent to every naval district, advising,

Do not be influenced by the absence of submarine activity off the coast to relax in the slightest degree the vigilance of patrol, both surface and air and under water. Give this immediate attention and impress it on all hands.[4]

Indeed, submarine-hunting groups were now encouraged to take a more offensive stance during their patrols, instead of merely reacting to incidents as they had previously.

Despite the increase in patrols and overall diligence of the Navy along the Eastern Seaboard, the threat of a U-boat attack still appeared to pervade the psyche of American merchantmen, and a state of anxiety was ubiquitous. Although no U-boats were operating within American waters at the time, reports were still being made by vessels claiming they were being attacked. Additionally, many American seamen, fearful of venturing too far away from coastal protection, hugged the shoreline and grounded themselves, while others ran into each other while they kept their ships unlit during the night.

A particularly disastrous example of the latter type of incident occurred shortly before 0500 on June 21, when the Navy gunboat USS *Schurz* collided with the tanker SS *Florida* off the coast of North Carolina. *Schurz*, formerly the German unprotected cruiser SMS *Geier* (seized by the US upon the declaration of war while she was interned in Hawaii), had been assigned to patrol and escort duties along the East Coast and the Caribbean and had departed New York City bound for Key West two days prior. On the morning of the twenty-first, she was running without lights when the *Florida* collided with her, resulting in the tanker penetrating 12 feet into the starboard side the ship.[5] This impact immediately killed one sailor, injured an additional twelve, and ultimately resulted in the *Schurz* sinking three hours later. Although casualties were somewhat light, considering there were 217 men and officers on board, USS *Schurz* was a total loss.

In the week that followed the sinking of USS *Schurz*, more vessels would be afflicted by the hypothetical threat of U-boats lurking just outside coastal protection. Just as Sims was sending a warning indicating that *U-156* was on her way westward on June 29, the steamship *Hattie Gage* ran aground while sailing just 400 yards off the Virginia coastline.[6] Her first mate would drown attempting to launch a lifeboat during the incident. Later, on July 2, the Canadian troop transport *City of Vienna* (6,111 GRT and with seven hundred Canadian soldiers on board) would follow suit, beaching herself at Black Rock, Nova Scotia. Although the crew and troops aboard the *City of Vienna* were rescued by two Navy converted yachts, USS *Aztec* (SP-590) and USS *Niagara* (SP-136), the troopship itself was unable to be salvaged. While the US awaited the arrival of *U-156*, sailors continued to perish, and material losses continued to add up without the Germans firing a single shot.

During this chaotic first week of July, Kapitänleutnant Feldt and his crew were actually nearly 500 miles southeast of Newfoundland and over 1,000 miles away from the nearest American port, completely unaware of the havoc being wrought in anticipation of their arrival. Here in the middle of the North Atlantic, the German submariners were approaching the New World on the surface, disguised as a steamship. Like von Müller, who added a bogus additional stack to the SMS *Emden* to make his cruiser appear to be a British warship, Feldt had his crew fashion a false funnel of their own, which was assembled around the U-boat's conning tower to accentuate the U-cruiser's natural ship-like surface silhouette. It was under this guise, on July 5, that they encountered USS *Lake Bridge* (ID-2990), a 1,984-ton, armed mine carrier, employed by the Navy to transport mines from the United States to the Northern Barrage minefield in the North Sea.[7]

Initially, it had appeared that Feldt's ruse was successful, since *U-156* was able to approach the armed cargo ship within 10,000 yds. / 9,144 m (well within the nearly 15,860 yd. / 14,500 m range of the U-cruiser's powerful 15 cm deck guns) unhindered. Perhaps out of fear of violating false-flag regulations or out of concern of the range of the American ship's guns, Feldt chose this moment to drop his facade and engage the mine carrier—removing his fabricated funnel and speeding toward the cargo ship as his gun crew opened fire. The American sailors aboard *Lake Bridge*, now recognizing the distant vessel as a U-boat, immediately began returning fire while their commanding officer, Lt. Cmdr. (USNRF) Charles Wall, ordered his ship to make steam and for a smoke screen to be laid down.

As USS *Lake Bridge* sped away from *U-156* at full speed, the distance between the two vessels had grown enough that only the shrapnel from the U-boat's explosive shells was able to reach the superstructure of the steamer. Although the projectiles from the 5-inch/51-caliber[8] deck gun on *Lake Bridge* (which had an identical range to *U-156*'s 15 cm guns) could be faring no better, they must have troubled Feldt, who deployed his own *Nebel-U-Boots-Anlage* in response. As both vessels hid behind their cloak of artificial fog, continuing to fire away at a now-impossible range, the superior surface speed of USS *Lake Bridge* allowed the American ship to escape unscathed. In what could be considered a German defeat, the brief, half-hour engagement left Richard Feldt with nothing to show for his expended rounds, and Charles Wall being awarded a Navy Cross for his.

Like von Nostitz who preceded him, Feldt was given orders to avoid detection until his minelaying mission had been completed. After violating his directives with the irresistible temptation of USS *Lake Bridge*, Feldt would revert back to his original instructions and *U-156* would engage only two sailing ships, incapable of escaping the U-cruiser or radioing for help, prior to her arrival off the American coast. The first of these ships was a Norwegian sailing ship, which came to a halt upon observing warning shots from *U-156* on July 7.

The *Marosa*, a 1,987-ton, three-masted barque, was en route from Newport News to Montevideo, Uruguay, with 3,171 tons of coal when she was stopped at 40°0' N, 50°35' W, or about 730 mi. / 1,175 km east-southeast of Nova Scotia. Here, the ship's captain and officers were interrogated by *U-156*'s second officer, Oberleutnant zur See Paul Richard Knöckel (incorrectly identified as "J" Knöckel in early American sources), concerning their cargo, as well as current and previous voyages. More specifically, the Germans were asking various questions concerning American coastal defenses, locations of American warships, and the general American sentiment toward the war.[9]

All this was information that the Admiralstab potentially wanted von Nostitz to pass on to Feldt personally when they were trying to establish a rendezvous between the two submarines in late June, but it would now have to be gleaned from a Norwegian crew with little motivation to provide accurate information. Whether or not valuable intel was provided to the Germans is unclear from the testimonies of the *Marosa*'s captain and chief officer, but it appeared that the Germans were satisfied with what they heard, since they were cordial to the Norwegian crew and allowed them to take whatever they needed from their ship prior to looting and sinking her. Interestingly, chief officer Holte remarked that the rationale for sinking the *Marosa* given by Oberleutnant Knöckel had nothing to do with their cargo of contraband, but instead that she was chartered by an American firm.[10] The fact that the cargo was intended for Uruguay, which had severed diplomatic relations with Germany and seized the German ships interned in her harbor back in October 1917, was likely also in the back of the *Oberleutnant*'s mind.

After being given instructions to travel westward, the Norwegians pushed off from their ship while the German prize crew prepared the barque with explosive charges and opened her hatches. The ship was still afloat when the Norwegian crew departed, and they would later report that they were uncertain of its eventual fate. As they continued on their heading, they would actually come across the second victim of *U-156* the next evening—spotting another fully rigged ship sitting idle at 40°0' N, 52°0' W, with her sails furled up and with the gray-and-black-camouflage-painted U-Kreuzer close beside her.

This unlucky vessel was the Norwegian barque *Manx King*, 1,751 GRT and transporting a cargo of oil, cotton, barbed wire, iron, and shoes from New York to Rio de Janeiro. It too would be sunk by *Sprengpatronen*. In this case, the Norwegian captain, Helgesen, argued that his ship was registered to Norway and was thus a neutral vessel and should not be sunk. The German retort, however, was that the ship's cargo was obviously contraband intended for Brazil, another South American nation who also declared war against Germany, in October 1917. Like the *Marosa*, the *Manx King*'s crew were given instructions to row west, where they would likely be picked up by a passing steamer—they also departed their vessel without actually seeing it sink.

Both Norwegian crews would be picked up by passing ships on July 9, with the crew of the *Marosa* being deposited off Nova Scotia on July 16, and the *Manx King*'s crew arriving in an unknown "Atlantic port" (in all likelihood New York City) on July 12. The latter crew reported to the *New York Times* that since they didn't see their ship sink, it was possible that it may have been converted to a surface raider—a theory the newspaper ran with.[11]

In a testament to Richard Feldt's ability to evade detection, nothing was seen of *U-156* from the sinking of the *Manx King* until July 17, when the auxiliary cruiser / troop transport USS *Harrisburg* (ID-1663) sent an "allo" message, noting her position of 40°10' N, 68°55' W—about 92 mi. / 148 km southeast of Nantucket. The American ship claimed that *U-156* was observed on the surface at a distance of approximately 10,000 yds. / 9,144 m, with neither the U-boat nor the transport making any attempt at combating one another.

There is speculation as to whether *U-156* was heading toward New York at this point to launch her Teka mines or had already done so and was on her way to another operational area. Since the *Kriegstagebuch* for *U-156* does not exist, one can only hypothesize, but the available evidence indicates that it is probable the mines had already been sown. The location of the U-boat, as noted by USS *Harrisburg*, was about 775 nautical miles (approximately 893 mi. / 1,437 km) from the location of the *Manx King* sinking. Assuming that *U-156* was traveling at a conservative average speed of 5 knots (her maximum surface speed was 12.4 knots), it would have taken only six and half days to reach the area, placing her ETA on July 15, instead of the seventeenth and making it doubtful that *U-156* hung around the area for two days before continuing on toward Long Island.

The question of why Feldt opted not to attack USS *Harrisburg* could then be asked, since his minelaying objective would've been completed, and he would no longer have to remain undetected. In this case, one can postulate that the distance was too far to chase the cruiser submerged and fire a torpedo, and that the U-Kreuzer was woefully outgunned by USS *Harrisburg*'s four 6-pound and four 3-pound guns if any attack was attempted on the surface. If it's assumed that the sequence of events is true, Kapitänleutnant Feldt likely entered American waters prior to being spotted and began his minelaying mission between the fifteenth and sixteenth. It would be here that one of the biggest victories of a U-boat against an American warship would take place.

Like *U-151*, *U-156* carried fourteen Teka mines on board, and according to historian Eberhard Rössler, Feldt would proverbially be placing all his "eggs in one basket" by releasing them all in a single location. This was likely not how events actually transpired. Given the number of mines recovered from the area, combined with the way that future events in *U-156*'s patrol unfolded, evidence exists of a secondary mining location, but that will be expanded on later in the chapter. For now, Feldt's destination would be the outer periphery of the Ambrose Channel, the gateway to the New York City harbor.[12] The payoff for his minefield arrived quickly on July 19, a mere two days after USS *Harrisburg* located the raider, when the armored cruiser USS *San Diego* (ACR-6 and former USS *California*) sailed toward New York City from the Portsmouth Naval Shipyard in New Hampshire.

USS *San Diego* (photo taken when she was still USS *California*) in the prewar years. *Author's collection*

USS *San Diego* was a Pennsylvania-class armored cruiser[13] of 13,680 tons, which had been the flagship of the Pacific Fleet in the years between 1907 and 1917. While the original, nineteenth-century concept of armored cruisers had been to place them on a nearly equal standing with battleships (relying on the cruisers' speed to engage the enemy to await the arrival of the main force), analysis of the Russo-Japanese War in 1904 revealed them to play more of an auxiliary role as scouts/escorts in the twentieth century.[14] This was the job *San Diego* would perform in the Pacific in the years leading up to the First World War, with her most dramatic action taking place as an "observation" ship, lying offshore during the Tampico Affair and subsequent occupation of Veracruz in 1914.

With the loss of the German naval base at Tsingtao (now Qingdao) and of Germany's remaining Pacific colonies, and the eventual British defeat of the German East Asian Squadron off the Falklands in 1914, the United States found itself without an enemy in the Pacific when war was declared in 1917. For this reason, USS *San Diego* was transferred to Atlantic service, where she began escorting convoys in September 1917. During this early-war period, her armament would also evolve along with the technology of the Great War, shedding twelve of her original eighteen 3-inch/50-caliber guns to accommodate extra ammunition for her four 8-inch/45-caliber guns, fourteen 6-inch/50-caliber guns, and two 18-inch torpedo tubes.[15] Tragically, one countermeasure intended for antisubmarine warfare was omitted from her complement during a refit in June 1918—"otter"-type paravanes.

After completing two successful transatlantic convoys to France and Britain (as well as other shorter trips escorting merchant convoys to meet their destroyer escorts), USS *San Diego* was drydocked for her third wartime refit. It was at this time that the cruiser was equipped with the mount for "otters," but the paravanes themselves were never installed.[16] The otters, unlike earlier British paravane designs, which were armed with 400 pounds of TNT and functioned like a towable depth charge, were mounted on the bow of warships in pairs and, instead of being armed with explosives, had cutting jaws to sever a submerged mine's anchoring cable, allowing it to float to the surface, where it could be safely destroyed.[17] These became standard equipment on American warships as early as January 1918, and it is unclear why their installation was neglected by the Portsmouth Navy Yard. Otterless, USS *San Diego* departed Portsmouth at 0915 on July 18, bound for her home port of New York City. Once there, she would resume escort duties but unfortunately would instead be sailing on a course for destruction.

At 0500 on July 19, Capt. Harley Hannibal Christy, the commander of *San Diego*, rounded the eastern tip of Long Island, adjusted his course, and ordered the ship to begin zigzagging at a speed of 15 knots; visibility on this hazy morning was noted as being up to 6 miles.[18] As the morning sun burned off the haze, *San Diego* paralleled the southern edge of Long Island in calm seas, with "small objects easily visible."[19]

Christy was an extremely qualified captain. He had begun his career with the Navy in 1887, serving as an ensign during the Spanish-American War and earning promotions that would lead to a total of nine commands (including *San Diego*) during his forty-seven-year career. Realizing that U-boats were expected in the area, Christy placed his ship in a state of battle readiness, with seventeen lookouts on watch, gun crews in position, fire control parties on standby, and the closing of all watertight doors (not to be opened unless given permission by an executive officer) on all unused "compartments or storerooms below the waterline."[20] If a U-boat was to be encountered in the area, Capt. Christy wanted to be prepared.

Five minutes after 1100 at 40°30' N, 73°W (about 12 mi. / 19 km south of Fire Island, New York), an explosion shook the port side of *San Diego*, throwing a column of water into the air and resulting in the instantaneous deaths of two sailors in the engine room. According to Christy, who was located in the wheelhouse, 8 feet above the forward bridge, this detonation was felt and heard to be "dull" and "seemed to lift the stern of the ship appreciably, but not violently."[21] This caused an immediate list to port of 10°, and, not knowing whether the ship was hit by a torpedo or a mine, the submarine defense alarm was sounded and gun crews were ordered to fire at any object resembling a periscope or submarine. These gun crews would later recount that they believed a submarine was in the area and was disguising its periscope as a floating barrel on the water's surface.[22]

Christy then ordered his ship to turn toward the shoals off the Long Island coastline at full speed, intending to engage his enemy and try to salvage the vessel. Unfortunately, the explosion damaged the linkage on the engine room telegraph, and when the order was given to proceed to full ahead, the annunciator in the engine room indicated full stop and then full astern. Ultimately, this would be the command the engine crew believed to be true.

Despite all of the precautions taken with the watertight doors when USS *San Diego* set sail, the explosion had jammed door #142 in an open position, resulting in Lt. J. P. Milton opening up other compartments on the starboard side of the cruiser in an attempt to correct the list.[23] While this initially stabilized the ship, as water continued to gush in (eventually reaching the 6-inch gun ports) the lean once again increased. During this period, realizing that the ship had an uncontrollable list and that no headway was being made toward the shoals, Capt. Christy gave the order to abandon ship. While the crew did their best to launch the lifeboats with the cruiser coming ever closer to capsizing, the gun crews continued to fire at anything looking remotely suspicious until their guns themselves became flooded and ceased to be operational. Nearly 1,000 of the 1,257 officers and men on board were forced to jump into the water and swim to launches.

When *San Diego* finally reached an angle of 35° to port, Capt. Christy, according to naval tradition, became the last man to depart the vessel—first jumping down from the bridge to the superstructure deck, next sliding down the armor belt to the bilge keel, and then to the docking keel, whereupon, being only 8 feet from the water, he jumped in and joined the rest of his crew in the New York / New Jersey bight.[24] *San Diego* would fully capsize just five minutes later and sink. The entire event, from initial explosion to sinking, lasted just over twenty minutes and resulted in the loss of six lives. At the time, there was still uncertainty as to whether a torpedo or mine had caused the explosion.

Unfortunately, the initial blast had rendered the ship's radio useless, so no SOS signals were able to be sent as the vessel proceeded to sink. In response to being unable to call for help, once Christy safely made it to a lifeboat, he ordered one of his lieutenants (C. J. Bright) to take his dory and row to Long Island to report the sinking and bring back aid—a process that would take over four hours. Simultaneously, a naval airman on patrol had heard *San Diego*'s gunfire, headed to the location, and witnessed the stricken sailors in the water, struggling to get to the lifeboats. The *New York Times* would later report the recollection of a survivor who claimed that the seaplane landed near the lifeboats, stopped to ask them some questions, and then took off again to issue the SOS.[25] This unidentified pilot then flew to the closest observation post and gave his report, which was then forwarded to the Fire Island wireless station and radioed to every vessel and naval station from Boston to Norfolk.[26]

This broadcast would trigger a flurry of activity, with the 3rd Naval District, the Coast Guard stations at Fire Island and Oak Island, and even the naval training station at Sayville dispatching all available surface craft to aid in the rescue.[27] In a somewhat embarrassing turn of events, the 1st Yale Unit (reserve naval aviators from Yale University, based in Huntington, Long Island) took to the skies to hunt the German raider and believed they had spotted it near the location of the sinking, lurking 100 ft. below water. As they proceeded to carpet the area with bombs, debris came to the surface in the form of paper materials and photographs, identifying the submerged object as USS *San Diego* herself.[28] There would be no confirmed sighting of *U-156* for another two days.

Ultimately, the sailors would be rescued by the steamships SS *Malden*, SS *Bussan*, and *E. P. Jones*, with the Coast Guard taking the men from the water and ferrying them to the awaiting steamers. Once the survivors of *San Diego* were taken aboard the troop transport USS *Maui* (ID-1514), their new temporary quarters, the investigation into her sinking began.

As early as 2330 on July 19, RAdm. Albert Gleaves telephoned Washington that he had been in contact with Capt. Christy, who was unable to assert with confidence as to whether or not a torpedo or mine struck the cruiser, telling Gleaves that he wished to "consult his officers and men to base a decision on."[29] While Christy would come to the conclusion that he was torpedoed the next day, the preliminary report sent to the Department of the Navy would be inconclusive, oddly discounting both the torpedo and mine theories, noting,

Captain of the *San Diego* reports after preliminary investigation of officers and men that he is inclined to the belief that the ship was sunk by torpedo. There are no conclusive factors, however, on which to base a definite opinion at present, in view of the following circumstances:

(1) No torpedo wake was seen
(2) No convincing evidence that periscope was seen
(3) No submarine appeared in spite of the fact that three unarmed rescue ships were in the vicinity for about two hours
(4) Weather fine; smooth sea
(5) Ship was struck about Frame 92 on port side abaft point of greatest beam, which discourages mine theory[30]

Had this report been made at the end of the day, it would have noted that minesweepers from the 3rd Naval District had recovered and destroyed three Teka mines, with two more being located on August 5.[31]

This crucial evidence would exonerate Capt. Christy in the subsequent naval court of inquiry regarding the sinking, resulting instead in commendations for the captain and his crew and further concluding that *San Diego* met her fate by the contact horns of a German mine. Had the Navy been able to read the war diary of *U-151*, they may have arrived at the conclusion even sooner—realizing that the length of time it took to prepare the mines for launching and to subsequently rearm the U-cruiser with torpedoes would not have supported the timetable of events.

Despite the fact that USS *San Diego* accounted for about 3 percent of the total American cruiser force in World War I (including auxiliary cruisers such as the recently lost *Schurz*) and over 10 percent of the active armored cruisers, Secretary Daniels was quick to downplay her loss and accentuate the positives of the convoy and transport service. Speaking in Norfolk, Virginia, on July 20, he claimed that

> the presence of German submarines on this side of the Atlantic is more or less of a menace of course, but they will not avail in stopping our transports going overseas with soldiers and more soldiers, as fast as we can send them. . . . I still consider it marvelous that we have succeeded in getting more than a million troops over the seas without the loss of a life or a ship.[32]

Of course, he was referring only to outbound vessels, later noting with regret that about two hundred men had been lost on return voyages thus far.[33] These statistics, although impressive, would ring hollow for U-boat victims of *U-151* and *U-156*, and one must wonder if the citizens of Orleans, Massachusetts, were reading his statement in the morning's newspaper on the twenty-first, when they too would come face to face with the North American U-boat scourge.

On the morning of July 21, the seaside community of Orleans, Massachusetts (on the center of the hooked landmass that forms Cape Cod), would fall victim to the first naval bombardment on the United States from a foreign power since the War of 1812. The action would start shortly after 1000, when *U-156*, having failed to sever the transatlantic telegraph cable from Orleans to France, headed closer to shore to resume the war on maritime commerce. She was first observed by the small seiner *Rose*, surfacing in the morning fog—whereupon the *Rose*'s captain, Marsi Schuill, promptly abandoned his fishing trip and sped toward shore, hoping that the fog would be his salvation. Perhaps the *Rose* was simply too small of a target or too far away, since the U-cruiser fired only about five shells at her before summarily ignoring her and continuing toward Cape Cod on the surface.

Shortly before 1030, Kapitänleutnant Richard Feldt found his eventual prey about 3 miles east-northeast of Orleans Coast Guard Station 40 (the approximate location being 41°46.5' N, 69°53' W) in the form of a tugboat (the *Perth Amboy*) with four barges in tow (the *Lansford* and barge numbers 403, 740, and 766), all owned by the Lehigh Valley Railroad Company. These were interesting targets, since only one of the four barges actually contained cargo (granite), and it can possibly be surmised that Feldt chose to sink them not for what they were currently transporting, but what they could potentially ship in the future. The book *When the U-boats Came to America* theorizes that the German commander may have actually mistaken them for something more lucrative, such as two colliers that had passed by Orleans earlier that day and had eluded him in the haze.

Unlike his predecessor von Nostitz, who preferred stopping unarmed vessels, allowing their crews to take to boats, and then sinking them with explosive charges, Feldt chose another tactic. His first engagement on the American East Coast would begin with *U-156* emerging from the cover of fog and firing upon the small American vessels with her twin 15 cm deck guns—without any warning whatsoever.

Both Charles Ainsleigh, the captain of the *Lansford*, and a deckhand on the *Perth Amboy* reported that they observed three streaks in the water heading for the tugboat, which they interpreted to be torpedoes, just prior to receiving shellfire from the U-boat. This is unlikely for a number of reasons. The first and most obvious is that since *U-156* was equipped with only two forward torpedo tubes, three torpedoes would be impossible to fire in quick succession. Another rationale for this account being dubious is that torpedoes were so precious to the U-boats that they were reserved for use while submerged (usually against an armed merchant or warship) or for the purpose of dispatching a large vessel quickly, when the use of deck guns would have been too dangerous or would have taken too long. They would not be wasted on undefended tugs and barges of negligible tonnage.

If one discounts the torpedo theory, then *U-156* must have initiated her attack on the *Perth Amboy* with explosive shells, knocking the helmsman unconscious and severing the hand of a sleeping crew member. The tug's captain, J. P. Tapley, was also roused from his nap by the firing and, after proceeding to the deck, braced himself to meet his fate. Fortunately, it appeared to him that the German gun crews were very poor shots, with many of the shells missing his boat. He recalled,

> I never saw a more glaring example of rotten marksmanship. Shots went wild repeatedly and but few that were fired scored hits.[34]

This sentiment was echoed by other bargemen and local townspeople, who witnessed shells missing by miles and heading toward land. These "wild" shots, however, may not immediately be discounted as misses. In fact, the local citizens may have been completely incredulous to the possibility of what was really occurring.

Prior to *U-156*'s current cruise to the United States under Feldt, she and her crew had spent months in the waters off North Africa and the Iberian Peninsula under the command of Kapitänleutnant Konrad Gansser. During this period, specifically on December 12, 1917, both *U-156* and *U-157* (commanded by Kapitänleutnant Max Valentiner) shelled the town of Funchal in Madeira for a little over a half hour, damaging the town's church and resulting in twenty civilian casualties (including three dead).[35] Indeed, this was actually the second time Valentiner shelled the town—his first attack occurring just over a year earlier when he commanded SM *U-38*.

In what could be considered a punitive attack against Portugal for declaring war against Germany in March of that year (1916), the German commander fired his guns at the port village for nearly two hours immediately following his sinkings of the berthed French gunboat *Surprise* and the depot ship *Kanguru*.[36] These, of course, paled in comparison to the Kaiserliche Marine's surface fleet's raids on Yarmouth, Scarborough, Hartlepool, and Whitby in 1914, of which a U-boat was utilized only for reconnaissance. Nonetheless, U-boat bombardments remained powerful psychological tools against the civilian populace, who were made to feel that their own forces were powerless to defend them.

Given the history of Germans bombarding the coastline at targets of questionable military significance, one could infer that Feldt's objective may have been to give a compelling fright to the local townspeople by bringing the war to their doorsteps, while simultaneously avoiding creating any unnecessary casualties. This was actually how Lt. Elijah Williams at the Chatham Naval Air Station interpreted the attack, claiming that *U-156* "would have destroyed Chatham or Orleans not because of any possible military value, but for the decided moral effect that such destruction would have had."[37] After all, numerous shells were confirmed to hit the shoreline, with others falling within the village of Orleans itself. One witness, Mrs. Weston Taylor, claimed that while she was working in her kitchen, a shell whizzed by just feet from her roof and landed about 100 yards away.[38] There could be only the slimmest possibility that this was a stray projectile aimed at one of the offshore barges, since her home was located a mile inland and over 4 miles from *U-156*'s location.

The author Henry James, observing the bombardment from nearby Provincetown (on the northern tip of Cape Cod), also interpreted the shelling of land-based targets as being both effective and intentional. He wrote,

> On the deck of the low gray hull of the *U-156* were two groups of men, manning the fore and after guns. The gunners' aim was almost perfect. Shell after shell ripped into the planking sending a shower of splinters and water skyward. One shell ricocheted shoreward burying itself in the sand. Another whistled overhead, and everybody drew his head into his shoulders turtle fashion. No one sought shelter. We were too engrossed in the whole incredible spectacle to think of personal safety.[39]

One of the surfmen from Coast Guard Station 40, witnessing from a closer vantage point, Nauset Beach, also noted that the Germans' aim was "damned good,"[40] with his captain debating whether to row into the maelstrom to rescue the distressed sailors and bargemen, or to wait until the situation had calmed down.

Indeed, the Kaiserliche Marine is often praised by historians for excelling at gunnery (Jutland being one such example), and the 15 cm cannons on the U-cruisers were noted for their accuracy. So many disparate shots at the assemblage of vessels from a range of about 300 meters is difficult to write off as ineptitude. Unfortunately, with the loss of *U-156*'s *Kriegstagebuch*, the truth has been lost to the depths of the sea.

Returning to the engagement on the water, once the *Perth Amboy* caught fire, the gun crews of *U-156* began focusing their aim on the barges in tow, giving the tugboat's captain and his fifteen deckhands a chance to board their lifeboat, raise a white flag, and head toward shore. The raider's next target was the *Lansford*, whose crew consisted of the barge's captain, his wife, their two sons, and the family dog.

The *Perth Amboy* seen towing barges similar to those destroyed off Cape Cod. *Author's collection*

Instead of immediately abandoning their barge (and subsequently their home) when *U-156* began her attack on the *Perth Amboy*, the family was dumbstruck and remained on deck—watching the spectacle up to the point the U-boat's deck guns began firing in their direction. After five to six shots struck the barge, upending the deck planks, blowing off hatches, and wounding Capt. Ainsleigh, the family quickly gathered what they could and abandoned ship. The captain's sons, Charles Jr. and Jack, retrieved a pump-action Winchester Model 1890 in .22-caliber and an American flag, respectively, with the former taking futile shots at the German submarine and the latter tying his flag to their departing lifeboat as they headed for Nauset Beach. The crews and families on the other barges did not wait for their turn to be sunk by *U-156* and also abandoned their vessels at this point.

About a half hour after *U-156* began her attack off Cape Cod, American defenses arrived in the form of a Curtiss HS-1L piloted by Ens. Eric Lingard (along with copilot Ens. Edward Shields and an observer, Chief Special Mechanic Edward Howard) from the nearby Chatham Naval Air Station. Ens. Shields would later recall that *U-156* was unlike any submarine he expected to see, instead resembling a small cruiser or destroyer.[41] Still, their seaplane was equipped with a single Mk. IV bomb, whose payload of 120 pounds of TNT would be more than adequate in critically damaging the U-boat, as long as it exploded within 100 yds. (91.44 m) of the target—but it wouldn't.

Despite *U-156* being dead center in the seaplane's bombsight when the bomb was finally released (initially the bomb release stuck, and Chief Mechanic Howard leapt out of the plane, grabbed a strut, and then reached down and released the bomb with his fingers), the Mk. IV bomb failed to explode, resulting in an anticlimactic splash a few feet from the U-boat. At this point, the German gun crews began firing antiaircraft, shrapnel-loaded projectiles at the seaplane, which remained close to the submarine, continuing to observe it.

As the disheartened seaplane crew continued to circle the U-boat, continuously keeping it in sight, another naval seaplane appeared on the horizon at 1120. This new arrival was a Curtiss R-9 (number 991), being flown by the Chatham Naval Air Station's commander, Capt. Philip Eaton, who had returned to base after completing his fruitless search for the missing naval blimp about twenty minutes earlier. His R-9 was similarly armed with just a single Mark IV bomb, which, after being dropped within 100 feet of the U-boat, also failed to explode. The captain would later state in a letter:

> Had the bomb functioned, the submarine would have been literally smashed. I circled about and tried to stay over the spot where the U-boat was, but it was too hazy and smoky. At this point of the coast the water is 95 fathoms deep by chart. The submarine submerged far down, turned, and escaped. Ensign Lingard was by this time far off to warn ships in the vicinity.[42]

U-156 would, in fact, submerge after the second bomb was dropped, but not for very long.

Approximately five minutes after escaping the watchful eye of Capt. Eaton (who had then thrown his toolkit at the Germans out of frustration), Feldt would resurface a few miles southwest and fire one parting shot (a miss) at the watchtower of Coast Guard Station 40 before once again going below the surface and departing the area. As *U-156* proceeded outbound, another R-9 from the Chatham Station arrived off Orleans and, believing that he spotted a periscope, would make another attempt at sinking the raider. Amazingly, his bomb also failed to detonate, as did another one of Ens. Lingard's, who made a second sortie that afternoon and dropped his payload on an oil slick observed on the water's surface.

The Naval Ordnance Bureau would later investigate why the Mk. IV bombs appeared to be duds, since the problem wasn't unique to the Chatham Naval Air Station, and would conclude that there was nothing technically deficient, stating,

> [The] Mark IV bomb is an efficient bomb when properly cared for and properly operated, but that its mechanism is too complicated for the average personnel in whose charge it is placed.[43]

Despite this, the bureau would call for a complete redesign of the bomb, making one question if the cause of failure was truly due to being too advanced of a device. Indeed, on September 30, the Office of Naval Intelligence sent a cablegram to Admiral Sims requesting a report on the percentage of British aerial bombs that were dropped on submarines that also failed to explode—specifically inquiring why they malfunctioned. It defeatedly concluded, "Our bombs do not appear effective."[44] Asking the British for help may have been misguided, however. As historian Dwight Messimer noted in his book *Find and Destroy*, the US Navy was unable to design a viable aerial depth charge for domestic defense for the duration of the war, since they relied on British-made fuses, "which did not always work or caused the bomb to explode prematurely."[45]

Certainly, a reliable bomb would have dramatically changed the outcome of the day, which stood at a tugboat and four barges sunk or damaged, amounting to just under 2,900 tons and $190,000 in costs, the shockingly low casualty count of three wounded (considering there were forty-one people on the water, including three women and five children), and the bombardment of Orleans for nearly an hour and half. The onus, however, can't be placed entirely on the Naval Ordnance Bureau or the aviators from Chatham. It must be remembered that the naval base at Provincetown, located just under 25 miles from the attack (where the Chatham pilots had been playing baseball against the minesweeper team), had been remarkably quiet during the encounter.

Aside from a brief mention in the war diary of the 1st Naval District, wherein the crew of the *Rose* describes seeing a naval patrol boat heading in the direction of the U-boat (after the *Rose* had already escaped the combat area), very little is mentioned in official records about the fleet of Section Patrol (SP) boats based in Provincetown. Local author Henry J. James once again can fill in some of the details:

> Back at the naval base at Provincetown the fleet of fifty-one submarine chasers spent the first precious hour arranging themselves in battle formation, an extended crescent formation. The flotilla steamed at full speed out of the harbor to meet the enemy. Off Peaked Hill Bar Buoy the officers received bewildering orders from their commander. The chasers were ordered to circle the buoy and return to their base.
>
> "Without a shot?" every man asked his shipmate.

The fleet commander had apparently resolved to be cautious. He realized that once he had rounded the bluffs at Highland Light the flotilla would be exposed to enemy fire.

The public has never been able to understand the commander's decision. His boats were armed. Surely their guns could have struck telling blows at the enemy's craft before being silenced. If indeed, several of the chasers had been put out of commission, there were still enough of them to run in close to the U-boat, and either sink of capture it.[46]

To elaborate on the specifics of his anecdote, the vessels he describes as submarine chasers were not the 110-foot boats specifically designed for the purpose but were instead the Section Patrol boats, which were converted yachts of various types. This being said, they were armed similarly to the SC-class chasers, with all having deck guns and machine guns and many receiving the stern-mounted "Y-gun" for the launching of depth charges. James goes on to claim that residents of Cape Cod ridiculed the crews of these vessels by referring to the "SP" that preceded the identification number as standing for "slacker patrol," and indeed a better chance to engage a U-boat never presented itself to this fleet for the rest of the war. *U-156*, having benefited from an extraordinary amount of luck, was now heading northward, to attack the New England fishing fleets.

USS *Malay* (SP-735) was present during the attack in Provincetown. While her forward deck gun is somewhat obscured, the stern-mounted Y-gun for throwing depth charges is clearly visible. *NH 45282, courtesy of the Naval History & Heritage Command*

The first fishing boat to meet the German marauder was the *Robert and Richard*, a 140-ton schooner that had just completed a two-week trip and was loaded with 30,000 pounds of halibut and 7,000 pounds of assorted fish.[47] She was stopped on the evening of July 22, after a warning shot was fired across her bow at 42°42' N, 68°23' W, about 114 mi. / 184 km southeast of Portland, Maine. Her captain, Robert Wharton, had actually observed *U-156* approach his ship in the distance and, like so many other American victims of the U-cruisers, believed it was a friendly patrol craft. His account of the incident is interesting not only for what actually occurred, but that his tone in describing it evolved the further time elapsed from the sinking.

His initial version of events, which was also the story he gave to naval intelligence officers, was that upon being fired upon, he and his crew boarded the ships dories, with his boat being ordered alongside the U-boat to pick up the German boarding party. Once the German prize crew (consisting of Oberleutnant Knöckel and two sailors) boarded the rowboat, they were taken back to the *Robert and Richard*, where Knöckel spoke to the captain as he took the ship's papers and an American flag. As the captain and the *Oberleutnant* conversed, Knöckel's crew prepared their single explosive charge. According to Capt. Wharton's testimony,

> I asked him what he was going to do with us, and he said he was not going to do anything, and when we got ashore, he wanted us to tell the authorities that we do not do anything to those on the vessels we sink. He said, "You think too much of what Wilson tells you." They acted as though they had plenty of time. They only brought one bomb aboard and carried this in a canvas bag. This they swung underneath the ship by the use of the sounding lead. They started on the stern end of the ship and pulled it up to about midships.[48]

He would go on to claim that when Knöckel took the ship's flag, he spoke about how it would be his second American flag, since he had another at his summer home in Maine (an assertion that has yet to be substantiated) and that another sailor remarked that he had operated a coastal towboat off New England in the prewar years. Indeed, naval authorities concluded that the German crew must have had excellent maps or very intimate knowledge of the local coastline, given how close they approached the shoals off Cape Cod the previous day.

After preparing the vessel for sinking, the German prize crew boarded a spare dinghy and rowed back to the submarine, while the ship's five lifeboats headed westward to the Maine coast, hearing the German bomb explode when they were about a mile on their way. Although the lifeboats were scantily supplied and became separated over the course of the night, all would be rescued without any casualties.

Days after being rescued and giving his account of the sinking to American naval intelligence officers, Capt. Wharton would give another, more detailed version to newspapers, with perhaps just a tinge of propaganda included. The *New York Tribune* article, which reported Wharton's story, even suggested it may have been somewhat exaggerated, given the time it took the sea captain to recall such detailed remarks. The article would go on to say this:

> While the U-boat officer was searching the cabin of the schooner, he picked up a photograph of Captain Wharton's young sons, Robert and Richard, for whom the boat was named. Commenting on the sturdy appearance of the boys, he added: "We got a big ship a few nights ago and turned the crew adrift. Among them was a boy six years old. It was pretty rough that night, and I doubt if they got ashore . . ."
>
> According to Captain Wharton, the submarine officer was very anxious to have him report on the "nice treatment" accorded him and his crew. "As they left us seventy miles at sea in an open boat with scanty supplies, I call it wanton cruelty."[49]

While everyone would agree that being stranded on the ocean so far from land is far from being treated humanely (though the alternative would be far worse), the statement about the captain's sons is so emotive and divorced from reality that it had probably been added for the purpose of stirring up American resentment toward the Germans.

Another interview, this time with the *Boston Daily Globe*, was even more detailed, claiming that Kapitänleutnant Richard Feldt spoke to Capt. Wharton in perfect English (in actuality, he could speak only broken English, which is why Oberleutnant Knöckel wrote out the receipts for sunk ships and acted as the prize crew's interrogator) and now substituted the ambiguous term "big ship" he alluded to in the *New York Tribune* with the very specific "*Perth Amboy* and the four barges sunk off Provincetown." In fact, it seemed that the more Wharton learned about the previous days' events, the more elaborate his narrative became. He would also claim that Feldt told him, "I have been sent here to annihilate the American fishing fleet and I am going to do it."[50] With this statement, Wharton was actually speaking some truth and giving the authorities valuable insight to the German objectives; unfortunately it would be mostly ignored.

Certainly, the Germans, who were themselves starving at home due to the British blockade, understood the effectiveness of disrupting the food supply of the civilian population. Given that meat and other major foodstuffs were given military priority in the United States by the summer of 1918, an interruption of the seafood supply, if serious enough, would be sure to have an effect on American morale. In fact, this objective echoes bullet points mentioned by von Nostitz in his postmission report with *U-151*. Strangely, given the character of the vessels sunk by *U-151* and *U-156* and Wharton's statement about Feldt's objectives, the US Navy persisted with their obsession about troopships.

Following the sinking of the *Robert and Richard*, RAdm. Spencer Wood (commandant of the 1st Naval District) issued a statement warning against any celebratory demonstrations made for troop transports departing ports, worrying that spies would relay their locations to awaiting U-boats. While this was a valid concern, what he said next was appallingly off-base given the clarity of twenty-first-century hindsight. He stated,

> It is well known by all that an enemy submarine is lurking in the waters adjacent to this coast, that the sinking of coal barges and fishing vessels is merely incidental to the real mission. To sink our transports, to mercilessly train machine gun fire on our men who may be struggling to save themselves from drowning, is the real purpose for which this submarine was sent 3,000 miles from her base.[51]

With language like that, it is no surprise that the passengers aboard the *Carolina* feared approaching *U-151* in their lifeboat when the Germans' intention was actually to save a stranded crew member or why future U-boat victims would be hesitant to accept the Germans' hospitality when it was offered.

In the nearly week and half following the sinking of the *Robert and Richard*, the German raiders were finding neither coal barges, fishing boats, nor troop transports to attack. This inactivity may have been intentional, with *U-156* avoiding contacts in order to lay down another minefield in secrecy, a supposition to be elaborated on later in this chapter. During this lull in action, Room 40 had advised Adm. Sims that although the Gulf of Maine was the primary area *U-156* would be patrolling, the U-boat would relocate to Delaware Bay if foggy weather was encountered off New England.[52] This notion was reinforced on the twenty-sixth, when Sims cabled Washington, advising that the Germans may be considering a bombardment of the "harbor works, cranes, etc.," at Wilmington.[53]

What neither the US Navy nor the British Admiralty was aware of at the time was that the U-boat heading for the American mid-Atlantic was SM *U-140*—a true U-Kreuzer that had departed Kiel on July 2 and was about to leave her own trail of destruction. Indeed, while the Navy received reports alluding to the southerly presence of *U-156* on the twenty-seventh (first by the *Florence Olson* off Barnegat Light, New Jersey, and later that evening by USS *Colhoun* (DD-85), which claimed she was being attacked in Delaware Bay), *U-140*'s war diary entry that day confirmed that Feldt never left New England. His actual position was noted as being 200 nautical miles ahead of *U-140*—placing her about 157 mi. / 252 km off Nova Scotia.[54] Since no U-boats were operating off the Jersey shore or in Delaware Bay on the twenty-seventh, one could only wonder what the sailors aboard *Colhoun* believed was attacking them.

U-156 would instead genuinely reveal herself in northern waters on August 2, 1918—firing two warning shots to stop a Canadian schooner at the entrance to the Bay of Fundy, halfway between the coasts of Nova Scotia and Maine (specifically at 44°17' N, 67° W). The schooner in question was the *Dornfontein*, 766 tons, equipped with an auxiliary motor and transporting lumber from St. John, New Brunswick, to the Port of Natal (now Durban) in South Africa.

In a departure from the brusque manner the Germans had treated the captain and crew of the *Robert and Richard*, Oberleutnant Knöckel and his prize crew ordered the Canadian sailors over to *U-156* while his team went to work looting and destroying the schooner. As the Canadian captain, Charles E. Dagwell, was kept on the deck of the U-boat for questioning, his crew of nine was put in a holding area beyond the U-boat's engine room, where they were offered a meal of bully beef and rice. They were assured by the German sailors that "they could eat the food without the fear of poison as the U-boat was not 'after them.'"[55] During this temporary imprisonment, the Canadians were also indulged with various sea tales from their captors, some of which were partial truths, while others were blatant lies.

Some of what could be considered legitimate statements were that they were responsible for sinking USS *San Diego*, that they had been sitting idly off the coast of Maine waiting for shipping to appear before heading toward the Bay of Fundy, and that there "were two larger submarines and one of the same size operating on the American coast."[56] This last claim was particularly revealing since, like von Nostitz, Feldt was aware that both *U-140* and *U-117* were destined (and had actually arrived) on the American coast and that he assumed *U-151* was still present somewhere in the vicinity.

During the nearly five hours the Canadians were aboard *U-156*, the German prize crew had been plundering the *Dornfontein* of every item of the crew's clothing and about six months' worth of provisions. Once the transfer of goods was completed, the Canadians were ordered off the U-boat and instructed to row their lifeboats toward the shore. At this point, instead of sinking the schooner with *Sprengpatronen*, the Germans set fires in the schooner's hold and departed the area, heading eastward toward the Nova Scotian coastline. Incredibly, the schooner would not sink, and much of her cargo would survive the blaze, being sold off after what was left of the vessel was towed to Eastport, Maine—the *Dornfontein* herself was declared a total loss.

Following the resurfacing of *U-156*, and the realization that *U-140* was now heading toward the United States, the Department of the Navy issued a war warning to the 1st through 8th Naval Districts, advising that U-boats "may be encountered in Western Atlantic between latitudes of Halifax and Cape Hatteras."[57] Despite the fact that the Americans were now fully aware that Feldt remained in the area, the proceeding days would essentially be a turkey shoot for the German sailors.

The hunt began at 1100 on August 3, when *U-156* encountered the 120-ton fishing schooner *Muriel* on the surface, about 45 miles west by north of Seal Island, Nova Scotia (at approximately 43°29' N, 66°53.5' W). Two warning shots stopped the American fishermen, who were then commanded to their lifeboats once the U-boat pulled up alongside their ship. After taking some provisions, the American flag, and the ship's papers, the German prize crew dispatched the *Muriel* by means of a single bomb. This same sequence repeated itself when *U-156* engaged the schooners *Sydney B. Atwood* (100 GRT) at 1300, the *Annie Perry* (116 GRT) at 1430, and the *Rob Roy* (112 GRT) at 1800—all sinking within the same area near the Nova Scotian coastline. The crews of all these ships were assured by the German sailors that no harm would come to them personally, but their vessels must be sunk. The men aboard the *Annie Perry*'s single dory were even given brandy and cigarettes for their troubles.

It would be more of the same on the fourth, with the sinking of the Canadian fishing schooner *Nelson A.* (72 GRT), as well as on the morning of the fifth—with *U-156* sinking the trawler *Agnes B. Holland* (100 GRT) at 0900 and damaging the schooner *Gladys M. Hollett* (203 GRT) an hour later (the *Gladys* would remain afloat and later be towed back to port and salvaged on August 9).

Interestingly, the fishermen from the latter two ships would echo the sentiment that the Germans must have been intimately familiar with the area, having been able to navigate the treacherous waters so effectively. The war diary of the 1st Naval District noted,

> The rumor that one of the officers of the submarine was well acquainted in the United States recurred continually.... Two men from different schooners that were sunk claim to have recognized a former acquaintance, who has changed little except that he has grown a beard since they last saw him.

Shipping men are satisfied that one of the officers of the submarine had an exact knowledge, as he operated the most dangerous waters in safety. The suspected man is said to know these waters, from Woods Hole, Mass., to Nova Scotia[,] as well as anyone who has ever sailed them.[58]

Regarding such opinions, Richard Feldt's continuous military service and mediocre command of English make it unlikely that he could have been another Paul König–type commander, well versed in English and selected specifically for the job due to his knowledge of local waters. Instead, these testimonies actually give some credence to Oberleutnant zur See Paul Knöckel's comment about residing in the US during his prewar summers.

Apparently satisfied with his work with the fishing vessels that morning, Feldt departed the La Have banks and proceeded in a northeasterly direction. At 1400, and now about 50 mi. / 80 km off Liverpool (43°48' N, 63°40' W), Nova Scotia, he would spot a much more lucrative target—the Canadian tanker *Luz Blanca*, 4,868 gross tons and en route to Tampico, Mexico, to take on a cargo of crude oil. In what was either a mere coincidence or a string of extremely bad luck, the Canadian tanker may have inadvertently been struck by *U-156* two separate times that day.

At 0640 that morning, with no U-boat warning being broadcast in the area, the *Luz Blanca* departed Halifax and, just five hours into her journey, experienced an explosion that rocked the ship and dented the plates of her hull. Finding the ship to still be seaworthy, her captain, J. Thomas, turned the tanker around and carefully headed back toward port to have the damage repaired. Unfortunately, he would unwittingly be sailing into the path of *U-156*, which would be spotted on the surface about two hours later.

The cause of this initial explosion is the source of considerable speculation to this day, though all historians attribute it to *U-156* in some shape or form. Some sources (namely, Clark's *When the U-boats Came to America*) theorize that *U-156* had already been stalking the *Luz Blanca* off Halifax that morning—resulting in the initial firing of a torpedo at 1140. Finding the torpedo to be ineffective, *U-156* would surface at 1400 to finish the job with her deck guns. Other sources attribute the detonation to an underwater mine, since no torpedo wake was observed, and there could be little justification for the Germans waiting over two hours after firing a torpedo to resume the attack. While neither theory can be confirmed without Feldt's war diary, the latter seems more probable and would help explain not only *U-156*'s relative inactivity in the time period between July 22 and August 2, but also the lack of mines recovered off Fire Island following the sinking of USS *San Diego*.

By the time Allied minesweeping had been discontinued off the North American coast in February 1919, only eight of the fourteen mines carried by *U-156* had been accounted for in the vicinity of the Fire Island lightship. While some of these mines could have broken off from their anchoring chains and drifted away, never to be discovered, this was (and is) one of the busiest maritime shipping lanes in the northeastern United States—to say nothing about being the departure point for most of the American troopships. It is extremely implausible that only about half of *U-156*'s complement of Teka mines would be definitively uncovered in such a well-patrolled area (from both on the sea and in the air), had they all been distributed within the Ambrose Channel. The question that then begs to be asked is, Where did the additional six mines go?

Less congested, but of equal military importance to the channels leading into the New York City harbor, were the waters off eastern Nova Scotia—specifically around Halifax. This port was the primary embarkation point for Canadian troopships and convoys and, by 1918, would also become an essential stopover for American vessels awaiting their escorts. Despite being such an essential link in the Allied supply chain, the British Admiralty (much like American Naval Command) considered the main battle with the U-boats to be on the European side of the Atlantic, and thus refused to sacrifice any of their modern destroyers for Canadian coastal defense.

As a result, and again mirroring American protocol, guarding of domestic waterways was entrusted to reservists on converted yachts, armed fishing trawlers, and a limited number of sub chasers. This lack of any modern antisubmarine patrol craft in any appreciable numbers left the Nova Scotia coastline nearly indefensible to a U-cruiser with the capability of laying a minefield without ever coming to the surface. Feldt could have easily launched his six remaining Teka mines in the waters off Halifax and subsequently departed the area—with Canadian coastal patrols none the wiser.

Correspondingly, by the war's end, three German mines would, in fact, be discovered in the vicinity of Halifax, with one being located and destroyed near the port itself on September 18, another drifting into St. Margaret's Bay (about 50 miles from where the *Luz Blanca* would be sunk) on October 10, and the last one beaching itself at Sable Island (about 180 mi. / 290 km east of the *Luz Blanca* sinking) on October 21, 1918.[59] If it can be assumed that the *Luz Blanca* did in fact contact a Teka mine on August 5, it would be the fourth confirmed mine in that operational area and would lead to a much more plausible twelve of *U-156*'s fourteen mines being accounted for.

The eleven-day gap in reported activity from *U-156* between July 22 and August 2 also reinforces this theory. It would have allowed Feldt adequate time to travel to eastern Nova Scotia, sow his remaining complement of mines, and then return to the Bay of Fundy to begin sinking the small

American fishing ships. When Feldt's crew told the sailors from the *Dornfontein* that they had been sitting idly off Maine awaiting ships to arrive, they probably weren't lying. There would have been at least a few days following their second minelaying mission to rest or search for more targets (or both). All these suppositions, combined with the knowledge that *U-156* was the only German submarine to operate off Nova Scotia for an extended period of time, greatly increase the prospect that it was a Teka mine, not a torpedo, that detonated alongside the tanker.

Regardless of what theory the reader chooses to accept to explain that morning's incident, at 1400 that afternoon, the *Luz Blanca* was definitely engaged by *U-156*'s deck guns—which opened fire on the tanker from a distance of 4–5 miles. Although the Canadians had been armed with a 12-pound, 3-inch/50-caliber, QF (quick firing) cannon mounted on the ship's stern, that morning's blast had tilted the cannon's mount downward—resulting in a significant reduction in its firing arc. The Germans appeared to notice this handicap and took advantage of it, positioning themselves just out of the tanker's reach, but well within the range of their 15 cm / 6-inch guns.

In just under an hour and a half, *U-156* had fired thirty high-explosive shells, resulting in the destruction of the tanker's propeller, the death of two of the *Luz Blanca*'s crew members, and the ship being completely set alight before it ultimately sunk below the surface. Although initial newspaper reports claimed that the German gun crews fired on the tanker's lifeboats,[60] the US Navy noted that these reports were "not borne out by the statements of the crew."[61] Interestingly, while a sub chaser would rescue two of the *Luz Blanca*'s boats (the third would reach shore on its own), no antisubmarine craft would proceed to the area where the tanker sunk in order to hunt the U-boat—at least not immediately.

The Royal Canadian Navy's dockyard in Halifax had, in fact, been aware of the *Luz Blanca*'s plight, both during the initial explosion and subsequent gunfight, but had difficulty in assembling enough patrol boats to proceed to the area and seek out the enemy U-boat. Once the group was able to depart Halifax, the time it took to reach the location of the *Luz Blanca* meant that she had already sunk, and the hunt squadron could only pick up the survivors. To add insult to injury, a torpedo boat from the US 1st Naval District, USS *Tingey* (TB-34), had actually been the closest Allied warship to *U-156* while the firefight was in progress, but was not notified of her presence until 1630—long after Feldt and his crew retired for the day. Once again, *U-156* appeared to be impervious to Allied patrols.

Completely unthreatened, over the next two days *U-156* would proceed in a southerly direction away from Nova Scotia and, on August 7 and 8, would happen upon two vessels claiming to be sailing on charity missions.

Despite their identical alibis, the proof they would provide the Germans would elicit two completely different reactions from Kapitänleutnant Feldt. While Chancellor Theobald von Bethmann-Hollweg had scoffed at the consequences of a "scrap of paper" back in 1914, in 1918 the same derision would be directed at the Kaiserliche Marine from a lowly Swedish steamship captain. This would be Feldt's first encounter with Belgian relief ships.

An example of a well-marked Belgian relief vessel, in this case the Danish *SS Ribe*. *Author's collection*

In 1914, the Commission for Relief in Belgium (CRB) had been formed in the United States as a response to German requisitions of already limited Belgian civilian food stocks during their occupation of the country. The CRB would charter ships for the purpose of transporting sustenance and clothing past the British blockade and German U-boat patrols, and into the hands of the American diplomatic mission for eventual distribution to the Belgian citizenry. The ships in service of the CRB were clearly marked as being for Belgian relief and were guaranteed safe passage both by the British and the Germans, with one crucial caveat. Germany would insist that any ships sailing for this purpose must carry a permit issued by the German government to ensure that their actual intention wasn't to resupply the Allies. This permit was on board the *Elizabeth von Belgie* when she was stopped by *U-156* on August 7, at 42°15' N, 64°17' W. As such, she was allowed to proceed on her way. The *SS Sydland*, on the other hand, lacked this paperwork when she was halted at 1430 the very next day.

This 3,031-ton steamer owned by Svenska Amerika Linien was on her way from Bergen, Norway, to Hampton Roads in ballast when two warning shots from *U-156* stopped her at 41°30' N, 65°22' W (about 135 mi. / 217 km south of Nova Scotia). Receiving the signal to approach the U-boat with the ship's papers, Capt. Alexander Larson and three members of his crew boarded a dory and rowed over to *U-156*'s deck, where Oberleutnant Knöckel and his prize crew awaited them.

After producing the ship's papers, Capt. Larson explained that while his ship had previously been involved with trade between Norway and the United States, it had now been chartered by the Allied governments and was proceeding to Hampton Roads to begin a Belgian relief mission. This prompted the German prize crew to return to the *Sydland* with the Swedes for an inspection and for the captain to produce his German-issued permit. Once it had been established that no such certificate existed on the ship and no other proof of the Belgian relief mission could be ascertained, the vexed *Oberleutnant* returned to *U-156* to confer with Feldt. At 1610, Knöckel returned with the unfortunate news—the crew must abandon ship since the *Sydland* would be sunk. This infuriated Larson, who then demanded a written explanation for the sinking. He was provided with the following receipt (written on the *Sydland*'s stationery):

I certify that the steamer *Sydland* was stopped by a German submarine on 8 August 1918. Due to the nature of the chartering party and the complete absence of any German certification that the ship is destined for the service of the Commission of Belgian Relief, the ship is captured because the suspicion of hostile intentions is considered proven.

Knöckel
Oblt. z. S [62]

An American naval intelligence aide would note that once the Swedes took to their boats, Larson was given a course for land but remarked that the German crew was "very insolent." At 2000, their ship had been sunk by three explosive charges. Proof of their Belgian relief mission has subsequently never been established.

While *U-156* once again departed the area and avoided contact for another three days (with *U-140* simultaneously making her presence known farther south), the US Navy was realigning its priorities toward American coastal defense. In a cablegram to VAdm. Sims, CNO Benson began to pull the reins on the number of sub chasers being sent abroad, stating,

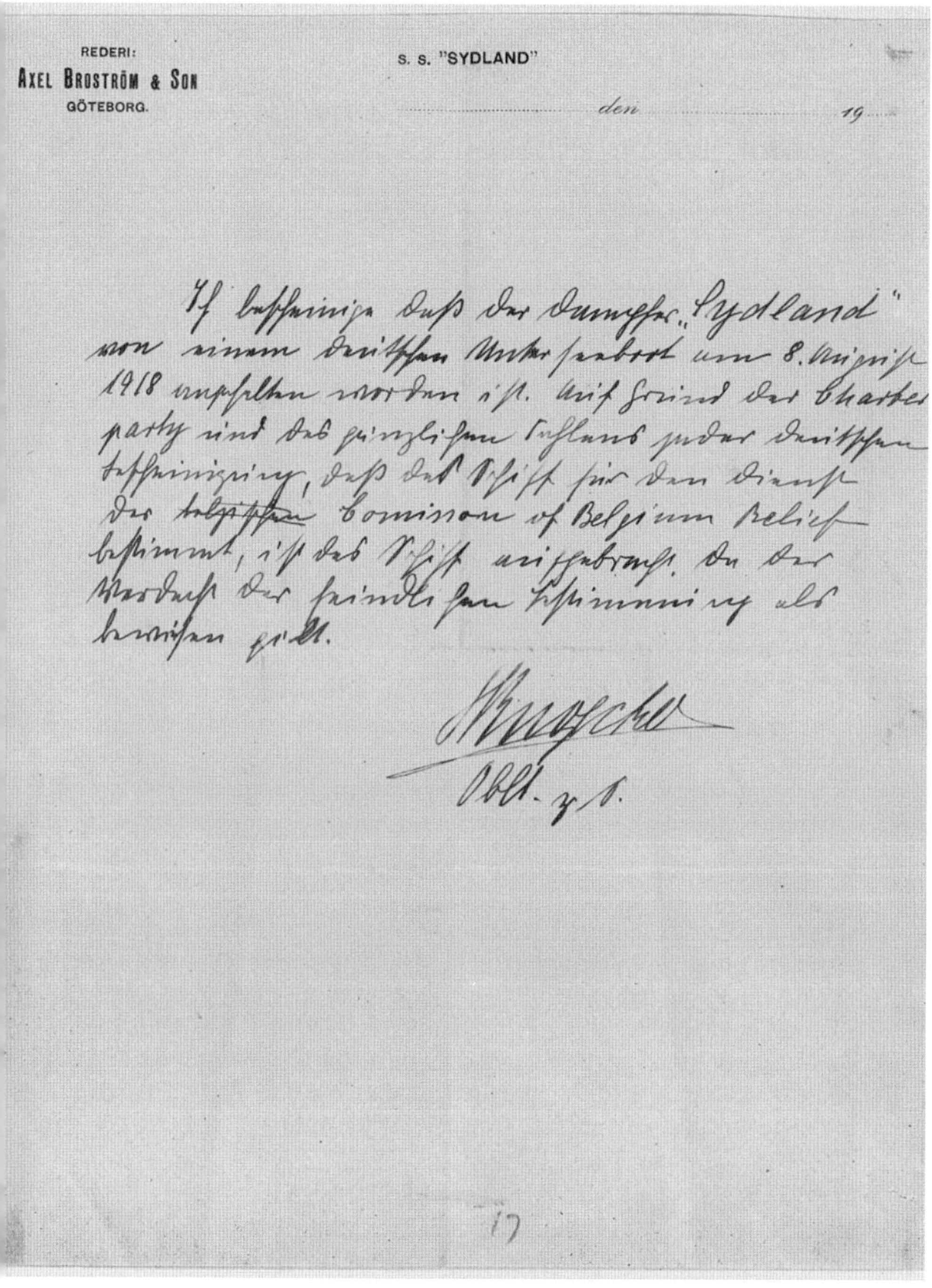

REDERI:
AXEL BROSTRÖM & SON
GÖTEBORG.

S. S. "SYDLAND"

den .... 19....

Ich bescheinige daß der Dampfer „Sydland" von einem deutschen Unterseeboot am 8. August 1918 angehalten worden ist. Auf Grund der Charter party und des gänzlichen Fehlens jeder deutschen Bescheinigung, daß das Schiff für den Dienst der ~~belgischen~~ Comission of Belgium Relief bestimmt, ist das Schiff aufgebracht. Da der Verdacht der feindlichen Bestimmung als bewiesen gilt.

[illegible signature]
Oblt. z. S.

17

The actual receipt given to Capt. Larson of the SS *Sydland*. *NH 115444, courtesy of the Naval History & Heritage Command*

Present conditions render it inadvisable to send any submarine chasers abroad in excess of the 144 already allotted before next spring. It is planned to allocate 36 Eagle Boats to Stations abroad at that time if they can be used there to advantage. Of the 144 submarine chasers previously allotted 41 [will] remain in home waters. Will be sent abroad as soon as the submarine chasers assigned Naval Districts can be properly equipped and organized for hunting out areas adjacent to our coast.[63]

Due to the fact that *U-156* was seemingly operating with impunity, Benson once again placed emphasis on sub chasers going on the offensive. Toward this purpose, he instructed Adm. Mayo, commander in chief of the Atlantic Fleet, and all naval district commanders to redistribute their chasers yet again, forming hunting groups that would be led by destroyers:

[The] Department has planned to organize a hunting group of submarine chasers to operate temporarily from Base Three [Hampton Roads, Virginia] composed following chasers: 11, 209, 270 from Naval District Base New London; 22, 23, 121, 232, 234, 245 from the Fleet; and three chasers from the Fifth Naval District as COMNAVDIS FIVE ["Commander of Naval District 5," Rear Admiral Augustus F. Fechteler] considers best fitted for the duty. Prepare these chasers for duty planned and direct them when in all respects ready for sea proceed Base Three and report COMNAVDIS FIVE not later than 20 August ready for duty. Department will assign destroyers to take command this detachment prior 20 August.[64]

The choice of the 5th Naval District as the base for these hunting squadrons appears to have been a compromise. It avoided placing these additional resources in the service of the 1st and 6th Naval Districts, where *U-156* and *U-140* (which will be discussed in detail in the next chapter) had been operating, respectively, and instead favored a point between each. As with most concessions, the objective of being able to fulfill the needs of both districts was effective at satisfying neither, and the Navy was forced back into a reactionary position when *U-156* resumed the offensive.

On the morning of August 11, about 83 mi. / 134 km east-southeast of where USS *Harrisburg* had sighted *U-156* on July 17, the German raiders had intercepted an eighteen-ship convoy bound for Bordeaux from New York City with a single armored cruiser as an escort. Observing the vessels at periscope depth, Feldt was able to single out one particular ship as the most vulnerable prey. This was the British cargo steamer SS *Penistone*

(4,139 GRT), which had been lagging behind the convoy since 0400. Despite her best efforts, and the urging of the cruiser escort to keep up at 0800, she could make no better than 8 knots and was not zigzagging.

After watching the steamer fall farther and farther behind the protection of the convoy, Feldt took his chance with a single torpedo shot at 1000. Although this torpedo found its target, striking the engine room on the starboard side, killing the ship's third engineer, and injuring a further four crew members in the process, it would not completely sink her. Even more amazingly, when the *Penistone*'s radio operator, W. Holloway, sent out an SOS signal prior to the order to abandon ship, the cruiser escort ignored it and sailed on with the remainder of the convoy. The failure of the escort to respond to the SOS, along with the local naval district, particular piqued the crew of the *Penistone*, who found sympathetic ears when they ironically reached the shores of Provincetown, Massachusetts, on August 16.

Here, the criticism of the US Navy remained fervent, and the local citizens provided an echo chamber for the sailors' sentiment that they had been left to fend for themselves. Historian Henry James noted that

> so caustic became the criticism against the Navy Department that a resolution was introduced in Congress on August 12 requesting the Secretary of the Navy to furnish the House with facts concerning recent attacks of German submarines on American shipping off the Cape Cod coast of Massachusetts. This resolution, H.R. 422, was submitted to the Naval Affairs Committee. No report was ever made.[65]

Returning to August 11, the absence of any American warship presence allowed for *U-156* to safely surface near the *Penistone*'s lifeboats, detain her captain, David Evans, and send him and the German boarding party back onto the ship. Here they would allow the captain time to retrieve the ship's papers, some clothing and shoes, and his bedding, since he was about to become a prisoner aboard the submarine. Rather than use the U-boat's deck guns to finish off the vessel, which would likely attract unwanted attention, the boarding party opted for their efficient *Sprengpatronen*. In an odd breach of etiquette, Oberleutnant Knöckel assigned this job to radio operator Holloway, who would later state that he personally dropped two timed bombs in two separate hatches, resulting in the eventual sinking of the *Penistone*[66] ten minutes later. Once the bombs had been placed, the four British lifeboats began their long journey toward Nantucket, while Evans and *U-156* proceeded northeast in the direction of the convoy—briefly engaging the American steamer *Herman Winter* on the surface before it was able to slip away.

The imprisonment of Capt. Evans was rather peculiar, since nothing was gained from the English captain in his brief stay aboard the U-boat. He consumed the submarine's supplies and took up valuable space, and he himself noted that the Germans "did not discuss the sinking of ships and they never asked me for any information whatsoever."[67] While no attempt was made at gathering intelligence from the merchant captain, the U-boat sailors were more than willing to volunteer their own intel, mainly about themselves and their mission. Additionally, Evans was given freedom of movement throughout the U-boat, which he used wisely, taking mental notes about the details of the submarine's armament, technical specifications, and general modus operandi—all of which were shared with naval intelligence officers after being rescued.

The only times he was restricted in what he could observe was when *U-156* sighted a vessel and sounded the alarm. When this occurred, he was ordered below to the quarters he shared with enlisted men, and could discern what was occurring only through the sounds he heard. Such was the case when *U-156* attacked the British tanker *Lackawanna* on August 16. Here, Evans recounted hearing about forty shots being fired from the U-boat's deck guns (noting that the vibrations were so significant that the guns were probably too large for the submarine to be used effectively).

What he couldn't know from his position was that Feldt initiated the attack submerged, firing two torpedoes, both of which failed to strike the tanker (one missed and the other was "diverted" by gunfire) before surfacing and initiating an artillery battle with his deck guns. Of the forty-odd shots Evans heard, twenty or so were actually return fire from the *Lackawanna*, which was able to escape through the use of a smoke screen and her greater surface speed. According to the *Lackawanna*'s crew, their shots were falling so close to the U-cruiser that she was forced to submerge and retreat. A somewhat better turn of events for the Germans would occur the next day, which would become Evans's last day aboard the U-boat.

On the morning of August 17, *U-156* surfaced near the Norwegian steamer *San Jose* (1,586 GRT), stopping the vessel with a warning shot across her bow. The *San Jose* had been en route from Bergen to New York to pick up a cargo of foodstuffs allegedly for the Norwegian Food Commission, and, like the *Sydland* that preceded her, her fate would be decided by paperwork. Upon being boarded by the German *Prisenkommando* crew, Capt. Hans Thorbjørnsen of the *San Jose* argued that his vessel was neutral and was likewise chartered to the government of Norway, not the Allied belligerents. When pressed to produce proof of this charter, he came up empty-handed. Once again, the German officers conferred and decided that the steamer would be sunk. The receipt provided to the

Norwegian captain explained that the last charter the steamer sailed under was from the British firm Furness-Wither & Company, and that "a communication of July 31, 1918, could not contradict this assumption."[68]

As the German boarding party prepared to sink the *San Jose* with explosives, Capt. Evans of the *Penistone* was given the option to remain with the U-boat or join the Norwegians in their lifeboats. His choice to take the boats was a wise one, not only because of *U-156*'s eventual fate, but because his rescue came quickly in the form of the British steamer *Derbyshire*, which, having heard the *San Jose* explode, arrived on the scene less than a day later. Upon releasing the British captain and sinking the Norwegian steamer, Feldt took inventory of *U-156*'s provisions and made the decision to set a course back toward Germany. This, however, should not imply that his hunting days were over. Traveling in a northeasterly direction, *U-156* once again returned to the Canadian fishing banks, whereupon the Germans would adopt yet another unconventional, and effective, tactic.

After sailing for three days and nearly 225 mi. / 362 km, Feldt returned to the Grand Banks off the eastern coast of Nova Scotia on August 20—he was in search of an auxiliary raider. Remarkably, the first vessel the Germans came across was an ideal candidate, the 239-ton Canadian steam trawler *Triumph*. This fishing boat had just arrived in the area and thus had enough coal for ten days of travel when she was stopped by a warning shot from *U-156* at 1210 that afternoon. The Canadian fishermen, not waiting to see what the Germans would do next, immediately took to their lifeboats, with "no belongings except a box of biscuits for each boat."[69] Luckily for them, Feldt and his crew would be very providing hosts.

Once *U-156* came within 50 yards of the lifeboats, the Canadians were ordered alongside the U-boat, where their captain, G. Myhre, was first taken aboard the submarine with the ship's papers. Shortly thereafter, the rest of the trawler's crew would follow suit while the German prize crew utilized their dinghy for the purpose of preparing the *Triumph* for action as a surface raider. According to the interned crew, the Germans transported the following armament to the trawler:

(a) Either one or two 3-pounders, not assembled, including base and all

(b) Approximately 25 high-explosive bombs, about 1 to 1½ feet in height and 6 to 9 inches in breadth, with time attachment visible

(c) A large sea bag, the contents of which were not visible or possible to learn, it being about twice the size of the Navy regulation sea bag

(d) Two large boxes of 3-pound shells[70]

It is difficult to establish what the 3-pounders being mentioned were without *U-156*'s war diary, especially since no other U-cruiser logs specify what arms were being supplied for the prize crew's use. A Uruguayan officer from the steamer *Infanta Isabel de Borbon*, stopped by SM *U-157* off the Canary Islands in March 1918, was given a tour of that converted U-Kreuzer and described the same guns to a British intelligence officer (Agent S.7) as being "two inoperable quick[-]firing guns in the interior of the submarine,"[71] but he neglected to elaborate any further.

In all likelihood they were probably the early 3.7 cm Maxim machine cannons that were removed from warship service in 1917 but were still being utilized for naval landing parties. These were certainly easier to assemble and transport via a rowboat, and they took up significantly less space on a cramped U-boat than the 5.2 cm SK L/55 and 5 cm SK L/40 guns that armed German torpedo and gun boats. In the case of the *Triumph*, two of these machine cannons were transferred from *U-156* and mounted on the trawler's bow and stern.

While this was occurring, the fishermen inside the U-Kreuzer were treated with brandy and cigars, had their pictures taken, and were regaled with sea tales from the German raiders. Just as they did with the crew of the *Dornfontein*, the Germans spoke to them in half-truths. Kapitänleutnant Feldt allegedly reiterated his intention to obliterate the New English / Canadian fishing fleets to Capt. Myhre, while Oberleutnant Knöckel imparted that *U-156* had sunk a large tanker off Sandy Hook, New Jersey, and taken the captain prisoner for a week (he was referring to the *Penistone*, which sank quite far from New Jersey). Interestingly, Knöckel also asserted that *U-156* was responsible for sinking USS *San Diego* with a torpedo, but offered this yarn only after the *Triumph*'s steward, Alton Geyer, confirmed to the *Oberleutnant* that the cruiser actually had sunk.[72]

This fraternization would be short lived, however, since the German sailors were able to complete their conversion of the trawler in less twenty minutes—with *U-156*'s entire prize crew complement of one officer and twenty men boarding the *Triumph* at 1235. By 1315, the Canadian fishermen were ordered back to the lifeboats and pointed toward the nearest landfall, while *U-156* (partially submerged so that only her conning tower remained above the waterline) and the freshly outfitted "SMS" *Triumph*, with the German war ensign flying proudly from her mast, proceeded north. They wasted no time in seeking out potential targets.

At 1445 that afternoon, the *Triumph* spotted the American schooner *A. Piatt Andrew*, 141 GRT and from Gloucester, in the approximate area of 44°21' N, 61°28' W. She would be the first of many victims that evening. With *U-156* remaining barely visible at a distance of 4–5 miles south of the armed trawler, the *Triumph*'s German crew fired warning shots ahead of the American fishermen and ordered them to come alongside the raider with their ship's papers. The *Andrew*'s captain, Wallace Bruce, was shocked to find Germans manning the trawler, particularly when three of them boarded his dory and rowed back to the schooner armed with bombs and revolvers. He would not be the only captain in a state of disbelief.

While the small German boarding party was aboard the *A. Piatt Andrew*, preparing the vessel with *Sprengpatronen*, Capt. Joseph P. Mequita, of the schooner *Francis J. O'Hara Jr.* (117 GRT), sailed toward the vessels to see how the fishing was going. Having been familiar with both the *Triumph* and the *A. Piatt Andrew* from earlier fishing trips, he was flabbergasted when he was ordered via megaphone to heave to. According to the captain,

> I thought the captain was joking with us[,] and kept on toward the *A. Piatt Andrew*, and the first thing we knew four shots were fired across our bow from rifles. We brought our vessel up in the wind and the beam trawler came up alongside of us and I then saw that she was manned by a German crew and had a German flag at her masthead. The captain ordered me to come aboard of his vessel with our papers, so I took one of my dories and with one of the crew rowed alongside of him and the German gave me quite a calling down for not stopping my vessel sooner and said that if we expected him to do the right thing, we would have to do the right thing by him.[73]

Another three members of the German crew boarded his dory and returned to the *O'Hara* to sink her. By 1530, both schooners had been destroyed. It wasn't until the fishermen had abandoned ship that they observed *U-156* in the distance, heading in the direction of another fishing vessel.

Not content with letting his prize crew get all the action, Kapitänleutnant Feldt directed his U-boat toward the Canadian fishing schooner *Uda A. Saunders*. This 124-ton sitting duck had been lying at anchor while the majority of her crew were out on the ship's dories, fishing nearly a mile away. Only the captain and three of his crew members were actually aboard the vessel when Feldt sent his own three-man boarding party over to sink the ship. The four Canadians were given ten minutes to gather what they could, while the Germans placed their bombs and returned to *U-156* with the ship's papers and flag. Unfortunately, the men already aboard the dories were not afforded any opportunity to return to the ship to get supplies or personal effects by the time the *Uda A. Saunders* exploded. Nearly 77 tons of fish and seven casks of oil were lost with the vessel.

Later that night, the *Triumph* would repeat the events of the afternoon by sinking the Canadian schooners *Lucille Schnare* (121 GRT) and *Pasadena* (119 GRT) at 2200 and midnight, respectively. The same would occur the next morning, when the French schooner *Notre Dame de la Garde* (145 GRT and loaded with 320 tons of fish) and the American schooner *Sylvania* (136 GRT) encountered the *Triumph* at 45°32' N, 58°57' W—now beyond the Nova Scotian coastline and approaching the Cabot Strait, the entrance of the Gulf of St. Lawrence. In the case of the latter ship, Capt. Jeff Thomas realized that the *Triumph* had been compromised, and attempted to escape; however, for once in their entire patrol the Germans possessed a craft with a superior surface speed and quickly caught up with the schooner and sank her.

As the *Triumph* and *U-156* were now departing the fishing banks of Nova Scotia, Feldt, deviating from Korvettenkapitän von Müller's tactics, understood that taking along a steamer that would need additional coal supplies on their homeward journey was more trouble than it was worth. After dispatching the *Sylvania* that twenty-first day of August, the prize crew was recalled, and the *Triumph* too was scuttled. Once again whole, the crew of *U-156* then continued onward toward the archipelago of St. Pierre and Miquelon, on the southwestern extreme of Newfoundland.

Not surprisingly, as the survivors of the fishing schooners began reaching shore and reporting their experiences, there was significant outrage both in the United States and Canada from populaces that felt as though nothing was being done to protect their commercial seamen. Senator Porter James McCumber of North Dakota captured this sentiment when he spoke on the floor of the Senate. According to the Congressional Record,

> He wanted to ask a member of the Naval Affairs Committee how it was possible for a little trawler, whose speed could not exceed twelve knots per hour, to destroy "fleet after fleet of our fishing smacks. . . . Where are those swift U-boat chasers we have been hearing about?" and "Where is there an end?"[74]

Apparently unbeknown to Senator McCumber, the Navy Department had, in fact, established patrols in the New England fishing grounds beginning on the seventeenth, but only at a level that wouldn't diminish the fleets available for convoy escorts. Following the sinking of the *San Jose*, on August 19 the 1st Naval District dispatched a hunter squadron with the specific aim of locating and sinking *U-156*. Unfortunately, since this search encompassed an area stretching from Nova Scotia to Nantucket, it was comparable to finding a needle in a haystack.

This was followed by another hunt in conjunction with Canadian coastal patrol vessels, involving all available antisubmarine craft (including destroyers and submarines) in the area of the Grand Banks on August 21, which, due to the *Triumph* being destroyed and *U-156* leaving the fishing banks, also resulted in naught. Feldt, for his part, did little in providing the American and Canadian patrols with any hints as to his current location, since he would remain quiet for nearly four more days.

U-156 would reemerge at 0130 on the morning of the twenty-fifth, approximately 125 mi. / 201 km north-northeast from where the *Notre Dame de la Garde* had sunk. She was still in the vicinity of the Cabot Strait but had now edged even closer to Newfoundland, being about 70 miles west-northwest of St. Pierre Island. Here Feldt and his crew would encounter the unarmed, British, steam-powered whaling ship *Erik*.

Although the *Erik* had been running without lights, the cloudless night and full moon allowed the German watch officers to observe her clearly from a distance of about 2 miles. It was from this range that a particularly concerning piece of equipment was observed through the lenses of their high-powered binoculars—the whaling ship's radio antenna. Apparently, the *Erik*'s ability to call for help troubled Feldt, since he broke protocol for the second time of this patrol and gave the order to open fire on the unarmed whaler without warning. Seven shots were fired in total, with the first destroying the whaler's wireless apparatus, the second her stack, and three of the remaining five shots striking the ship's deck, resulting in five of the *Erik*'s crew members being wounded and all but one of the lifeboats being put out of service. The whaling ship came to a stop immediately.

Once it had been established that the vessel had been silenced and immobilized, *U-156* approached the steamer to inquire if anyone had been killed during the barrage. When the response came back in the negative, an unidentified officer on board the U-boat (assumed to be Feldt or his first officer, Kapitänleutnant Arnold Vorkampff-Laue) "said that he was glad, as he was after ships not lives."[75] The Canadian crew, making multiple trips on their single remaining lifeboat, then transferred themselves into *U-156*'s hull, where the wounded were treated by the U-boat's doctor, Marineoberassistenzarzt Martin Schlemm. The *Erik*'s captain, W. Lane, remained on the U-boat's deck with Kapitänleutnant Feldt and his officers for questioning.

It was during this interrogation that Capt. Lane was informed that he and his men would be staying with the Germans for the immediate future. Realizing that his shells had turned most of the *Erik*'s dories into splinters, Feldt pledged to keep the Canadians on board his U-boat until a vessel with adequate lifeboats could be located. Although U-boat commanders, by nature, had to be somewhat coldhearted, he was not about to abandon a crew of eighteen men on a lifeboat that could fit only four. Since it seemed to be the custom, coffee, brandy, and tobacco were once again offered to *U-156*'s new guests to make their stay more comfortable while Oberleutnant Knöckel's boarding party prepared to finish off their whaling ship.

As Feldt watched his prize crew prepare the *Erik* with explosive charges, he turned to Capt. Lane and asked if he had seen any other fishing ships earlier that night. Whether or not the Canadian captain understood the rationale behind this question is uncertain, but he responded in the affirmative and then gave the vessel's approximate position. *U-156* then proceeded on a southerly course to seek her out.

Just after dawn, salvation for the Canadian whalers came in the form of the schooner *Willie G.*, out of Newfoundland. Rather than fire any warning shots at the sailing ship, Kapitänleutnant Feldt brought his U-boat alongside the vessel so he could make an inquiry as to how many lifeboats were stowed on board. While it had been his intention to ultimately sink the *Willie G.*, he was willing to do so only if there were enough boats on board to accommodate the schooner's crew in addition to his eighteen interned whalers. Unfortunately for the Germans, there wasn't. Disappointed, Feldt then transferred his prisoners to the *Willie G.* and allowed her to remain afloat and go on her way while he continued onward to seek more targets. It would be this course of action that nearly became his undoing.

By 1030, *U-156* happened upon six fishing vessels at 46°33' N, 57°33' W (about 58 mi. / 93 km from St. Pierre and Miquelon). These were the schooners *E. B. Walters* (126 GRT), *C. M. Walters* (107 GRT), *Verna D. Adams* (132 GRT), and *J. J. Flaherty* (162 GRT) and the smaller fishing ships *Clayton W. Walters* (116 GRT), and *Marion Adams* (99 GRT). All had been at anchor, and none made any attempt to escape. Like so many other seamen before them, their crews had mistaken the massive U-Kreuzer to be a Canadian patrol boat.

U-156 focused on the *E. B. Walters* first—instructing her crew to abandon ship. The schooner's captain, Cyrus Walters, approached the U-boat in his dory and, rather pathetically, asked, "You are not going to sink my schooner, are you?"[76] Expectedly, the response from the Germans was that they were, and the German prize crew subsequently boarded Walters's dory to take the ship's papers, canned provisions, and other needed supplies before planting their bombs. The same sequence repeated itself until all six vessels had been scuttled, with the *J. J. Flaherty* being the last to go down. The ships' captains noted that the Germans placed a particular emphasis on looting the foodstuffs, though it didn't seem to occur to them that the Germans were essentially stocking up before they headed back across the Atlantic.

While the oblivious German raiders occupied themselves with their task at hand, a Royal Canadian Navy patrol consisting of a converted yacht (HMCS *Hochelaga*), a converted surveying ship (HMCS *Cartier*), and two armed trawlers (unimaginatively named *Trawler 22* and *Trawler 32*) had meandered into their vicinity. This four-ship hunting squadron (a fifth ship, the HMCS *Stadacona*, had left the party earlier) had actually been searching for *U-156* and the *Triumph* since the twenty-first and now found themselves as the first Canadian patrol to ever come face to face with an enemy U-boat in domestic waters.

The HMCS *Hochelaga. Royal Canadian Navy*

A lookout on the *Hochelaga* had initially spotted the idle fishing schooners (though he wasn't aware they were being boarded) from a distance of 12 miles. Upon this discovery, the converted yacht's commander, Lt. Robert Douglas Legate, then redirected the ship's course toward the vessels in an effort to warn them about *U-156* and her depredations from earlier that week. When the *Hochelaga* got within 4 miles of the ships, one of the schooners suddenly blew up, at which point the yacht's signalman, Harold Gates, claimed he had spotted the U-cruiser lurking nearby. Lt. Legate now found himself in a predicament.

Realizing that his vessel was armed only with a QF 12-pounder (12 cwt)⁷⁷ cannon and was thus significantly outgunned by *U-156*'s twin 15 cm deck guns (to say nothing about the torpedoes),

> Lieutenant Legate made a decision that was to prove lethal to his career in the RCN. Rather than advance to engage the submarine, he turned *Hochelaga* back towards HMCS *Cartier*, commanded by Lieutenant Henry Francis McGuirk, who was the senior officer on patrol. *Cartier*, upon seeing *Hochelaga* alter course, turned to intercept, and read the signals the *Hochelaga* was making [these vessels were not equipped with radios and had to resort to flag signals]. The signal read by *Cartier* was "submarine bearing east." Lieutenant McGuirk immediately ordered all four ships on patrol to alter course towards the last bearing of the submarine and proceed at full speed to engage it. Upon receiving this signal *Hochelaga* again held back from the attack[,] signaling that she thought it best to await reinforcements.⁷⁸

By the time the patrol reached the location that *U-156* had last been sighted, the submarine was gone.

The only chance the Royal Canadian Navy ever had at engaging the enemy in their home waters was completely squandered. For his decision to break off the initial engagement, Lt. Legate would be court-martialed and found guilty of violating section 2 of the Naval Discipline Act, specifically for failing to "use his utmost exertion to bring his ship into action" upon sighting "a ship of the enemy which it may be his duty to engage."⁷⁹ Whether this was the tactically correct decision or not, Legate lost his commission and was dismissed from the RCN, while Feldt and *U-156* once again escaped unscathed.

As *U-156* continued south toward the forty-fourth parallel (where she would resume her easterly course toward home), she encountered one last Canadian schooner—again without any sign of Allied patrols. This was the *Gloaming*, 130 tons out of Nova Scotia, which was sunk in the same fashion as the prior fishing vessels. Her loss would not even merit front-page news in any American or Canadian newspapers. Aside from that relatively minor engagement, *U-156* found little in the way of contacts on her homeward voyage on the American side of the Atlantic, save for a brief, twenty-minute gun battle with USS *West Haven* (ID-2159) about 235 mi. / 379 km south-southeast of St. Johns, Newfoundland. The skirmish ended rather anticlimactically, with *U-156* giving up the fight and turning away. Although Kapitänleutnant Feldt and his crew were able to continue on their way unharmed and untroubled, their situation became considerably more perilous the closer they got to home.

Like von Nostitz who preceded him, Feldt was presented with two different courses to reach home: the shorter route through the narrower and more heavily mined and patrolled English Channel, or the more sparsely defended northern route that he had taken on his outbound voyage. Like most U-boat commanders, he opted for the latter, but this still was not without risk, since the Allies had continuously been sowing more minefields in an effort to create an impregnable seawall between Scotland and Norway.

Dazzle-camouflaged US Navy minelayers sowing mines in the Northern Barrage in the summer of 1918. *NH 41736, courtesy of the Naval History & Heritage Command*

While the British had initiated this process at the outbreak of war, over the years they could keep up neither with the production of mines nor the minelaying itself. This resulted in the minefields being permeable, allowing careful U-boat commanders to travel through them successfully. The Royal Navy also tended to concentrate their mines closer to their own coastline, in a location later designated by the Allies as "Area B." The US Navy, on the other hand, found this to be unacceptable and was determined to plug all the holes in this North Sea barricade.

Shortly after entering the war, a bureau was established to "develop a new design of mine and to arrange for its manufacture at the rate of approximately 1,000 a day, or four and two-tenths times the production that Great Britain had succeeded in reaching"[80]—a figure well within the industrial capability of the US, but also one Britain deemed impossible to achieve. How successful the United States was in accomplishing the unsurmountable can be ascertained by the following data:

In all, 70,263 mines were laid, 56,611 being American mines, laid by the United States Mining Squadron. Area "A" [the middle section of the North Sea between Scotland and Norway], which was originally allotted as the United States portion of the barrage, was completed except for 6,400 mines more, which could have been laid in approximately 10 days. Besides mining Area "A" exclusively, the United States mining squadron had laid 10,440 mines in Area "B," and 5,980 mines in Area "C." [the section closest to the Norwegian coastline] Thus it will be seen that in addition to mining the part of the barrage originally assigned to the United States Government, we had in addition laid more mines in the British Areas "B" and "C" than they themselves had put down.[81]

American mines in storage before being sown in the Northern Barrage. *NHF-136-G.01, courtesy of the Naval History & Heritage Command*

The US Navy had originally intended for the Northern Barrage to have been completed by September 1918, but delays attributed to insufficient Grand Fleet escorts and uncooperative British minelayers resulted in the mining process being unremitting up to the date of the Armistice. This meant that U-boats returning from a patrol they began months prior were now presented with a significantly denser minefield than the one they had traversed at the beginning of their cruises. What may have been a gaping hole before was now teeming with antisubmarine countermeasures.

To improve their chances of breaking through, U-boat commanders remained in contact with one another, trying to establish which routes remained somewhat clear. This had been one of the reasons von Nostitz had repeatedly tried to contact Feldt once it had been determined that *U-156* made it to the open Atlantic. It was also the rationale behind Feldt's orders to send regular updates on his location when radio contact with Nauen was resumed. Unfortunately, this radio traffic led only to additional problems for the German raiders.

Nearly every message broadcast to Nauen or other U-boats in the North Atlantic was being intercepted by the British and deciphered in Room 40. It was due to *U-151*'s incessant wireless updates that von Nostitz encountered at least four British submarines on his homeward voyage—resulting in him having to dodge torpedoes on top of navigating the minefields. When Feldt contacted SM *U-139* on the twentieth, and later *U-161* on the twenty-third, noting his location and seeking information on the Northern Barrage, he was essentially setting himself up for the same type of ambush. Unfortunately for *U-156*, Feldt's attempt to escape from this trap would prove fatal.

On September 25, *U-156* made her final broadcast, radioing her current position and her intended route through the barrage. Upon receipt of this message, the ever-listening Royal Navy consequently dispatched the destroyer HMS *Marksman* and the submarine *L-8* to cut off the U-cruiser at the minefields' periphery, with the latter spotting a "vessel, nature undistinguishable"[82] at 0740 in the area of *U-156*'s last broadcast.

While *L-8* would be unsuccessful in sinking *U-156* through direct combat, losing contact with *U-156* shortly after diving to attack, her actions compelled *U-156* to also submerge as a means of evasion. In doing so, Feldt was forced to negotiate the minefields blindly, a stratagem that ultimately determined the fates of himself and his crew. Contrary to some early American and British sources that claim some crew members from *U-156* arrived in Norway shortly after the encounter with *L-8* and were repatriated after the war, *U-156* would never resurface. Her entire crew would perish that twenty-fifth of September—their names being immortalized on the Möltenort U-boat Memorial outside Kiel in 1930.

In what could be considered poetic justice, it would be the US Navy that would ultimately take credit for sinking the elusive U-Kreuzer, albeit on the other side of the Atlantic. Specifically, the Navy attributed *U-156*'s downfall to American mines located in "Area A," sown sometime during the minelaying excursions of the tenth through twelfth.[83] In an odd twist of fate, the mines responsible for sinking *U-156* may have even been the ones offloaded by USS *Lake Bridge*, which had managed to escape Feldt's 15 cm deck guns back in July. Still, the mine theory is just that—a supposition based on what most likely occurred.

The US Navy actually noted that there was a 66 percent likelihood of passing through the barrage successfully if a U-boat was submerged, specifically between the depths of 50 and 250 feet. If a submarine was traveling on the surface or above 50 feet in depth, the odds of avoiding a mine dropped to 33 percent.[84] With this in mind, Feldt's decision to dive to escape *L-8* was actually the best option to break through the barrage, even if it wasn't made with that intention. While some historians have attempted to posit exactly where *U-156* sank, her wreckage has yet to be discovered, and thus a concrete explanation for her sinking has yet to be determined.

Regardless of the mystery behind *U-156*'s final circumstances, the hard facts surrounding her cruise continued to demonstrate the U-Kreuzer as being an effective instrument against the Allies (irrespective of how many troopships were or were not being sunk). The tally of thirty-eight vessels being sunk or damaged, for a total of 42,415 tons, once again exceeded Sims's 30,000–40,000-ton estimate, and *U-156*'s focus on the New English / Canadian fishing industry resulted in over a month-long disruption of operations.

German minesweepers destroying a British mine and showing its devastating effects. *Author's collection*

Additionally, the deaths caused by *U-156* that made it past the censors (twenty-two in all) were difficult for a civilian populace to swallow—particularly since the Navy had little to show for combating the German submarine threat. In fact, the sinking of USS *San Diego*, the lack of a response from the Provincetown section patrol boats, and the fact that *U-156* was able to operate in the shoals so close to the coastline only bolstered the U-boats' demoralizing effect. To make matters worse, *U-156* was only one of three German submarines operating off the North American coast in the period between late July and August 1918. *U-140* and *U-117* had also arrived shortly after *U-156* and had been busy making their own contributions to the *Handelskrieg* in American waters.

CHAPTER 9
A Tale of Two Cruisers

August 13, 1918, 1700. The tanker *Frederic R. Kellogg* is currently sailing in a northeasterly direction, about 5 miles offshore from Seaside Heights, New Jersey. A vessel of the Pan-American Oil and Transportation Company's fleet, she is en route to Boston with a cargo of 70,000 barrels of crude oil intended for the US government, which had been taken on in Tampico, Mexico, the week prior. Her captain, C. H. White, anticipates reaching his destination early the next day, and his men have already begun to make plans for their respective shore leaves.

Below deck, most of the crew is having supper, but two young Naval Reserve cadets have already eaten and retired to their cabin for the evening—Quartermasters (3rd Class) Chester C. Cubberley and William T. Stillman. This would be the first voyage for the twenty-one-year-old Cubberley, since he had been transferred into the Naval Auxiliary Reserve only in July. His excitement for his new duties is reflected in the tone of the letters he sends home to his mother and to his former school, Rutgers College. Although he left academia in order to enlist back in 1917, he still maintains contact with Earl Reed Silvers of the Rutgers War Service Bureau, who regularly publishes updates on alumni serving in the Great War. The twenty-nine-year-old Stillman, resting on his bunk across from Cubberley, is a bit more world-weary.

Staring at a photo of his wife, Helen, pictured standing in front of their home in Shelton, Connecticut, Stillman calls over to Cubberley: "Say, Chester, why don't you ease up on the writing. We're going to be home in a few days; you can tell all your college buddies about your heroic feats in person." Cubberley, not allowing his train of thought to be interrupted, finishes writing his sentence and retorts, "Well, Bill, inquiring minds want to know what it's like to be in the Merchant Marine, dodging Hun torpedoes and mines on board a ship with a belly full of flammable oil. Maybe someday you'll get a fan club of your own requiring your correspondence. Besides, once we get back, I'll be heading straight back to Long Branch to see my mother."

Their conversation is briefly interrupted by a loud crash in the galley, immediately followed by the squawking of a parrot and what sounds like someone saying, "Don't forget poor Polly."[1] Cubberley and Stillman both share a chuckle. Cubberley remarks, "I guess Polly's dinner just ended up on the floor. I bet old Cookie is kicking himself for teaching that bird so many words." Stillman, nodding his head in agreement, returns to their original conversation. "You know, Chester, we should be sailing by Long Branch in a few hours; maybe we can sneak you onto one of the dories and send you off early; it would sure be a swell surprise for your mother. I don't see them serving much purpose otherwise; it sounds like all of the U-boats are preoccupied off Hatteras and New England."

A look of unease sweeps over Cubberley's face when presented with this prospect, and he appears to be lost in thought. "You all right, buddy?" posits Stillman, who himself is oddly beginning to feel his young shipmate's same sense of dread. Cubberley turns to Stillman and looks him dead in the eyes: "I really wish I could do just that, Bill. I've got a real bad feeling about this last night at sea. We've been hearing war warnings up and down the coast, and what did we see, maybe one patrol boat off North Carolina the whole trip? We're getting close to where *San Diego* went down; who's to say that the same U-boat responsible for the cruiser isn't out there waiting for us right now?"

Stillman, now visibly troubled by the young man's intuition, tries his best to exude confidence and attempts to reassure Cubberley that everything will be fine. "You're just feeling jittery since this was your first trip so far from home. In fact, you're probably overexcited that's it's almost finished. We've been at sea for almost a month now; don't you think if something was going to happen it would've already?" Cubberley thinks this over in his head for a minute, and a slight smile begins to emerge at the corner of his lips. "I guess you're right, Bill. We'll be safely back on land soon enough. It'll sure be nice to swap some of these butterflies in my stomach for some of my mother's delicious home-cooked meals. You're welcome to join me if your wife's cooking isn't on the level." "After a month at sea, the last thing I want to do is head down to Jersey to share a meal with your mom," retorts Stillman. "Me and Helen have some other catching up to do that doesn't involve cooking, if you catch my drift."

This change of tone seems to satisfy the misgivings of both men, and they each return to their own thoughts—it is now 1709. Just a minute later, a torpedo would strike the port side of the tanker, blowing a huge hole in the combined engine and fireroom and quickly flooding the lower decks of the ship. Within minutes, the *Frederic R. Kellogg* would sink in the shallow waters off the Jersey shore, attacked without any warning. Of the forty-two officers and crew on board, seven wouldn't survive, including the two young naval reserve cadets. The U-boat responsible for the attack was SM *U-117*, which, along with SM *U-140 "Kapitänleutnant Weddigen,"*[2] departed Germany shorty after *U-156* on July 11 and July 2, respectively. They were unlike any U-boats that had previously operated off the North American coast that summer.

U-140, commanded by Korvettenkapitän Waldemar Kophamel (a veteran officer who had previously commanded the Pola Flotilla, SM *U-35*, and later SM *U-151* during her North African patrol in 1917), was the first true U-cruiser, being developed from the ground up specifically for long-range, extended-period combat operations (as opposed to being a converted merchant submarine). She was given orders to resume the *Handelskrieg* beginning in area between the Nantucket lightship and New York and then continuing onward as far south as Cape Hatteras. Nineteen torpedoes were stowed on board, and unlike *U-151* and *U-156*, she would not be armed with any Teka mines.

Korvettenkapitän Waldemar Kophamel. *NH 65861, courtesy of the Naval History & Heritage Command*

Mining duties would instead be taken up by *U-117*, under the command of Kapitänleutnant Otto Dröscher—a U-boat commander since 1913 who had the honor of being the first German officer to circumnavigate Britain (with SM *U-20*) in October 1914. She was the first of her class of cruiser-minelayers, whose complement of forty-two 100 cm UC 200 and thirty 50 cm *Torpedo Kaliber* mines was designated for six separate minefields off the coasts of New York City, New Jersey, Delaware, Virginia, and North Carolina. Twenty torpedoes were also on board for the sinking of any targets of opportunity while traveling to and from the intended minefields, though there appeared to be some miscommunication between headquarters and the commander as to which task took priority (minelaying or commerce raiding).

SM *U-117* departing Kiel. *Courtesy of Deutsches U-Boot-Museum*

Some British and American sources, basing their claims on radiograms from Adm. Sims, also claim that one of *U-117*'s tertiary missions was to bombard shipyards, bases, and factories with her 15 cm deck gun. German records, however, do not confirm that coastal attacks were ever part of *U-117*'s orders, a fact Dröscher was quick to point out to his men when such an opportunity would present itself.

It had been intended that both *U-140* and *U-117* would operate off North America in conjunction with *U-151* and *U-156* that summer. Unfortunately for the German U-cruiser command, this wouldn't occur as planned, since late-war shortages both of material and skilled labor resulted in poor-quality U-boat construction, which significantly delayed their readiness.

Korvettenkapitän Kophamel was particularly damning of these issues during the evaluation of his new submarine and the training of his crew in the period between March 28 and July 1, 1918. He noted that the entire U-boat was leaking and that the bilge system had failed as early as April 20. These concerns seemed only to worsen as the weeks went on, with leaks being a recurring problem. On April 26, he returned back to the Germania Shipyard for urgent repairs, noting,

> Boat still leaking. Despite blowing tanks, the boat continues to fall. Bilge and blow-out lines are not in order. Since the boat is so unstable, it is now suggested, in order to finally make improvements, to undertake considerable upgrades. . . . It is impossible for the boat to go to sea in this condition.[3]

Despite spending nearly two weeks at the repair dock, material and workmanship issues continued to manifest, and problems with the U-cruiser persisted.

On May 17, Kophamel noted that even his periscopes had to be replaced, since they were "unusable when they were put into service."[4] The failure of such an essential device for submersible warfare is inexcusable, yet it seemed trivial compared to the ongoing issue with leaks. You can sense the veteran commander's frustration when he made the following reports:

> May 25—The boat is still 230 metric tons stern-heavy; the leaks, especially with diving tank 1, have not been repaired. Trim device doesn't work yet. Trim and regulating tanks flood heavily.
> June 4—Leaks have hardly been reduced; reported issue to the U-cruiser unit.
> June 6—Laid aground at a depth of 27 m for leak testing. Boat still leaks very badly. Oil leaks not yet eliminated. Trim pumps doubtful.

Report made to U-cruiser unit.

June 29—Went out to test to trim and incline. When blowing tanks, the starboard reserve bunker #4 must also be blown due to leaks.[5]

It should be noted that in the days following Kophamel's war diary entry on June 29, *U-140* actually departed Kiel for Warnemünde, whereupon she would begin her mission to the American East Coast on July 2. There would be no time allotted for additional repairs, and the problems that surfaced during *U-140*'s evaluation would follow her into her cruise.

Indeed, in the period between July 2 and 8, while *U-140* was attempting to break through the Northern Barrage and dodge enemy submarines off the northern tip of Scotland, Kophamel had nothing but doubts about the integrity of his submarine. Instead of leaks, stability now became his prime concern. He noted that during surface travel, the submarine often listed about 35° due to water washing over the deck (he figured about 50–70 tons), entering the structure, and draining far too slowly. He could somewhat improve the situation by partially flooding his tanks, but ultimately keeping the U-boat on course was to be a constant struggle. Eventually, Kophamel ordered his crew to cut more drain holes into the upper deck on July 12 (and later on July 18) to help alleviate the drainage issues.

Batteries spilling over due to the extreme banking of the U-boat also became a frequent problem, as did the reliability of his equipment. Operation of *U-140*'s main bilge pump continued to be erratic, and just two days into the cruise, both radio antenna supports had been wrecked due to rough seas (they would be somewhat repaired by the tenth). Kophamel noted that even in good weather, ammunition had to be stored below deck, and that it was impossible for the hatches to be opened for any extended period of time. In bad weather, the submarine was almost unbearable. By the time *U-140* made it to open seas, about 320 mi. / 515 km west of the Outer Hebrides, Kophamel resentfully wrote in his war diary that "the condition [of *U-140*] is embarrassing."[6]

Interestingly, Fregattenkapitän von Koch, chief of the Unterseekreuzer Flotilla, would discount in his report the factor of substandard raw materials or wartime manufacturing shortages playing any role in Kophamel's complaints. Instead, he opted to place the onus on the Germania Shipyard—namely, the management and workers—noting,

> The regrettable delay in the front readiness "U 140" can be traced back to two circumstances: on the one hand to the [U-boat's] insufficient stability, which forced extensive upgrades, and on the other hand to the poor construction in terms of shipbuilding. It was only after a long layover at the shipyard that it was possible to get the pressure hull tight. There should

be no doubt that these deficiencies could have been avoided with more careful construction. It is beyond my judgment whether the shipyard alone or also the [Germania] supervision is responsible for this. After a change occurred in the latter . . . it is to be hoped that the next U-cruisers from the shipyard will not have the same technical defects.[7]

These accusations may have had some basis in truth, since labor strikes, personnel shortages, and supply issues became more frequent in 1918 (particularly at shipyards); however, the problems with quality control were not unique to Germaniawerft.

SM *U-117* fared much the same on her maiden cruise, despite being built at Vulkan Werke in Hamburg. Unlike *U-140*, which identified and attempted to remedy issues before the mission, the most-serious issues concerning poor workmanship and inferior materials with *U-117* surfaced only after her patrol began. Her chief engineer, Oberingenieur Adolf Beckmann, must have had an inkling of what was to come. He would later recall that when Dröscher inspected the crew before the voyage, the commander asked him, "*Alles in Butter?*" (a German phrase literally translating to "Is everything in the butter?," and meaning "All good?"). Beckmann's disheartening reply was "Still partly margarine."[8] Having departed Kiel on July 11, it would take only one day before the first malady struck—leaky fuel tanks that, besides wasting valuable fuel, resulted in a visible trail of oil accompanying the U-boat. This problem would only be compounded by more-serious concerns in the coming weeks.

On July 15, while attempting to evade an unidentified enemy submarine in the North Sea, *U-117* would inadvertently get into an uncontrollable dive—eventually leveling off at a depth of 60 m. It was only after numerous attempts were made to blow the tanks that the U-boat finally came to the surface. Unfortunately, the quickly escaping water had a side effect of further damaging the submarine's external fuel tanks and augmenting the U-boat's fuel loss and accompanying iridescent course marker. While an unmanageable plummeting could be considered the worst-case scenario for a U-boat, the failure to submerge altogether would be a close second. This, inauspiciously, was the next issue that was beginning to manifest itself on *U-117*.

Dröscher noted that as the voyage went on, the clutches on the diesel engines became increasingly unreliable and oftentimes would not disengage themselves during dive attempts. This was a serious dilemma because the electric motors that were required for underwater travel could not be started until the diesels had first been uncoupled from the drivetrain. Every time this issue occurred, the dive had to be aborted—sowing seeds of doubt in the minds of the commander and crew as to the reliability of their submarine in critical combat situations. After numerous attempts at regrinding the friction disks, resulting in no observable improvements, Kapitänleutnant Dröscher was ultimately forced to concede that "there [was] always the uncertainty that, in spite of all care, the clutches [would] not be disengaged in time."[9] Still, *U-117*'s troubles would continue to worsen.

On July 17, the stuffing box on the port diesel engine began to leak, causing the exhaust to emit a plume of thick, white smoke. Later, on July 20, the aft bearing on the starboard-side engine heated up and failed, resulting in it having to be removed for inspection and remachining. This, however, was only the first indication of more-significant problems, and, over the course of the next couple days, both the portside diesel engine and the starboard-side electric motor had to be completely disassembled and overhauled at sea. As if this wasn't enough already, a final insult arrived on July 23, when the freshwater production system broke down.

The freshwater generator had been essential for the U-cruisers, since it allowed them a nearly unlimited supply of drinking, cooking, and cleaning water for the duration of their patrols (or as long as the diesel supply lasted). It functioned by desalinating seawater by piping it into an evaporator heated by the diesel exhausts. Once the seawater was converted to steam, it would lose its salt and mineral content and would then be piped away to be cooled and condensed back to a liquid state and filtered.

When Oberingenieur Beckmann investigated the breakdown, it was found that the system's piping was made from iron, instead of copper or another alloy less susceptible to rusting away, and was already full of holes. A more perfect manifestation of the destitute state of the German war industry in late 1918 would be tough to come by. This incident also served to reinforce just how important the earlier voyage of the *Deutschland* as well as the seizure of the *Vindeggen*'s copper by von Nostitz and *U-151* were.

Kapitänleutnant Dröscher's war diary entry explains the seriousness of the situation:

> Both evaporators are uncertain. On closer examination it turns out that the pipe system is made of unsuitable material (iron). . . . Recovery is not guaranteed. This is a matter of concern. The drinking[-]water supply is currently 3.6 cubic meters. Extreme conservation of water will commence.[10]

To put this into perspective, 3.6 cubic meters of water is just over half of the water supply Hans Rose had on board when he departed for Rhode Island back in 1916, and that was a trip intended to be as short as possible.

Although a makeshift repair was made to the system on the twenty-fifth, Dröscher was also competing with a loss of fuel from several diesel bunkers and was only halfway across the Atlantic. He had an important decision to make—press on or turn back. He, like his colleague commanding *U-140*, decided on the former.

When Fregattenkapitän von Koch commented on the delays in getting *U-140* into service, he also noted that the training of the crew had "been reduced to the lowest possible level, which was only possible because the commander and all the officers had extensive submarine experience."[11] Indeed, both Kophamel and Dröscher were by far the most-seasoned commanders to journey toward North America up to that point. If they were to overcome the technological and mechanical shortfalls of their U-boats and complete their missions, they would have to rely on their own cunning, since both their vessels seemed to be actively working against their success. They would certainly have to work much harder than von Nostitz and Feldt in their endeavors.

The first intimation that Kophamel and Dröscher were en route toward North America arrived on July 14, when USS *Harrisburg* (the same vessel that spotted *U-156* on the seventeenth) sent an "allo" message purporting to have seen *U-140* at 45°33' N, 41° W. At the time, *U-140* was actually in a position 475 mi. / 765 km east of the American troop transport and had already attempted to engage an Allied convoy three days prior. This occurred at noon on the eleventh, when Kophamel spotted eight steamers being escorted by what he described as a British "Bacchante-class cruiser"[12] at 53°56' N, 26° W. After ordering his submarine to periscope depth to initiate a torpedo strike, Kophamel found only more faults with his U-Kreuzer, which ultimately led to the attack being broken off.

First, he noted that *U-140* did not behave like previous U-boats he commanded while traveling at periscope depth. Instead of rolling with the ocean swells, the vessel's contact with each individual wave would cause the U-Kreuzer to come to a stop, allowing the convoy to increase its distance from the pursuer. Even more worrisome, it had been observed that although the crests of the waves traveled over the periscope, their troughs would expose the conning tower, giving away Kophamel's position. Amazingly, the cruiser escort never seemed to notice, and the convoy sped away.

The same sequence of events was repeated on the fifteenth, when *U-140* encountered four unescorted, outbound troopships at 44°38' N, 32°48' W, or still about 400 mi. / 643 km east of *Harrisburg*'s "allo" report. These were USS *Agamemnon* (ID-3004, formerly SS *Kaiser Wilhelm II*), USS *Mount Vernon* (ID-4508, formerly SS *Kronprinzessin Cecilie*), USS *George Washington* (ID-3018, formerly SS *George Washington* of the Norddeutcher Lloyd Line), and the HMS *Tuberose* (or RMS *Mauretania* if going by the Cunard designation). They had a combined displacement of just over 96,000 GRT and were choice targets for a U-boat, if only one were able to engage them.

The *Mauretania* in service with the Royal Navy as the HMS *Tuberose*. New York Tribune

In *U-140*'s case, within a half hour of spotting the convoy they were already out of sight. Korvettenkapitän Kophamel was forced to lament that "because of their high speed, the great distance and the heavy seas, a pursuit could not be considered at all."[13] The German commander would go on to note their size and course when he radioed his location report that evening, but, much to the chagrin of the chief of the U-Kreuzer Flotilla, this message never made it back to Germany due to the poor condition of the U-boat's wireless apparatus. Ultimately, the small convoy would reach France unmolested, and all the vessels would survive the war.

Curiously, American sources unanimously claim that a straggler from the aforementioned convoy, the American tanker *Joseph Cudahy*, reported herself as being shelled by *U-140*'s deck guns on July 18 at 45°33' N, 41° W. Despite traveling at the slow speed of 9 knots (well below *U-140*'s maximum surface speed of 15.8 knots), and her 3-inch stern guns being outranged by the U-Kreuzer's 15 cm cannons, she was miraculously able to escape unscathed and without ever having to return fire.

This event cannot be corroborated with *U-140*'s war diary, except for the fact that Kophamel intercepted the tanker's signal and was himself confused by it. He assumed it to have originated from a lone, separated steamer he encountered, but one he did not attack (in fact, he expressly ruled out use of the deck guns), on July 16 at 45°38' N, 36°10' W. Upon picking up the dubious broadcast on July 19, he recorded,

"Allo" message intercepted in which [our] boat is being reported. It's pretty wrong, but it being another vessel is out of the question. It is assumed that the steamer saw our boat and steered away—otherwise its disappearance could not be explained. The night was so dark and impenetrable that I hadn't believed we could be observed, especially since we only had the steamer in sight for about 2 minutes. Instructions being broadcast from New York warn that all preparations should be made between 35°–45° north latitude.[14]

Interestingly, the war warnings being intercepted by *U-140* could be traced back to the American protected cruiser USS *Galveston* (C-17), which also heard the tanker's curious "allo" message.

Like Kophamel, Capt. Francis L. Chadwick, the commander of *Galveston*, also originally cast doubt on the signal's accuracy—instead believing it to be a trap. For reasons unexplained, he later established the signal as being legitimate, and relayed the warning back to the 3rd Naval District, which would go on to dispatch a submarine hunter squadron consisting of fifteen sub chasers and the destroyer USS *Jouett* (DD-41) the next week. Regrettably, they would never venture any farther than 60 mi. / 96 km from the coastline, leaving *U-140* free to continue her hunt unhindered.

In the time that elapsed between this strange "allo" transmission and the time concrete evidence of *U-140* would actually be established by the Allied navies, Kophamel would stop two additional steamers on the nineteenth and the twenty-fifth. The first was the Danish *Olaf Maersk*, transporting oil and gas for the Swiss government, and the second was the Swedish *Uppland*, carrying phosphate from Florida to Sweden. Both would have to be let go since they were confirmed neutrals. Considering he was commanding one of the newest "super-subs," Kophamel must have been dumbfounded that after making so many contacts, his log's *Liste versenkter Schiffe* was still entirely blank.

Dröscher, too, was not finding any success with attacks in the open Atlantic. Shortly after *U-117* departed Kiel on July 11, he encountered a "correctly badged" Belgian relief ship that he had to let go on the sixteenth, then he made a fruitless deck gun attack on an unidentified steamer about 250 mi. / 402 km northwest of Ireland on the twentieth. In the latter case, the steamer was able to escape due to her superior speed and a combination of overcast skies and the evening darkness.

While that vessel never broadcast an "allo" signal reporting *U-117*'s presence, the British cargo ship *Baron Napier* would do so on the twenty-sixth. In this instance, the U-boat and the steamer fired at each other with their respective deck guns (two 12 cm cannons on the cargo ship, and the 15 cm and 8.8 cm guns on the U-boat) from an extreme distance, with neither registering any hits. Dröscher noted that the *Baron Napier* was loudly broadcasting SOS signals and that he had decided to "break off the battle due to the hopelessness to achieve success."[15] This was mostly due to extreme ocean swells that only continued to worsen. In what was an uncharacteristic lapse on the part of British Intelligence in Room 40, this would be their first indication that *U-117* had already left port. Worryingly for the British and Americans, by this point she was already halfway across the Atlantic, at 44°28' N, 34°8' W.

Even more troubling news arrived on that same day, when actual positive identification of *U-140* was first reported at 38°40' N, 60°50' W—nearly 1,435 mi. / 2,309 km west of *U-117* and just 700 mi. / 1,126 km east of the New York City harbor. Here *U-140* broke off an attack with a distant, unidentified vessel and instead stalked the 13,967-ton, armed, British steamer *Melita* for nearly three hours, beginning at 0930 that day. Despite initially planning on a submerged torpedo attack, Kophamel reacted to the steamer's superior speed, zigzag course, and dazzle camouflage by ordering *U-140* to the surface and initiating an artillery battle at 1245. Although seventeen shots were fired from the twin 15-cm deck guns, none registered any hits and the *Melita* slipped away.

With no time to waste dwelling on the failed pursuit, Kophamel then steered for additional smoke clouds observed to the west. These originated from the 4,147-ton British tanker *British Major*, which would be the second vessel to report *U-140*'s location that day. Finding he had no time to submerge, Kophamel once again opted for an artillery duel with the distant tanker, opening fire at a range of 12,200 meters. In response, the tanker increased her speed from 10 to 15 knots (now nearly matching the surface speed of the U-Kreuzer) and returned fire with her single 4-inch gun. Although she was too distant for her shots to be effective, this strategy seemed to be just enough for her to elude the German raider. Neither vessel was able to gain an advantage on the other during the nearly five-hour battle that ensued, and the encounter ultimately resulted in the *British Major* escaping to safety. A total of 139 of *U-140*'s complement of 1,030 shells would be wasted in the attempt.[16]

Now realizing he had allowed nearly 115,000 tons of shipping (excluding the nine-vessel convoy from the eleventh) to slip through his fingers since the start of his cruise, Kophamel wrote an unusually long entry in his log, explaining his rationale for breaking off the latest attack. He noted, with a tinge of derision, that since you have to stop to shoot, the distance [between the steamer and *U-140*] increases. Firing must be temporarily stopped in order to be able to steam on. The steamer shoots at us from a range up to about 120 hm, with the projectiles' impact landing about 50 m from the boat. Resumed firing again at 110 hm. This distance can be maintained only if we fire from the forward gun. Before the onset of darkness, we once again turn away to bring both guns into use. The distance becomes too great, and firing is stopped. The attack is given up because the difference in speed between the vessels is too small and I can't catch up. . . . I will probably lose the steamer in the dark until the moon has risen and under these circumstances I cannot continue with the attack. In the end, the pursuit will only have resulted in consuming a lot of fuel. It has to be conserved because more than a third of the supply has already been used up and I only reached the upper border of my operational area.[17]

U-140 had indeed just entered her operational zone and, with *U-117* on the way and *U-156* going silent after sinking the *Robert and Richard* four days earlier, the Allied navies were left utterly bemused as to where the Germans would strike next. Correspondingly, anxious commercial traffic resumed the practice of hugging the coastline, just as they had pending the arrival of *U-156* in late June, with similarly disastrous results. Nine lives would be lost from this point in July up to the first week of August due to collisions and sinkings, but none at the hands of a German U-boat.

Kophamel would finally find success on July 27, when *U-140* stopped and sank the Portuguese barque *Porto* (1,079 GRT) at 39°18' N, 60°40' W (about 340 nautical miles off Cape Sable Island, Nova Scotia). The three-masted sailing ship was bound for Oporto, Portugal, from Savannah, Georgia, with a cargo of six hundred bales of cotton and barrel staves, but the German crew seemed to be more interested in the ship's provisions.

Although nothing is mentioned in the German logs other than that the vessel was sunk with explosives and the ship's papers were retained, the *Porto*'s captain, José Tude d'Oliveisa da Velha, disclosed to American naval intelligence that *U-140*'s crew spent five hours confiscating the entirety of the ship's stores, including all the pork and chickens kept on board. This was accomplished by means of planks placed on the barque's deck while the vessel was tied off to the U-boat.[18] While the Germans may have eaten well that evening, the victory was bittersweet, since it appeared that *U-140*'s streak of bad luck was about to resume for the next six days.

Immediately following the sinking of the *Porto*, *U-140* intercepted an "allo" message indicating that *U-156* was about 200 nautical miles ahead of her. Kophamel, recognizing the opportunity for cooperation, would spend the upcoming week attempting to contact her, all the while making failed bids at sinking further vessels. The first of these attempts occurred on July 29, when *U-140* spotted smoke clouds from the 4,753-ton British tanker *Vitruvia* at 39°6' N, 62°39' W. Yet again, *U-140* was too far away to make a worthwhile chase, and the tanker steamed away to the north after observing the German submarine and sending out an "allo" giving her identity and location. Oddly, historian William Bell Clark claimed that it would have been impossible for *U-140* to be in the position given by the *Vitruvia*, and he dismissed the U-boat sighting as an error.[19]

Later that day, with *U-156* now noted as being 60 nautical miles distant from *U-140*, an SOS signal was intercepted from the 12,000-ton British troopship *Osterley*[20] from a location approximately 200 mi. / 320 km southwest. Smelling blood, Kophamel had his radio operator send a signal to the liner via the U-boat's Marconi transmitter (utilizing American escort nomenclature), stating, "O, please course and speed," with the full intention of intercepting her. Following the trend of the cruise so far, it fell on deaf ears. Kophamel recorded that *U-156* was "deliberately not called [about the plan] in order not to reveal the presence of a second submarine."[21]

Success would further elude *U-140* when she encountered the American steamer *Kermanshah* (4,947 GRT) on July 30, about 350 mi. / 562 km from the New Jersey coastline (specifically at 38°27' N, 67°50' W). In this case, Kophamel noted that the steamer was on a strong zigzag course, and, after observing its stern-mounted 4-inch deck gun and forward 2-pounder (being manned US Navy gun crews), opted to submerge and attempt his first torpedo attack of the patrol. In Kophamel's words:

> Dove to initiate the underwater attack. Torpedo tube 5 "launch." Distance about 300 m. Angle 90°. Depth 3 m. The [torpedo] bubbles go well toward the [ship's] stern. No detonation . . . Turned off for bow shot. Torpedo tube 1 "launch." Miss.
>
> Surfaced. There was so much sea that the torpedo went below the target due to the swells, at least that was absolutely certain with the first shot. I shouldn't have let myself be tempted to take the second shot. . . . Further pursuit on the surface had to be refrained from due to too much sea distance needing to be covered. Steamer sends allo signal and gives its name "Kermanshah" (according to estimates 4–5,000 t) and opens fire from a great distance.[22]

The version of the event that was recounted to US Navy intelligence by the *Kermanshah*'s master, Robert H. Smith, was far more dramatic.

According to the American captain, the first torpedo did not travel below the steamer but instead missed the stern of the ship by 10–15 feet—the result of Smith observing its wake and taking evasive action. Likewise, when the second torpedo track was spotted, he turned the steamer onto a parallel course to the projectile, which caused it to miss the starboard bow by approximately 5 feet. Additionally,

> As soon as the second wake was sighted[,] the commander of the armed guard [USN chief gunner's mate M. Coffey] fired one round from the 4-inch gun astern, the shot being directed at the spot the wake started from. The explosion that followed sounded like the bursting of the shell against a hard object, which gave the captain the impression that a hit had been made. . . . As the submarine made no attempt to chase or fire on the ship, the captain believes there is some basis for assuming that the first shot had some effect.[23]

While the belief that the single shell fired from the deck gun critically wounded *U-140* may have been good for American morale, a more offensive posture from the Americans may very well have bested a dejected U-boat ace who was now second-guessing all of his decisions. Although the captain of the *Kermanshah* took the correct course of action at the time, just like the encounter between USS *Von Steuben* and SM *U-151*, a potential opportunity for an American victory had been once again been left unexploited.

To cap off Kophamel's disappointing day, he finally gave up trying to contact *U-156*, since no signals were ever received back from his sister *Kreuzer*, and then he had to dodge two small enemy vessels in the evening hours—one of which was thought to have been an American submarine. For a man who already had sunk forty-eight ships, accounting for 126,879 tons at this point in the war, he must have been completely dejected. He, however, was not suffering alone. Two days later and 1,155 mi. / 1,860 km east, *U-117* was having nearly identical issues with her own torpedo attacks.

On August 1, at 40°30' N, 46°8.8' W (approximately 545 mi. / 878 km southeast of Newfoundland), Kapitänleutnant Dröscher also decided to try his luck attacking an Allied warship. The encounter unfolded as follows:

> Blacked[-]out vessel in sight. Distance 2 nm at 50°. Maneuvered for a nighttime torpedo attack on the surface. When approaching, observed 3 funnels and a long, smooth deck, apparently a small cruiser, course 240°, 11 nm. Shot at a distance of approx. 600 with 15° angle shot, tube 1, depth setting 2 m (G6AV* Torp.). Observed torpedo trajectory in part, then submerged. No detonation. Since a missed shot cannot be explained,

having observed the torpedo run its course, it must be concluded that the torpedo passed underneath the vessel, as it was probably a torpedo boat destroyer. Depth setting was 2 m. There cannot be any gross error in the distance estimate, as the vehicle and the wake were clearly visible. Resurfaced after ¼ hour. Nothing more to be seen of the vessel.[24]

On the basis of Dröscher's description of the craft, it was probably either USS *Perkins* (DD-26) or USS *Mayrant* (DD-31). These were two of the ten three-stacked variants of the Paulding class of destroyers, and the only ones designated for cross-Atlantic escort service. Although there were some flush-decked Caldwell-class destroyers with three funnels, only two were commissioned by August 1918, and only one was actually in service, albeit in European waters.[25] Both destroyer classes had a draft of just under 2.5 m.

In retrospect, Dröscher should have been thankful that the destroyer disappeared following the failed torpedo strike. Had it truly been a Paulding-class destroyer, her five 3-inch/50-caliber deck guns, six 18-inch torpedo tubes, and depth charge racks (combined with a top speed of nearly 30 knots) would have been more than enough to deal with the cumbersome cruiser-minelayer. Instead, he remained undeterred and attempted to challenge even-more-formidable opponents the next day.

In the afternoon hours of August 2, now about 720 mi. / 1,159 km east-southeast from the Nova Scotian coastline, *U-117* found herself in attacking range of an outbound convoy escorted by two or three cruisers. Despite being in extremely rough seas and outnumbered by superior enemy warships, Dröscher decided to once again take his chances with a submerged assault. Unfortunately, the hunt had to be called off just as quickly as it began. Echoing Kophamel's *Kriegstagebuch* entry from July 26, Dröscher felt compelled to explain his rationale for ultimately breaking off the attack:

> Although the position of the boat is unfavorable, diving is carried out for an underwater attack. The ocean swells are too high to hold the boat at periscope depth. It also seems impossible that a torpedo will run smoothly.
> Surfaced. Convoy out of sight.

U-117 encountering heavy seas. *Courtesy of Deutsches U-Boot-Museum*

Pursuit must be avoided because of the fuel supply. It turns out that the daily consumption is a good deal higher than the travel curve suggested. The boat also shows a constant oil trail, so that a loss of fuel oil, which is difficult to assess, must occur persistently.[26]

While the failure to sink any vessels thus far in his cruise must have been extremely frustrating to the German commander, Dröscher should have once again thanked his lucky stars. Had he fired upon the convoy and subsequently been chased down by the escorting cruisers, his incessantly leaking fuel tanks would have easily revealed his submerged position and made his U-boat extremely vulnerable to the inevitable depth charge counterattack.

As *U-117* was dealing with her own troubles at the beginning of August, the first of the month would actually mark a change in fortunes of *U-140*. Even though that morning a Swedish steamer was allowed to escape Kophamel (on the account of rough seas), and *U-140* was once again outrun by a faster steamer early that afternoon, at 1840 that day, better luck arrived in the form of a zigzagging, 7,029-ton Japanese steamer.

The *Tokuyama Maru* had been en route from London to New York City with a cargo of 1,300 tons of aluminum oxide[27] when she crossed paths with *U-140*. Although she had sailed across the Atlantic as part of a convoy, she had been released to continue the last leg of the voyage on her own. She was about 225 mi. / 362 km east-southeast of her destination (specifically at 39°3' N, 70°26' W) when Kophamel, having observed two deck guns through his periscope, ordered a submerged torpedo attack.

Firing from tube 5 at 2010, *U-140*'s single G6AV* torpedo would find its target, detonating on the starboard side of the steamer, below her bridge. This, however, would not be enough to sink her. Instead, her Japanese crew was able to close her watertight compartments and isolate the leak, with Kophamel noting that although she was now overweight, she remained afloat. As the *Tokuyama Maru* sent out an "allo" message following the strike, Kophamel decided to remain near her for the duration of the night, awaiting potential victims in the form of rescue ships. Unfortunately for both parties involved, no one was coming.

At 0700 the next day, with the entire eighty-five-man crew of the *Tokuyama Maru* now safely in their ship's lifeboats, *U-140* came to the surface to finish off the wounded steamer with her 15 cm deck guns. It was at this point that the *Maru*'s captain imparted that his ship had originally been in a convoy and disclosed the fleet's last known coordinates and course to the German commander. Without taking the time to reward the stricken Japanese crew for their intel or supply them with water or the direction of the nearest landfall, *U-140* instead sped away westward toward the New Jersey coastline in an attempt to intercept the convoy's remaining vessels. Astonishingly, the Germans were actually able to locate some of the convoy's stragglers by 1600. Just 55 mi. / 88 km away from the sunken Japanese steamer, at 38°55' N, 71°6' W (about 178 mi. / 286 km from Atlantic City), *U-140* spotted an unidentified tanker and the convoy's escort, the cruiser USS *Albany* (CL-23).

Unlike Otto Dröscher in *U-117*, who apparently had no reservations about attacking warships, Kophamel was spooked by the presence of the protected cruiser and specifically noted in his war diary that the American warship must be avoided. A submerged attack was felt to be completely out of the question.[28] USS *Albany*, for her part, did not notice *U-140* in the distance and, prioritizing the protection of the tanker, proceeded onward toward her destination. Despite being so close to the *Tokuyama Maru*, neither the tanker nor the escort altered course to provide aid. Instead, the Japanese sailors were later rescued by an American schooner who happened upon them by accident, later depositing them in Nova Scotia on August 7.

Kophamel, disregarding the abundance of large vessels encountered thus far in his patrol, somewhat strangely chose this point to alter his course southward toward Cape Hatteras, North Carolina. He noted,

> Since only incoming traffic was encountered in this area, the more important outgoing traffic should be searched for. It is intended, according to the orders (compare wireless about later departure of "U 117"), to go south to Hatteras first. Then from the 10th through the 11th, the favorable moonlight will be utilized and operations will resume by the Nantucket Lightship.[29]

While it was true that his orders assigned him an operational zone between Nantucket and New York City pending *U-117*'s arrival, *U-117* was still in the middle of the Atlantic on August 2—some 750 mi. / 1,207 km from the nearest landfall in Nova Scotia. There was still ample time to spend in his current location. In all likelihood, Kophamel wanted a change of scenery and a shot at less defended targets. He would be rewarded for his foresight just days later.

After spending the entire next day sailing toward new hunting grounds, on August 4, *U-140* would come across one the largest victims of her cruise—the *O. B. Jennings*. This 10,289-ton American tanker was sailing from Southampton, England, to Newport News, Virginia, in ballast when she narrowly avoided one of *U-140*'s torpedoes at 36°36' N, 74°20' W (about 90 mi. / 145 km off Virginia Beach). According to *U-140*'s war diary, the *O. B. Jennings* had been painted with dazzle camouflage and had a 12 cm stern gun, which predicated her being attacked without any warning. In a case of the dazzle pattern actually doing its job, Kophamel conceded that his torpedo missed "because the size of the steamer had been significantly underestimated."[30] The events, according to the *Jennings*'s captain, George W. Nordstrom, proceeded as follows:

> A torpedo was sighted about 1,000 yards, four points on port bow; by maneuvering ship, torpedo missed and passed 3 to 4 feet astern. At 9:30 a.m. [there is an hour time difference in the German records] the submarine opened fire from a distance of about 8 miles, and we immediately hoisted our flag and opened fire, after we broke out our smoke boxes and made a smoke screen, changing course often to hide ship behind smoke screen. . . . The submarine followed us and kept shelling until 11:40 a.m., having our range finely all the time, several shells bursting so close to the ship that the ship's side was punctured in several places. At 11:40 a.m. a direct shot hit the engine room through the counter, smashing port engine and wrecking main steam line. Several men were wounded. At the same time another shell hit magazine and exploded, destroying all ammunition. Previous to this[,] one man was killed by gunfire and some minor wounded on deck. I pulled my colors and sent out wireless calls. I surrendered at 11:45 a.m., ordered all hands in the boats, and abandoned ship. Pulling away from the ship, the submarine came up and interrogated boat crews, took second officer prisoner, asking the boat crew where the captain was, and the crew answered that the captain was killed. Then the submarine returned to ship and commenced to shell her.[31]

The dazzle-camouflaged *O. B. Jennings. NH 44573, courtesy of the Naval History & Heritage Command*

The captain, being able to give his testimony, was obviously alive. To prevent him from being taken prisoner, his men swapped his uniform with that of the only crew member killed, the second steward, leaving the newly promoted steward's body on the deck of the tanker. For their part, the Germans did not investigate the matter any further, nor did they need to. With the "captured" second officer, they now had a man on board who was willing to tell them everything they wanted to know and more.

While Capt. Nordstrom's description of the sinking of his tanker mirrors the description from *U-140*'s war diary almost exactly, the case of the second officer being taken captive is where intrigue enters the narrative. According to the testimonies of other American survivors, the second officer, Rene Bastin, was a Belgian national who had just joined the crew before departing Southampton. His fluency in Flemish, French, and German immediately raised suspicions among his fellow crew members, who feared he may have been a German spy. This sentiment was amplified when Bastin "insisted that he be permitted to speak with the officer on the submarine and, despite the fact that he was slightly wounded, jumped from the lifeboat to the deck of the submarine and began speaking rapidly in German to the officer and men on the deck, finally shaking hands with them and without further conversation with his companions in the lifeboat, went below decks of the submarine and never returned."[32]

In contrast to the treacherous optics of his actions, Bastin would go on to claim he was a victim of the circumstances. After spending the remainder of the war in a German POW camp and desiring to be transported to the United States upon its conclusion, he explained to the American consulate, as well as Standard Oil's *The Lamp* magazine (Standard Oil owned the *O. B. Jennings*), that he was merely translating for the crew members being interrogated by the German officers. When the Germans were told the captain had been killed, they replied that he, as an officer of the ship, would have to be taken prisoner instead. In Bastin's words,

> He [the German officer believed to be Kophamel] asked for the next in charge; we shrugged our shoulders and said we did not know who was in charge. Then he came closer to my boat and said to me, "If you do not know where the captain is[,] you come here." I saw the submarine dropping alongside the boat with machine guns and pistols aimed at us. As I knew there was nothing else to do, I jumped on the submarine, making the jump so as to not fall in between the boat and the submarine. . . . As I landed . . . the captain said, "You are an officer of the ship, so I must keep you on board as a prisoner of war."[33]

He would go on to describe the inner workings of the U-Kreuzer, giving suspect accounts of events from *U-140*'s patrol and claiming that he was treated poorly, particularly from the U-boat's doctor, who was alleged to have completely ignored his wounds. The consulate and subsequent American publications bought the excuse, though they did not have the benefit of being able to check his story against *U-140*'s *Kriegstagebuch*.

Had German records been easily accessible at the time, it would have been realized that Bastin, contrary to being simply caught up in an unfortunate situation, appeared to be a man willing to sell out his comrades and assist anyone who could possibly benefit him. Indeed, *U-140*'s log confirms that reality was more closely aligned with what the rest of the *O. B. Jenning*s crew observed. Kophamel would record that it was Bastin who insisted on being taken onto *U-140* and promptly sang like a canary once inside, noting,

> The steamer's 2nd officer was taken on board as a prisoner at his urgent request. The man seemed capable of giving important statements. His statements are compiled in a special report.[34]

This special report seems to have been lost to time; however, Bastin, referred to as *der Gefangene* (the prisoner) from that point on, is repeatedly mentioned in future *Kriegstagebuch* entries as providing essential tips that not only would help Kophamel find targets but would ultimately help *U-140* get home safely.

Although Capt. George Nordstrom claimed to American authorities that the Belgian prisoner couldn't have provided anything of a confidential nature to his captors, he was apparently familiar with American merchant traffic and would be pointing the Germans in the direction of where to find it. His knowledge about Allied countermeasures on the European side of the Atlantic would also prove invaluable both to *U-140* and *U-117* later in the cruise. Even though Rene Bastin was not a German spy, as will be seen later in this chapter, he was certainly a man guilty of aiding and abetting the enemy and then lying about his experiences when it suited him.

In one of the Belgian's dubious, colorful reminisces, he claimed that Kophamel taunted him shortly after becoming a prisoner, cuttingly remarking, "Just have a look at your ship; I am going to show you how she sinks; where are your destroyers and your navy?"[35] While this was most likely a fabricated statement uttered for the purpose of gaining sympathy from his American examiners, it is nonetheless a valid question. Where were the American patrols?

As *U-156* was busy sinking fishing ships off Nova Scotia with impunity on August 4, Navy patrols were actually less than 100 miles from *U-140*'s location, guarding the immediate coastal waters off Cape Henry. Upon receipt of the distress calls from the *O. B. Jennings*, the 5th Naval District, headquartered at nearby Norfolk, immediately ordered the formation of a submarine hunter squadron consisting of the destroyer USS *Hull* (the destroyer that stymied one of *U-151*'s attacks) and a complement of sub chasers. Unfortunately, by the time the warships left port and reached the approximate location of the attack, darkness had already set in and *U-140* was already well on her way to the Outer Banks. Undeterred, the destroyer and sub chasers persisted in combing the area for the enemy and searching for survivors. It was to be a long, ill-fated night.

Things immediately got off to a shaky start when the sub chaser, *SC-187*, struck an unlit Norwegian steamer (the SS *Capto*) and sank. She would be one of just six sub chasers lost during the Great War, of which half sank as a result of a collision with another vessel.[36] Thankfully, no lives were lost in the incident, although there were casualties in the form of two injured sailors and the embarrassment of handing *U-140* an indirect victory over an American warship.[37] Although this was nearly a disaster, this would not be the end of the night's problems.

When USS *Hull* eventually located the survivors of the *O. B. Jennings* at 0220 on August 5, only two lifeboats (those of the first officer and chief engineer) were observed. She then spent the next half hour scouring the area for the missing third boat belonging to the captain, before giving up and heading back to Norfolk. Ironically, Capt. Nordstrom and the remaining crew were nearby but were intentionally hiding from the destroyer since they believed that her silhouette was that of another enemy submarine. They would ultimately be rescued by the Italian steamer *Umbria* at approximately 0830 that same day.

Just three hours after the *Umbria* took on the remaining survivors from the *O. B. Jennings*, *U-140* was already nearly 125 mi. / 200 km south, and about 133 mi. / 214 km off Cape Hatteras, at 34°58' N, 73°20' W. Here the German raider spotted the *Stanley M. Seaman*, a 1,060 GRT, four-masted schooner transporting coal from Newport News, Virginia, to Puerto Plata, Dominican Republic (then Santo Domingo and under occupation by the United States). A single warning shot not only halted the vessel but sent her captain, William McAloney, and his eight-man crew hastily into their boats. They abandoned their vessel so quickly and without consideration that they neglected to take any water or food and, despite being over 100 miles offshore, launched their rowboat instead of their motorized dinghy.

It is unclear from the German records whether Kophamel was amused at what he saw or instead felt pity on the stricken seamen. In any case, he wasn't prepared to leave them in their current state. After taking it upon himself to chastise McAloney for being so careless in abandoning his ship and putting the lives of his men in jeopardy, Kophamel ordered their boat to be towed back to the schooner so they could take on provisions and then board their motor launch instead. The Germans too boarded the schooner, helping themselves to some of the Americans' supplies before sinking her with a single explosive charge. Despite having the benefit of a gasoline engine on their boat to aid in traveling toward the coastline, the crew of the *Stanley M. Seaman* wouldn't be rescued for another three days. One could only imagine what their fate would have been had they been left in a rowboat without any food.

The next day, *U-140* remained in the waters of Cape Hatteras, patrolling on the surface in extremely hazy conditions. Surprisingly, it would be one of the most exciting days for *U-140*, with Kophamel actively engaging four separate vessels, still without any protection from the US Navy. The afternoon action proceeded as follows:

1320: Steamer with 1 funnel and 2 masts in sight, latitude 35°5' N, longitude 75°19' W. Shortly afterwards a second steamer is observed behind her. Fired one shot in front of the bow of both. While the first appears to be stopping, the second turns away from the first ship, with sharp changes in course. This steamer is painted in a camouflage pattern. Opened fire. [The steamer] takes hits, starts to burn and the crew gets out. It is now recognized that the other steamer is the *Diamond* [Shoals] *Lightship* [LV-71]; it transmits wireless signals while the other steamer is being bombarded. In order not to disturb my operations, it too had to be fired upon for a short period of time. Approached the first steamer and, as two more steamers came into sight and came closer, sunk it with a torpedo. It is the American (formerly Dutch steamer) *Merak* (3,024 t) with 5,600 t of coal from Norfolk to South America [Chile]. Concerning the last steamers observed, one apparently has seen the attack and stopped, the other is still close by. Both steamers signal to each other and then race towards land. For a while afterward we continued to fire [at the steamers], then I had to turn away because the water was too shallow. According to the layout of the map, they must have set a course for the beach. Exactly where could not be determined because the visibility became even poorer, and the steamers could no longer be seen in the haze at 120 hm.

1650: Returned to the Lightship[,] which had already been left by the crew. It was then sunk.

1800: Steamer sighted that is heading for the lightship from the south. A rear gun is able to be made out. Opened fire. According to her wireless transmissions, she is the English steamer "Bencleuch[,]" 4,159 t. She turns away and returns fire. Since my position is outwardly unfavorable—steamer is still firing at our boat from the better horizon, while she can no longer be recognized in the haze—the battle was broken off.
1820: Headed for deeper water again. Will hold off during the hazy night. By daytime tomorrow I will continue to stay on the steamer routes.[38]

In the interest of being concise in his logs, Kophamel left out a few important details concerning the sinkings of the *Merak* and the Diamond Shoals lightship that are nonetheless worth mentioning.

In the case of the former, after the *Merak* altered course for the shore and began zigzagging, she ran aground. Being unarmed, she was essentially a sitting duck for the approaching U-boat. It should be noted that Kophamel specifically referred to the *Merak* as being camouflage-painted, but not necessarily armed, before giving the order to open fire. Both he and Otto Dröscher were alike in this respect, apparently assuming that camouflage automatically established a vessel as being belligerent and thus provided justification for them being attacked without any warning. Although unrestricted submarine warfare did not differentiate between commercial vessels and warships, past practices of U-boat commanders along the coast of North America showed that prize rules were still being respected up to that point, and sudden attacks on unarmed vessels were far from the norm. Since the veteran commanders Kophamel and Dröscher both seemed to feel a need to justify their actions on such vessels in their logs, it can be assumed that they, still recognizing prize rules, were not acting out of bloodlust, but instead out of self-preservation.

This notion is given credence by testimony from the *Merak*'s crew. Once the crew had taken to their boats (and the lightship's radio had been silenced), *U-140* approached them and inquired about their vessel. According to one of the *Merak*'s officers,

> The submarine came to within a boat's length and an officer, speaking perfect English, asked our name, nationality, cargo and where we came from. He did not seem to place us and he told one of his men to go below and get him Lloyd's Register. Examining the book, he said, "Oh, your ship was a Hollander, was it?" He then asked if we had a sail and on being told we did, he advised us to hoist it, with the remark that the coast was only ten miles distant to the westward. Another officer said,

"You are going to let them go, aren't you?" He replied, "Yes, I don't want them, they can go." He waved us goodbye and started after two ships that were visible about four or five miles away. He was seen shooting at both vessels.[39]

The men on the *Merak* also claimed that explosives were used to dispatch their vessel, though their vantage point, combined with the fog, may have obscured their view of the torpedo that really sank their ship.

Concerning the Diamond Shoals lightship, once her radio had been silenced, her crew immediately took to lifeboats and rowed ashore. Only when *U-140* returned to the vessel and found it abandoned hours later was it destroyed with three shots from the U-Kreuzer's 15 cm deck gun. Kophamel is often given more credit than he is due for sinking the lightship, since it was believed that he intentionally targeted her for tactical reasons. Due to the hazardous waters off Cape Hatteras, a missing lightship could cause just as much destruction on coastal shipping as a minefield. Unfortunately, going against Kophamel's assumed brilliance, his own war diary indicates that LV-71 had been just another target of opportunity.

Apart from the aforementioned missing details in the German account, the sequence of events described by Kophamel most likely represent what occurred in reality that day. They were succinct, emotionless, and to the point. By contrast, American accounts of the incident were both speculative and sensationalized.

One of the more fanciful versions of the day's events originated with a supposed eyewitness aboard the U-boat, the Belgian prisoner Rene Bastin. Once again attempting to paint himself as a victim of his merciless "captors," his account describes Kophamel as a man out to ensure no one survived the day's attacks, not only shooting at lifeboats but also utilizing poison gas. He claimed,

> I noticed the smoke of these shells was yellow[,] and I think the shells fired at the *O. B. Jennings* were smokeless. I concluded[,] therefore, that the submarine was firing gas shells at the *Diamond Shoal*. I think she did that in order that none of the Light Vessel [*sic*] crew might escape. The Light Vessel blew up in a few minutes[,] and I saw her lee boat pulling away at a few hundred yards['] distance. The submarine was shelling the boat with a 4-inch gun but missed it[,] and the submarine could not go any further in as it was shallow water. That is how the shoal light boat escaped.[40]

This narrative was an obvious embellishment. Neither *U-140* nor any other U-boats ever used poison gas during World War I, and it is doubtful that a prisoner would have been allowed on deck in the midst of combat. This being said, Bastin was not the only person to report its use off the Carolinas that August.

Although Bastin's story was not published until after the war, meaning his tale could not have influenced other American citizens, on August 10, the 6th Naval District advised that a gas attack had also occurred on Smith Island, North Carolina (over 175 mi. / 282 km west-southwest of Hatteras). According to the dispatch, at 1700 that Saturday, "three large oil spots, each over an acre in extent" were observed passing by the island's Coast Guard station, which subsequently generated a vapor reminiscent of mustard gas. It had been believed that a U-boat released the chemical into the channel, hoping that the tide would bring the poison inland to go to work in a more populated area such as Wilmington.

Unfortunately, this mysterious fog appeared to have settled on the island, and, consequently, the lighthouse keeper, his wife, an assistant, and three lifeguards "all suffered from the gas for half an hour."[41] Even the station's chicken coop was affected, with all the kept poultry reportedly dying shortly after being exposed to the unknown chemical agent. Col. Chase, of the Army's Coastal Artillery Corps in Fort Caswell, made the assurance that the "entire matter will be investigated and [a] report made."[42] Indeed, the truth was established the following day, but the findings were much less reported on. The poison gas was nothing more than "the aroma of a particularly nasty load of oily sludge that a passing steamer had pumped out of its bilges."[43]

In reality, by the time the reported gas attack had occurred, *U-140* was already well away from the North Carolina coast. On the morning of August 7, less than a day after the attack off Cape Hatteras, Kophamel made the decision to return to northern waters. After encountering an American coastal submarine, but little else in the way of targets, he noted,

> 0855: About 4,000 m away, a submarine is sighted whose tower comes out of the water twice with poor depth control. Dodged.
>
> 1200: Crossed Hatteras during the day, but no more traffic observed, it can be assumed that it is blocked [from leaving port] or relocated. This area should therefore be abandoned, and a slow northerly course should be taken in order to gradually get to Nantucket.
>
> First, a location will be approached that the prisoner conveniently gave me.[44]

Instead of proceeding on a direct course toward Nantucket, Bastin advised Kophamel to detour back toward the entrance to Chesapeake Bay. Here, he would be certain to encounter outbound convoys. Ironically, the same day and nearly 300 mi. / 483 km north, the US Navy was busy defending such a convoy from a reported U-boat attack. Unfortunately for the Navy, the submarine in question wasn't German at all.

In a case of Allied vessels actually going on the offensive on the American side of the Atlantic, a convoy being escorted by USS *Paul Jones* (DD-10) encountered what they believed to be an enemy submarine off the coast of Cape May, New Jersey. In actuality, it was the diminutive USS *O-6*, on a defensive coastal patrol. An unidentified, armed British steamer was the first to spot the submarine and began firing upon her, with several shells damaging the sub's conning tower and 3-inch gun pit—forcing her into crash dive.[45] After waiting for the steamer to leave the area, *O-6*'s commander, Lt. Cmdr. Carroll Wright, gave the order to surface, only to receive additional shots into her hull from the awaiting destroyer *Paul Jones*. Shooting wouldn't cease until another one of the submarine's officers, Lt. Glann, was able to make it to the deck and identify the craft as American.

Once Lt. Leo Thebaud, the offending destroyer's commander, realized his mistake, *Paul Jones* escorted *O-6* to Cape May for repairs and then returned to the convoy. For their part in saving the submarine, both *O-6*'s commander and first officer were awarded with the Distinguished Service Medal and Navy Cross, respectively. *O-6* would ultimately survive the war and even go on to serve in a limited capacity in World War II.

O-6 (*second from left*) pictured in Boston in 1921. *NH 103193, courtesy of the Naval History & Heritage Command*

Although retiring due to friendly fire is the least optimal outcome of a patrol, it was quite common during the First World War, and there were some important takeaways from the incident. On one hand, the fact that USS *Paul Jones* (another outdated Bainbridge-class destroyer like USS *Hull*) was able to speed to the last known location of the submarine, with an aim to ambush her, indicated that the US Navy was gaining valuable experience in antisubmarine warfare and had the confidence to engage (had it been a U-cruiser) a much-better-armed enemy. On the other hand, the fact that the destroyer's gun crews, armed with two 3-inch and five 6-pounder deck guns, weren't able to sink a submarine with a total displacement of 639 tons that wasn't shooting back, to say nothing of not dropping depth charges prior to *O-6* surfacing, was a bit concerning. The US Navy would get another shot at proving themselves three days later, when *U-140* encountered a Brazilian steamer approximately 135 mi. / 217 km off Virginia Beach.

At 0530 on August 10, *U-140* spotted the passenger/cargo ship SS *Uberaba* (formerly the German SS *Henry Woermann*, seized by Brazil in 1917) at 36°32' N, 73°32' W. Included in her complement of 350 passengers were a hundred officers and sailors from the US Navy, bound for the Atlantic Fleet in Norfolk, Virginia, from the small American base in Rio de Janeiro. After observing the vessel from a distance of about 5,000 m, Kophamel ordered a warning shot to be fired across her bridge. Immediately, the *Uberaba* sent out an SOS signal and turned away, resulting in *U-140* firing more 15 cm shells, whose shrapnel struck the deck of the steamer and the wireless operator's room. Apparently, the Brazilians were unsure of what type of craft was firing at them, since between sending out SOS signals, they also radioed *U-140*, demanding that whoever was attacking them to please give their name. *U-140*'s radio operator simply replied in English, "Stop and send a boat."[46] The request went unanswered.

Instead, *U-140* intercepted wireless transmissions from the 5th Naval District, advising that four destroyers had been dispatched, with one already quite close by. Undeterred, Kophamel ordered his submarine to close the distance to the steamer and continue the attack. Just as firing was about to resume, the *Uberaba*'s salvation arrived in the form of USS *Stringham* (DD-83), one of the modern, flush-decked Wickes class of destroyers. The *Stringham* wasted no time in engaging the enemy, speeding toward *U-140* in a zigzag pattern. According to Kophamel,

> When the attempt was made to resume [firing the deck guns], the aforementioned destroyer came into view; the attack had to be given up and [we] submerged. The destroyer easily found the oil sheen that trailed the boat and bombed us[47]. . . . 16 depth charges[48] were dropped in considerable

proximity to us. Since the first bombs were already very well placed, we went to a depth of 75 m. After a short time, there was a major water ingress at the central hatch between the bracket screws and the hatch ring. The leakage couldn't be sealed from the inside. Additionally, there were other major leaks. After the batteries were completely discharged, the bilges weren't allowed to be emptied because the destroyer remained above us, the situation became critical due to the penetrating water. The boat could only be held by blowing into the diving tanks. In total, about 40–45 t of water entered the boat. With the flowing water in the boat and tanks, depth control became very difficult. In order to reduce the pressure of the penetrating water, we went back to [a depth of] 40 m.[49]

For once, Rene Bastin gave a somewhat reliable eyewitness account of the action, although he nearly trebled the depth *U-140* settled at. Most importantly, he was able to provide details on what Kophamel was doing to avoid being sunk, specifically the following:

On an order from the officer in charge to straighten her [*U-140*] up, everybody rushed toward the stern. I can tell you, during those few minutes we all thought our last moment had come. When the submarine got straight, she was steaming at a very slow speed—about two knots—so the destroyers with their submarine telephones could not hear the motion of the propeller. Another depth charge burst right on top of us, blowing up the middle hatch, putting the lights out and giving the submarine a list of forty degrees. I felt water dripping on me while I was sitting in the bow torpedo room. Two more depth charges dropped on top of us and then the submarine felt as though she were straightening up. I heard water rushing everywhere and this kept up for it seemed about three hours. Temporary lights were used, and the submarine kept on steaming slowly at 415 feet depth in all kinds of angles, now down by the stern, now up by the head, or with a list of forty degrees to port, etc. At 12 p.m., the lights came on again. I learned that the dynamo room had received fifty-five tons of water through leaks, the pipes bursting, but the submarine, with her powerful pumps, which were worked by compressed air, could blow out 500 tons a minute.[50]

True to Bastin's account, it wouldn't be until noon that the depth charge attack ceased, and a proper damage report could be taken. Kophamel noted a series of significant leaks, including the noted "major ingress" around the central hatch, and further heavy leaks in the diesel room, diving tank 2, and the bow, stern, and living quarters. Not giving USS *Stringham*'s commander,

Lt. Cmdr. Neil E. Nichols, any credit for a well-placed bombardment, he concluded that "all of the leaks can be traced back to inadequate workmanship at the Germania shipyard."[51] Smaller leaks were also noted in every other compartment, and contrary to Bastin's claim that all the water could be dealt with, Kophamel realized that he would not be able to save his submarine if he continued to remain submerged for much longer.

After spending an additional two hours biding his time, Kophamel made the difficult decision to blow all his tanks and resurface. To his relief, no vessels were observed on the horizon when *U-140* emerged from the depths. Yet again, he snubbed the abilities of Cmdr. Nichols, feeling that it was only due to his lack of experience that he wasn't able to finish the job on the U-cruiser.[52] This was more than a bit unfair. Even during World War II, where much-better submarine detection equipment existed, oil that made its way to the surface still sufficed as positive confirmation of a U-boat sinking. In *U-140*'s case, there was plenty of fuel to sample due to her leaking tanks. Indeed, Cmdr. Nichols, after distributing all seventeen (one more than Kophamel logged) of his depth charges, observed a "large and noticeable patch of oil, five-hundred yards long and three-hundred yards wide, with noticeable fresh penetrating odor."[53] Understanding the surface sheen to be a sign that *U-140* was no longer a threat, he, having been successful in defending the *Uberaba*, considered his mission complete. Unbeknown to Nichols or anyone else in the US Navy at the time, it was this attack that led Kophamel to retreat out to sea to make repairs and reassess the rest of his patrol.

USS *Stringham* in 1919. NH 50020, courtesy of the Naval History & Heritage Command

After initially believing to have sealed all the leaks in his submarine by midnight on the eleventh, Kophamel was forced to admit that conditions remained quite bad. Upon ordering a test dive to a modest 30 m at 0200, it was found that many of the leaks believed to have been repaired "reappear[ed] quite strongly."[54] Additionally, the outer doors on torpedo tubes 1 and 2 were loosened and damaged so badly that they were rendered unusable, with Kophamel claiming that it was possible for a person to be able to lie down in the gap. Taking this into consideration, the decision was made to head toward the Nantucket lightship and eventually set a course for home. While this was the first step toward ending Kophamel's cruise off North America, like a wild animal, *U-140* was only wounded and still remained dangerous. She had not yet given up the fight and would continue to pursue targets on her homeward march.

The forward torpedo room of *U-140* in the process of being dismantled after the war. *19-N-3853, courtesy of the National Archives*

CHAPTER 10
An Unending Trail of Destruction, and Oil . . .

At about the same time *U-140* was busy getting depth-charged on the tenth, 450 mi. / 724 km northwest, *U-117* finally made her presence known in the waters off New England. This, however, did not come as a surprise to the US Navy. On August 7, shortly after the Diamond Shoals lightship was sunk, a war warning was issued for the entire coastline between Cape Race and Charleston. Later that day, Adm. Sims sent an additional, more specific warning to CNO Benson, stating,

> HIGHLY SECRET . . . URGENT . . . We feel so certain that minelaying submarine will operate in Vineyard Sound and Nantucket Sound August 10 that counter measures in mining are recommended.[1]

Although Dröscher would not be sowing any minefields in New England or operating there for an extended period, he was indeed headed in that direction.

Incredibly, *U-117* had nearly destroyed herself just a day after Sims's warning, on August 8, when a torpedo got stuck in its tube during a failed attack on a twenty-two-ship convoy at 40°7' N, 61°45' W (still some 435 mi. / 700 km from New England). The submarine was spared when the projectile was dislodged by a cresting wave, falling safely to the ocean floor. No further attempts were made on the convoy, whose escorting cruiser was completely unaware of the German invader lurking just 1,000 m distant. On August 10, the morning of her projected arrival, *U-117* was now only about 175 mi. / 282 km from Sims's approximation of 40°30' N, 66°48' W. Here, Kapitänleutnant Dröscher would briefly resume the war on the coastal fishing fleets that *U-156* had initiated back in July.

In a day that began at 0830 and ended nearly ten hours later, *U-117* was able to sink nine small fishing vessels off Georges Bank, completely unopposed. Dröscher, rather surprisingly, recorded few details of the day's events in the war log, and those he did log were incorrect. He undercounted the number of vessels sunk, overestimated their average tonnage (claiming 75 tons), and noted only the initial time the fishing vessels were observed. Luckily, the American and Canadian survivors, as well as *U-117*'s chief engineer, help fill in the blanks and reveal important details concerning both *U-117*'s mission and the effects of Allied propaganda on the fishermen.

The first vessels to encounter the German minelayer were the schooners *Aleda May* (31 GRT), *William H. Starbuck* (53 GRT), *Progress* (34 GRT), *Reliance* (19 GRT), and *Earl and Nettie* (24 GRT), with a crew member of the *Starbuck* being the first to spot the approaching raider. By the time the five vessels were able to start their auxiliary motors, warning shots from *U-117* were already raining down in their vicinity, with one shell severing the main sail of the *Aleda May* and the others sending shrapnel onto the deck of the *William H. Starbuck*[2]—immediately prompting their crews to their dories. Once all five vessels had been abandoned by their crews, *U-117* prepared to plunder and sink them.

Chief Engineer Adolf Beckmann rather eloquently described *U-117*'s arrival as being "like a pike in carp pond" suddenly emerging from a "baseless depth."[3] He also indicated that there was some reluctance to sink the innocuous fishing boats, and, unlike American authorities who believed that such attacks were merely a distraction meant to steer escorts away from troopships, understood such vessels as being essential to the Allied war effort. He recalled,

> In and of itself we were of such harmless natures that we faced peaceful people—even if it was in hostile waters—in an equally peaceful manner. But unfortunately, we also had to tell ourselves that a large part of the catches captured here would be used for the purpose of stocking up the supplies of the enemy armed forces and that the hunger blockade meant that our own people were withheld even the smallest fraction of the tasty food that was easily caught here in vast quantities.[4]

The officers of *U-117*. Kapitänleutnant Otto Dröscher is pictured third from the left, Oberingenieur Adolf Beckmann is believed to be the officer wearing a white jacket. *Courtesy of Deutsches U-Boot-Museum*

Indeed, like *U-140* with the *Porto*, the crew of *U-117* seemed anxious to get ahold of as many delectable, and plentiful, American provisions as they could.

As Dröscher first approached the lifeboats of the *Aleda May*, he ordered her captain, her chief engineer, and a sailor off their dory and into the U-boat—replacing them with one of his own officers and two sailors. The three Germans and remaining fishermen in the launch then returned to the schooner for the purpose of requisitioning supplies and eventually dispatching her with a bomb. The same sequence would repeat itself for the remaining four schooners, with the *Aleda May*'s dory being utilized for each vessel. The *Aleda May*'s chief engineer, a French Canadian named Fred Doucette, provided a considerable amount of insight about his captors following his eventual rescue.

Unlike earlier U-boat crews, who seemed fond of telling their prisoners fantastic tales and embellishments, he recalled that the men of *U-117* seemed much more honest and curious. After feeding Doucette pea soup (he was the only man of his party willing to accept it), they sought coastal charts and intelligence on American minefields, which seemed to be their most particular concern, and one the fishermen claimed to know nothing about these. They also wanted to know what Americans thought of the war, and additionally how many American troops made it to France already—apparently believing the actual American presence to amount to between only 100 and 100,000 soldiers (a figure actually well over a million at that point in 1918). It was during these conversations that Doucette noticed a certain war-weariness among *U-117*'s officers. When the topic of who would win the war came up, an unidentified German officer (in all probability Kapitänleutnant Dröscher) stated that he believed there would be no winners, and when the *Aleda May* was sunk, the German boarding officer commented, with a tinge of compunction, "There she is; that is war."[5]

Of the five initial schooners sunk by *U-117* that afternoon, the *Earl and Nettie* was the last to go down at about 1500, with her crew experiencing much less amicable treatment by the German boarding party. Instead of being fed and socialized with, they were rushed to their lifeboats, robbed of personal trinkets, and experienced their ship being shelled before they had the chance to push off (a story corroborated by Capt. R. Sanchez of the *William H. Starbuck*).[6] It was at this point that Fred Doucette, Capt. Lynch, and the other captives of the *Aleda May* were finally released back to their dory and sent on their way.

By 1600, the Germans were already approaching another group of fishing vessels—the *Cruiser* (28 GRT), *Old Time* (18 GRT), and *Mary E. Sennett* (27 GRT). These were akin to the vessels that initially encountered *U-151*, and Capt. Manuel Dias of the *Mary E. Sennett* recalled that little concern was given to the shellfire heard in the distance that afternoon. He also, strangely, claimed another U-boat was present that evening, working with *U-117* to ensnare the fishermen. According to his statement to naval intelligence,

> The *Cruiser* from Boston, a fishing boat, told me that they heard some shots east of them and that they thought we had better go to port, but owing to the fact that the captain had heard these reports from other fishermen from time to time, did not pay attention to this report. *Cruiser*, *Old Time*, and this boat, the *Mary E. Sennett*, were all fishing together around 1 o'clock, and the captain was on mast looking for swordfish when two submarines were sighted ESE of where this boat was. One submerged and was never seen again, and the other was making circles trying to fool the fishing boats—that is, the submarine zigzagged around so that the fishing boats would come near to it. Whereas the captain thought these were other fishing boats at first, and sailed toward them. *Cruiser* and *Old Time* sighted and recognized what they really were.[7]

It is unknown what Capt. Dias believed to be a second vessel that afternoon, since conditions were clear and the sun was still shining; however, once *U-117* was positively identified, the fishermen quickly realized they couldn't outrun her and abandoned ship. This time, the Germans made no attempt at boarding the fishing boats. Instead, they opted to immediately sink each vessel with the use of their deck guns before proceeding farther westward to engage their final victim of the day—the *Katie L. Palmer*.

The *Katie L. Palmer* (21 GRT) had been fishing in a location approximately 8 miles west of where *U-117* sank the initial cluster of five fishing schooners that morning. Her captain, Edward Russel, had also both heard and disregarded the distant sounds of gunfire throughout the day. It wasn't until the crew of the *Reliance* (who had rowed vigorously for nearly three hours to be rescued by the *Palmer*) warned him about *U-117* that he made the decision to flee the area. Despite getting a head start, the *Katie L. Palmer*'s paltry top speed of 6 knots wasn't enough to escape the fast-approaching minelayer, which quickly caught up with her at about 1645. Not waiting for a warning shot, the crews of both fishing vessels sullenly took to their dories and awaited their fate.

Returning to the practice of earlier that day, Dröscher decided to send a boarding party over to his latest prize and once again required an occupied dory to do so. As a result, Capt. Edward Russel and crew members Fred Quinlan, Forman Belliveau, and Louis Amirault were removed from their lifeboat and taken aboard *U-117*, being replaced by Dröscher's men, who utilized it in pillaging and sinking the schooner. Like the transitory prisoners from the *Aleda May*, the men of the *Katie L. Palmer* were offered food and drinks and interrogated about potential minefields along the East Coast during their nearly three-hour-long stay aboard the U-boat. Once again, the Germans were left frustrated, being informed that any information pertaining to such defenses was kept secret from ordinary fishermen. Unbeknown to all parties that evening, the real reason for the lack of any minefield intelligence was because there weren't any mines in the first place.

Although Adm. Sims had suggested placing antisubmarine minefields in the shipping channels off the northeastern American coastline earlier that month, the Department of the Navy had already decided back in February that they would be counterproductive and dangerous to domestic vessels. A special board created to establish defense plans for domestic waters noted that under no circumstances were minefields to be considered for offensive purposes against enemy submarines or surface craft. They concluded,

> Mines which are submerged at a depth which is dangerous to surface vessels, including submarines (sub-surface mine fields) would be a greater embarrassment to our vessels in the situation under consideration than to the enemy's. We cannot afford to endanger or restrict the movements of our own vessels, which are at best very limited in number, and there being no hostile surface vessels involved, the Board concludes that no sub-surface mine fields should be included in the present plans.[8]

In actuality, Allied vessels were far from being "limited in number," since American shipbuilders had been setting production records throughout all of 1918. Just days before *U-117*'s arrival, Charles Schwab, of Bethlehem Steel, even went so far as to gloat that the U-boat threat had been all but checkmated by the combined Allied shipping industries, which were outproducing vessels being sunk by U-boats by a ratio of 1.43:1 in just the first quarter of that year![9] The real concern of the board was that minefields would impede this rapid flow of industrial output.

Ironically, there was such a demand for mines overseas that had the board actually been keen on the minelaying concept, American munitions factories wouldn't have been able to allot any for domestic use. Even if manufacturing suddenly caught up and provided a surplus of mines, the regulations concerning where the fields could be placed allowed for such ample passageways through them that their effectiveness would have been essentially negated. Despite advising that there might be benefits to announcing fictitious minefields to scare off potential raiders, the board emphasized that shipping would ultimately "be patrolled and protected by other means"—essentially the sub chasers, destroyers, and SP boats already performing the task. Apparently, Sims's earlier advice that any losses from the U-cruisers would be minimal and could be shouldered by the United States was still being accepted as a viable policy.

While Dröscher and his crew were justifiably concerned about the presence of a second American mine barrage, the fear of character assassination by the American press also seemed to linger strongly in their minds, just as it had for von Nostitz and his men. Even though the United States was fully committed to an Allied victory at this point in the war, the officers aboard *U-117* specifically instructed survivors not to fabricate stories about their experiences and to present the Germans in a truthful light. When Capt. Russel and the other prisoners from the *Katie L. Palmer* were eventually released on the evening of the tenth, Dröscher (or a man believed to be the commander) yelled to them, "We are not baby killers, so don't tell any lies about us when you reach land."[10] Even thirteen years after the war, Chief Engineer Beckmann bemoaned the fantastic stories about the U-boat crews being published by Allied newspapers, as well as their effects on their victims.

Writing about the events of August 10 in his memoir, he appeared to have combined his experiences fraternizing with the crews of the *Aleda May*, the *Katie L. Palmer*, and the *Elsie Porter* (a similar type of fishing vessel sunk weeks later on August 30, off Newfoundland) into one singular interaction. He wrote,

> The hostages in our submarine were initially terrified. The work of raising the lifeboats had already taken four hours. I wanted to get a little conversation going with the aforementioned senior of the first boat's crew, which apparently did not succeed. Suddenly the old man turned around, looked at the small clock in our mess and said clearly [in German]: "It's almost twelve o'clock!" Surprise to my side: "Do you speak German?"—"A little; grandfather emigrated from Germany, fisherman . . . Boston!"
>
> Wasn't it a tremendous stab in your own heart when we had to take action against peaceful people with German blood flowing in their veins? Wasn't it terrible when the old man, when asked his name, answered in a clear voice: Eisermann! Even if the act of war itself was bloodless, it was as unsympathetic as possible in the face of such facts.
>
> I took the white-haired old man into my heart, I offered him something to eat, he shook his head. I flavored a glass of water for him with raspberry juice, he again vigorously shook his white head and held out his hands defensively. But his eyes seemed to desire it. I sensed the connection. I took a sip myself, sat down and said to him: "No poison!"

Then the old man tore the glass out of my hands, emptied it quickly, then gratefully shook my hands. What he read in the newspapers caused him to be defensive; sad, sad, but unfortunately only too true.[11]

The "Eisermann" referred to by the *Oberingenieur* was in all certainty the Canadian captain Irvin Eisenhauer of the *Elsie Porter*, who matched Beckmann's description perfectly and was noted to have spoken German. Regardless of this apparent lapse in memory, the other fishermen did confirm much of what he was trying to convey in this elaborate yarn.

Capt. Russel and the men of the *Palmer* did in fact share drinks with Beckmann, who was noted as appearing to be the second mate and dressed in a white uniform. While Russel said nothing about the possibility of the drinks being poisoned in his statement, Amirault felt it important to mention that he was specifically advised by the German officer "to drink it as it was not poison"[12] in his. This notion of being murdered by their captors was also the reason Doucette was the only member of his party to accept the offer of pea soup earlier in the day. Paradoxically, the Germans weren't averse to using the threat of murder as a scare tactic to ensure the fishermen remained alive as the U-boat war went on.

Before he and his comrades were finally released at 2000, Louis Amirault allegedly received a warning from one of the mates on *U-117*, advising against mounting any guns on fishing vessels since the Germans would "consider you pirates and cut your throat."[13] This hyperbolic statement was by no means an empty threat. Although the Germans wouldn't literally be severing the arteries of any captured crews, the presence of a deck gun would significantly increase the chances of a vessel being sunk by torpedo without any warning, thus preventing them from being taken captive in the first place. The Germans clearly wanted to make certain that the Americans, who were minimally affected by the war overseas, understood the consequences of "unrestricted submarine warfare."

Luckily for the mental well-being of Dröscher and his men, the survivors of the *Katie L. Palmer* did not appear to make up any wild stories about their time on board the submarine when they were rescued later that evening. Even more providentially, the only mines *U-117* would have to concern herself with for her entire patrol would be those already left by *U-151* and *U-156*. Even so, the approach to the northeastern United States was not without coastal hazards, particularly as *U-117* entered the waters surrounding New York City.

The gateway to the New York City harbor had been of considerable military and commercial significance since the days of the Revolutionary War and was thus heavily defended. There were four forts composing the city's harbor defenses, with the Army's Coastal Artillery Corps' base at Fort Hancock on Sandy Hook, New Jersey, being the most formidable (the other three were Fort Wadsworth in Staten Island, New York; Fort Lafayette within the Narrows; and Fort Hamilton in Brooklyn, New York). It was this fort that would be the first to be encountered upon entering the New York / New Jersey Bight.

Although the large-caliber coastal artillery and mortar batteries at Fort Hancock were intended for late-nineteenth-century surface vessels (and were already obsolete by the time they were completed), they were abundant in number and more than capable of dispatching a minimally armored submarine. Still, as the United States observed the changes in modern warfare from afar, measures had been taken to upgrade the defenses to specifically combat an enemy U-boat. As early as February 1917, construction had begun on a steel-wire antisubmarine net designed to stretch between Sandy Hook and the Ambrose Channel. Interestingly, this was to be utilized only at night, while Navy seaplane and sub chaser patrols were deemed to be adequate defense against U-boats in the daylight hours.[14]

Additionally, the larger, antiquated artillery pieces were removed to be utilized by the Allied armies as railway and field guns on the western front in Europe, leaving the fort to rely on the more practical (and effective) 6-inch M1900 and M1903 and 3-inch M1898 and M1903 guns. While these guns would never be directed at an enemy vessel during the war, they would regularly be fired for training purposes. These drills, combined with frequent ordnance tests from the Sandy Hook Proving Ground on the northernmost tip of the spit, would lead to rumors about a coastal bombardment from *U-117*—an event that will be discussed later in the chapter.

A 6-inch M1900 gun at Fort Hancock. While installed at Battery Gunnison in 1943, this would have been at the fort's Battery Peck during World War I. *Author's photo*

Kapitänleutnant Dröscher must have been aware of these defenses, since, unlike the other U-boat commanders operating off North America that summer, he had specifically marked Sandy Hook's location on his *Minenskizze* (minefield sketch) map. Despite the Lower New York and the Sandy Hook Bays being ideal for minelaying (Adolf Beckmann noted that they had actually been designated minefield zones), Dröscher did his best to avoid them entirely. While he was still some 70 mi. / 113 km east of Fort Hancock, he would begin to adjust his course to the southwest, but not before engaging any targets of opportunity making their approach to New York City.

On August 12, *U-117* entered the congested steamer route, and *U-156*'s former minefield, just south of Fire Island. Unfortunately for the German raiders, an extremely thick fog blanketed the entire area. With visibility thus significantly reduced, it was extremely dangerous to travel on the surface due to the chances of a colliding with a passing vessel. Despite the hazards, Dröscher appeared determined to take advantage of his hunting grounds and initiate an attack. The day's events, according to his war diary, proceeded as follows:

0715: A steamer sighted in close proximity; distance 800 m, course 290°. Turned away. A second vessel comes into view. As far as can be discerned in the fog it is an elongated, low craft, apparently 2 stacked. Since it is probably a torpedo boat, submerged.

0807: Surfaced. As the tanks were being blown out, another steamer came into view approximately 1,000 m away, course 100°; it had cleared up a bit by now—initiated underwater attack.

Steamer had a gun at the stern.

Launched torpedo—hit. Tube 3. Depth setting 2 m, shooting distance 400 m (G6AV* torp.) The steamer sinks shortly thereafter. Estimated size 3,000 t. Course 300 degrees 9 nm towards New York.

[hour illegible]: Lifeboats come out of sight again in increasing fog. Popped up. Proceeded on the surface as the fog has cleared up somewhat.

1155: Submerged. Proceeded underwater due to thick fog.

[hour illegible]: Surfaced, proceeded above water.

[hour illegible]: Several vessels in sight. Steered away from them. The steamer observed to be in the closest vicinity (lights set) is running a course that intersects ours. Submerged as there is a risk of ramming in the fog.

[hour illegible]: Laid aground due to fog.[15]

The reward for Dröscher's persistence was the Norwegian steamer *Sommerstad* (3,875 GRT), chartered by the US government and en route from Bergen to New York in ballast. She was sunk at 40°10' N, 72°45' W, or about 26 mi. / 43 km south-southeast from where USS *San Diego* went down back in July.

Although Dröscher's log makes no mention of any unusual course taken by his torpedo, Capt. Jørgen Hansen of the *Sommerstad* reported that it had initially passed beneath the steamer and subsequently circled back, striking the vessel's port side and sinking her four minutes later. This had led to speculation that the Germans were using radio controls to guide their torpedoes, a theory the US Navy was quick to debunk.

Naval experts pointed out that the torpedo's gyroscope could be set to travel in an arc that would ultimately return toward the submarine—a setting commonly used by the American navy during exercises to allow for easier retrieval of the projectiles.[16] They further asserted that this was a known tactic used by the Germans to double their chances of success if a vessel increased speed to avoid the initial track of the torpedo. Chief Engineer Beckmann provides a counterpoint to this theory.

In explaining his trepidation toward attacking vessels with torpedoes (he seemed to feel that deck gun battles were safer and more honorable), he insinuated that any instances of torpedoes returning toward the U-boat were solely due to gyroscope malfunctions. He wrote,

> Torpedo shots! With a grain of salt! You can easily get run over by objects that have gone wild, yes . . . you can even kill yourself by a so-called circular runner à la a boomerang if the steering control of the torpedo fails and it comes back in a circle.[17]

The fact that he does not mention the circular track as being caused by a missed shot indicates that this was likely never a common practice in the Kaiserliche Marine or, at the very least, not a tactic employed by any of the commanders he served under.

Regardless of whether the torpedo's arc had been intentional or not, it seemed that *U-117* once again narrowly avoided destruction from one of her own missiles, this time courtesy of a Norwegian captain attempting evasive maneuvers. She would remain quiet for the rest of August 12 and much of the morning of the thirteenth as her crew rested on the seabed about 12 mi. / 19 km off Lavallette, New Jersey, waiting for the dense fog to clear. It was only after visibility improved that afternoon that *U-117* would surface and resume her southerly course.

Interestingly, there is an oft-repeated claim that the armed British steamer *Pyrrhus* engaged in a two-hour battle with *U-117* a mile north of the Fire Island lightship at 0600 that same day. It is a myth that has been cited as fact, with minor variations, in nearly every publication covering the U-boat war off North America for the past 103 years. Tragically, in assuming the *Pyrrhus*'s account to be true, each work failed to illustrate how this mistaken encounter actually contributed to *U-117*'s successes later that day.

According to testimony from the *Pyrrhus*'s officers, the British freighter fired about seventy-five shells at the distant *U-117* and was able to "destroy or divert" two of her fired torpedoes through the use of depth charges.[18] While the story was convincing both to naval authorities and subsequent historians, neither *U-117*, *U-156*, nor *U-140* was anywhere close to their vicinity. Amusingly, even Kophamel, hundreds of miles away to the south on *U-140*, was convinced of the tale. His prisoner, Rene Bastin, had been given the job of interpreting various intercepted Allied wireless transmissions and, on the basis of the transcripts that morning, concluded that besides destroyers being located off Hatteras, a submarine was being reported near Long Island.[19]

Given the prevailing hazy conditions of that morning, combined with the anxiety of being in the same area where the *Sommerstad* had sunk the day prior, the captain of the *Pyrrhus* could be excused for making a victimless error—if only it were actually victimless. In actuality, the *Pyrrhus*'s erroneous "allo" message tied up the sub chasers of the 3rd Naval District searching for a U-boat that didn't exist. These chasers, which would otherwise have been making patrols along the New Jersey coastline (down to the border of Monmouth and Ocean Counties, specifically off Brielle), were now being concentrated off Long Island and the New York Harbor, leaving *U-117* free to travel on her southerly course unhindered.

As the 3rd Naval District focused their efforts on the New York Harbor entrances, *U-117* was now nearly 75 mi. / 121 km southeast, en route to sow a minefield in the busy shipping lanes off Barnegat Light, New Jersey—on the northern periphery of the 4th Naval District's patrol zone. Although Dröscher would allow two sailing ships and a steamer to escape his sights due to his focus on his "imminent mining task," one target would overcome his devotion toward his primary objective. This would be a fully laden, dazzle-camouflaged, 7,127-ton tanker some 12 miles north of his destination at 39°55' N, 73°54' W.

The sighted tanker was the *Frederic R. Kellogg*, transporting 70,000 barrels of crude oil from Tampico, Mexico, to Boston, Massachusetts. Upon observing the vessel, Kapitänleutnant Dröscher ordered *U-117* to submerge in order to observe it more safely. Besides complimenting its "well-done outboard paint job"[20] in his war diary, he also noted the presence of a deck gun mounted on the *Kellogg*'s stern. Deciding to not take any chances with a possible artillery battle on the surface, since his boat had already been prepped for minelaying, he opted to attack with a torpedo.

The single G6AV* torpedo, having been fired from a distance of only 450 m, quickly found its prey, striking the tanker in its aft engine room at 1710 that evening and killing three of the tanker's crew members instantly. Four more would drown less than a minute later, being trapped in their quarters as the vessel quickly took on water.[21] According to the *Kellogg*'s captain, C. H. White, it took only fifteen seconds for the tanker to sink (other accounts claim a more realistic four minutes), and even though she had been measured for gun platforms on a previous cruise, the ship was actually completely unarmed.[22]

The *Frederic R. Kellogg* with her bow remaining above water. *USN Historical Section*

Despite the exceptional loss of life and the haste at which the tanker flooded, she was not a complete loss. Due to the relatively shallow depth of the coastal waters (about 89 ft. / 27 m), the stern of the ship struck the seafloor and kept the bow and a portion of the bridge above the surface. She would be salvaged two weeks later. The surviving crew members, numbering thirty-six in all, would be rescued three hours after abandoning ship by a passing steamer in the vicinity of Sandy Hook, while *U-117* continued onward to lay mines in the Barnegat Inlet—a task completed between 2015 and 2100 that evening with nine mines being sown, each 900 m apart, between 39°41' N, 73°54' W and 39°42' N, 73°59' W (according to *U-117*'s coordinates).[23] Unlike previous U-cruisers that summer, every mine was launched while *U-117* was submerged.

Further illustrating the effects of the *Pyrrhus*'s fallacious encounter earlier that day, the *Frederic R. Kellogg*'s radio operator was able to transmit an SOS signal just before he fled the sinking tanker, which was received by the 3rd Naval District less than fifty minutes later. Unfortunately, they were forced to relay it to the 4th Naval District, based in Philadelphia, who had no idea a U-boat was expected in their operational zone. By the time a hunting squadron was formed and dispatched to Barnegat, *U-117* had long since departed the area—remaining some 25 mi. / 40 km offshore and heading south toward Delaware. Amazingly, none of the sub chasers in the pursuing squadron struck any of the freshly planted mines, which wouldn't find any victims until October.

Given the actual circumstances of that evening, it is lamentable that the *Pyrrhus* incident was given so much credence by the US Navy; however, it wasn't the only myth to propagate that August 13. Reporters from the *Asbury Park Press*, after hearing about the sinkings of the *Sommerstad* and the *Frederic R. Kellogg*, began to reevaluate the routine firing of the guns on Fort Hancock. In a censored article published on August 14, 1918, regarding the sinking of the *Kellogg*, the front-page story read as follows:

> Residents along the shore yesterday afternoon heard the great guns at Sandy Hook firing, and in addition to the rumble of the giant discharges, thought they could distinguish between the burst of shells. . . . Between 3 and 4 o'clock, apparently off to sea to the northeast, came the sound of what seemed to be bursts of firing, from three to six shots being heard, repeated at intervals of 10 to 15 minutes. The firing caused little comment, it being presumed it was the often-heard practice firing at Fort Hancock.[24]

Three months later, and with the Armistice now signed, the same article was revisited by the newspaper with the new headline: "Did a Daring U-boat Shell Sandy Hook?" In this new, uncensored version, the reporter stated that "the Press has had confidential advises, which the end of the war now releases, that the Hook was shelled on the afternoon of August 13 during a fog."[25] It was now being reported that *U-117* surfaced on the extreme north end of the hook (coincidentally near the Coast Guard station), under the cover of the day's heavy fog, and fired sixteen shells, with the only noted damage being a crater in the earth about 50 feet in front of the fort's guard shack. What the newspaper didn't elucidate on was the possibility that this damage had been caused by American guns. It certainly didn't expand on the Sandy Hook Proving Ground's proof battery's long history of misfires, with ordnance regularly landing within Fort Hancock.

During World War I, there had been no fewer than six close calls, with "friendly fire" at Sandy Hook. Some of the more colorful stories include an officer narrowly avoiding being decapitated by a bursting antiaircraft shell fired from the proof battery on August 25, 1917, a 6-inch shell ripping through a tent and missing a soldier by 10 feet in November 1917, and a fragment of a ricocheted, high-explosive shell falling near an occupied tent near Battery Granger on April 13, 1918.[26] Indeed, during August 1918, when the rumor about *U-117* bombarding the coastline started,

> several shells, some as big as 10 inches, impacted at various points on the Fort Hancock reservation. Barracks and other structures occupied by troops had been endangered. Colonel Brady, who had replaced Colonel Harris [as the commanding officer of Sandy Hook defenses], called these incidents to the attention of his superiors. When asked for an explanation, Col. William A. Phillips of the proving ground reported that his people took every reasonable precaution but "Fort Hancock is in dangerous proximity to the proof battery." Premature explosions or other accidents were impossible to foresee or control.[27]

This report lends considerable credence to the notion that it was the proof battery doing all the firing that August 13—with shells yet again landing near sensitive areas on the Fort Hancock grounds.

Given that the U-boat bombardment legend didn't truly take on legs until after the Armistice, it is likely that Army personnel, after being badgered by reporters about the earlier incident, spared themselves embarrassment by leaking a complete fabrication. Since the discerning eyes of a censor were no longer required, it would be easy to conjure up a U-boat tale by using pieces of information they had heard in the local news that August, combined with Adm. Sims's warnings in July that coastal bombardments were imminent. The fact that this myth is still being debated in historical circles to this day is proof of its plausibility. Thankfully, it can finally be put to rest.

Interestingly, it appeared that Kapitänleutnant Dröscher was the only man standing in the way of such myths becoming reality. At the end of the month, when *U-117* returned to Delaware Bay on the homeward leg of her patrol, an auspicious moment to shell coastal shipyards presented itself. As Oberingenieur Beckmann recalled, the crew was strongly in favor of taking such action against the American maritime industry in order to make a bigger impact in the war. Unfortunately for the German war effort, Dröscher, ever the stickler for following orders to the letter, quickly put a kibosh on the idea. According to Beckmann,

This time we were all of Wilhelm's[28] view and took the position: something has to happen here for something to happen! Not so our commander. Even if it seemed to us as if all fingers were twitching to hit the cannon really hard, instead, as such a technical term went, he replied[,] "*Hahn in Ruh*,"[29] because that went against the operational orders that we had received. It is a shame that these people on land never found out how we actually waged the submarine war, and that we have long been using the word for ourselves what they claim to be: Gentlemen![30]

This, along with *U-117*'s debriefing, make it very clear that coastal bombardment was not a mission of the U-cruisers, contrary to the British Admiralty and Adm. Sims's earlier advisories from July 26 (see previous chapter). Aside from the odd, and debatable, case of *U-156*, any subsequent claims that U-boats successfully shelled the mainland United States can be regarded as mere local lore.

Returning to the actual events of August 13, *U-117* wasn't the only U-boat on the offensive. Approximately 380 mi. / 611 km southwest, *U-140* was having her own run-in with a large steamer, USS *Pastores* (ID-4540), at 35°30' N, 69°30' W. According to *U-140*'s log, *Pastores* was running a zigzag course and was both camouflaged and armed. Still, perhaps due to *Pastores* being the second-largest target of his cruise thus far, at 7781 GRT, Kophamel found it impossible to resist attempting a pursuit. After stalking the steamer for a little over an hour, he ordered *U-140* to the surface for a long-range deck gun attack. USS *Pastores*'s war diary records the details of the assault, and its subsequent futility:

> At 5.32 p.m., G.M.T. [1332 local time] . . . this vessel changed course from 269° true to 330° true in order to cross a restricted area in approach route before moonset. Zigzag combined plans Nos. 1 and 2 had been carried on all day. At 5.43 p.m., G.M.T., the officer of the deck noted a splash about 2,500 yards distant . . . and heard the report of a gun. With his glasses he discovered a large enemy submarine lying athwart our course 6 or 7 miles distant . . . and firing at this ship, apparently with two guns. From [the] size of [the] splash it appeared that these guns were of about 6 inches in caliber. Went to battle stations and commenced firing at submarine at extreme range with armor-piercing shell at 5.46 p.m., G.M.T. The enemy fired about 15 shots, none of which came more than 1,500 yards, after which she headed around toward us or away from us and ceased firing. This ship fired nine rounds at extreme range from after 5-inch 40-caliber guns, all of which fell

more than 3,000 yards short. Ceased firing at 5.50 p.m., G.M.T., after enemy had ceased, and proceeded on course at full speed. Submarine disappeared about 5 minutes later.[31]

Kophamel did little to justify the failure of his pursuit other than noting that *Pastores*'s superior speed ultimately allowed her to escape. He did, however, go into lengthy detail about the test dive he ordered at the engagement's conclusion, which speaks volumes about why he may have been less aggressive in carrying out the assault. He noted,

> When going at a depth of 15 m the leaks now hold fairly tight; still, greater depths must be avoided. The leaky bunkers have been pumped out so only the best are filled; nevertheless, a trail of oil can be followed as far as the horizon. Also, the diving tanks . . . leak a considerable amount of fuel with every flooding and blowing out. A great loss [of fuel] must be expected. A stop [in the leakages] will only come about when another bunker will be empty in the next few days, and it will be possible for additional pumping can be resumed.
>
> The condition of the boat no longer allows it to operate close to the coast. The boat could not withstand a systematic pursuit. Nantucket lightship must be abandoned, and we must relocate to an area where only sporadic patrols can be expected.[32]

In the days that followed, Kophamel headed farther into the ocean but found it to be better patrolled than the coastal waters. He had to dodge an American submarine, two destroyers escorting a tanker, and even an "old gunboat" and a destroyer, which he felt may have been dispatched from Bermuda (he was now about 475 mi. / 765 km off North Carolina). Here, he once again reassessed the condition of his U-boat, logging on August 17 that

> after pumping over the fuel oil, it turns out that in addition to the previous loss, a new loss is set after 45 days at sea to 35 cbm, which is only due to the inadequate shipbuilding design of the bunkers and additional bunkers by the Germania shipyard.
>
> The oil supply is only sufficient to cross the lightship north on the roads to Nantucket for 1–2 days. Then the march home must be started.[33]

On the basis of his reevaluation, it seemed he was not entirely prepared to give up the fight and would make on final effort off the American coast before turning back. Meanwhile, *U-117* remained on the hunt off the southern tip of New Jersey and the northern coast of Delaware. While Kophamel was making a fruitless attack on USS *Pastores* days earlier, Dröscher was adding to his tonnage tally, with nearly fatal consequences.

Shortly after midnight on August 14, *U-117* found herself at the entrance to Delaware Bay, approximately 25 mi. / 40 km southeast from Cape May. The fog that hampered her earlier operations off Fire Island seemed to be following the U-boat down the coastline. Because conditions were so hazy, the practice of vessels running without lights was particularly effective. Although Dröscher would make an attempt at pursuing a large steamer in the darkness, it wasn't until daylight arrived that *U-117* was finally able to find success. This occurred shortly after 0900, when *U-117* fired a warning shot at the *Dorothy B. Barrett*, a 2,088-ton, five-masted schooner transporting coal from New York to Norfolk. Upon its receipt, the American merchantmen aboard the schooner immediately took to their motor launch and abandoned ship without requiring any further prompting.

The *Dorothy B. Barrett* being sunk by *U-117*'s 15 cm deck gun. *Courtesy of Deutsches U-Boot-Museum*

At this point, testimony from the *Dorothy B. Barrett*'s captain, William Merritt, describes *U-117* behaving rather confusedly. He recalled that after he and his ten crew members headed northwest on their launch to get help, the U-boat at first appeared to follow them, make a circle, dive, and then resurface. Unbeknown to the American sailors, shortly after their vessel was stopped, Dröscher observed a much more worthwhile target on the horizon in the form of what he believed was a distant steamer (in actuality a tanker, the *William Green*). The strange course of action taken by *U-117* was due to initially submerging to attack, losing sight of the vessel in the fog, and then abandoning pursuit to return to the *Barrett* to sink her.

Despite breaking off the attempt on the tanker just as quickly as it began, *U-117* did not escape the binoculars of the *William Green*'s ever observant watch. Even in the hazy conditions, the *William Green* sent out an "allo" message, accurately reporting the enemy raider's position. It would be intercepted immediately by sub chasers *SC-71, 72, 73*, and *144*; submarine *N-7*; and seaplane A-1859 (a Curtiss HS-2L), which, in turn, rushed to the radioed coordinates. All these craft belonged the 4th Naval District, and, for once, all were located within 10 miles of the attack. This was to mark the beginning of what was to become an incredibly bewildering day.

Back at the schooner, Dröscher was struggling to sink her. He reported that the type of shells initially used in his first attempt were ineffective because the ship was constructed of timber. He then concluded that the schooner would have to be "sunk with a torpedo because of the close proximity to the shore."[34] A single torpedo would be fired, which consequently traveled below the vessel, since it was set too deeply, and missed. Finally, the German commander had to resign himself to the use of deck guns to get the coal-laden ship to go down.

SC-71, *SP-544*, a Curtiss HS-2L, and an auxiliary minesweeper at Cape May Naval Base. *NH 42453, courtesy of the Naval History & Heritage Command*

As this was occurring, the survivors of the *Barrett* had reached the American minesweeper USS *Kingfisher* (AM-25) some 2.5 miles northwest. Once aboard, Capt. Merritt implored the sweeper's commander, Lt. C. L. Greene, to fight the raider, but, after discovering the vessel was armed only with 3-inch guns, advised him that "the submarine was too big for him to tackle."[35] Heeding this advice, Lt. Greene ordered *Kingfisher* to retreat to the nearby shoals, where *U-117* wouldn't be able to submerge. As they proceeded to the shallows, the men aboard USS *Kingfisher* spotted the distant *William Green*, and, fearing she would soon become *U-117*'s next victim, Greene ordered his gun crews to open fire on the U-boat from afar.

USS *Kingfisher*. NH 667, courtesy of the Naval History & Heritage Command

Meanwhile, on *U-117*, Dröscher was completely oblivious to the developing situation. While *U-117* was on the surface dispatching the *Dorothy B. Barrett*, Dröscher spotted USS *Kingfisher*, noting her as a steamer "which evidently wants to leave the Delaware Bay, but, because of our presence, is seemingly staying far inshore in shallower water."[36] When the minesweeper's guns were heard by the Germans, they were never recognized as originating from *Kingfisher* or even being aimed at them. Instead, *U-117*'s war diary describes a "protective rumbling" that was misinterpreted as being 15 cm projectiles being fired from *U-140* (which was nowhere near Delaware Bay)!

The Germans could be forgiven for not realizing they were being attacked, since *Kingfisher*'s shells were all very poorly placed, with none whatsoever landing near the U-boat. This was, in all likelihood, due to the prevailing fog, since neither Capt. Merritt nor Lt. Greene on board the minesweeper realized that the black smoke they saw suddenly rise up from the water when *U-117* ceased firing was the burning *Dorothy B. Barrett*. This notion was further reinforced during Capt. Merritt's postbattle interview by naval intelligence. In it, he admonished the US Navy, remarking, "If we only had one of your fast submarine[-]chasing boats there we could have gotten that fellow because he was in shallow water and could not turn very fast."[37] The problem with his dressing-down of the intelligence officer was that *SC-71*, *SC-73*, and *SC-144* were all, in fact, present at the time, with the latter approaching and remaining with *Kingfisher* (even firing a shot at *U-117*) while *SC-71* and *SC-73* rushed to the aid of the *Barrett*.[38] Visibility was so poor that Capt. Merritt had no idea.

SC-144. NH 2691, courtesy of the Naval History & Heritage Command

The existence of the sub chasers in the battle was confirmed not only by the 4th Naval District but also Kapitänleutnant Dröscher, who wrote that "during the bombardment, two patrol vessels were sighted which proceeded toward the sailing ship."[39] It was the presence of these two chasers that led Dröscher to make the decision to submerge and remain hidden temporarily. Once he observed the two sub chasers split up and begin searching in the wrong area (they were actually putting themselves into positions to utilize their hydrophones), he ordered *U-117* back to the surface and headed in a southeasterly direction, away from the engagement. *U-117*'s time spent traveling on the surface, however, would be extremely brief, since just a few hours later, the seaplane HS-2L A-1859 arrived on the scene and quickly spotted her making her escape. The Germans too noticed the inbound seaplane and immediately sounded the enemy aircraft alarm, initiating a crash dive, but it was already too late. By 1312, the American patrols were back on their scent, and bombs and depth charges soon began raining down on them.

The first to make an attack was the seaplane, which reportedly dropped her bombs within 75 feet of the U-boat. Like the bombs dropped on *U-156* off Cape Cod the previous month, they must also have been duds or, as Oberingenieur Beckmann later suggested in his memoir, had an incorrect depth setting that caused them to explode on the surface. Had they actually fallen and detonated within 75 feet of the U-boat as was claimed, they would have been close enough to have seriously damaged, if not sunk, *U-117*. The sub chasers *SC-73* and *SC-71* were next in making a pass. After following A-1859 to *U-117*'s approximate location, where the seaplane fired her machine gun into the water to mark the submarine's position, both chasers began dropping their depth charges over an area where the commander of *SC-73* claimed that "bubbles were observed."[40] As it turned out, this was precisely were *U-117* was hiding.

Below the surface, Dröscher was completely incredulous as to how his submarine could have been spotted. Believing he was being attacked only by the single seaplane, he noted,

> Aerial bombs dropped. Apparently, the U-boat can be observed closely by the aircraft. Current depth about 25 m. One after the other, 9 bombs fall in an interval of 50 minutes, each time closer. How it recognized the boat is difficult to determine. Either from the trace of oil or compressed air bubbles or the gray exterior paintwork that has been lightly washed by the sea.[41]

The bubbles, being the true cause of his discovery, were already a known issue to Dröscher. Earlier that week, he noted in his war diary that the "compressed air lines on the upper deck are leaking; bubbles can be seen through the periscope when traveling underwater."[42] It must be assumed that since the lines had not yet been repaired in the three days leading up to his current situation, he felt they were a low priority in comparison to the other major issues with his U-boat; namely, the massive fuel leaks. These defects, rather paradoxically, proved to be his salvation.

Just as with *U-140* and USS *Stringham*, *U-117*'s flaws were deemed to be sufficient evidence by the sub chasers and seaplane that the U-boat had been sunk. Ens. James Clarke of *SC-73* noted that he continuously observed the bubbles for a half hour before dropping a buoy on the spot and heading toward USS *Kingfisher*. The commander of *SC-71*, C. Raymond Shaw, reinspected this position an hour after the initial bombardment and, realizing that bubbles continued to rise to the surface, then proceeded toward the *Five Fathom* lightship to begin a 20-mile radius patrol along with *SC-144* and the late arrival *SC-210*. It was only after this search came up fruitless that they left the area and headed home. Certainly, a lack of experience on the part of the sub chaser commanders may have played a role in allowing *U-117* to escape, though, unlike Kophamel, Dröscher doesn't allude to this or deride them in his log. Given Dröscher's next courses of action that day, he was seemingly more accepting of the fact that he had been soundly beaten. Although *U-117* obviously survived the bombardment, so did the *William Green* and the other vessels within Delaware Bay that day, marking another partial victory for the US Navy.

In a perfect example of what could be achieved when adequate patrol craft were given timely and accurate information about a U-boat's presence, the US Navy prevented further sinkings that day by forcing *U-117* below the surface for nearly seven hours—allowing the vulnerable surface traffic to escape. Indeed, when *U-117* finally popped back up at 1900, she immediately set a course to lay down her second minefield near Fenwick Island, Delaware. Much to the consternation of his superiors after the patrol, Dröscher would make no attempt at engaging any more vessels that evening, despite spotting two well-lit and unescorted steamers at 2130 and 2330, respectively.

U-117, pictured as a prize after the war, being escorted into an American harbor by *SC-415*. Courtesy of Deutsches U-Boot-Museum

Given the success of the sub chasers that day, CNO Benson's later advisories to the commanders of the 1st–7th Naval Districts on August 16 appear to be counterproductive. After concluding that German U-boat activities would continue off the American coast, at a minimum through the upcoming winter, he reassessed the role of domestic patrol craft, specifically American submarines and sub chasers. Instead of learning from the lessons of the fourteenth, where only half of the available craft that intercepted the *William Green*'s "allo" message were able to respond to the call, he further restricted how domestic patrols could operate.

First, he acknowledged that the submarines available for domestic patrols were lacking in number, and, still believing Sims's earlier guidance that the best countermeasures for U-boats were other submarines, ordered them to guard areas away from seaplane patrols. This made sense in a way, since it extended the coverage of American patrols while at the same time reduced the chances of an American submarine failing prey to friendly fire. However, his proviso that "aircraft, surface hunting units and other surface patrol or scouting craft must not be sent on anti-submarine missions into areas known to be occupied by our own submarines"[43] essentially tied the hands of the only craft that had actually engaged enemy submarines in US waters up to that point.

The domestic sub chasers were further restrained by Benson's continued insistence on concentrating them in hunter squadrons. Once again ignoring the fact that just two chasers effectively ended *U-117*'s assault on the fourteenth (simply by being lucky enough to be the closest of four sub chasers to reach the area and respond to the call for help), he advised,

> In view of the lack of special equipment and special training of some submarine chasers assigned to Naval Districts, and the necessity of using these vessels at certain places for escort work, etc., it is not considered practicable, at present, for the Naval Districts to efficiently patrol all those areas adjacent to the coast, with the submarine chasers available for that purpose.
>
> The Department has therefore organized three special hunting squadrons of submarine chasers. Each squadron is composed of a certain number of submarine chaser hunting groups and a vessel of the cruiser or destroyer type, with sufficient gunpower to back up the operations of the submarine chasers and maintain the control of the surface. . . . The first squadron to operate on the Atlantic Coast to the northward of latitude 40° north; the second squadron to operate on the Atlantic Coast between the latitudes 30° north and 40° north; the third squadron to operate in waters to the southward of latitude 30° north.[44]

By concentrating the additional sub chasers into three operational zones, Benson essentially stripped them of their offensive capabilities. Given their numerical superiority over the domestic submarine and destroyer forces, they were ideally suited to be spread out along the coastline in small groups, patrolling and listening for enemy submarines. In that role they would be the first to warn of a U-boat's presence and the first to engage, pinning the U-boat while more-powerful warships traveled to the area. By assigning them to a more reactive role, they would be forced to respond in a group that may or may not be near the location of a U-boat.

Additionally, their speed disadvantage would be a handicap to the cruiser or destroyer in their pursuit squadron. With an actual top speed of 14–16 knots (nearly half as fast as the early Bainbridge-class destroyers and just about as quick as a U-boat traveling on the surface), their presence would dramatically slow the hunting group's response time when an "allo" or SOS signal was received, guaranteeing that the U-boat would already be gone by the time they arrived. The relative failure of sub chasers to make a meaningful impact on the U-boat war off North America from this point onward is proof of the failed tactic. Indeed, as *U-117* continued her southerly course to sow her remaining mines, she encountered very little in the way of resistance.

At 0230 on August 15, *U-117* found herself just over 20 miles southeast of Fenwick Island, Delaware, and began depositing her mines precisely where the observed steamers from the previous night had passed. In total, seven mines were thrown between 38°15' N, 74°42.5' W and 38°16' N, 74°46' W, a line stretching approximately 3 nm. Deciding not to spend any time waiting for any vessels to approach the area, Dröscher proceeded farther south toward his third minefield location. On the way he happened across a four-masted, motorized schooner, but realizing it was on the same course as *U-117*, he decided to wait until he dropped his next set of mines before making an attack.

Oberingenieur Beckmann provides some insight as to why *U-117*, being a cruiser-minelayer, was more hesitant to make attacks while prepped for minelaying than other U-cruisers. Because the U-151-class submarines relied on Teka mines to be thrown from the deck or launched through torpedo tubes, the UE II–class minelayers had a much more involved process, involving variables that von Nostitz and Feldt never had to deal with. Beckmann recalled,

> Now imagine two large, very long tubes aft in the boat, one on the starboard side and one on the port side, which can each hold three mines at the same time. There goes a drudgery and a drill in the back of the mine room with an elevator and lifting platform, where you can have your clever friends as spectators or annoyances if you're supposed to keep the boat at an even depth.
>
> As with the torpedo armament, we have a hatch on the inside and a large slide on the outside of each tube. The ejection of the three mines loaded into the tubes is not carried out with compressed air, but mechanically using gears and racks, which are located on the mine's base. Display devices inside the boat clearly show whether the "egg" has been properly dispersed.

The weight and trim phenomena and their regulation proceed exactly as in torpedo firing. They only have a greater effect on the continued "laying of eggs," so that the chief engineer in the central command post has his hands full. Sometimes it looks funny when the boat is tilted forwards or aft with unequal weight and many hands are hanging on the deck frames so that their corresponding legs don't slip.

The tragic comedy usually takes place in sea depths of 30 to 60 m and at a sailing depth of 20 m. It is of immense importance that one knows mathematically precisely where the mine barrier is located, where one threw the first mine, which direction the barrier is going and where the last mine is waiting for the untender awakening from its sweet slumber.[45]

The laborious task described by *U-117*'s chief engineer would be completed by 0630 that day, with an additional eight mines being planted near the *Winter Quarter* lightship off Virginia, in a line between 37°44.7' N, 74°54.3' W and 37°44.7' N, 74°57' W (just over 2 nm). With his primary task for the day now completed, Kapitänleutnant Dröscher then turned his attention to the schooner at 0745.

The schooner in question was the *Madrugada*, transporting 1,000 tons of cement and other general cargo from New York City to Santos, Brazil. In a clear indication that Dröscher had been spooked by the previous day's depth charge bombardment, he ordered the unarmed vessel to be stopped and sunk by using his deck guns, without allowing any time for the crew aboard to gather their belongings and take to lifeboats. He noted that the ship was already on fire and sinking within a half hour of the first shot being fired. This was confirmed by the schooner's captain, Frederick Rouse, who reported that three shots had been fired over his ship from *U-117* by the time he was able to stop his engines, and then two more were quickly fired into it before he and his crew could take to their boats. No signal to stop or abandon ship was ever received from *U-117*.

Although he recalled that the Germans didn't appear to be firing at their lifeboats, they continued to lay shells into the schooner, with a total of ten being fired before the ship began to burn and sink. The *Madrugada*'s radio operator, a navy electrician named Frederick Cook, was the only man who didn't abandon ship immediately. Instead, he remained on board sending out an SOS transmission prior to jumping overboard when the ship began to go down. While his actions are mentioned in American sources, the same sources claim that his calls went unanswered, since he and his other crew members weren't rescued for another four hours by a passing steamer. *U-117*'s war diary indicates that this may not have been the case.

At about 0830, just as Dröscher spotted a steamer on a northerly course that was in a position he wouldn't be able to attack, he mentioned that SOS signals were intercepted that were believed to be coming from the *Winter Quarter* lightship. These were likely the transmissions being sent by Fred Cook aboard the *Madrugada*, but if not, they were an indication that his message had been received and was being relayed. Although no immediate signs of a US Navy response were observed, by 1115 a naval seaplane arrived just as *U-117* was preparing to sink an unidentified, three-masted, fully rigged ship. It was at this point that Dröscher was forced to break off the attack and dive to avoid being bombed. He would spend the next two hours and forty minutes submerged before coming back to the surface and setting a course for Cape Hatteras—the location of his final minefield.

When Dröscher arrived off the Outer Banks at 0630 the next day, he observed his first convoy since his last, nearly disastrous encounter on August 8. Although *U-117* had already been prepped for minelaying, for once Dröscher seemed prepared to put his primary objective on the back burner. He would spend the next six hours stalking the convoy, alternating between the surface and periscope depth in an attempt to come into striking range with the nine unescorted vessels that were running an "irregular course." Despite his best efforts, he would ultimately give up, concluding that the distance was too great and that he would instead proceed submerged to the Wimble Shoals light buoy in order to lay down a line of nine mines between 35°36' N, 75°18' W and 35°36' N, 75°20.6' W.

While this was certainly a disappointment, just hours later his luck would dramatically change. The SS *Mirlo*, a 6,978 GRT British tanker en route from New Orleans to London with a belly full of gasoline (and a small cargo of kerosene), was about to wander directly in the path of *U-117*. The course of events, according to Dröscher's war diary, proceeded as follows:

1330: Wimble Shoals light buoy in sight.

1445: Started launching mines. During the minelaying, a steamer came into sight, distance 4 nm bearing 200°, which steered on a northerly course along the coast, passing through the gap between the previously laid mines and the light buoy. Since I can move the mine barrage in geographical latitude without prejudice to its effect, I decide to interrupt mine launching for a short time and attack the steamer first. The distance to the buoy was about 1.5 nm. A second steamer comes into view, steering from the north, distance 4 nm bearing 330°. Their courses intersect in front of my bow, but I decide to attack the steamer that I saw first. Laden tanker about 2,500 t [a gross underestimation of tonnage], fantasy painting; of its two masts, one painted very light, the other painted entirely black. This type of coating makes it very difficult to determine the course and has been observed several times, but not properly recognized.

1530: Torpedo Shot–Hit (G6AV*). Tube 1, depth setting 3 m, shooting distance 400 m. The steamer immediately catches fire. The second steamer sighted is Dutch with neutral insignias. After the attack held off a little to the south—continued mine throwing in the direction of the light buoy. Navigated to a depth of 20 m to avoid any aircraft in the shallow water.

1730: At periscope depth. Steamer still burns with extraordinary smoke. At a distance of approx. 2 nm, a second steamer is burning with much[-]heavier smoke. No detonation was heard, a second tanker must have struck a mine thrown before the first tanker. A number of smaller steamers nearby.[46]

Dröscher's version of the sinking is significant for a number of reasons; namely, that the *Mirlo* avoided his first cluster of mines and was sunk by a torpedo, that the Germans had finally figured out why Allied ships were painted so fantastically, and that another vessel was believed to have sunk shortly thereafter.

Capt. William Roose Williams of the *Mirlo* would have especially liked to see the German log, since he seemed to be the only one convinced of his ship's true fate. The US Navy, and much of the immediate postwar texts surrounding the U-boat war, placed the onus of the sinking on a German mine. After all, no torpedo wake (or U-boat) had been observed in the vicinity by Williams or any of the nine steamers that witnessed the event, and *U-117*'s minefield had been conveniently discovered the following day. Even presented with those facts, the British captain was adamant not only that his ship was struck aft on the starboard side by a torpedo, but that a second followed immediately (in actuality, this was his flammable cargo igniting)—destroying the ship's dynamos, engines, telegraph, and wireless apparatus. He further justified his theory by noting that his ship, unlike USS *San Diego*, had been towing "otter" paravanes since entering the open Atlantic from the Gulf of Mexico, making the loss of the ship by mine significantly less probable. Whatever frustration he may have borne arguing his case to naval authorities, however, unquestionably paled in comparison to the thankfulness he felt that he and 113 of the 123 total crew members aboard the tanker survived.[47]

This in and of itself was miraculous. As Dröscher's log indicated, he believed that a second ship was sinking nearby the *Mirlo*, even though he didn't hear another detonation. This other burning hulk was the *Mirlo* itself, having split in two due to the violent explosions emanating from her hazardous cargo. It was only through the quick action taken by the US Coast Guard Life Saving Station 179 (under the leadership of Capt. John Allen Midgett, who braved the rough sea alight with burning petroleum to rescue the stricken sailors) that there were so few casualties. In fact, six more may have died had they not been pulled from the water when their lifeboat capsized.

As Leroy Midgett, who had initially been on watch duty at the station that morning, recalled in 1959: "'Captain Johnny' and his men snatched six exhausted, burned, and blackened sailors from the jaws of death. The heat from the fire was so intense that it scorched and blistered the paint on the rescue boat. It was 'hot country.'"[48] These men had survived by remaining underwater, away from the flames, until they could no longer hold their breath, at which point they returned to the surface and then quickly retreated below. The only nine deaths of the incident originated from the same capsized lifeboat, with those crew members being assumed to have drowned.

Even with the horrific scene presenting itself through his periscope lens, Dröscher still wanted to continue with his assault. Just twenty minutes after observing what he believed were two flaming wrecks on the horizon, and still at periscope depth, he spotted another steamer approaching from the south, some 7 nm distant. Although he intended to make another torpedo strike, an approaching plane was spotted that forced him to abandon the chase and dive deeper to a depth of 30 m. Apparently, he was still reeling from the seaplane attack two days prior. When *U-117* resurfaced just under two hours later, Dröscher, much like Kophamel, reassessed his patrol, taking into account his objectives and the poor state of his U-boat. He noted,

> 1930: Surfaced. Proceeded north above water. The two steamers are still burning. Now that the mining task has been carried out, the intention at Cape Hatteras is to conduct a trade war off the Chesapeake and Delaware Bays and then to start the retreat home. The observations of the last few days also give reason to expect a very good success. However, the overview of the fuel oil inventory does not permit this plan. Only 107 cbm of the total stock of 224 cbm fuel oil are still available. Therefore, there is only a very small reserve because the route via Cape Race is about 400 nm shorter than the outward march. Thus, I have made up my mind to head back. It is also difficult to overlook the extent of the fuel oil loss to be expected in the end. Furthermore, diving tanks III and VI can no longer be blown out because of their crushed vents, with the result that the boat lies too low and therefore loses speed.
>
> Retreat started.[49]

Also, as with Kophamel, the northerly change of course did not necessarily imply that Dröscher would remain nonconfrontational. Less than twenty-four hours later, *U-117* was back on the attack.

The crew of *U-117*. *Courtesy of Deutsches U-Boot-Museum*

On the morning of August 17, just as Kophamel was making his decision to plot a course for home due to *U-140*'s heavy loss of fuel, Dröscher and *U-117* were now situated about 150 mi. / 241 km east of Norfolk, Virginia, and almost exactly 350 mi. / 563 km west of *U-140*'s location. Apparently trying to coordinate plans with his sister U-boat, Dröscher made repeated calls for *U-140* throughout the night; however, all went unanswered. As a result, both commanders would be simultaneously heading toward Nantucket to begin their homeward journeys, completely unaware of each other's intentions. As *U-117* continued northward, Dröscher decided to stop the first vessel he saw that morning, a four-masted, Norwegian barque.

This was the 2,846 GRT *Nordhav*, transporting linseed from Buenos Aires to New York City. Because she was flying neutral colors, unlike the American *Madrugada* days prior, the barque would have to be stopped and inspected prior to being sunk. Her captain, Sven Marcussen, was particularly vague in describing the encounter to US intelligence after being rescued by the battleship USS *Kearsarge* (BB-5) over a day later. According to the Norwegian captain, the *Nordhav* was stopped at 0700 by three warning shots, at which point he and twelve crew members took to a rowboat and headed toward *U-117* with the ship's papers. When the Germans realized that his cargo consisted entirely of linseed, which was considered contraband, they explained that the vessel would have to be sunk. He then noted that he and his crew returned to the barque, along with a German boarding party of four men who then prepped the vessel with *Sprengpatronen*, hanging them over the ship's sides. Once the bombs were placed, the entire party then returned to *U-117*, where Capt. Marcussen and eight of his crewmen were ordered below. For reasons he didn't elaborate on, they were kept there for nearly four hours, after which they came to the deck to observe their ship already in the process of sinking. This four-hour internment leaves much to the imagination, and *U-117*'s war diary offers no help in explaining it.

In fact, Dröscher's log doesn't mention any interaction with the captain or his crew and simply notes that "as linseed is contraband and the entire cargo consists of it, the Norwegian barque is subject to destruction."[50] The time of sinking was recorded as being 1230 that afternoon, thus confirming, but not elucidating on, the large delay in completing a job that should have taken no longer than a half hour. Oberingenieur Beckmann once again helps fill in the details. He claimed that the missing time was spent looting the ship of her cargo, stating,

> We took 300 sacks of the best linseed from the load to take home with us for oil production. It was quite an extensive job, and if we had known that later the "Central Purchasing Company" would confiscate the whole swindle without us ever seeing or hearing anything about it again, we probably wouldn't have been half as tormented. A two-hundred-weight sack fell through the tower hatch on my skull in such a way that I saw lightning and stars everywhere![51]

He would also go on to assert that while Capt. Marcussen was aboard *U-117*, most of his Norwegian crew was left on the *Nordhav*, along with the German boarding party offloading the sacks of linseed. According to his version of the events, the Norwegians took the opportunity to raid the ship's alcohol stores, resulting in one of the drunken crew members severely injuring his foot with a broken bottle and having to be taken to *U-117* so the submarine's doctor could stitch and bandage the wound. This in itself resulted in further drama (involving the drunken Norwegian insisting on giving the German doctor a gift) that contributed to the long interval that elapsed. If Beckmann's account is true, it can certainly be understood why Capt. Marcussen would have omitted those details from his testimony, but it does little in explaining Dröscher's silence.

In the case of the latter, his absentmindedness may be attributed to the fact that he placed much more importance on recording in his war diary the strange behavior of two other vessels observed during that same period. These mysterious vessels, a three-masted schooner and a "motorized vessel," had been approaching *U-117* very slowly since the first warning shots were fired at the *Nordhav*. What was felt to be unusual by Dröscher and his officers was that the schooner did not appear to have its sails positioned correctly for utilizing the wind and instead appeared to be "walking around in place." Additionally, the motorized vessel appeared to constantly seek cover behind the larger schooner, continually going in and out of view. According to Dröscher's now much more descriptive log,

> Next to this, but at a greater distance, a second vessel comes into view, which can't be made out at this point. However, this vessel is approaching so quickly that it cannot be a sailing vessel, as was initially assumed. Then it disappears behind the three-masted schooner and then all of a sudden, with a very high speed, the front of the bow [Dröscher uses the German term *Bugwelle*, literally "bow wave," which describes the front, pointed shape of a ship's bow] shoots out along with two thin masts, one of which seems to be flying a flag. Then the masts suddenly disappear, and the vehicle is suddenly no longer visible. Submerged, went to 30 m. It is not clear what type of vessel this was. The previous exercise with the sails of the three-masted schooner and the sudden appearance of the fast vessel, however, make a submarine trap seem likely. Whether vessel is a submarine hunter or another submarine can't be determined. Noise reception revealed nothing as the receiver is not completely in order. With this uncertainty, a surface attack is avoided. The schooner (approx. 400 t) is too small for an underwater attack. After about half an hour, went to periscope depth, only the sailing ship can be observed at a great distance.[52]

While Capt. Marcussen of the *Nordhav* makes no mention of seeing any other ships in his vicinity (he was likely preoccupied with abandoning his ship), both *U-117*'s log and Beckmann's postwar account clearly describe the same incident unfolding. Despite the fact that American postwar sources do not record any decoy vessels making any positive U-boat sightings, the men aboard *U-117* correctly identified (and avoided) an American U-boat trap in the form of the decoy ship USS *Helvetia* (SP-3096) in the process of towing the coastal submarine *E-2*.

Unlike the British Q-ships, which were designed to fight off U-boats on their own, CNO Benson's ingenious deception relied on a decoy ship luring a U-boat toward it, while a towed submarine would do the attacking.

In this case, the bait was *Helvetia*, a 157.5-foot, 499-ton, three-masted schooner that had previously been employed as a civilian vessel. In July 1918, she was bought by the Navy and refurbished with listening devices, a radio, and a cargo hold full of small arms. Her crew, consisting of naval seamen, like their British counterparts, dressed the part of ordinary sailors and mostly remained hidden below deck.

The Navy assumed that like other sailing ships, USS *Helvetia* was too small to waste a torpedo on (confirmed by Dröscher's log, though it had not stopped him previously) and would have to be stopped, boarded, and sunk with explosives like so many other schooners sunk earlier that summer. It would be at this point that the hidden crew would pounce on the German boarding party, while the submerged submarine being towed would then be utilized in sinking the immobile U-boat. It was a clever plan, but there were numerous pitfalls; namely, that the submarine in tow had to remain out of sight for the trap to work, and when submerged its radio couldn't communicate with the mother ship. If the American submarine wanted to know what was going on, she'd have to return to the surface.

USS *Helvetia* was one of three American "Q" ships operating in American waters that summer, but the only one of two operating off Norfolk that was three masted. The others, USS *Robert H. McCurdy* (SP-3157) and USS *Charles Whittemore* (ID-3232), were both larger and four masted, with the latter being assigned to the 2nd Naval District and operating off New England. Most often these ships were spotted by merchant vessels, who believed they were being towed by U-boats as traps instead of the other way around. Up to this point, none were thought to have come into contact with an enemy U-boat.

A photo of USS *Helvetia* taken from the deck of the submarine *E-2*, in tow. *NH 78920, courtesy of the Naval History & Heritage Command*

Nevertheless, USS *Helvetia* was indeed spotted by the officers of *U-117*, who recognized her true nature and, after resurfacing that evening, opted to leave her be and continue on their way. For her part, *Helvetia* also saw *U-117* and had ordered *E-2* to submerge and attack, but after *U-117* went below the surface and "was not seen again,"[53] the U-boat trap was never fully executed—*Helvetia* simply sailed onward, not even stopping to take on the survivors of the *Nordhav* (which were noted as being observed in her log).

Over the next three days, both Dröscher and Kophamel would make various attempts at engaging additional vessels on their respective northerly courses. Unfortunately, many had to be broken off due to the poor state of their U-boats.

In the case of *U-140*, an attack on a camouflaged, armed steamer had to be abandoned on the eighteenth just over 400 mi. / 644 km off Delaware due to the vessel's superior speed. Two days later, and now some 350 mi. / 563 km east of Long Island, New York, a fire started on the submarine, which ended an underwater pursuit of an unidentified French steamer. Apparently, while *U-140* was running her electric motors at maximum speed to catch up with the quick steamer, one of the batteries heated up and ignited, resulting in flames that then spread to the U-boat's stock of provisions. Kophamel noted that the amount of smoke was "disturbing," and ordered the bulkheads to be closed while his crew prepared to fight the fire. Amazingly, once the fire was put out, the battery was found to be undamaged; however, in a big blow to Kophamel's sunken-tonnage record, the vessel was able to escape in the process. According to *U-140*'s log, the ship was believed to be either the *Espagne*, which Lloyd's Register noted as being a massive 11,115 GRT, or the *Flandre*, which was also quite large at 8,503 GRT.

Meanwhile, a day earlier and couple of hundred miles west, *U-117*'s problems with her diesel engines' clutches not disengaging resurfaced during the pursuit of an unidentified steamer off the coast of Delaware. This occurred just as *U-117* was attempting to dive to attack and avoid detection. Although the clutches were eventually freed, the steamer had spotted *U-117* during her delay in submerging and was able to escape. Rough seas prevented Dröscher from making any further attempts at sinking the vessel that morning. Additional issues would follow him into the next day.

On August 20, now about 200 mi. / 322 km east of Cape May, New Jersey, *U-117* initiated a failed surface attack on the 5,310-ton, well-armed Italian steamer *Ansaldo III*. In what turned out to be a nearly three-hour artillery duel between the two vessels, *U-117* (although being completely unscathed in the battle) was able to damage only the aft gun of the steamer, subsequently wounding three Italian sailors in the process. As Dröscher explained in his log,

The steamer shoots back from three guns. Their positions are aft, behind the bridge, and the stern. The two front guns are medium caliber, the rear gun is a light caliber. At times the steamer's middle and aft guns make marked impacts [in the water]. They fall 300 m or more short, although they are placed well laterally. The boat [*U-117*] had a constant list, a defect that had already appeared in the previous artillery battles. This deficiency could only be remedied for a short time by frequent blowing out, flooding and counter-flooding [the dive tanks]. The list also changed frequently. This circumstance influenced the shooting—as in the past—considerably. Due to the irregular canting of the gun's trunnions, shots often lay sideways, so that these were out of the question for observation. Battle was conducted at an average of 120 hm. Shorter distance sought, but steamer continues to travel at about 12 knots. A direct hit put the aft gun out of action. A well-placed shot with double detonation observed. After about 100 shots, a break had to be taken because all the live shells had been fired and new shells had to be armed. During the pause that has occurred, the steamer continues at a higher speed, but our boat follows without coming much closer. Distance has since increased. Pursued with "maximum power" for a while but gave up the pursuit because there was little prospect of catching up with the steamer and because of the lack of fuel.[54]

The appearance of a sub chaser on the horizon later that evening spoiled any further offensive plans for *U-117* that day. Nevertheless, going into the morning of the twenty-first, both *U-117* and *U-140* remained undeterred in waging their *Handelskrieg* as they continued toward New England.

In the case of the former, the day elapsed from one frustration to another. At 0615, an attempt at a large, four-stacked steamer had to be abandoned because it was too far away to engage. Hours later, another steamer, the 4,343 GRT *Thespis* from Manchester, was spotted well within *U-117*'s attacking radius, but the single G6AV* torpedo fired from the minelayer had a malfunction and, after changing course twice, ultimately missed its target. According to the statements given by the *Thespis*'s crew, even with the gyroscope failure, the torpedo avoided the ship by a margin of only 20 yards.[55] They would also claim that *U-117* popped back up shortly thereafter and engaged in a futile deck gun battle for about a half hour, wherein the *Thespis* was able to speed away. This is not corroborated in any German sources. While Beckmann seemed to have forgotten the day's events entirely, Dröscher indicated in his log that he observed the steamer's deck gun at periscope depth but made no attempt at dueling with it. Instead, he waited just over three hours before returning to the surface, only to be forced back down by a naval seaplane at 1320. *U-117* wouldn't reemerge from hiding until 1600 that day.

When smoke clouds from a lone steamer were observed on the horizon at 1615, it appeared that Dröscher was finally about to secure a victory that day; however, this too would merely lead to further disappointment. After carefully positioning himself for another submerged attack, just as the order to launch a torpedo was about to be given, the vessel was identified as being Swedish, with a "large neutral insignia on the ship's side."[56] This was the last straw. Giving the command to resurface for the third time in nearly as many hours, Dröscher ordered the vessel to be halted with warning shots so it could be inspected. He was looking for any reason to send the neutral vessel to the ocean floor, and the unknowing Swedish captain opposite him nearly gave him one.

Although Dröscher's war diary entry that day is written very matter-of-factly and devoid of emotions, Capt. Eric Risberg, of the *Algeria*, recalled encountering a very irritable German commander, bent on destroying his ship. Upon stopping his vessel after seeing the first warning shot fall 200 yards off the port beam, Risberg observed *U-117* raising letter signals reading "T.A.R," to which he replied, "I can see your letters but cannot make out the meaning."[57] The German response to his reply arrived in the form of another warning shot, prompting the Swedish captain to take to his boat and proceed toward *U-117* with his papers. According to Risberg's statement to naval intelligence:

> When he approached the submarine he was told to go up on the conning tower, and when he got on the conning tower the commander first said to him, "Why did you not lower a boat at once when you saw the submarine; your actions were not those of a neutral." The captain answered, "You were showing no flag, and it not being the first submarine I have seen and being so close to American waters, I assumed it to be an American submarine." He then asked where the captain was bound. He replied to Gothenburg to Sandy Hook for orders.
>
> He then took the *Algeria*'s log and examined it, and when he found that she had been operating on the United States coast, he said that was the "end." The captain replied, "You should not be guided by what I have been doing in the past but by what I am doing in the present." The chief officer of the submarine said to the captain of the submarine that the captain of the *Algeria* was correct; that they had nothing to do with what he had been doing before. At this point several of the officers of the submarine joined in the conversation, all of which was in German, and took the side of the chief officer, stating among other things that if they sank the *Algeria* the German Government would have to pay for it.[58]

This impromptu conference lasted the better part of an hour and resulted in the Germans allowing the ship to go free. Apparently Dröscher conceded to his own officers, who, despite Risberg advising that he was going to Sandy Hook "for orders," believed a contrary excuse given by Risberg, which claimed that he was traveling to the United States only to pick up foodstuffs for his native Sweden.[59] Dröscher, quite expectedly, remained skeptical.

Upon allowing the *Algeria* to depart, Dröscher insisted on Risberg giving his word of honor that he was not chartered by the US Shipping Board—leaving him with the warning that if he were caught again, he would be sunk. When the question "You would not sink us without warning, would you?" was posed by one of the *Algeria*'s officers, Dröscher was reported to have cynically replied, "Don't be so sure of that—best not take any chances."[60] The final entry in the U-boat's war diary for the day rather dejectedly read that while the steamer would assuredly make stops at numerous American ports, she had to be dismissed since *U-117* lacked the authority to sink her. Meanwhile, 210 mi. / 338 km east of *U-117*, *U-140* was having somewhat better results on her hunt.

Kophamel's day began early on the twenty-first and also appeared to be setting off on the wrong foot. Like Dröscher, at 0150, his first attempt at engaging a vessel had to be broken off because *U-140* was simply too slow to catch up with the much-faster unidentified steamer. Then at 0410, Fortune delivered a gift right into *U-140*'s path in the form of a 7,523 GRT British cargo ship, the *Diomed*.

The *Diomed* was just one of an eight-ship convoy of transports traveling back to the United States from Liverpool in ballast. She had the unfortunate luck of being spotted by *U-140* at 40°40' N, 65°14' W (about 460 mi. / 740 km from New York City), just days after the convoy had broken up. It should be noted that the convoy's eight initial destroyer escorts abandoned it some 330 miles off the coast of Portugal. In lieu of American warships being assigned on the other side of the Atlantic to resume escorting duties, each vessel in the convoy had been instructed to sail to their destinations independently, using a preassigned route. Kophamel, aware that she was armed, at first endeavored to make a submerged torpedo attack but quickly abandoned that plan after realizing his maximum underwater speed was once again completely inadequate to remain in contact with the target. Consequently, he decided to surface and utilize his twin 15 cm guns against what he believed was a single, British 10 cm gun (in actuality a 4.7-inch / 12 cm gun) from a range of about 5 km.

According to the *Diomed*'s chief officer, Alfred E. Batt, *U-140* had been spotted on the horizon when Kophamel came to the surface, but the British officer, not yet knowing if it was an enemy U-boat or an American submarine or torpedo boat, ordered his gunners to stand by until positive confirmation could be made. This was a fatal error, since it allowed *U-140* to take the initiative in opening fire. Once *U-140* began shelling the *Diomed*, the splashes in the water from her missed shots completely obstructed the British gunners' view, making sighting in the U-Kreuzer nearly impossible. Nonetheless, the British fired back the best they could, although nothing would land close to the raider. Meanwhile, *U-140* continued to home in on her target, and by her fourth shot, which struck the ship's starboard quarters, she found her range and began hitting more-critical areas on the ship. Batt noted that after the *Diomed* had fired twelve shots, one of *U-140*'s "carried away" the steam line connected to the ship's steering gear, disabling it and subsequently blocking access to the ammunition locker, thus inhibiting any return fire. In order to prevent any further loss of life (two sailors had already been killed and an additional twelve had been wounded by shellfire, with the ship's boilers exploding), the ship was then abandoned.

Prior to sending the final blows into the *Diomed*, Kophamel was reported to have ordered his U-boat toward the steamer's lifeboats to inquire if any of the ship's wounded needed treatment from his surgeon. This offer fell on deaf ears, since the British officers on the launches believed it was just a trick to get them to reveal themselves so they could be taken prisoner (a somewhat odd concern, since two-thirds of the ship's crew were Chinese). Although *U-140*'s Belgian prisoner, Rene Bastin, would later make the claim that "one man was taken on board the *U-140* and had a large 'No. 6' chalked on his back,"[61] Kophamel never made a note in his log of any medical services being provided or additional prisoners being taken on board. Apparently, the only prisoners he was interested in taking on were men like Bastin, who enthusiastically gave themselves up and were eager to collaborate with the Germans. With no British officers fitting that description, *U-140* instead quickly sank the *Diomed* with four shots from her 15 cm guns and then sped away, since a small craft, believed to be a sub chaser, was observed on the horizon at 0850. Kophamel bemoaned, "Because the oil trail would be spotted and reported, the boat should be avoided."[62]

After losing the purported patrol craft, *U-140* spotted a quick-traveling, three-masted steamer at 1057 but made no further attempts on attacking any vessels for the day, again because of *U-140*'s significant fuel leaks. Following the sinking of the *Diomed* that morning, Kophamel calculated that *U-140* lost 5 m^3 of diesel in that attack alone, emptying another of his fuel bunkers and bringing his total fuel loss to 40 cbm. When he was presented with the choice of chasing the second steamer that day, he resigned himself to the fact that "no more oil can be used without a chance of success."[63] Additionally, he could afford no changes to his current course back home—any future vessels he would attack would have to lie in his path. Not surprisingly, the *Diomed* would be Kophamel's final victory of the patrol, but not from a lack of trying.

In the weeks that followed the sinking of the *Diomed*, Kophamel encountered no fewer than eight worthwhile targets, some of which were attacked, but all were unable to be pursued to an end because of his fuel situation. The most notable of these contacts were the *Pleiades* on August 22, a 5,000-ton unidentified steamer on the twenty-fourth, and *Frank H. Buck* (wrongly attributed to *U-155* in nearly all other publications) on September 1.

Crew on the deck of a U-cruiser, with one of the 15 cm deck guns clearly visible. *Author's collection*

In the case of the 3,753 GRT American cargo ship, *Pleiades* (en route from Le Havre to New York), *U-140* opened fired upon on her at distance at 39°43' N, 63°11' W (about 450 mi. / 725 km east-southeast of Providence, Rhode Island). In a battle that lasted only fifteen minutes, the two vessels fought a very brief artillery duel, with neither registering any hits on the other. Although the first officer of the *Pleiades* claimed that *U-140* broke off the attack because the shots from his 4-inch/40-caliber stern gun were so well placed, Kophamel instead blamed his retiring on his poor positioning. He noted that while *U-140* was in the moonlight, the *Pleiades* was on the dark horizon, and the shots from his deck guns could no longer be observed.

The story was much the same with the 6,077 GRT American tanker *Frank H. Buck*, encountered 720 mi. / 1,159 km east of St. John's, Newfoundland, at 45°50' N, 37°32' W. Although this battle lasted ten minutes longer than that with the *Pleiades*, rough seas combined with the tanker's superior speed meant that Kophamel once again had to break off the battle and continue eastward toward home. Comically, the steamer's captain reported to the Navy that his vessel had sunk *U-140*, claiming, "Two shots were observed to have hit the submarine, which sank after a terrific explosion."[64]

The best chance that *U-140* had for adding another ship to her tonnage totals was the unidentified steamer engaged on August 24—it was also a vessel that Kophamel was bemused not to have sunk. After firing a single torpedo from a distance of only 700 m, he appeared to be grasping at straws as to why it missed. According to his log,

> Missed shot cannot be explained because the attack was very easy. Even with a rough estimate of the target data, a hit should still have been achieved. It must be assumed that the ocean swells caused changes in depth and that the steamer was undershot. . . . I cannot extend the pursuit to the west until dawn because of lack of oil.[65]

The unremitting fuel leakages would prove to be the bane of Kophamel's existence for the remainder of his cruise. He would repeatedly stress over lost amounts and took pains to calculate how much fuel remained and how it could be economized into getting him back home safely. A perfect example of this was on August 27, when Kophamel recorded the following:

> With the emptying of another bunker, a significant oil loss turns out again. From the contents of this 27 cbm bunker alone 7.5 cbm were missing. The total loss is now 47.6 cbm.
> The lowest speed is used in order to use the Gulf Stream for as long as possible.[66]

And then less than twenty-four hours later, on August 28:

> New leaks appear at one of the new additional bunkers. Pumping is no longer possible, as all empty bunkers are even worse.[67]

These serious deficiencies would be his rationale for not attacking a convoy on the twenty-eighth and two steamers on the fourth and sixth of September, respectively. He would remain adamant about keeping to his course and avoiding any unnecessary fuel expenditures.

Dröscher, on the other hand, was experiencing the same types of fuel leaks and shortages on *U-117* but showed none of the meticulous care in calculating his remaining supply that Kophamel had. Correspondingly, he failed to display any outward concern for holding his course to conserve fuel. Instead, he appeared to fly by the seat of his pants and was thus finding more success by being carelessly aggressive.

A heinous disregard for fuel consumption occurred on August 22, about 260 mi. / 419 km east of Long Island. Here, he spent hours chasing down a distant steamer, which was pursued even after he was sidetracked dodging a destroyer in the process of escorting a second steamship. At the end of the day, neither the steamers nor destroyer were fired upon, because both were found to be too far away for a successful attack to have been possible.

Even more fuel was wasted the next day, when *U-117* steered to investigate an "unmanned, drifting lifeboat" about 215 mi. / 347 km southeast of Nova Scotia. Incredibly, this was the abandoned lifeboat from the *San Jose*, which had drifted more than 100 miles farther out to sea following *U-156*'s attack six days earlier. While the sight was certainly a curiosity, Dröscher had nothing to gain from its inspection—it was neither a threat to his U-boat nor anything worth sinking.

His efforts did finally reap some rewards, quite literally, on August 24 (now about 140 mi. / 225 km south of Nova Scotia), when *U-117* came across a white-painted Canadian schooner that, according to Dröscher, more closely resembled a yacht. This was the *Bianca* (408 GRT), en route to Halifax from Bahia, Brazil, with a cargo of tobacco. Her crew abandoned her following *U-117*'s warning shot, at which point a German crew boarded her to prep her with a single *Sprengpatrone*. Like the *Nordhav* incident a week prior, much occurred in this encounter than Dröscher let on in his log. According to Chief Engineer Beckmann (who couldn't recall the correct name of the vessel),

> Tobacco was loaded the next day. Huge bales—*Felix Brasil*—as far as I can remember, enough to supply the entire submarine force with tobacco. The maneuver necessary to take over the cargo was somewhat difficult, for the sea was rough and it took a long time before we had stowed thirty-five of the gigantic bales in our empty mine room. Even the inside of the tower had to be half dismantled for this purpose, because we could not open other hatches because of the [ocean] swells. This tobacco became a very welcome affair for us on the way, because strangely enough, all other smoking materials began to mold shortly after our departure from Kiel. As we had such an unexpected joy, I would also like to tell you a very unfortunate affair.
>
> Due to some misunderstanding, the explosive charges we used to send the ship into the depths were triggered too early. Our people had to disembark the vessel head over heels. With almost tearful eyes I saw the Reserve Lieutenant looking over at the ship because, at the last moment, he noticed that the ship contained a whole compartment of rolled cigars, which now did not go up in smoke, but instead sank unused into the bottomless depths. In the age of dried beech leaves, it was a precious treasure. So, this day ended with deep sadness.[68]

Had *U-117* remained in the area, there would have been an even-greater reason to be depressed. As it turned out, the additional bales of tobacco that remained in the ship's hold swelled when they became wet and subsequently plugged the holes in the ship made by the Germans' bomb. The *Bianca* would ultimately remain afloat and would be recovered and towed to Halifax days later.

More bad news arrived the following morning, when Dröscher once again took inventory of his quickly diminishing fuel supply—reaffirming his sentiment from the sixteenth that *U-117* would have to return to Germany by taking the shortest route possible, via Cape Race, Newfoundland. He further noted that his original intention of heading toward Halifax "and waging trade wars in this area must be avoided."[69] That statement, however, stood in stark contrast to his actual behavior over the next two weeks. Just the very next day, *U-117* went back on the offensive, seemingly adopting the survival tactics of the German surface raiders.

Now about 160 mi. / 257 km east of Canso, Nova Scotia (specifically at 44°39' N, 57°52' W), *U-117* approached what was described in her log as being a large schooner. In reality, this was an American 162 GRT, steam-powered fishing trawler, the *Rush*, from Boston. Yet again, Dröscher was eerily reticent in his log about what transpired during the encounter, writing only that the vessel was sunk with a single explosive charge. This may have been because he didn't want to incriminate himself to his superiors in his log if he revealed just how bad *U-117*'s fuel situation really was.

A seaman from the *Rush*, Joseph Golart, later informed American naval intelligence that he, his captain, and two other crewmates were ordered into *U-117* by the Germans, who then kept them captive for about three hours. He would go on to claim that "I think they were short of fuel, for when we came aboard, they measured their oil tanks and found only four inches in the tanks. They took 1,200 gallons of fuel oil from our vessel."[70] Being below deck, he wouldn't have been able to observe how the fuel transfer was executed, and this time Beckmann's account doesn't help with filling in any of the details (in fact, the *Oberingenieur* fails to mention the encounter at all). Certainly, the fuel transfer was plausible and, if true, was a good practice run for another weeks later. In the meantime, *U-117* continued to aggressively pursue additional vessels.

On August 27, *U-117* encountered the 2,555 GRT Norwegian cargo ship *Bergsdalen*, about 120 mi. / 193 km south of St. Pierre and Miquelon (specifically at 45°14' N, 55°12' W). At the time, Dröscher had no idea as to the vessel's name, nationality, or cargo, noting only that it was armed with a deck gun on its stern. To him, this was enough justification to order *U-117* to dive and attack with a torpedo. The single G6AV* fired from *U-117*'s tube 2 quickly found its target and caused to the freighter to sink immediately. The haste in which the *Bergsdalen* went down was such that not all lifeboats could be launched in time, and one man died while jumping overboard. Had Dröscher been aware that the vessel was Norwegian, and thus neutral, the situation may have ended in an entirely different manner, with *U-117* more likely stopping the steamer and allowing her crew to escape before sinking her. As it was, Dröscher had been lucky to avoid being charged with a war crime, and he averted an international incident only because the *Bergsdalen* had, in fact, been chartered by the Allies and was en route from La Pallice (the main port in La Rochelle), France, to Baltimore in ballast—a detail he wouldn't find out about until after the war, if ever.

Three days later, and now about 145 mi. / 233 km southeast of St. John's, Newfoundland, *U-117* continued to seek victims. This time, she encountered the Canadian fishing schooners *Elsie Porter* and *Potentate*, each 136 GRT and fully laden with a season's haul of fish. They both would be looted and sunk by *Sprengpatronen* within four hours of each other.

The first to be sunk was the *Elsie Porter*, whose crew took to lifeboats after a warning shot was fired across her bow. Dröscher noted that her crew were all "German speaking, German-Americans,"[71] though in actuality they were German Canadians from Lunenburg. Although nothing is mentioned in *U-117*'s logs, the *Elsie Porter*'s captain, Irvin Eisenhauer (alluded to by Beckmann earlier as "Eisermann," or the anglicized name "Eisenham" in period Canadian newspapers), his son Warren Eisenhauer, and another crew member, Ferris Cross, all were taken as temporary prisoners aboard the minelayer while the rest of the crew was allowed to row away. Before the rest of the fishermen departed, they claimed to have overheard Dröscher threatening that he would take their master back to Germany to do pilot work. This, however, was likely just misconstrued jeering, since their captain himself reported that "they were treated to no insults, but every remark the pirate captain or his officers uttered was full of sarcasm."[68] Indeed, the younger Eisenhauer later remarked, "We found the U-boat crew quite interested in who we were . . . and what food what had on board."[72] Capt. Eisenhauer believed that the true reasoning behind the imprisonment was "to fool them regarding their position,"[73] so that they wouldn't be able to report *U-117*'s location accurately when they were eventually rescued.

When the *Potentate* was sunk hours later, the same process repeated itself and another three fishermen were taken captive: Capt. Gerhardt, Albert Bell, and Angus Erns. It wouldn't be nightfall until the prisoners were released, now even farther away from land. While all the crews that were initially allowed to depart on their lifeboats were rescued by the next day, the fishermen taken captive would not be rescued until June 2, when a passing ship took them aboard.

As the Canadian fishermen fought for their lives in their lifeboats, the crew aboard *U-117* prepared a feast with the looted provisions and their freshly caught fish. Beckmann recalled,

> When I think of how we put together a dinner on the Newfoundland Banks where the first, second, and third courses were fresh cod with a mustard dipping sauce and new American potatoes ... I don't understand why I didn't just live on cod and fresh potatoes in the future.[74]

Also on the menu were freshly baked bread, eggs, and various roasts, which, due to the worsening sea conditions, many men aboard *U-117* couldn't manage to keep down. Their time to revel in their new food supply would be short lived, however, as Dröscher continued to press on for more "kills" despite his earlier insistence on taking the shortest route home possible.

More of his limited supply of fuel was wasted on September 1, when he positioned himself for a submerged attack on a steamer, only to discover that it flew a Dutch flag. He lamented that he would have made an attempt to stop it and investigate, had the weather not been so unfavorable and the steamer not in ballast. Then a day later, even more was used up when he attempted to chase down a group of steamships. According to his log,

> Three Steamers sighted off port. Distance 7 nm, bearing 360°. Sighting bearing requires full steam ahead. Boat catches up at first, then no longer, even with extreme effort. Although little prospect for success, submerged for underwater attack. Unable to reach steamer for torpedo shot despite high speed. Surfaced. Artillery attack, distance about 90 hm. Distance increases rapidly while priming the diesel engines. Steamer pursued without significant convergence. Chase abandoned after ¾ hours due to lack of fuel oil.[75]

Still, he continued to be ambitious in his pursuit of tonnage despite his fuel concerns, not relenting until after his nearly catastrophic encounter with the British tanker *War Ranee* on September 5.

During this attack, *U-117* approached the tanker submerged and fired a torpedo, only to watch it pass harmlessly below the ship's engine room. This may have been due to the tanker being empty and thus running with a high draft, or to a torpedo malfunction, or to an error on the part of Kapitänleutnant Dröscher, who noted that the tanker was "strangely alien" in appearance, and, due to its "single mast and its paint scheme, the course and position were very difficult to determine."[76] He was actually so astounded by the *War Ranee*'s appearance that he drew a sketch of it to include in his war diary. While the missed torpedo shot wasn't in itself ruinous, all hell would break loose aboard the U-boat as *U-117* continued to engage the tanker.

As *U-117* continued to travel at a periscope depth in the direction of the *War Ranee*, suddenly her front hydroplane failed and the middle got stuck, resulting in the U-boat heading back toward the surface uncontrollably. Dröscher, observing that the tanker was armed, recognized the gravity of his situation immediately, and Beckmann, who was in charge of keeping the submarine at the correct depth, ordered all hands forward in a desperate attempt to change *U-117*'s trajectory. In what seemed like an eternity to the men aboard *U-117*, but what in reality was only a matter of minutes, Beckmann was able to restore control of the submarine through a combination of flooding and managing to free the front elevator. You can still sense his excitement and frustration decades later, when he wrote,

> Even at such moments one would like to have a hundred arms to accelerate the speed of the counter-maneuvers to be taken at such moments, because in such a situation all the necessary measures are concentrated in the brain and presence of mind of the chief engineer of a submarine. Flooding, trimming, draining, operating the compressed air equipment, eliminating any faults, orders here, reports from there, one thing follows the other. Just one wrong measure or one taken too late could spell the end for the boat and crew.[77]

Amazingly, just as *U-117* returned to periscope depth, Dröscher observed the *War Ranee* to be stopped and in the process of lowering a lifeboat. According to the report given by the officers of the tanker, their failure to flee the area was due to having to make minor engine repairs; however, in reality, they were probably in the process of abandoning ship, having been frightened by the torpedo that narrowly missed their ship. In Beckmann's recollection of the same event, he noted,

> The steamer must have become a bit mad at the unusual sight of a half-surfaced boat driving like mad in circles, because it stopped immediately in anticipation of the torpedo that was long overdue, had launched boats and probably thought: sauve qui peut![78] But when it was noticed that we had enough to do ourselves to get away from the steamer, its people got back on board as quickly as possible, left some of the boats and drove away like madmen.[79]

Coincidentally, it was at the exact time that *U-117* was observed by the *War Ranee*, and her crew returned to the ship, that her engines suddenly started working and she began to speed away, following a zigzag course. Dröscher, not yet willing to give up the hunt, ordered *U-117* back to surface and pursued the tanker at maximum power, despite his "low oil stocks." This lasted for over two and a half hours, during which *U-117* failed to make any gains on the *War Ranee* (who was making repeated SOS calls throughout the chase). Eventually, some sense prevailed with the German commander, who realized he was only wasting more fuel in a pursuit that offered "little chance of success."

Indeed, the fuel situation on *U-117* had finally come to a head. The next day, Dröscher finally addressed the continued losses yet remained strangely optimistic. He wrote,

> The question of fuel oil is becoming more and more unpleasant every day. The successively empty bunkers constantly indicate losses. The diving tank III used as an additional bunker alone shows a loss of 9 cbm. Such heavy losses had not been expected. At least there still seems to be enough fuel oil to get home with an economical trip.[80]

This wishful thinking was only temporary. Two days later he began radioing *U-140* for fuel.

Even with *U-140*'s dwindling fuel supply, Kophamel still found some to spare to save his reckless comrades. At Kophamel's suggestion, a rendezvous for the fuel transfer was set for 0800 on September 9, in the calmer waters off the Faroe Islands. Upon meeting up, the two U-boats traveled for an additional three days to find adequate "land protection" before the transfer could actually begin. It would take over thirty hours of constant toil to complete the process.

With no means to efficiently send over the fuel oil, the officers of both submarines formulated a plan in which a 600 m handline would be looped between the two U-boats (themselves separated by a gap of 100–200 m). Attached to this line were the empty containers for the 15 cm shells (not the cartridge shells, but U-boat-specific ammo carriers that were pressure resistant and hermetically sealed) for the U-cruisers' deck guns. These would serve both as buoys and as receptacles with which the precious diesel would be filled and then funneled into *U-117*'s empty tanks. To emphasize how laborious the process was, Dröscher noted that it took seventy-five cases to transfer just 1 m³ of fuel. Due to the sea conditions worsening over the course of the day, only 7 cbm were transferred on the twelfth, with the final

12 cbm being transferred on the thirteenth (at total of 19 cbm or 19,000 liters). Amazingly, Kophamel estimated that only 1 m³ of diesel was lost during the entire exchange. With the handover complete, and with both U-boats now equally low on fuel, at 1900 on the thirteenth, *U-140* and *U-117* proceeded into the Allied blockade area together.

A view of the rendezvous between *U-117* and *U-140*. Photo taken from the deck of *U-117*, with Oberingenieur Beckmann supervising. *Courtesy of Deutsches U-Boot-Museum*

In the four days Dröscher and Kophamel spent traversing the northern tip of the United Kingdom, only two small vessels were spotted, traveling as a pair 10 nm north of the blockade's border. Fortunately for the Germans, they continued on unobserved, but there was still one final obstacle to overcome—the Northern Barrage. *U-117* and *U-140*, and only those two submarines, would enter the minefields together as close to the Norwegian coastline as they could legally get, with Kophamel taking the lead. This would be where *U-140*'s "prisoner," Rene Bastin, provided his most useful intel to the Germans of the entire cruise.

According to Bastin, U-boats *102*, *156*, *100*, *117*, and *140* all met to advance through the Northern Barrage together. Adding more fabrications to his already fanciful story, he would even claim that he personally observed *U-156* striking a mine and blowing up, while the remaining U-boats simply sped on and escaped the area. This fantastic tale was probably conjured up to mask his own treacherous behavior in which he provided *U-140* with the key to getting through the minefield safely. As Kophamel noted in his log,

> In the restricted area, 3 round red wooden or cork buoys were passed close to port. . . . According to the prisoner, such buoys serve as floats for light nets (drifting nets) in the channel. Another floater was seen to the starboard on the field's southern border. In my opinion, the buoys were drifting, but the possibility that nets can lie there cannot be denied. I would pass the restricted area in the same place in the future.[81]

Indeed, per the US Navy, these buoys weren't supporting nets but were instead markers that were placed to mark the minefields' outer edges.[82]

As Beckmann recalled, *U-117* would follow closely behind *U-140* through the barrage, often having to stop so that *U-140* could back up and make sharp course alterations according to where the buoys (which he described as being "glass balls and other unfriendly objects") were placed. Although the hours that went by probably took years off the lives of the U-boat crews, both U-boats successfully broke through without incident. Afterward, they were forced to go their separate ways, primarily because of *U-117*'s continued fuel issues. Kophamel and *U-140* would continue on the "safer" route, hugging the Norwegian coast, and Dröscher and *U-117* would take the more direct route toward Kiel via Jutland.

Besides passing two dimly lit vessels on the evening of the seventeenth, Kophamel found little in the way of obstacles on his way home. On the eighteenth, *U-140* would see her first signs of Germany when *U-91* was spotted just over 20 mi. / 32 km off the southern tip of Norway. Kophamel and *U-91*'s commander (Kapitänleutnant Alfred von Glasenapp) took the opportunity to exchange stories about their experiences and then continued on their respective courses. Then, as *U-140* entered the Kattegat on the nineteenth, she met up with *U-100* and *UB-87* to await a German torpedo boat escort back to port. Despite being just 175 mi. / 281 km from Kiel, Kophamel was still taking copious notes on his remaining stock of fuel. Indeed, when *U-140* entered Kiel's harbor at noon the next day, concluding his patrol, he closed out his war diary with one final fuel calculation:

Total oil consumption: 348 cbm
Losses: 65.8 cbm
Given to "U 117": 19 cbm

Remainder: 12 cbm[83]

The surplus 12,000 liters of diesel would have been of significant benefit to *U-117*, which, although taking a more direct route home, was having a much more difficult time getting there.

After *U-117* and *U-140* split up on the seventeenth, Dröscher proceeded in a southerly direction on a zigzag course. On the twentieth, while *U-140* was safely moored in port, *U-117* was still miles away in the Kattegat when her fuel bunkers ran dry. According to Dröscher, there were 4.5 m³ less oil than was calculated, which, according to his log, must have been a fault of the U-boat designers at Vulkan Werke. He concluded that a loss of this quantity due to the submarine's perpetual leaks was "completely out of the question." Oddly, Beckmann supported this claim in his memoir, feeling that the actual, usable dimensions of *U-117*'s fuel bunkers were significantly smaller than what was indicated on the blueprints. Regardless of what actually transpired, *U-117* was still out of fuel and had a range of only 35 nm on her electric motors. Rather ignominiously, Dröscher was forced to radio for a tow back to port, prior to discharging the remainder of his batteries as he traveled onward with his electric motors.

In just a few hours, help arrived in the form of two German torpedo boats, but *U-117* was still not out of the woods. Besides the German vessels, a Danish patrol boat also simultaneously arrived and approached the immobilized U-boat from the stern—her war ensign visibly waving atop her mast. As Dröscher prepared for the worst, the Danish warship came within 30 m and then swerved to port, paying a tribute to the stunned officers aboard *U-117*. With the crisis averted, a line was then attached to one of the torpedo boats, and *U-117* was taken away in tow. Unfortunately for the war-weary U-boat crew, this still didn't spell the end of their troubles.

Less than an hour later, the tow line broke and *U-117* was once again dead in the water. After transferring 2.5 cbm of diesel from one of the torpedo boats into *U-117*'s bunkers, she was able to continue her journey on her own power, arriving alongside the pre-dreadnaught SMS *Hannover* (performing patrol duties in the Danish Straits) at 0200 on the twenty-first. Here more fuel had to be taken on, allowing *U-117* to finally reach the Unterseekreuzer Unit's base at 1000 on the twenty-second. Despite her inglorious return home, and the fact that *U-117* would never go on another war patrol for the remainder of the war, she was still racking up victories courtesy of her numerous minefields along North America's East Coast.

USS *Minnesota. Author's collection*

The first of these successes occurred at 0315 on September 29, when the battleship USS *Minnesota* (BB-22) struck one of *U-117*'s UC 200 (200 kg charge) mines off Fenwick Island. Traveling just 32 mi. / 51 km off the Delaware coast, with the destroyer USS *Israel* as an escort, her commander, Capt. Jehu Valentine Chase, reported a "heavy explosion under the starboard bow."[84] This detonation immediately caused a list due to the rapid ingress of water in the lower compartments. Despite part of the ship's structure being "practically obliterated," the ship's reinforced bulkheads isolated the flooding and the battleship remained afloat, allowing her to limp to the Philadelphia Navy Yard for repairs. There were no casualties.

Although the men on board had taken to their battle stations (it should be noted that USS *Minnesota* was a training ship for gunners and engineers at this point in the war), unlike with USS *San Diego*, no shots were fired haphazardly into the water in hopes of striking a U-boat. Capt. Chase seemed certain from the outset that a mine was responsible for the damage instead of a torpedo. While *Minnesota* ultimately did not sink, the damage incurred from *U-117*'s mine kept her out of the remainder of the war. She would ultimately return to service in 1919, for the purpose of bringing back American soldiers from Europe.

The damage inflicted on the hull of USS *Minnesota* from one of *U-117*'s mines. *NH 46026, courtesy of the Naval History & Heritage Command*

The next vessel to meet her fate at the hands of *U-117* was the 2,458 GRT steamer *San Saba*, bound for Tampa from New York with general cargo. She would contact one of *U-117*'s mines off Barnegat Light on October 4. The effect of the UC 200 on a smaller, commercial vessel was much more devastating than its effect on an American battleship. The steamer would sink within five minutes, leaving no time for any lifeboats to be launched. Of the thirty-four crewmen, only five escaped the wreck, and of these only three survived (one through the use of a life ring, and the other two by floating on a makeshift raft comprising pieces of wreckage). This would be the second-highest loss of life suffered at the hands of a German U-boat along the American coast during the war.

Just over three weeks elapsed before another ship was lost in one of *U-117*'s minefields. This was the Cuban steamship *Chaparra* (1510 GRT), en route to New York from Cuba with a cargo of 14,000 bags of sugar. She too would contact one of *U-117*'s mines off Barnegat Light on October 27. Despite the steamer capsizing and sinking in only two and a half minutes, nearly 80 percent of the twenty-nine-man crew survived the incident, since, miraculously, two lifeboats were able to be launched in that short time period.

Although the *Chaparra* was another one of *U-117*'s Barnegat Light minefield victims, it was not out of negligence from the US Navy. As early as September 7, mines were being discovered in the area, with two being recovered by the Navy and another being found on Sandy Hook nearly a month prior to the *San Saba* sinking. Following the *San Saba* disaster, an additional four mines were destroyed by the minesweepers USS *Teal* and USS *Freehold* between October 10 and 16. It was just bad luck that the *Chaparra* made the unfortunate discovery of *U-117*'s final mine, just two weeks before the Armistice.

Even unluckier than the *Chaparra* was USS *Saetia* (ID-2317), which sank just two days prior to the war's end. This 2,873-ton cargo ship was assigned to the Naval Overseas Transport Service, making frequent trips to France with ammunition and supplies for the Allies. It was while she was returning from one of these trips in ballast that she hit a UC 200 mine off Fenwick Island. In this case, the US Navy could bear some of the responsibility. Following the incident with USS *Minnesota*, no efforts were made to mine-sweep the area; in fact, minesweeping wouldn't occur until January 1919 (long after Adm. Sims advised of German minefield locations on November 18 and 27). Although USS *Saetia* would be lost, thankfully the only casualties consisted of thirteen of the eighty-five crew members being injured.

Taking into account the vessels lost after *U-117*'s patrol, Dröscher was able to sink twenty-two ships for a total of 34,612 tons (including the *Frederic R. Kellogg*) and damaging a further three (23,667 tons). Kophamel, although sinking far fewer vessels, with a total of seven, was still responsible for sending 30,594 tons of shipping to the ocean's floor. Although these totals fell within Sims's "acceptable" range of 30,000–40,000 tons lost, they were far from insignificant, particularly when one takes into account the seaworthiness of the U-boats upon leaving port. The fact that both U-boats were able to travel a combined total of 20,031 nautical miles,[85] despite being badly constructed, incessantly leaking, and having to end their patrols prematurely, was in and of itself remarkable; however, the sentiment that more could have been achieved if the submarines were in better condition was echoed in the postmission statements made by the *Befehlshaber der U-Boote* (BdU; Command Headquarters of the U-boat Force).

In the case of *U-140*, it was noted that although Kophamel's cruise yielded rewards and was worth undertaking, particularly along the American coastline, "the result fell short of expectations . . . partly due to the fact that the operation had to be terminated prematurely as a result of the high fuel losses—almost 18% . . . and water leaks."[86] Like Kophamel, the BdU blamed the patrol's shortcomings on the Germania Shipyard, concluding that the amount of time required to fix the various defects in *U-140* was significantly disproportionate to her relatively short cruise. Kophamel's concerns about surface stability were noted as being "in dire need of improvement";[87] however, this was a costly design flaw and would not be addressed in any of the U-139-class U-boats.

Concerning, *U-117*, the patrol was met with "general approval," even before the results of the sown minefields were known. Oddly, considering his behavior with his dwindling fuel supply, Dröscher was criticized for a lack of aggression. The headquarters' findings read,

- The commander specifies throwing mines as his main task in his "Experiences." That is not right. The main task is the sinking of vessels. Therefore, contact should have been maintained with the convoy on August 2 and August 8, if necessary, until the ammunition was used up. There was probably still an opportunity to throw mines.
- During the escort attack, all torpedo tubes should have been flooded and two torpedoes should have been shot at the ship at the end of the ship. The fact that the torpedo started in the tube on August 8 was probably a serious operating error.
- The fact that no double shots were fired on August 21 and September 5 cannot be justified.
- Otherwise, the enterprise is carried out with skillful exploitation of the attack opportunities. In particular, the active interruption of minelaying on August 16, which led to the destruction of an American steamer, deserves recognition. The mines were thrown in busy places, they will not fail to have the effect.

- Extending the stay in the operational area until the last oil reserve is used up can easily become disastrous. The boat was lucky that it met *U-140* and could get oil from him.[88]

No mention was made of the fuel bunkers actually being smaller in reality than in design, as both Dröscher and Beckmann claimed, nor were any deficiencies in *U-117*'s construction directly attributed to the Vulkan Works (as Germaniawerft had been in *U-140*'s brief).

The US Navy's performance during the period could also be considered a mixed bag of successes and failures. On the positive side, the new sub chasers had performed admirably in countering *U-117* in Delaware Bay. Additionally, the destroyer USS *Stringham* was nearly successful in sinking *U-140*. In both cases, the depth charges had been launched accurately, and effectively, although ultimately not enough effort was made to ensure the U-boats remained submerged permanently.

The importance of airpower was also clearly exhibited, even though it was perhaps not fully recognized at the time. Unlike Feldt in *U-156*, who attempted to fight off the attacking seaplanes, both Dröscher and Kophamel immediately dove at the sight of an aircraft on the horizon. The advantages of aircraft in antisubmarine warfare would be further illustrated in 1921, when *U-117* (having been awarded to the United States as war booty) would finally be sunk by three Navy F5L flying boats off Cape Charles, Virginia.

Still, the Navy continued to suffer from self-inflicted wounds and unforced errors. While *U-117* was busy torpedoing the *Bergsdalen* on August 27 off Newfoundland, 37 mi. / 60 km off the coast of New Jersey the freighter *Felix Taussig* (which would become USS *Felix Taussig*, ID 2282, two days later) was training her 4-inch/50-caliber and 3-inch/50-caliber deck guns on what she believed was a German U-boat. Unfortunately, it was the American sub chaser *SC-209*, which was destroyed before *Felix Taussig* realized her mistake and ceased firing. Eighteen of the twenty-six sailors aboard *SC-209* were killed.[89]

In a much less deadly incident, the same day *U-140* was sinking the *Diomed* nearly 500 miles east of New York City, one of CNO Benson's imaginative U-boat traps finally succeeded in damaging a submarine—the American *N-5* (SS-57), 80 mi. / 129 km south of Long Island. In this case, *N-5* managed to collide with USS *Charles Whittemore*, the schooner that had been towing her, resulting in a leak developing in her battery compartment. After hours of bailing water and caulking the seams of the submarine with "oakum and soft copper wire"[90] to stop the leaks, the flooding was finally brought under control. Still, *N-5* could not rest easy.

On the same patrol, shortly after being released from her tow line due to rough seas, she was fired upon by an armed naval auxiliary under the assumption that she was an enemy U-boat. Ironically, when this occurred (September 7), there were no German U-boats present off the United States' seaboard. Thankfully, this incident did not result like that of *Felix Taussig* and *SC-209*. All shots would miss *N-5*, and she was able to proceed to New London, Connecticut, safely.[91]

While these outcomes were far from what the Navy desired from its coastal defense forces, it did appear that, for the most part, things were moving in the right direction. Although no U-boats had been sunk on the American side of the Atlantic, the tonnage sunk per U-boat had been falling since *U-151*'s high watermark of 51,009. Despite this, the Germans would continue with the war against American shipping on the East Coast, this time sending a U-boat that had already made the trip twice already. For the third time in two years, the *Deutschland* would be returning to American waters.

CHAPTER 11
The Final Voyage of the *U-Deutschland*

"I was the last of the seven commanders of *U-155*, the old *U-Deutschland*," began Korvettenkapitän Ferdinand Studt on September 12, 1928. He was writing from the German Diplomatic Legation in Asunción, Paraguay. "I came back to Kiel after the outbreak of the revolution following a successful long-distance journey that had taken us past Newfoundland, Scotland, New York, and the Azores."[1]

This very general statement was written as a preface in a letter to RAdm. Arno Spindler (the administrator of the Marinearchiv and a U-boat historian) in reference to why his war diary was not in the possession of the German Naval Archives. Apparently, he was applying for the position of "inspecting director" of the newly formed Argentinian submarine force in Mar del Plata and required his *Kriegstagebuch* as a reference. He noted that up to that point, the Argentinians did "not know anything about this side of my multifaceted existence"[2] and needed proof of his previous command. He was, perhaps, overselling his experiences somewhat.

He was not the seventh commander of *U-155*, nor was his time spent on submarines extensive. Although he had begun his career in the Kaiserliche Marine as early as 1898 (earning numerous prewar awards, including the Iron Cross, First and Second Classes), he wouldn't actually enter the U-boat service until May 1917. Just as with *U-155*'s three previous masters (including König), this would be his first actual U-boat assignment. His wartime service aboard a U-boat would also be the shortest of the men who led *U-155* into combat. Still, the legendary *U-Deutschland* was far from being a typical submarine, and his time aboard her afforded him situations that many other U-boat veterans would have otherwise never experienced. In fact, by the time Studt took control of her reins, she was in her third (and final) evolution, with the ultimate phase of development occurring under the supervision of Studt's predecessor from October through December 1917.

Following Kapitänleutnant Karl Meusel's malfunction-prone maiden patrol off the Azores during the summer of 1917, *U-155*'s next commander, Korvettenkapitän Erich Eckelmann, was put in charge of ensuring that numerous upgrades took place to put the U-boat on par with the rest of the U-151-class U-cruisers. Most of these built off Meusel's existing litany of complaints. The major modifications were as follows:

1. Removal of the previous lattice torpedo tubes and installation of two inner torpedo tubes in the bow
2. Replacing the old 15 cm guns with 15 cm C/16 torpedo boat guns[3] and changing the ammunition stowage for the longer shells of the new guns. Increasing the standby ammunition to around 100 rounds.
3. Installation of a cutting device for underwater cables
4. Installation of a new periscope
5. Renewal of the upper deck[4]

While these were certainly critical updates, many of Meusel's and Eckelmann's important wish-list items would not be installed, primarily due to time constraints (the refurbishment was not allowed to exceed three months). Interestingly, two upgrades that should have been considered essential—additional torpedo stowage and the installation of 8.8 cm antiaircraft guns—had to be omitted solely because of the time required for installation.

Although Eckelmann may have lamented the exclusion of much of his desired modifications, there was something to appreciate about *U-155* being hurried back into service. At this earlier point in the war, the quality control at Germaniawerft was still quite good. Unlike Kophamel's test runs with *U-140* in the spring of 1918, when *U-155* spent forty-two hours between December 13 and 20, 1917, lying on the seabed testing for leaks, she emerged watertight.[5] Additionally, the problems Eckelmann experienced on his first patrol to the Azores, between January and May 1918, had little to do with the shipyard and instead lay with *U-155*'s inherent design flaws.

The diesel engines, which had been intended for auxiliary battleship generators, still continued to disappoint, as did his torpedoes, which had a success rate of less than 40 percent. Unlike the torpedo failings of *U-155*'s first cruise, these misses and duds could not be attributed to prolonged exposure to seawater from being mounted in external tubes—they were simply bad directly from the factory. Despite the perpetual torpedo issues, *U-155*'s new deck guns, now identical to the ones equipped on every other U-cruiser, proved to be excellent. In fact, the accuracy and range of the 15 cm cannons greatly contributed to Eckelmann being able to sink sixteen vessels for 50,522 tons (just 2,981 tons and three vessels less than what Meusel sank on *U-155*'s maiden war patrol).

Considering that the barometer of *U-155*'s performance was more than fifteen ships sunk for 50,000-plus tons, Studt had much to live up to when he took command of her in June 1918—particularly when considering the diminishing tonnage being sunk off North America following *U-151*'s initial patrol. Unlike the waters off Northwest Africa, the North American coastline had sparser targets, yet was being defended by significantly more coastal patrols, whose efficacy was improving with every passing week. Adding to the pressure being put on the green commander, his orders were far from simple. He was to mine the entrances to the ports of Halifax and St. John's (Newfoundland), though Studt would question this and ignore it entirely later, cut the transatlantic telegraph cables northwest of Sable Island (Nova Scotia), resume the trade war between Cape Cod and Cape Hatteras,[6] and, "if possible without endangering himself," shell any harbor or shipyard facilities of opportunity.[7] The legacy of the *U-Deutschland* would rest in his hands.

After spending the two months following Eckelmann's patrol being repaired and given a fresh camouflage paint job (reminiscent of the patterns encountered on Allied vessels), *U-155*, now under Studt, spent the time between mid-July and early August in the Baltic—acclimating the new commander to his crew and the U-cruiser. It wouldn't be until August 11 that *U-155* would finally depart Kiel in tow of torpedo boat *T-134* to make her way toward Canada and New England. Not surprisingly, Allied intelligence was already aware of her anticipated departure, with Sims confiding nearly a month later that she "would be one of the two converted mercantile type which were expected to sail from Germany about the middle of August, and she would reach the American coast about September 15."[8] The other U-boat was *U-152* (to be discussed in the next chapter), which, unbeknown to Sims at this time, would not leave port until September 5.

The final iteration of *U-155*, pictured with her new camouflage paint job. *Author's collection*

Regardless of *U-155*'s known departure time frame, she met little in the way of opposition upon leaving Kiel. By August 17, she had successfully traversed "Area C" of the Northern Barrage and, in the nearly two weeks that followed, only encountered but did not sink a neutral Norwegian steamer, the *Svarfard*, on August 18. Despite the colorful story recounted by USS *Ticonderoga* (then in the company of the *Montoso* and *Rondo*) about spotting a torpedo wake from *U-155* and then exchanging fire with her on the twenty-seventh, the first actual contact with the U-cruiser occurred on August 31, when *U-155* intercepted a 315 GRT Portuguese schooner, *Gamo*, just over 900 nm west-southwest of Ireland (specifically at 46°10' N, 32°0' W).

The *Gamo* had been en route from Lisbon to St. John's, Newfoundland, with a cargo of fish, and although she was hardly an exceptional target, she would have great ramifications on Studt's patrol. An "Englishman" aboard the schooner was able to convince the German commander, prior to the vessel being sunk with explosives, that there was nothing to be gained by mining the waters off St. John's. According to *U-155*'s war diary on September 1,

> Studying the nautical material, together with the statements of the Englishman aboard the Portuguese sailing vessel *Gamo*[, which I] sank on 31 August, lead me to believe that the harbor of St. John's where I am supposed to lay mines is really St. John in the Bay of Fundy.[9]

This hypothesis was not based solely on conjecture. Considering that St. John's, Newfoundland, was primarily a rural community in 1918, whose main industry was commercial fishing, it offered little in the way of industrial output or manpower that would have to be shipped aboard. As prior U-boat commanders had already realized, they were more likely to encounter small fishing vessels off Newfoundland than tankers or steamships.

On the other hand, St. John, New Brunswick, was on the mainland and, being an essential railway hub, was a terminus for Europe-bound, Canadian-manufactured war materiel. One of the primary sources of such equipment was the T. McAvity & Son Munition Factory, located just a few miles inland from the Bay of Fundy. This plant was responsible for manufacturing 4.7-inch shells for the British/Canadians, all of which would have to be shipped to France on large cargo ships.[10] By sidestepping St. John's, Newfoundland, and setting a course for New Brunswick, Studt could still complete his objectives off Nova Scotia without having to stray from his more direct route. In doing so, he would cut miles and days off his patrol, thus greatly conserving his precious fuel supply.

The concept of saving fuel was almost certainly on his mind when he wrote his log entry on the first, since nearly three hours after sinking the *Gamo*, he tried, and failed, to chase down three unescorted steamers traveling at a high speed. These potential victims were the 24,666-ton troopship SS *France*, and two unidentified vessels Studt described as being akin to the SS *Kronprinzessin Cecile* and the *Burdigala*, respectively.

In the case of the former, it was in all likelihood the 19,400-ton troopship USS *Mount Vernon* (ID-4508),[11] which had been heading toward Brest during that period, fully laden with American servicemen. All three vessels were prime targets and represented the first time a North American–bound U-Kreuzer had an opportunity to sink an outbound troop transport, but alas, it was not to be. Assuming the third vessel was of identical tonnage to the *Burdigala* (the actual vessel had sunk on November 14, 1916), Studt had allowed just over 56,500 tons of shipping and thousands of soldiers to escape his grasp and wasted a significant amount of fuel in the process. The *Korvettenkapitän* was beginning to realize that *U-155*, like the U-cruisers that preceded her, was far too slow to effectively pursue a large vessel making full steam.

It would take less than forty-eight hours for Studt to find some consolation for his failed prospect. On September 2, about 380 mi. / 611 km north-northwest of Lajes das Flores (the Azores), he spotted a much-slower Norwegian steamer that had been separated from her convoy. This was the *Stortind* (2,560 GRT), en route from Norfolk to La Pallice with general cargo. After halting her with a warning shot and inspecting her papers, her crew was told to abandon ship. She was then promptly sunk by *U-155*'s deck guns.[12]

Although Studt would continue to spot, but not pursue, distant vessels in the following five days, it wouldn't be until September 7 that *U-155* once again went on the offensive. According to nearly every postwar publication written in English, that morning Studt would open fire on the 4,078-ton British steamer *Monmouth* at 43°N, 45°40' W, which in turn reported her location and radioed that she had escaped.

Studt's diary, for once fairly legible, confirms the event taking place, noting that *U-155* engaged an armed steamer from a distance of 90 hm; however, he clearly identifies the Allied vessel as being the smaller, 2,594-ton French steamer *Pomone*. Her identity was gleaned not only through observation, but also from her intercepted "allo" message that was sent following her escape (once again due to her superior surface speed). Studt further specifically noted the *Pomone* on his course chart and included her in his list of "observed transatlantic ship traffic that was partially attacked and escaped."

It is unclear how such a disparity in identifying the steamer could exist, particularly when both sides agree on the date, time, and location of the event. Nevertheless, the steamer, whichever ship she was, would escape and

U-155's position would now be known for certain—prompting Adm. Sims to finally share his intelligence about *U-155*'s course and destination with Washington two days later. Unfortunately, a small Portuguese sailing ship, apparently without a radio, would fail to hear the "allo" signal.

About four hours after breaking off the battle with the *Pomone*, Studt would stop and scuttle the 162-ton fishing vessel *Sophia* at 43°20' N, 46°8' W, sending her cargo of codfish back to the sea. He was now on the periphery of his operational zone, some 400 mi. / 643 km southeast of Newfoundland. As Studt decided earlier, he would not be heading north toward St. John's but would instead be continuing on his current course in the direction of Sable Island to proceed with his cable-cutting mission[13]—picking off targets of opportunity along the way.

After nearly five days of sailing, with few vessels being spotted on the horizon, *U-155* finally found her next victim in the form of a 3,245 GRT Portuguese steamer on the morning of September 12, at 42°12' N, 57°23' W (approximately 300 mi. / 482 km southwest of Nova Scotia). The *Leixões*, traveling from Hull, England, to Boston in ballast, had previously been a German vessel, the *Cheruskia* of the Hamburg-Amerika Line (a fact Studt was quick to point out in his log), and had been requisitioned by Portugal after her German crew interned her at the outbreak of the war.[14] Studt, observing that she was armed with a deck gun, ordered *U-155* below the surface, whereupon a torpedo was launched shortly after 0600. According to the captain of the *Leixões*, Joaquim F. Sucena,

> The torpedo struck on the starboard side of No. 4 hatch; the submarine was not visible. As soon as the ship was hit I saw she was going to sink, and I ordered all hands to take to the lifeboats, and all my confidential books were sunk. . . . Fifteen minutes after the ship was struck[,] the submarine appeared on the starboard beam about one-quarter mile distant. Our vessel sank in about 15 minutes and before we got alongside of the submarine.[15]

One sailor died during the attack, believed to have been asleep in his bunk when the ship went down, but an additional eleven would die from exposure when one of the four launched lifeboats was lost at sea.[16] Although nothing is mentioned in *U-155*'s log, Sucena claimed that Studt inquired if there were any Englishmen on board before inspecting the crew on the deck of the U-boat. Apparently satisfied, he was then alleged to have ordered, rather brusquely, the Portuguese sailors to shove off, without supplying them with any provisions or the direction toward the closest landfall. According to Sucena, Studt was "of light complexion, dark mustache, and wore no uniform, but had on a cap; was heavy set and spoke splendid English, very much like an American."[17]

The following day, *U-155* made another submerged attack on an armed steamer, although this time without any success. This attempt took place just before 1000 at 42°18' N, 58°22' W, and involved the British merchant ship *Newby Hall* (4,391 GRT), en route to New York City from Milford Haven in ballast. Unluckily for both the steamship and the U-boat, she separated from her convoy ten days earlier and was proceeding to her destination alone.

Following Studt's failed torpedo shot, which narrowly missed the steamship by 6 feet, *U-155* was ordered to the surface to continue the attack with her long-range 15 cm guns, opening fire from a distance of 6,000 m.[18] The gun crews aboard the *Newby Hall* immediately responded with artillery from their aft 4-inch gun while the vessel made steam and proceeded on a zigzag course, keeping *U-155* astern of her at all times. The *Hall*'s captain, F. O. Seaborne, would claim that *U-155* fired a combination of high-explosive and shrapnel shells during the attack, with only the latter actually reaching the steamship and resulting in no damage.

In contrast to the Germans, he alleged that his crew's return fire was quite effective, scoring three critical hits on the U-boat and taking out one of the 15 cm guns completely. For once, an Allied mercantile captain was not stretching the truth. Although no damage was done to the forward 15 cm gun, one British shell struck *U-155*'s bow and dented her armor plating (Studt noting this occurred from a distance of 10 km), and others smashed into *U-155*'s pressure hull, causing leaks that prevented the U-boat from being able to submerge until they were repaired. Like so many other vessels that attacked U-boats that summer, the *Newby Hall*, in her haste to flee, failed to land the final, fatal blows on her opponent. Instead, she escaped using her superior speed, all the while sending distress signals and throwing all her "secret books and codes" overboard.[19] Once she reached a distance of 13,000 yards from *U-155*, the engagement was over.

Although the US Navy had replied to the *Newby Hall*'s SOS calls, by the time they reached the area there was nothing to be found of the German raider. In response, a general war warning was broadcast on the fifteenth to the 1st through 8th Naval Districts, advising of new, inbound enemy submarines. Studt, also intercepting the same wireless signals, took this as his cue to begin his minelaying mission.

In the four days Studt spent traveling toward his minefield locations, the American and Canadian navies mobilized antisubmarine patrols around Halifax, rightly believing that the attack on the *Newby Hall* was a precursor to future assaults. They would be patrolling precisely where Studt intended to sow his mines. According to historians Michael Hadley and Roger Sarty,

Admiral Story at *Halifax* immediately deployed his most effective ships—the American submarine chasers and HMCS *Grilse* [a converted yacht]. While the *Grilse* made an unusually long, three-day patrol at the harbor entrance, the American ships undertook daily patrols and hydrophone[-]listening watches along the sea lane from Halifax to Sambro Island. All shipping sailed under escort, including air cover by the US Navy flying boats.[20]

Indeed, much was now being expected of the listening capabilities of the American sub chasers. Admiral Sims noted in an Intelligence Section bulletin that as their crews became more experienced, they were able to realize that sounds previously attributed to periscope noises and U-boat signals were naturally occurring phenomena (whales, dolphins, tidal currents, etc.; it must be remembered that technology of this type was still in its infancy). As such, the SC boats were now no longer chasing down marine mammals and the reflecting resonances of underwater wrecks but could identify vessels approaching at some distance. Sims, in the same dispatch, went on to note a particularly fruitful listening session, stating,

> During a hunt lately by US sub-chasers, an excellent demonstration took place of the use of detection devices (in this case a "C" tube) in connection with scouting. The listener heard, and definitely stated, that a convoy was approaching on a certain bearing, although nothing was in sight in that direction. Half an hour later, smoke was sighted, and eventually 2 steamers escorted by 2 destroyers appeared over the horizon. This convoy must have been located at a distance of at least 25 miles.[21]

He would also go on to claim that a crew member on another chaser was able to pick up a message "in plain German which, translated, read 'Keep quiet, do not move.'"

Given these gains in sub chaser crews' capabilities, it is somewhat surprising that those dispatched to Halifax would fail to detect *U-155*'s presence in the area, despite it being right under their hulls. This being said, their appearance off Halifax in and of itself served as a deterrent for *U-155*. Studt, well aware of their existence, having repeatedly observed them through his periscope, was dissuaded from making any attacks on surface vessels during this period out of fear of being depth-charged.

Instead, between 0500 and 0900 on the seventeenth, Studt launched his first complement of six Teka mines (out of a total of fourteen on board) while submerged, which, according to his log, were placed "at one-mile intervals approximately 5 miles south of Betty Island near St. John."[22] In actuality, this was the Betty Island near Halifax, not the Bay of Fundy (being that Studt clearly marked the mining location off Halifax on his chart, one can only wonder why he was confused in his log). After brief interruptions due to the presence of Allied patrols, the aforementioned *Grilse*, and sub chasers (he didn't mention observing any aircraft in his log), he deposited the remaining mines on the eighteenth, with four being sown between "Sambro Lightship and Sambro Ledge" at 0100, and the rest being launched "right in front of the entrance" to Halifax's harbor at 0255.[23]

Although there is a handwritten notation in *U-155*'s log by Arno Spindler attributing one of the mines to the sinking of the *Chaparra* (actually sunk by *U-117*'s mines; see previous chapter), none of the Teka mines succeeded in damaging any Allied shipping. It is unclear if this was because of an error in the depth setting or the poor construction of the mines at this point in the war. According to Hadley and Sarty, "Most broke loose from their moorings and were thus rendered 'safe'; fishermen recovered several of them and received twenty-five-dollar rewards."[24] If Studt wanted to add to his tonnage total this patrol, he was going to have to do it the hard way, but first he had to complete his cable-cutting mission.

Proceeding in a northeasterly direction through the evening of the eighteenth, at 0049 on the nineteenth Studt ordered *U-155* to the surface on a course "to begin, in 90 m of water, cutting the six NW Sable Island cables."[25] Unfortunately, he would almost immediately have to crash-dive in order to dodge a sailing ship, two blacked-out steamers, and a destroyer. Unlike with von Nostitz, it appeared that Studt was willing to use his cable cutter only while traveling on the surface and made no attempt at testing his device during submerged travel.

As a result, it wouldn't be until the afternoon hours that he would finally begin his operation. Once *U-155* finally began towing the cutter, the process proceeded much like it had with *U-151* off New York City—using a dynamometer to measure the tension on *U-155*'s towing line. The first indication that a line had been cut occurred shortly after 1430, when a rise in tension to 2.8–3.4 tons was observed. The next occurred nearly two hours later, when again, the dynamometer climbed first to 1.8, then to 2.2–2.6 tons. This led Studt to conclude that three of the transatlantic cables had been cut at 44°34' N, 60°57' 10 W (about 64 mi. / 103 km northwest of Sable Island). Despite continuing the process until about 1930, no other lines would be severed. Assuming that his cutting mission was a great success (in reality, the three cut cables would not interrupt Canadian/British communication in the slightest), Studt then returned his priorities to resuming the trade war south of Nova Scotia. He wouldn't have to travel very far to find his next prey.

At 0930 on the twentieth, *U-155* happened upon the 353-ton American steam-powered trawler *Kingfisher* (a different vessel than the minesweeper of the same name encountered by *U-117*), about 78 mi. / 125 km southeast of Halifax. Although initial, sensationalized newspaper reports claimed the small fishing vessel was torpedoed without warning, her captain, known in publications only by his surname, "Riley," affirmed that an initial warning shot from *U-155*'s deck gun prompted him to begin launching his boats, and a second, which passed directly over the trawler's stack, compelled him and his crew to immediately abandon ship.[26]

After being questioned about the specifics of himself, his ship, and his crew (as well as whether or not they had observed any "large ships") by an unidentified German officer, Capt. Riley noted that a boarding party was sent from *U-155* to the trawler, and she was subsequently sunk with bombs. He also went into detail about the appearance of the U-cruiser, describing her cable cutter and her unique camouflage paint job, with the former looking "like a large pair of steel scissors over her stern and rudder" and the latter being "freshly painted with grey, blue, and white."[27] Although the crew of the *Kingfisher*, much like the crew of the *Leixões*, were not afforded any time to take provisions, their proximity to land allowed them to reach shore by 1000 on the twenty-first, with all twenty-six crew members surviving the ordeal.

News of their arrival in West Quoddy, Nova Scotia, appeared to reignite U-boat fears much farther south. Despite the fact that both *U-117* and *U-140* were safely back in Kiel at the time (and *U-155* was still in Canadian waters), reports of multiple U-boats near the Ambrose Channel lightship on the twenty-third led the 4th Naval District to dispatch a hunter squadron to the area. This group, led by USS *Patterson*, was given orders to patrol "north of Lat.40° to southern shore Long Island then return Delaware Breakwater,"[28] with the 3rd and 5th Naval Districts also being put on standby. As expected, their efforts bore no fruit.

British Intelligence in Room 40, on the other hand, seemed to be much more in tune with *U-155*'s actual location. Two days after the fool's errand involving USS *Patterson*, RAdm. Hall advised Sims of his intentions to lure *U-155* into a trap, cabling the following:

MOST SECRET

Admiral Sims

The following false information has been conveyed to the enemy: Convoys rendezvous at St. John's Newfoundland, ships proceeding thither by the following route:

From 5 miles off Cape Race to 47°25' North 52°11' West, thence to harbor entrance.[29]

This message, as well as later broadcasts reporting troop transports leaving Halifax, would be intercepted by *U-155*, but Studt refused to take the bait. Whether it was due to his cautious nature, or the need to conserve fuel, he would not be reversing his course. Instead, he lingered south of Cape Sable Island before continuing on a southerly course toward the area of Georges Bank.

In retrospect, the decision to avoid such high-profile targets (even if they were traps) was peculiar, especially considering that the *Kingfisher* would be the last vessel encountered by *U-155* for nearly a week. Although *U-155* made a futile pursuit of an unidentified steamer (which consequently sent an "allo" reporting *U-155* at 43°15' N, 65°W) in the area of Cape Sable on the morning of the twenty-sixth, no real targets of opportunity presented themselves.

Studt's luck appeared to change on the morning of the twenty-ninth, when *U-155* entered American waters. Here, nearly 150 nm east-southeast of Cape Cod, he spotted a 2,246 GRT, armed British steamer, the *Reginolite*, on a zigzag course heading northwest. After stalking the vessel at periscope depth for two hours, he gave the order to surface, and *U-155* opened fire on the merchant ship from a distance of approximately 5,000 meters. In turn, the British gun crew replied with their aft gun while the *Reginolite* made steam, began sending SOS signals, and increased her distance from *U-155*.

After thirty-nine minutes of back-and-forth artillery fire (with no vessel scoring any hits), Studt observed what he believed to be a destroyer approaching, and crash-dove, abandoning the attack. On the basis of his description of the vessel in his log, this was likely not a destroyer, but instead either a section patrol boat or a similar auxiliary vessel, if anything at all. Curiously, the *Reginolite* made no such reference to any other vessels in her SOS broadcasts. In fact, her final message radioed during the battle stated, "Proceeding unassisted. Submarine submerging 40-40, 66-59."[30] Whatever the case may have been, Studt wasn't taking any chances. He would remain below the surface for more than two hours, and by the time *U-155* resurfaced at 1130, neither the *Reginolite* nor the "destroyer" was in sight. This experience was a sign of things to come.

Over the next few days, *U-155* came nearer to the American coastline but saw little improvement in her prospects. On September 30, with *U-155* now 100 nm east of Nantucket, smoke clouds were observed, but *U-155* was too slow to make any pursuit. Such was the case the following day (with a Bibby Line passenger ship of the Warwickshire type, approximately 8,000 tons), and again on October 2, when *U-155* made a hopeless deck gun attack on the British steamer *Nevasa* (the same vessel that *U-151* failed to sink with her deck guns on July 3), from a distance of 9,000 m. In the case of the *Nevasa*, the only reward Studt received was an "allo" message notifying the Allied navies of his new position. Had USS *Patterson*'s hunting squadron been a week later in their patrol, they may have had a chance at combating *U-155*. Instead, when *U-155* resumed the offensive on October 3, she did so unopposed.

Now about 420 mi. / 676 km east of Cape May, *U-155* began her morning stalking what Studt described as a "giant cargo steamship." After submerging and positioning himself for a torpedo attack, at 0450 Studt gave the order to fire. Unfortunately for the German raiders, the single torpedo malfunctioned and would fail to find its target. The unidentified steamer, apparently oblivious to her situation, simply sped along on her way, with *U-155* being too slow to continue the pursuit. Whatever disappointment Studt may have felt would be short lived, however, since there were still more smoke clouds on the horizon.

Returning to the surface at 0554, *U-155* continued southward toward her new prey. The target now in Studt's sights was the 3,838-ton Italian cargo ship *Alberto Treves*, en route from Cartagena, Colombia, to New York City. After closing the distance to the vessel, at 0700 Studt noted in his log: "Submerged at 60 hm. Drove to attack. Steamer is armed."[31] The last sentence, being the most critical piece of information in his entry, would seal the fate of the Italian sailors. This time, the single G6AV* torpedo fired from *U-155* found its mark, and the steamship went down in less than twenty minutes. Of the crew's total complement of thirty-four sailors, twenty-one would perish when their lifeboats became lost at sea.

The next day, and about 55 mi. / 88 km southeast of where the *Alberto Treves* was sunk, the trend of *U-155* being too slow to engage distant steamers started anew, with the exception that this time Studt got a consolation prize. After breaking off an artillery battle from a distance of 10 km on an unidentified steamer, Studt found a much more vulnerable victim in the form of a 330-ton Canadian schooner, the *Industrial*. Traveling from the Turks and Caicos islands back to Nova Scotia with a cargo of salt, she was unarmed and, more importantly to *U-155*, far too slow to escape. Being no threat to the Germans, her crew was allowed ample time to collect their belongings and abandon ship before a boarding party dispatched her with explosives—all would be rescued shortly thereafter.

Unbeknown to the crew of *U-155* at this time, back in Europe the western front was collapsing, and the German High Command, under Generals Hindenburg and Ludendorff, began seeking an end to hostilities. Following the resignation of Chancellor von Hertling and his cabinet, staunch conservatives who were committed to an absolute German victory, on October 3 (after much urging from the kaiser) Prince Maximilian von Baden accepted his appointment as the new German chancellor. He was stunned when he discovered that his first duty on the job was to approach the Allies for an armistice.

As *U-155* was busy sinking the *Industrial* on the fourth, von Baden was preparing a missive for President Wilson, seeking a resolution based on his Fourteen Points—it would be sent the very next day. In a strange coincidence, it was exactly on September 5 that the weather changed for the worse on *U-155*'s patrol, and despite the crew observing numerous steamers, use of the U-cruiser's weapons was completely ruled out. This would continue until October 10, when news of the peace offering finally reached Studt. Although Wilson wouldn't demand the cessation of submarine hostilities until October 23, U-boat command, in an effort to avoid upsetting negotiations with the US, instructed Studt to end the *Handelskrieg* off North America and instead resume it in the Azores. Apparently misinterpreting the spirit of his new instructions, Studt would have two final goes at American vessels on his eastward journey toward his new operational zone.

The first of these occurred on October 12, just over 700 mi. / 1,126 km off the Virginia coast, and involved USS *Amphion* (ID-1888, 7,410 GRT). Formerly the SS *Köln* of the Norddeutscher Lloyd, she had been interned in the US at the outbreak of the war and seized upon the United States' entry into it. When *U-155* caught up with her, she was returning from France in ballast, having already safely deposited her cargo of mules, horses, and other equipment.

After stalking the steamer at periscope depth for just over an hour, Studt ordered *U-155* to the surface at 1000 to "initiate an artillery battle" from a distance of 9 km. His first salvo proved to be very effective, since one shot destroyed the *Amphion*'s wireless apparatus, ruling out any chance she had of reporting *U-155*'s position or calling for help. Subsequent shots critically wounded two sailors (with one succumbing to his injuries in Bermuda after the ship landed there for emergency assistance), damaged the ship's superstructure, and "riddled" the steamer's lifeboats with shrapnel.[32] Despite the continuous return fire from the *Amphion*'s naval gun crew, the battle looked to be well in favor of the Germans—at least initially.

Up to this point, *U-155* had been traveling in pursuit of the steamer and, due to her positioning, could fire only her forward 15 cm deck gun. After 120 rounds had been fired, it malfunctioned, with *U-155*'s gun crew being unable to quickly repair it. In order to continue the battle, Studt ordered his submarine on a diagonal course to bring her rear deck gun into action, but in doing so lost speed, and the *Amphion* gradually began pulling away. Eventually the distance between the vessels exceeded the range of *U-155*'s deck guns, and Studt was forced to retire from the battle.

Although no Allied tonnage was lost in the engagement, the single death and multiple wounds inflicted on the American crew by *U-155* certainly gave the impression that Studt was acting contrary to his latest instructions, despite his outbound course. Indeed, Studt wasn't yet finished with his assault on the United States.

His second attempt on an American vessel would prove to be far more devastating. This occurred on October 17, at 38°4' N, 50°50' W, about 1,260 mi. / 2,028 km east of Atlantic City, New Jersey, and involved the 6,744 GRT SS *Lucia*—a vessel believed to have been "unsinkable." Like the *Amphion*, the *Lucia* had also originally been a steamer belonging to the Central Powers, which had been interned and then seized (though this time she was Austro-Hungarian instead of German). Unlike the *Amphion*, she was given a more than $200,000 upgrade in the form of an experimental engineering design to prevent her from being sunk. It consisted of "a buoyancy arrangement . . . of air-filled boxes which lined [her] hold and cabins" and, according to its inventor, would be able to keep the steamer afloat "no matter how much water was taken in through holes torn in the side."[33] *U-155* would put the system to the test with just one, albeit large, gash.

Air escaping from one of the *Lucia*'s buoyancy compartments during *U-155*'s attack. *NH 51461, courtesy of the Naval History & Heritage Command*

At 1510 on the seventeenth, while *U-155* was traveling on the surface, Studt observed numerous smoke clouds on the horizon and quickly realized he had happened across an unescorted convoy consisting of the *Lucia* and the 5,670 GRT SS *Hawaiian*. After spending the next hour and a half positioning *U-155* for a submerged torpedo attack, he set his sights on the larger *Lucia*, hanging to the rear, launching a single torpedo from a distance of 360 m.[34] According to C. F. Leary, the captain of the *Lucia*,

At 5:30 p.m. [*U-155*'s log gives the actual time at 5:40] on October 17, 1918, the *U.S.A.C.T. Lucia* . . . was torpedoed in the engine-room on the port side, killing four men. . . . There was no sign of any submarine to be seen. I had just finished my supper and was going on the bridge. The commander of the armed guard, who was on top of the chart house several minutes before I got on the bridge, said he saw the wake of the torpedo about 100 yards off, and had guns trained in that direction. There was an efficient lookout kept at all times. . . . We immediately sent out SOS calls and our position and semaphored the guide ship *Hawaiian*, to broadcast same.[35]

The captain would go on to note that he expected another torpedo to be forthcoming, and thus made the decision to board the lifeboats but not yet lower them into the sea. This choice would ultimately save the lives of his men.

The experimental buoyancy system, while not wholly preventing the ship from sinking, was actually significantly delaying the inevitable. It would take nearly nine hours for the afterdecks to fully flood, despite the "engine room and fireroom and No. 4 and No. 5" holds being full of water,[36] and an additional thirteen hours for the sea to engulf the remainder of the ship. Given that the boats were still attached to the ship until her final moments, the crew was able to continue to gather provisions as needed and avoid needlessly spending time in the rough seas below. The lifeboats wouldn't actually be completely released until 1515 on the eighteenth—nearly an entire day after the *Lucia* began flooding and only five minutes before the *Lucia* disappeared. It wouldn't be until 2126 on the nineteenth

USS *Fairfax* pictured after rescuing the survivors of the *Lucia*. *NH 54134, courtesy of the Naval History & Heritage Command*

that the crew of the *Lucia* would be rescued by the destroyer USS *Fairfax* (DD-93), and not a moment too soon. According to Capt. Leary: "If the *Fairfax* had not arrived at the time it did, I do not think our boats would have weathered the heavy seas, as they were all overloaded."[37]

The determination not to fire a second torpedo or attack the *Hawaiian* was made by Studt at 1920 on the seventeenth. After coming to the surface and observing the *Lucia* already beginning to list, *U-155* began intercepting her numerous SOS calls, which led Studt to opt against lingering in the area much longer. With the end of the war seemingly in sight, it simply wasn't worth leading his crew into any unnecessary risks with any responding warships.

U-155 would spend the next four days continuing on a course toward the Azores, though she'd never actually make it there. On October 21, at 40°15' N, 40°15' W, about 500 mi. / 805 km west of Santa Cruz das Flores, Studt received the order to return home. Although peace negotiations had begun in earnest, he still had enough fuel for fifty-eight days of travel, three torpedoes, and nearly 75 percent of his deck gun ammunition.[38] Apparently, he didn't want his supplies to go to waste, since he continued to pursue additional targets while proceeding on a northerly course toward the Shetland Islands.

Indeed, two half-hearted attempts were made at engaging vessels on the twenty-third, with one vessel being described as a "giant" steamer with "1 stack and 4 masts" and the other being the British hospital ship *Oxfordshire*. Thankfully, Studt wouldn't follow through with either attack. Although postwar sources claim that *U-155* made a final, unsuccessful assault on the British steamer *Clan MacArthur* at 41°20' N, 32°30' W, Studt's log indicates he was actually miles away, at 46°37' N, 31°42' W, at the time, with no vessels in sight. Instead, his final chase would actually occur on November 1 (about 280 mi. / 451 km northwest of Ireland), when *U-155* spotted another unidentified steamer; however, this pursuit would also come to naught.

In the weeks that followed, as *U-155* rounded the northern periphery of Scotland and negotiated the Northern Barrage, there was a flurry of wireless traffic noted in her log. Most of these transmissions revolved around other U-boats coordinating their efforts to reach home, with Studt specifically noting signals from *U-151*, *U-153*, and *U-139* (all of which will be discussed in the next chapter). Although sentiment can't be ascertained from Studt's war diary, he must have experienced an overwhelming sense of disillusionment.

This would only be amplified when *U-155* finally returned to Kiel on November 14, to a Germany no one on board *U-155* would recognize. Instead of receiving a heroes' welcome with the black, white, and red banners of imperial Germany waving in the air, the men aboard *U-155* were met by mutineers and presented with the red flags of revolution. Even more ignominy awaited *U-155* later that month, when she would be surrendered to the British and used as an exhibition piece before ultimately being sold for scrap—thus painfully ending the legendary career of the *U-Deutschland*, now the embodiment of the ruined state of the once-mighty German Empire.

Adding to the disappointing demise of the *U-Deutschland*, Studt's patrol would be the least effective of any of the U-cruisers that arrived in North American waters, though the burden of this failure can't rest entirely on his shoulders. In most cases, his U-boat was simply too slow to make any successful pursuits while traveling on the surface. For every one vessel he was actually able to sink, five were able to escape. He lamented these circumstances earlier in his cruise, when he noted in his war diary, "It's becoming increasingly recognized that U-cruisers are slow, and that a steamer can often save itself by tough resistance while running off at high speed."[39]

Certainly, the 17,592 tons of shipping he was able to destroy paled in comparison to the tonnage sunk by the equally slow and unwieldy *U-151*, but focusing solely on figures ignores the wider circumstances of Studt's patrol. Given that *U-155*'s operation was ended prematurely and precisely at the point she was approaching more-congested shipping lanes, Studt was never able to advance toward the coastline as closely as previous commanders that summer. Because of this, he was never afforded the opportunity to focus his efforts on the large concentration of vessels making their way in and out of ports (it must also be remembered that *U-155*'s war record did not benefit from any vessels being sunk by her Teka mines). Still, a closer patrol off the mainland United States wasn't in and of itself a guarantee of greater successes, even if *U-155* was able to continue her trade war all the way down to Cape Hatteras. As evidenced by the downward trend of tonnage totals sunk by *U-117* and *U-140*, whose patrols were not interrupted by political developments, there were other factors playing a role in reducing the effectiveness of the U-cruisers.

The fact that Studt, Kophamel, and Dröscher all incurred damage to their U-boats both from mercantile and naval vessels (forcing them to adjust the conduct of their patrols) was indicative that the sailors on the North American side of the Atlantic were becoming much more proficient in countering the U-boat threat. Just as Sims noted the vast improvements of the sub chaser crews in utilizing their listening devices, the recent engagements between American patrol craft and the U-cruisers demonstrated that Allied antisubmarine warfare in North America was only continuing to get better as the war went on. The shock over *U-151*'s arrival earlier that summer had clearly worn off.

Unfortunately, the US and Canadian navies wouldn't be able to further exhibit the lessons learned from that summer, since no other U-boats would reach North America for the remainder of the war. This, however, should not imply that more weren't en route or that the deaths of American sailors would suddenly subside. Just as it seemed that the US and Canadian navies had finally weathered the storm, four more U-boats departed for North America in September/October 1918, and one of these was about to inflict the greatest loss of life of the entire campaign.

CHAPTER 12
The Howling Wolves Fell Silent

Montenegro, the Austro-Hungarian Empire, late September 1918. Korvettenkapitän Georg von Trapp, commander of the Kaiserliche und Königliche Marine[1] base in Cattaro (now Kotor), is presiding over a feast he had planned for his comrades in the neighboring German U-boat station. The Germans, although being located just a few miles farther down the gulf, may as well have been a world away. While the Austro-Hungarian navy had been struggling through the war with tiny, antiquated, gasoline-powered U-boats, contracted German UB submarines, or whatever they could salvage (such as von Trapp's former command, SM *U-14*, formerly the French submarine *Curie*), the Kaiserliche Marine was equipped with the state of the art in large, submersible craft. Earlier that day, as he watched three of his men tending to the spit, then roasting the evening's main course, he reminisced about his first encounter with a U-boat belonging to his Teutonic cousins.

This occurred back in May 1915, when Kapitänleutnant Otto Hersing arrived in Cattaro with SM *U-21*. "Only three years ago, yet it seems like an eternity," von Trapp thinks to himself. Back then, upon being given a tour of the U-19-class submarine, he was left in a state of envious awe, remarking,

> What this boat has is unbelievable! Powerful diesels, the engine room separated from the other parts by bulkheads . . . one large control room to handle the diving maneuver, a spacious conning tower, two periscopes that are electrically raised or lowered . . . torpedo shafts fore and aft. The men have proper berths, the commander even has an honest-to-goodness cabin with an electric lamp next to his bed . . . Like a luxury steamer compared to my old boat . . . It is like being in Wonderland and the Germans are not even aware of it. They act as if this were commonplace.[2]

When Hersing returned the courtesy and visited SM *U-5* (von Trapp's command from June 8, 1914, through April 22, 1915), he was flabbergasted. After taking a quick look around at the archaic submarine, he, rather coarsely, was only able to remark, "I would refuse to travel in this crate."[3]

Von Trapp would never get to see a U-Kreuzer in the flesh, but had he been given the opportunity, he would certainly have been even more impressed than he was with *U-21*—even as a jaded, career naval man. Likewise, the citizens of the German and Austro-Hungarian Empires, whose only knowledge of U-boats came from photos and newspapers, would be even more enthralled by their giant, ocean-traversing wonder weapons. Indeed, even in late 1918, postcards advertised the "newest U-cruisers," praising them as the "largest submarines in the world," taking care to avoid mentioning the slow speed and poor maneuverability that came with their girth. Such marvels of German engineering, such as the earlier zeppelins, promised the populace (at least to those who still believed the propaganda of the period) that the long-awaited victory would finally be forthcoming. The men in Cattaro are much less certain, but just as hopeful.

U-139 departing Kiel. *Author's collection*

As the evening festivities continue, and the Dalmatian wine flows more freely, the German and Austro-Hungarian sailors begin to sing imperial anthems and sea shanties. The jovial scene, standing in stark contrast to the Allied air raid earlier that day, is only superficial. Even with the fine food and ample distractions, the dire state of the war pervades the atmosphere. The ambience takes a particularly dramatic shift when the happy melodies of songs begin to fade from the air, being replaced by news from home, rumors, and war stories.

Even the host of the party isn't immune to the gossip, and in a short while he and his old friend, Linienschiffleutnant Hugo von Seyffertitz (commander of the Austrian U-boat SM *U-47*), begin discussing the latter's recent sinking of the French submarine *Circé*. Apparently, only one of the French sailors was able to survive the attack (the watch officer), and his name was broadcast unencrypted so that news of his survival would eventually reach his wife. Korvettenkapitän von Trapp, no longer surprised by anything he hears, can only shake his head in a sober appreciation that the ones who didn't make it could have been any of his colleagues instead of enemy Frenchmen. The conversation continues:

"By the way—he was called Lapéreyre. Almost like Arnauld. Where is Arnauld now?"

"He's commanding a U-cruiser and might be in the Atlantic. Do you know how much he has sunk so far? About 400,000 tons!

"Yes, yes, he is a terrific fellow . . . God, please let our U-boat war succeed! At home it looks terrible!"[4]

The man the Austrians were pinning their hopes on was the U-boat ace of aces, Kapitänleutnant Lothar von Arnauld de la Perière. After spending much of the war in the Mediterranean commanding SM *U-35*, he was indeed now in the Atlantic, at the helm of the U-Kreuzer *U-139*, "*Walther Schwieger*." He was just one of four German commanders making one final push toward the United States.

The others were Kapitänleutnant Adolf Franz in *U-152*, Korvettenkapitän Paul Pastuszyk in *U-153*, and, making his second patrol toward the US, Korvettenkapitän Heinrich von Nostitz und Jänckendorf in *U-151*. Given that the U-cruiser command considered the previous missions to North America to be successful (despite Allied insistence to the contrary), these vessels would be dispatched westward to continue the exact same strategy as their predecessors: minelaying combined with waging a trade war.

U-152 was the first of the quartet to depart. Although originally scheduled to weigh anchor in mid-August (with *U-155*), she had been held up in the Imperial Dockyard in Kiel for repairs to her diving tanks and fuel bunkers. Ironically, the damage was incurred between July 20 and August 12, when *U-152* and *U-139* were testing a fuel transfer at sea (à la *U-117* and *U-140*) utilizing a conventional fuel hose.[5] It wouldn't be until September 5 that she would finally leave port, with orders to sow fourteen Teka mines between Atlantic City, New Jersey, and Currituck Beach, Virginia, attacking any targets of opportunity along the way.

U-139 was next to sail, departing Kiel on September 11. Just like her sister submarine, *U-140*, she would not be equipped with any mines and would instead focus solely on the *Handelskrieg*, beginning off Cape Hatteras and proceeding northward. If favorable weather was encountered on her return leg, she was also to operate off Halifax for as long as provisions allowed. Unlike prior U-cruisers, she would set a southerly course toward the Azores and Canaries before turning westward and proceeding toward the United States.

U-151 and *U-153* were the last to head out and, although sharing the same general goals as their predecessors, would employ tactics more reminiscent of FdU Hermann Bauer's original designs for the U-cruisers. In this case, both U-boats were given very specific directives to operate off North

America concurrently and cooperatively, or, as their jointly issued orders put it, "hand in hand." While prior U-boats had been dispatched in close sequence and given vague instructions about each other's objectives, these two would depart together on October 1, separating only as they neared Cape Hatteras—with *U-151* then proceeding northward, and *U-153* sailing south toward the Florida Straits. During their "outward march," they were instructed to

> be on the lookout for weakly protected steamers. Sail back if necessary, using the Gulf Stream. Maintain contact with convoys bound for Europe within the restricted area around Great Britain for as long as possible and try to get other boats to attack by radio. Where shipyards, docks and other military installations can be identified from the sea and fired upon with prospects of success that won't endanger the cruiser, they may be fired upon.[6]

They were also given diagrams showing where the previous U-cruisers had sown their mines (including *U-152*'s intended field) and given much more precise mining instructions than their predecessors. These read as such:

a) *U-151*

1.) South to east of the barrier laid by *U-117* at Wimble Shoals, but not more than 10 nm from Wimble Shoals Lighthouse, based on observations to be made beforehand.

2.) From a point: Bodie Island light buoy at 290° to the right. 15 nm direction 90°. Shift due to traffic observations in direction 90° up to a nautical mile permitted from the boundary of the specified mining area. Depth setting: 4.5 m below spring low tide. The barriers should be placed in quick succession, if possible, on the same day.

b) *U-153* lay mines at a maximum distance of 10 nm from:

1.) Martins-Industry Lightship (Savannah)

2.) Charleston Lightship. Depth setting: 4.5 m below spring low tide. The barriers should be placed in quick succession, if possible, on the same day.[7]

Finally, having realized that *U-155* wasn't entirely successful in her cable-cutting mission, *U-151* was given the task of finishing the job (*U-153* would not be equipped with cable cutters). This, however, was only a tertiary objective, as the orders noted:

North of Sable Island the cables leading to Europe are to be cut. This task takes a back seat to the trade war, insofar as there are any prospects for this to be successful. However, it should be pursued with vigor if it can be accomplished on the return journey without a significant loss of time.[8]

These were the most-coordinated and most-detailed orders drawn up to that point and exhibited a foresightfulness (particularly with the scouting mission off Britain) for how U-boats would successfully operate in the future. Unfortunately for the Germans, the payoff of these plans wouldn't be realized until decades later. Due to their late departure date, *U-151* and *U-153* would be recalled just days after successfully negotiating the Northern Barrage. Whatever final blows were going to be struck against North America would have to come from *U-152* and *U-139*.

In the case of the latter, she would be beginning her patrol with many of the same design handicaps and workmanship flaws as *U-140*. Additionally (given that *U-140* arrived back in Kiel over a week after *U-139* headed out), von Arnauld would lack the benefit of hearing about Kophamel's experiences with his cumbersome U-Kreuzer. This meant that von Arnauld and his crew would encounter many of the same exact issues as their colleagues and would be forced to adapt to them in situ. Akin to *U-140*, problems were encountered immediately after departing Kiel.

Although *U-139*'s logs were destroyed after the Armistice (out of fears that Rügen would be occupied by the Royal Navy), the specifics of *U-139*'s cruise can still be gleaned from postwar interviews and memoirs. Thankfully, the son of Hans Fechter, *U-139*'s chief engineer, was able to provide some of his father's records to the historian Eberhard Rössler (who subsequently published them in his book *Die Deutschen U-Kreuzer und Transport U-Boote*). It is striking how closely some of these notes resemble what was described in Kophamel's war diary, particularly with the U-boat's various faults.

The first issue experienced by the crew of *U-139* occurred in the stormy waters of the North Sea and concerned the U-cruiser's stability. In words that could have been copied verbatim from *U-140*'s *Kriegstagebuch*, Fechter's narrative reads as follows:

> The U-cruiser was heavily loaded and lay deep in the water. The overflowing seas could not drain through the openings in the upper deck and made the cruiser top-heavy. She remained lying in the sea with a list of 15°, could not right herself and was heeled by the overcoming seas up to 52°, only to then very slowly right herself again to 15° before the next sea brought her back to the point of capsizing. . . . This danger could only be eliminated by blowing out the diving tanks, which were also filled with fuel and served as bunkers.[9]

Had von Arnauld been able to speak with Kophamel before leaving Kiel, this problem could have been alleviated by drilling the additional drainage holes into the upper deck while still in port. It doesn't appear that Fechter was ever able to arrive at the same solution. Next came the problem of fuel shortages:

> After the first dive bunkers were emptied, it was found that, after adding up the measured fuel consumption, they had received 15% less fuel. It was impossible to determine how this error could have occurred. We now didn't have enough fuel on board to wage war on the American east coast for more than two or three weeks.[10]

This is interesting since, like Dröscher and Beckmann, Fechter seemed to blame his situation on some nebulous, indeterminable error, potentially with the design of the tanks deviating from how they were actually manufactured. Although nothing is mentioned either by von Arnauld or his chief engineer about an oil sheen accompanying them on their cruise, the significance of the fuel deviation couldn't have been anything other than the same leaks that affected *U-117* and *U-140*. Fortunately for von Arnauld and *U-139*, all of their engagements occurred on the European side of the Atlantic, and fuel shortages would not haunt them as they had Kophamel and Dröscher.

Indeed, the first victories of *U-139*'s very short patrol occurred about 195 mi. / 313 km north-northwest of Cape Finisterre (the west coast of Spain) on the morning of October 1—her initial attack nearly being her last. Here, von Arnauld spotted a large convoy on the horizon, being escorted by two British auxiliary cruisers and a complement of British ML boats. After positioning himself for a submerged torpedo shot, intentionally lying in wait for the convoy to sail in front of *U-139*, he launched a single G6AV* torpedo in the direction of a large freighter at 1145, only to have it miss. Considering he was the highest-scoring submarine ace of all time, his next plan of attack seemed downright reckless.

While still at periscope depth, he could hear the "huge rushing and whirring sound ... of many propellors"[11] over his U-boat, indicating that the convoy had changed direction and its extremities were now passing above him. Instead of diving, at 1320 he opted to surface (navigating upward by the sound of the steamers' screws) to use his twin deck guns against the nearby ships. Not surprisingly, once *U-139* opened up the artillery battle, she immediately received return fire from the armed steamships and one of the approaching auxiliary cruisers, the HMS *Perth*. Von Arnauld was quickly forced back down, but not before his shells damaged the *Perth* and inflicted two casualties, both of which resulted in death.[12] The only consolation for the British was that one of the *Perth*'s high-explosive shells was able to damage *U-139*'s conning tower. The

ML boats' depth charge attack that immediately followed the shelling was completely ineffective. Although the British cruisers and sub chasers gave up the pursuit at this point, von Arnauld was just getting started.

Following the bombardment, von Arnauld ordered *U-139* back to periscope depth to observe the convoy steaming away to the north. Not content with escaping with himself and his command being fully intact, he once again decided to surface and steer toward the convoy at maximum speed in an attempt to engage it with his deck guns—it would take him nearly two hours to catch up. According to von Arnauld,

> This time luck favored us. The auxiliary cruisers were slow and gave us time to get the range. In good shooting distance, we had a few minutes of precious target practice. We sent out shells as fast as we could at the nearest steamer. She stopped, badly hit. Then we turned on the next one. A few shells, and she was disabled. By this time one of the cruisers was headed for us at full speed, firing and trying to ram us.
>
> The ocean swallowed us, and in a minute depth bombs came looking for us with their ugly banging voices. When they had their say we returned to periscope depth to see what could be done. The first steamer we had hit was sinking. The cruiser that had attacked us was taking aboard the stricken vessel's crew. The second steamer we had hit was lying well afloat. Patrol boats were standing by, and one of the larger vessels was preparing to take it in tow.[13]

To clarify what von Arnauld described: the steamer in the process of sinking was the British SS *Bylands* (3,309 GRT), which had been en route to Dublin with a cargo of phosphate—she would eventually go under at 1855 that evening; the disabled cargo ship was the Italian SS *Manin* (2,691 GRT), which was en route to Glasgow (von Arnauld was not yet done with her); and the HMS *Perth* was once again the auxiliary cruiser that engaged *U-139*, firing at her from "an extreme range"[14] for an hour and a half.

After observing the rescue operation at periscope depth until the convoy once again departed the area at 1930, von Arnauld decided to finally finish off the (now abandoned) *Manin* with a torpedo under the cover of darkness—this was to nearly become his undoing. According to von Arnauld's version of events, he observed the *Manin* as "a looming shadow in the twilight" and, without spending any time to inspect the area, fired a torpedo at close range, giving the order to dive to immediately thereafter. In doing so, he was taking *U-139* directly below the sinking ship, which subsequently impacted the conning tower of the submarine, broke her periscopes, and began taking the U-boat down with her.

Postwar statements from 1st Artillerie-Offizier (gunnery officer) Korvettenkapitän Pistor and Oberingenieur Fechter portray the commander as being even more rash. Their narratives claimed that

> during the attack von Arnauld was at the periscope, the 1.AO [Pistor] was under the tower hatch and the Obersteuermann [chief helmsman, the senior NCO and navigator] and the combat helmsman were in the turret. After looking through the periscope, the 1.AO remarked, "Damn close." The commander replied, "It doesn't matter—shoot—go quickly to 50 m." The tower hatch was pushed open by the impact of the sinking steamer, but the 1.AO was able to close it again against the flooding water. However, water continued to splash into the tower through the cracked rivets.[15]

Both von Arnauld's and his crew's narratives are identical otherwise, describing in vivid detail the mayhem that ensued.

As they lay below the sinking steamer, water continued to pour in, and it wasn't until they reached a depth of 60 m that the tanks were blown and *U-139* was able to free herself from the wreck. This, however, did not mark the end of their problems. As they shot to the surface, there were still British patrol boats waiting in the area, and *U-139*, now blind and immobile, presented an easy target.

Just as quickly as *U-139* emerged from the depths, she was forced to crash-dive to avoid the incoming shells. Evasive maneuvers then had to be taken to escape the imminent depth charge salvo. Amazingly, von Arnauld was able to steer *U-139* to safety and, by 2300, was even able to surface and proceed on a northwesterly course unhindered. What was even more incredible was that when Fechter inspected the U-boat for his damage report, besides the periscopes and leaky conning tower, he found the rest of the submarine's compartments to be undamaged and "watertight."

They next day, now about 334 mi. / 537 km northwest of Cape Prior, the blind and wounded *U-139* encountered a small Portuguese lugger—the 301-ton *Rio Cavado*. This was fortuitous not only because she was slow and unarmed, but also because she had a cargo of port wine (which the Germans were happy to confiscate to calm their nerves from the previous night). After the Portuguese crew boarded their launch and the Germans finished looting the sailing ship, the *Rio Cavado* was then sunk with explosives. Her crew would survive, eventually reaching Spain without any casualties.

Following this engagement, von Arnauld realized that his U-cruiser, now lacking the ability to dive because of the conning-tower leaks, was basically a weakly armed surface raider and would be useful only in attacking small, unarmed vessels. After considering his circumstances, he decided to head home for repairs—it was obvious that his U-boat was no longer in the condition to make a worthwhile assault off North America. This assessment was reinforced a few days later, when von Arnauld spotted the *Mauretania* in the Bay of Biscay. Although this was a prime target, *U-139* was woefully outgunned on the surface, and the cumbersome U-cruiser's slow speed would have made a successful pursuit in rough seas extremely difficult. Von Arnauld, disappointedly, had to let her go. Then, on October 9, he picked up a wireless transmission that forced him to once again reevaluate his patrol.

On this day, *U-139* received the message being sent to all operational U-boats, explaining that Germany was attempting to begin peace negotiations with the Allies through the United States. This early indication of defeat seemed to spark a patriotic fervor in von Arnauld, since he, instead of continuing back toward Kiel, then radioed headquarters with his intentions to continue his patrol solely off the Azores—attacking any vulnerable vessels he could find with his deck guns. He must have been extremely cautious, however, since no attempts were made on any vessels until the fourteenth, when *U-139* spotted the 2,557-ton Portuguese steamer *San Miguel* being escorted by one of the Marinha Portuguesa's auxiliary minelayers, the 487-ton trawler *Augusto de Castilho*. According to von Arnauld, the engagement unfolded as follows:

> We sighted a big steamer escorted by a Portuguese gunboat. We gave chase, but the steamer was too fast. The gunboat attacked us. It was a puny, antiquated thing and had no guns to match ours [it was armed with only a 7.5 cm and a 4.7 cm gun] and had only half as many men aboard as we had. I have never seen a braver fight than that old piece of junk put up. Those Portuguese fought like devils, firing shell after shell from their popguns while we raked them from stem to stern. Fourteen of their forty men lay dead on deck and most of the rest were wounded before the boat surrendered. We took the survivors aboard as prisoners and sank their vessel. Later in the day we sighted a ship, stopped it, put our prisoners aboard, and sent them home.[16]

Ironically, just a day before *U-139* left Kiel, the Portuguese government recommended to Adm. Sims that the "United States furnish Portugal several submarine chasers on account of present inadequate patrols [of the] Portuguese coast maintained by few Portuguese vessels in bad condition."[17] They also wanted the Navy to supply them with gasoline for their seaplanes, since they apparently lacked enough fuel to get any in the air. Not surprisingly, Sims advised against sending any sub chasers, since they were "needed in other areas which it is more important to cover," but did suggest that CNO Benson spare some gas for aerial patrols.

One could only speculate how the gun battle on the fourteenth may have gone if von Arnauld was met by a 110-foot sub chaser instead of an antiquated trawler. Certainly, even if *U-139* survived the attack, it would have been unlikely that they would have found supplies on a sub chaser that would have helped repair the U-Kreuzer. Indeed, finding such a cargo was a detail missing from von Arnauld's aforementioned narrative about the *Augusto de Castilho*, which, when being interviewed by Lowell Thomas, he mistakenly attributed to his earlier encounter with the *Rio Cavado*.

According to Chief Engineer Fechter, prior to sinking the *Augusto de Castilho* with *U-139*'s deck guns, the German boarding party discovered two barrels of cement on board. While seemingly goods of negligible significance, Fechter had them brought over to *U-139*, where he began "chiseling off the loose and damaged parts [of the U-boat], [and] had the leaky areas of the [conning] tower ceiling poured [with the cement] and thus temporarily sealed."[18] In his version of the event, a subsequent test dive proved that the conning tower was now watertight up to a depth of 20 m. Von Arnauld, pleased with the repair, later remarked, "We were still without periscopes but . . . could still navigate the depths again—a blind fish, to be sure, but still a fish."[19] Unfortunately for *U-139*, this repair would fail to have a meaningful impact on their patrol, since another more serious breakdown was about to occur.

The next day, as *U-139* pursued a convoy of unescorted tankers, a counterweight within the starboard engine sheared off, lodging itself between the crankshaft and its base plate. The result was a destroyed bearing and a damaged crankcase, rendering the engine useless. It would be rebuilt at sea in a process that lasted the better part of eight days. During this downtime, *U-139* received instructions to cease attacking merchant ships and instead focus solely on warships. This was out of the question for *U-139* in her current condition, and thus her patrol had effectively ended. As she proceeded back to Germany, successfully crossing the Allied minefields and dodging the torpedoes of a British submarine, *U-139*'s final orders of the war oddly directed her to act against her countrymen.

According to Fechter, as *U-139* approached Copenhagen on October 26, a wireless transmission was received instructing naval officers to occupy the wireless stations at Nauen and Rügen. This was followed by an additional directive from FdU Kommodore Michelsen advising U-boats to "shoot at any vessels with red flags"![20] The final message of the day came from the Workers and Soldiers' Council in Kiel, countermanding all previous orders and signifying that the revolution had fully taken hold. Instead of going back to Kiel under these conditions, von Arnauld instead sailed for Sassnitz (on the island of Rügen) to better assess the situation and dispose of his logs—*U-139* would ultimately arrive in Kiel on November 14.

With *U-139* never actually having turned westward for the United States (prior to her eventual retirement), the only U-Kreuzer still en route to North America in late September / early October 1918 was SM *U-152*, which had departed Kiel a week earlier than *U-139*, on September 5. Given that she had already been commissioned as a converted merchant U-boat since 1917 (and had already completed two prior war patrols), she experienced none of the initial teething issues suffered by *U-139* but *would* have to contend with completely worn-out engines. The only change she would receive from her original configuration was a fresh camouflage paint job reminiscent of the one painted on *U-155*.

Despite his rather ominous departure, where the towing line from *U-152* to her torpedo boat escort (*T-139*) broke twice, Kapitänleutnant Adolf Franz had a mostly uneventful trip from Kiel, through the Kattegat, and eventually through the Northern Barrage. While radio messages from Rügen warned of "enemy submarines being observed day and night"[21] in the Skagerrak, along with enemy minelayers and aircraft, *U-152* traversed the restricted zone around Great Britain completely undetected. In fact, it wouldn't be until September 27 that Adm. Sims warned that in the period between September 8 and 14,

> there is a converted mercantile submarine [*U-155*] bound for the American coast, and another outward-bound north of the British Isles probably to operate off the American coast. The submarine that operated off the coast of Portugal [*U-157*] has been lost track of and may have entered the Mediterranean. The converted mercantile operating about the Canaries is probably still there [*U-139*; Sims often mistook all U-cruisers as being of the U-151 type].[22]

U-152, being the other converted mercantile submarine north of Britain, had already attacked a vessel by that point, the Danish schooner *Constance* (sometimes referred to as *Constanza*, even within Franz's log) on September 11 at 62°30' N, 0°35' W (about 180 mi. / 290 km west of the Norwegian coast).

This innocuous vessel had the misfortune of transporting lumber (wooden planks) in the restricted zone, where her neutrality no longer protected her. Although her captain specified that the cargo originated in Bergen, Norway, and was destined for Gothenburg, Sweden, the *Constance*'s presence so far out at sea (well away from any logical course to Sweden) raised Franz's suspicions that the cargo was really destined for the Allies. After noting that contract from the Swedish consignee was "not on board," there was "no corresponding declaration from a neutral government," and a crew member had a British passport,[23] he concluded that she would have to be sunk. Unfortunately for Franz, this was easier said than done.

After allowing the Danish crew to gather provisions and board their lifeboat, a German prize crew placed three bombs on board, which failed to sink the schooner since her cargo was keeping her afloat. Next, numerous 15 cm shells were fired at the *Constance*, which also yielded no result. Finally, at 1650, Franz dejectedly logged, "Abandoned wreck, did not observe sinking."[24] Ultimately, the *Constance* was recovered later and towed back to port. This would be the first of many disappointments for the *Kapitänleutnant* in the coming week and a half.

Beginning in the early hours of September 13, *U-152* began experiencing problems with both of her diesel engines. After spending two and a quarter hours fixing the ignition on the starboard diesel, a complete overhaul of the port engine was initiated (both the starboard and portside engines would require constant, almost daily attention from this point on in the patrol). Interestingly, just hours after the repair work began, three Danish fishing luggers were observed, and instead of making any attempt at engaging the vessels, Franz ordered a British war ensign to be raised on the U-boat and then heaved to—masking his true identity. The stratagem appeared to have worked (though the luggers in all likelihood didn't have radios), since *U-152* remained in place for nearly eight hours, completing the overhaul in peace. At 2300 that evening, "full speed ahead with both engines" was resumed and a course of 240° was set, but this too was to be short lived. By 0450 the following day, *U-152* once again had to stop because the oil mast was found to be full of water. This repair would delay the U-boat's cruise for another two hours.

More frustration followed when smoke clouds were observed on the horizon at 1605 that day. After going to periscope depth and positioning *U-152* to attack the steamship, Franz spotted the words "Belgian Relief" painted clearly on the side of the ship's hull.[25] Dismayed but not defeated, he ordered *U-152* to the surface to fire a warning shot and investigate the vessel further. Unfortunately for the Germans, the steamer was found to be the Norwegian *Bjørnstjerne Bjørnson*, transporting over 8,000 tons of wheat from New York to Rotterdam with all the necessary paperwork confirming her mission—she had to be released. So did the next vessel, halted by *U-152* at 2055, a Danish three-masted schooner (the *Ellen Benzo*) transporting salt from Cádiz to the neutral, Danish-controlled Faroe Islands.

This lack of viable targets was clearly on Franz's mind on the fifteenth. With *U-152* now 220 mi. / 353 km southeast of Iceland and seeing nothing on the horizon, he noted in his war diary the following:

> Glorious weather, wireless masts erected, lookouts stationed. . . . In today's weather, a reconnaissance aircraft would do excellent service. Leaving at night would cause the least trouble [for the aircraft].[26]

This idea of utilizing aerial scouts was not unique. The concept had actually been tested as early as January 15, 1915, when SM *U-12* launched an FF-29 floatplane outside Zeebrugge (coincidentally piloted by Oberleutnant zur See Friedrich von Arnauld de la Perière, the brother of Lothar von Arnauld de la Perière) specifically for increasing the patrolling range of the seaplanes. In the case of *U-152*, her distance so far from Germany would have required a zeppelin for the job. In fact, the lack of dirigible surveillance over the Atlantic was one of the biggest missed opportunities for the Kaiserliche Marine during the Great War.

Had the naval airships been sent over the Atlantic Ocean during the U-Kreuzer campaign, instead of being used primarily for patrols in the North Sea or for bombing missions over England (resulting in a loss of nearly half their airships and crews), they could have fulfilled the role the BdU was asking of *U-151* and *U-153*—spotting convoys over the wide swaths of the ocean, radioing their positions and courses, and coordinating U-boat attacks far from the protection of Allied aircraft and coastal patrols. They had a superior range (at this point in the war nearly 7,500 mi. / 12,000 km for *L70*/X-class zeppelins) and could stay afloat for weeks on end. Instead, the oceangoing U-boats were left to pursue anything they happened on by chance, or if they were fortuitous, to have received a contact report from another vessel in their immediate vicinity. As it was, Kapitänleutnant Franz would spend the next three days after making his observation as he traveled over 500 nautical miles with nothing in sight.

This changed at 0700 on September 18, when *U-152* intercepted radio transmissions from an American cruiser attempting to make contact with a convoy it was escorting. According to Franz, when a response was broadcast at 0800 he was able to estimate their distance as being 80 nm away. By 1230, *U-152* made contact. Upon the initial sighting of smoke clouds, Franz assessed the group as consisting of twelve steamers and two small cruiser escorts. He immediately ordered *U-152* to be submerged to periscope depth to move in for an attack. The rough seas and stormy weather were both a blessing and curse for the U-boat that afternoon. On the one hand, they prevented his submarine and its periscope from being spotted by the escorts; on the other hand, Franz found *U-152* to be extremely slow and difficult to keep level in such conditions.

Over the course of the next hour and twenty minutes, Franz repeatedly tried to pursue the convoy submerged, struggling to keep *U-152* at a level trim. He noted that his depth consistently varied from 20 to 30 meters, and that due to a "lack of glass level gauges" (apparently his were malfunctioning), depth had to be ascertained through the use of the periscope, which, due to the heavy ocean swells, could get a clear picture of the convoy only if he went to a depth of 13 m. At 1350 he surfaced to make one final attempt at the convoy but could no longer close the distance. All he could do was radio Rügen, reporting the convoy's size and course. Rather naively, he was under the impression that he would have been successful in his pursuit if he had a U-139-class U-boat, concluding,

> The helplessness of the old U-cruiser under today's circumstances was clearly demonstrated. Low surface and submerged speed, poor diving characteristics in rough seas . . . and in addition bad depth control characteristics made it impossible to get close enough to the convoy to maintain contact for a long period of time. A new U-cruiser would not have let go of this convoy.[27]

The experiences of the eighteenth followed him into the afternoon of the following day, when the same tactics were used against a lone, fast, zigzagging steamer that Franz believed was either the *Mauretania* or the *France*. Despite having both torpedo tubes flooded and being ready to fire, that attack also had to be broken off after three hours, since *U-152* was unable to catch up with the steamer either above or below the surface. Nothing else would be observed for the next five days.

The crew of *U-152* (and two American prisoners). Franz is pictured seated in the center. He was described by a survivor of the *Stifinder* as being dressed "like a chauffeur" with a short khaki overcoat with a large sheepskin collar. *NH 44371, courtesy of the Naval History & Heritage Command*

As *U-152* continued toward North America, Franz, like his predecessors, began to question the amount of fuel being consumed by the U-cruiser in relation to the original estimations. On September 23, now nearly 800 nautical miles southwest of the Irish coast (and almost halfway across the Atlantic), he began a series of calculations about his objectives, his course, the days traveled thus far, and the fuel used up. He was not optimistic. In fact, he was already anticipating his patrol being forcibly curtailed by his diminishing fuel supply. The fact that he learned of *U-117*'s and *U-140*'s oil shortages the following day did little to quell his reservations. Nevertheless, he pressed on, and by the evening of the twenty-fourth he had more-important things to worry about. *U-152* finally happened across another potential victim, the 5,223 GRT British steamer *Alban*.

The *Alban* was encountered at 44°22' N, 29°45' W, and, for reasons never explained in *U-152*'s war diary or postwar notes, Franz opted to fire a warning shot at her instead of immediately attacking the armed merchant ship. His poor judgment resulted in the British quickly turning the tables on the U-boat, and subsequently augmented *U-152*'s existing fuel woes. According to Kapitänleutnant Franz,

> The steamer immediately returned fire [she was armed with two 4-inch guns], steered a zigzag course, made artificial fog, and finally escaped in the haze of the horizon due to her superior speed, the result of a temporary malfunction in one of our diesel engines. To our great chagrin, early the next morning it turned out that the previous day's fruitless artillery pursuit had not been without dire consequences for us. By daybreak, to our great horror, a wide trail of oil streaks had been noticed in the cruiser's wake as far as our eyes could see. The damage that caused the estimated oil loss of around 13,000 liters during the night, which was later determined to be 16,000 liters, was due to the loosening of a valve on an oil bunker vent line caused by the sheet metal over the pressure hull of the ship loosening due to hammering of the sea or from the recoil of the deck guns. "With on-board means" it was repaired as quickly as possible.[28]

Even with the loss of 16 cbm of fuel and the persistent issues with his diesel engines, Franz remained undeterred and continued his patrol toward North America on the busy steamer routes between Gibraltar and the United States. Despite his course, it would take another five days for *U-152* to spot another vessel.

After lamenting on the twenty-eighth that the weather would have once again been ideal for a reconnaissance plane to lead him to a convoy or to scare shipping in his direction, on the morning of the twenty-ninth, *U-152* encountered a large, armed oil tanker at 43°40' N, 37°42' W (just over 750 mi. / 1,207 km east-southeast of Newfoundland). This was the 6,936 GRT USS *George G. Henry* (ID-1560), returning to the US from France in ballast. Yet again, Franz's inexperience as a U-boat commander was revealed, first by firing warning shots at an armed vessel instead of going in for the kill, and next from being much too far away to make a successful attack with his slow U-cruiser. When he recalled the event a decade later, he appeared to be cognizant of both of these facts, though he was completely unaware of just how close he came to sinking the vessel. In his words,

> On September 29, at 7:35 in the morning . . . the hoped-for steamer came into view in the form of smoke clouds, 4 points to starboard astern. . . . Since a submerged attack was impossible due to our unfavorable position and being too great a distance away, an artillery attack was carried out at a distance of approx. 8,000 m after several warning shots were fired, to which the steamer immediately returned fire. After *U-152* had fired at the enemy, the latter turned away, ran zigzag courses and at times quite skillfully made an artificial fog, so that he was completely out of sight for about 15 minutes and often only the tips of his masts protruded from the cloud of fog. Besides continuing to return the artillery fire against us, the steamer also shot . . . into the water in order to disguise [our shells'] impacts from us and thereby make it very difficult [for us] to observe our own shots. Without us having observed a hit from our gunfire on the enemy, the latter flashed with intensely burning flames on his stern lasting several minutes, at the same time the wireless call for help "SOS" suddenly rang out. It was either a powder explosion from the steamer's rear gun or the appearance of fire was a deliberate deception.[29]

According to American records, this *was* actually an explosion in the tanker's magazine. The only reason the fire didn't spread through the rest of the vessel was because the navy hose crew was actively fighting the inferno, and one man, 2nd Class Engineer William Vail, "climbed a red-hot ladder" to isolate the other compartments near the magazine—succeeding in his task and "suffering great physical punishment."[30] The damage control parties were able to clear the dense, asphyxiating smoke only by "breaking air-ports and cutting away the aft companion hatch."[31] Continuing with Kapitänleutnant Franz's narrative:

> We pursued this adversary utilizing all the naval arts of war and running . . . with the utmost power from both our diesel engines. Our cruiser suffered considerably, [and] at times seas swept over our forecastle and

the front 15 cm gun, which made shooting quite difficult for us. At around 1030, at a distance of approx. 130 hm from the enemy, we finally gave up the pursuit because of the lack of prospects and an enormous, but unfortunately futile, consumption of ammunition by our standards: "116 shots." The steamer continued on her course for about 12 nm. Unfortunately, we couldn't catch up. We learned our lesson from this experience: "Get closer to the enemy before opening fire!" So, as the sailor says, this 7,000-ton American tanker had slipped through our fingers. . . . The smoke continued to be followed until 2pm in the hope that "G Henry" would . . . return to his old general course and run into us again.[32]

As the German commander emphasized, the battle was indeed a learning experience. Franz would recall that after the engagement he was "somewhat contrite and dissatisfied," particularly with the expenditure of 116 shells.

Having previously been the artillery officer on the SMS *Thüringen* (earning the Iron Cross, First Class, for his efforts during the Battle of Jutland), he "tried to console the artillery officer of the U-cruiser by saying that he couldn't do anything about the gunfire landing in the sea and that we wanted to do better next time."[33] He reiterated the need to get close to enemy vessels and abstain from firing prematurely. The men on *U-152* wouldn't have to wait long to put these lessons into practice. On the following day, *U-152* was about to initiate one of the most intense and deadly U-boat attacks on American naval forces of the war.

After the failed pursuit of the *George G. Henry*, Franz found himself 50–60 nautical miles north of his previous course, forcing *U-152* to spend the entire night heading to the west in hopes of reentering the busy steamer routes. Shortly before 0600 on the thirtieth, while the *Kapitänleutnant* was still asleep, his overnight watch spotted USS *Ticonderoga* (ID-1958) during a momentary clearing in the early morning haze. This 5,130 GRT steamship had formerly been the SS *Kamilla Rickmers*, an interned German transport ship appropriated by the US Navy upon America's entry into the war in 1917. She was en route to France with a cargo of railroad ties and, besides her crew of naval personnel, also had 115 soldiers from the ordnance branch of the US Army on board.

During the night of the twenty-ninth, as *U-152* was traveling westward to get back on course, USS *Ticonderoga* fell behind her convoy due to engine trouble and was making only about 8 knots. When *U-152* caught up with her, neither the remainder of the convoy (another seventeen ships) nor the escorting protected cruiser, USS *Galveston* (the same cruiser involved with the convoy spotted by Kophamel), was in sight. Still, she was far from helpless since she was painted in an elaborate dazzle camouflage pattern and was armed with both a 6-inch (15.2 cm) aft gun and 3-inch (7.6 cm) forward gun.

USS *Ticonderoga. NH 42415, courtesy of the Naval History & Heritage Command*

According to Franz, the engagement began as follows (his entire perspective can be found in appendix C of this book):

> At 5:50 a.m. . . . the officer on watch had spotted a steamer going in the opposite direction about 7 points to port at a distance of about 2,500 to 3,000 m. . . . The steamer was similar to yesterday's, i.e., painted in completely mixed-up patterns, chessboard-shaped and stripes, so that in the brightness of the day the bow and stern were difficult to distinguish and thus the direction of its course was difficult to determine. The officer on watch might have turned towards the steamer a little too eagerly and bravely, and as a result of a misunderstanding, I took the bow of the steamer for its stern for a short time and wanted to continue turning to port, first bringing the stern of the steamer to the starboard side of my cruiser and follow in the steamer's wake. This error, i.e., the mix-up of bow and stern, was recognized immediately, but it was no longer possible to stop the cruiser's strong turn once it had been initiated. At the same time . . . we noticed that the steamer also turned to port towards us in order, after it had probably sighted us, to turn its broadside away from a possible launched torpedo or to ram us. With my appearance on the tower, the entire crew of the cruiser was alerted and immediately manned the guns to begin the artillery attack. A quick dive and an attempt at a submerged attack did not come into my consideration for a second in the situation that suddenly stood in front of us[,] and we had to continue

turning extremely quickly. An attempt to dive . . . would have been our undoing. With the water as smooth as glass, U-152 had been able to submerge in about 40 to 60 seconds several times. In normal weather and a wind force of 3 to 4, depending on the sea and swell, you could expect 2, 3, 4, or more minutes until you had the tower under water, so there was enough time for the steamer, in the given situation and weather, to run over the heap of us.[34]

USS *Ticonderoga* had, in fact, spotted *U-152* and was turning toward her precisely to open fire on and ram her. Ens. Gustav Ringelman, who was on the steamer's deck at the time, noted that *Ticonderoga* had narrowly missed ramming *U-152* by 25 feet, and just before the ship's forward 3-inch gun could get a shot off, Franz's gun crews were already opening up on the steamship (this time without a warning shot) with high-explosive shells.[35]

The artillery from *U-152* was extremely effective, since one of the initial shots succeeded in striking the steamer's bridge—instantly killing the helmsman, breaking the steering gear, disabling the radio, starting a fire, and severely wounding *Ticonderoga*'s captain, Lt. Cmdr. James J. Madison. This was impressive, given the circumstances, and was reflective of Franz's previous experience as an artillery officer. According to him, his gun crews could not see the sights on the 15 cm guns in the morning darkness, so he and his artillery officer instructed them to set the guns for night firing at a default distance of 1,200 m and aim for the steamer's stacks. Subsequent shots disabled the Americans' forward gun, killing the gun crew in the process, destroyed numerous lifeboats, and continued to strike down anyone unlucky enough to be in the proximity of the German shells. As Ringelman noted, "During this time[,] most everybody on board our ship was either killed or wounded to such an extent that they were practically helpless from shrapnel."[36] Then the firing stopped.

This sudden ceasefire on the part of the Germans was not because of an abrupt sense of mercy; instead it was due to Franz observing "flashes of fire" originating from a distant "vessel with 2 to 3 smokestacks," which was identified as a cruiser, firing at them, and approaching on a zigzag course at high speed. This was USS *Galveston*, mistakenly thinking that the *Feltore,* another naval transport ship within her convoy, was being attacked. While Franz ordered *U-152* to submerge to evade the warship, USS *Galveston*

> sped toward the spot [where] "a second set of gun flashes" was seen and [since] they were so close together . . . the cruiser stopped firing, for fear of "hitting a friendly vessel." Then the *Galveston* observed a fire break out but noted that it was soon extinguished." And then "the *Galveston* returned to her position with the convoy."[37]

Since USS *Galveston* had been running on reduced power due to a shortage of engineers (resulting from a flu outbreak), her commander, Capt. Chadwick, concerned about further submarine attacks on the greater part of his convoy, wanted to rejoin it before his slow speed placed him too far away to mount an adequate defense. Franz would place a significant amount of blame on *Galveston* for the massive loss of life that would result from the sinking of USS *Ticonderoga*—not only because she fled the area and abandoned the survivors, but also because her sudden presence during the attack dissuaded *U-152* from remaining in the area to provide any German aid to the American sailors (see appendix C). Whether such an onus could be placed on Capt. Chadwick is debatable, but what cannot be argued is that *Galveston*'s retirement from the engagement sealed the fate of *Ticonderoga*.

Although Franz positioned *U-152* to fire two torpedoes at the wounded steamer while he was submerged, due to the vessel "always turning in large circles to port," both attempts were abandoned. Instead, he waited until the escort departed and then resumed the artillery assault. He noted,

> In order to prevent the steamer from escaping, I surfaced, blowing out all the diving tanks. . . . As soon as our tower emerged from the water, the steamer immediately opened fire on us again with its stern gun. At a distance of 25 to 35 hm we returned fire using the so-called high-explosive shells and shrapnel shells that, depending on the setting of their fuses, burst in mid-air before hitting the ground. I could only decide on this ammunition with a heavy heart, since I knew how devastating it would be if the detonation point was in the right position. . . . As before, the ship began smoking and we observed numerous hits in the ship's side and in the deck structures of the steamer. The enemy, however, also shot excellently with his 15.2 cm guns, albeit without hitting us, with the fragments of his shells that burst in our vicinity whizzing around our ears. A piece of shrapnel wounded our excellent gunner at the front gun, not insignificantly, in the knee, another smashed into the inner protective wall of the conning tower right next to my arm. At a distance of about 25 hm I bypassed the stern of the steamer being pursued in favor of its starboard and windward side in order to facilitate our gunners' task, which had been made more difficult by the smoke from the steamer drifting toward us. . . . At about 0745 . . . we could make out people with raised arms on the superstructure decks of the steamer with our binoculars. After the enemy apparently stopped firing, I also stopped firing. The stern of the steamer sank visibly lower. In order to question survivors and possibly take them on board, I had the cruiser steered towards the shot-up life rafts and wreckage floating

nearby. The steamer gradually sank further and finally over its stern into the depths, after it had raised its bow almost bolt upright out of the water towards the sky. A horrible sight! Our ammunition consumption was 35 before and 48 rounds after diving, in total 83 rounds![38]

Nearly all the testimonies from the survivors of USS *Ticonderoga* claimed that *U-152* fired a torpedo at the steamer, which ultimately resulted in her sinking. German records do not corroborate this, instead attributing her loss to be exclusively from shellfire. Given that there is an unanimity among the American narratives that an explosion of some type occurred, it must be assumed that this internal detonation originated from an exploding boiler or igniting coal dust instead of a projectile.

Another point of contention between German and American sources is what occurred when *U-152* approached the survivors. According to nearly all the men interviewed by American naval intelligence, Kapitänleutnant Franz appeared to be coldhearted and short. He was claimed to have mocked and threatened the survivors (refusing to provide them with provisions or aid) and even went as far as ordering the lifeboats to be fired upon. He was also described as being particularly interested in locating the captain of the ship (who was lying on a lifeboat, unconscious and out of sight) and the chief gunner, who had been killed, but was believed by the Germans to have been responsible for the rear gun of *Ticonderoga* firing on the U-boat while a white flag was raised. It should be noted that, whether true or not, those statements are based solely on the translations from two of *Ticonderoga*'s German-speaking crew members (Ens. Gustav Ringelman and Chief Machinist Mate Rudolf Alicke) of their conversations with the German officers.

Given the circumstances, it is more than likely that Germans spoke in a succinct, no-nonsense manner, but the truth of what was actually said lies only with the men present that morning. One would expect that the Germans, after having survived being fired upon (with some crew members being wounded) would have been less than warm to their vanquished opponents. *U-152*'s commander, however, provides an opposing viewpoint.

From Franz's perspective, he was presented with a moral quandary. On the one hand, he had to keep his sights on his mission and the welfare of his crew and submarine; on the other hand, it would be extremely difficult to ignore the cries for help from the many wounded survivors. When he reflected on the incident years later, it was apparent that he had an extremely emotional reaction to the scene he was presented with. He noted (though it must be expected that one would present themselves in the best possible light) that his decision was based entirely on rationality:

The fight was over. The commander was faced with what was perhaps the most difficult decision of his life. We found ourselves in the midst of a debris field filled with surviving people, some of whom were seriously wounded and half or completely swimming in the water, and the remains of ships and boats. At the same time, we expected a reappearance of enemy forces on each side. The cries for help of the agonizing people hanging on life belts, beams and other debris went to our bones. The full horror of war was before our eyes now that the fighting was over. While we were still contemplating what nationality our heroic and now[-]defeated enemies might belong to, who had defended their lives on a cow-ferry steamer up to the last moment and had tried to destroy us, we saw to our greatest astonishment that all the survivors were dressed in uniforms [American sources contradict this claim, noting that only the officers were wearing uniforms], American uniforms[,] and hearing these people begging us for help and rescue, some in our own native language. German-Americans! How terrible and cruel is this war, it pierced our hearts! What to do and where to start with this pitiful and wretched remnant of partly shredded human remains that were swimming in the water (make a hospital ship out of our warship)? How many could there be, whose fate now stirred our hearts violently? Was it even possible to help many of them with their torn limbs and open wounds that turned the water around them red!? Wouldn't taking all the survivors and wounded on board endanger the health of my own crew!? Was it at all possible to take everyone on board and accommodate them without seriously endangering our boat ourselves? . . .

We were supposed to take care of, bandage[,] and heal those who were to be taken on board, but how should they be able to stand or lie in a boat with a crew of 77, for which every little corner, nook[,] and cranny was completely taken up and used? Our own crew lived and slept for weeks on end between ammunition stacks, torpedoes, and mines; when the weather was bad the air inside the boat was often almost unbearable for healthy people. Which survivor should be turned away from boarding? At 5, 10, 20, 30, 40, 50, or were there even more of them!? . . .

We were out here in the middle of the ocean to wage war, on our own. Concern for my own crew was the first priority for me as commander. . . . Humanity has its limits in war! Just as we would probably have had to sail around the ocean for days and weeks with several dozen survivors on board . . . it was to be expected, on the other hand, that that American escort cruiser, which had disappeared from the scene so remarkably quickly, would reappear any minute and take up the fight against us . . . forcing our boat, which was overcrowded by the rescued people, to dive without us having the probability . . . for any success.

In the event of such an unsuccessful attempt to dive, would the enemy not suspect anything and not shoot at us and his own fellow countrymen or try to run over us? Or should we set the white flag when the enemy appears in order to hand over the rescued?[39]

Ultimately, only two survivors were actually taken on board as prisoners—executive officer Lt. Frank Muller and 1st Assistant Engineer Junius Fulcher. These were the highest-ranking officers (apart from the captain, who was being hidden by his crew) to survive the attack.

The former had to be pulled from the water by German volunteers, who tied themselves off and dove into the sea, and the latter, being heavily wounded by shrapnel, was carefully extracted from his lifeboat. Both were taken inside the U-boat and, after some brief initial questioning, were separated and tended to. Muller was led to the officers' mess, where he was "undressed, toweled and wrapped in warm woolen blankets and received a very strong sip of rum,"[40] and Fulcher was allotted the chief engineer's room (voluntarily given up by Leitender Ingenieur Heine). Here his leg was successfully operated on by the U-boat's doctor, coincidentally having a homophonous surname—he would remain in this accommodation for the remainder of the patrol.

Once Fulcher and Muller had recovered somewhat from the ordeal, during the evening of the thirtieth the U-boat's English-speaking prize officer, known to Muller as "Lt. Wille," began a full interrogation of the prisoners, establishing the name of their vessel, the nature of the convoy, and more specifics of the battle. From that point on, the two Americans were treated as if they were part of the German crew, being given cigarettes, allowed to go on deck, and provided with the same meals as their captors.

Lt. Frank Muller (*left*) and 1st Assistant Engineer Fulcher (*right*) pictured on board *U-152*. *NH 2472, courtesy of the Naval History & Heritage Command*

In sharp contrast to how the two prisoners were handled, the remaining men of USS *Ticonderoga* were left to fend for themselves on the open ocean. As Franz alluded to in his narrative, and was confirmed by the American survivors, requests for medical assistance were denied to those aboard the lifeboats and floating wreckage, as were any additional provisions. In fact, when Chief Machinist Mate Alicke finished translating Fulcher's initial interrogation, he was ordered back to his raft and, after pleading with Fulcher to put in a word to save him, was allegedly told by Franz, "Get back on the raft. What do you mean by fighting against us, against your country [Alicke was born in Hamburg]? Only God can save such as you now!"[41]

Indeed, at 0945, *U-152* left the area, continuing on her course toward the United States. Franz noted the position of USS *Ticonderoga* as being at 44°7' N, 37°25' W—about 765 mi. / 1,231 km away from the nearest landfall at St. John's, Newfoundland. It wouldn't be until the afternoon of October 3 that the remaining survivors (only twenty-two out of a total complement of 237 naval and army personnel[42]) would be rescued by a passing British steamer, the *Moorish Prince*. The sinking of *Ticonderoga* would be the second-greatest loss of life on an American vessel during World War I—the first being the mysterious loss of USS *Cyclops* / AC-4, resulting in 306 lives lost.

During the nearly two weeks that followed the battle with *Ticonderoga*, *U-152* saw very little in the way of excitement. Besides a brief encounter with what was initially believed to have been a fully rigged ship but was actually a large steamer that the Germans couldn't catch up to on October 2 (Franz later noted that it was likely the steamer that rescued what remained of *Ticonderoga*'s survivors), the only tasks that kept the U-boat's crew occupied were numerous engine overhauls and continuous fuel calculations. Then, on October 11, *U-152* received the same radio transmission as *U-155*, advising Franz to give up his cruise toward the US and proceed east to the Azores. At this point, *U-152* was just under 750 mi. / 1,207 km from the American coast, located precisely between Bermuda and Newfoundland (at 38°53' N, 56°10' W).

This change of course almost immediately produced results for the crew of *U-152*. Although a convoy was spotted and pursued for nearly four hours before abandoning the chase on the twelfth, a much-smaller but well-provisioned victim fell into the lap of the Germans on the thirteenth. This was the three-masted, 1,745-ton Norwegian barque *Stifinder*, transporting various light-petroleum products, including naphtha and turpentine, from New York City to Fremantle, Australia.

At around lunchtime, on what Franz sardonically noted as being the "7th flying weather day," a lookout atop one of *U-152*'s radio masts spotted the sailing ship due to her "brand new" (it had actually just been replaced that morning), white mast shimmering in the sun—she was promptly halted by three warning shots. When the Norwegian crew sailed over to *U-152* with the ship's papers, they were instructed that their vessel would have to be sunk, since it was carrying contraband between two enemy countries. No amount of protesting from the Norwegians or the American captives on board the U-boat would change Franz's mind. Alas, the coldheartedness shown to the survivors of *Ticonderoga* who were not taken prisoner was about to be exhibited once again.

Although the Norwegians were allowed all the time they required to return to the *Stifinder* and gather possessions, supplies, and navigational tools prior to the German prize crew sinking the vessel (*U-152*'s navigator was called upon to provide them with a map), they were still nearly 650 mi. / 1,048 km from the nearest landfall in Nova Scotia (specifically at 37°25' N, 53°40' W)—a circumstance that meant little to Franz. Given that he and the crew of *U-152* were just about to have a very "frugal" lunch when the vessel was spotted, they considered the *Stifinder*'s presence in the area to have been a gift from Providence, and were overjoyed about what could be looted from her. The welfare of the Norwegian sailors was the last thing on their minds.

A view of the *Stifinder* from the deck of *U-152*. One of the German crew members appears to have taken a bath in the sea during the extended stop and is seen drying off. *NH 110776, courtesy of the Naval History & Heritage Command*

Apart from cases of turpentine, which the Germans desired for the war effort at home, they pilfered: one large and two small live pigs, crates of potatoes, the "best American wheat flour," butter, condensed milk, preserved fruits, tobacco, and other tasty luxuries. They would spend the entire night securing their booty before eventually sinking the *Stifinder* with three *Sprengpatronen* at 1010 on the fourteenth. The Norwegian crew (which departed the night of the thirteenth on two lifeboats), on the other hand, would endure tremendous hardships during the following weeks.

The men in the luckier of the two boats would spend fifteen days at sea before they were eventually rescued by the American sub chaser *SC-294*, which deposited them in New York City two days later. The other sailors would spend nearly a month on the ocean, having been separated from the other lifeboat during a storm and, even worse, having their boat capsize, with a loss of much of their provisions.[43] After attempting to sail for Bermuda, they eventually landed much farther southwest in the Turks and Caicos on November 5. Unbelievably, there were no casualties. *U-152*, meanwhile, continued on her course toward the Azores, seeking out additional prey, but without finding any further victories. In fact, on October 15, Franz nearly bit off more he could chew while attempting an attack on the British steamer *Messina*.

This encounter unfolded like so many other abandoned attacks involving U-cruisers and would hardly be worth mentioning if it weren't for the dissimilarities between German and Allied records. Both sides agree that the *Messina* (4,271 GRT), traveling in ballast from Plymouth (England) to Baltimore, was engaged in the middle of the Atlantic (about 720 mi. / 1,158 km southeast of Nova Scotia), and that a nearly two-hour, long-range artillery duel ensued. Additionally, all concur that the fire from *U-152* succeeded in damaging the steamer, with Franz noting that he was able to observe hits and "well-placed shrapnel" that destroyed some lifeboats secured on the *Messina*'s deck, and the British documenting strikes landing on the "port side . . . abaft of the bridge, fracturing two steel plates."[44] This prompted SOS calls to be sent from the *Messina* giving her location and that she was being shot at. This is where the parallels end.

While Franz attributed ceasing fire on the steamship due to the extreme distance of 120 hm and rough seas, he claimed that he was ultimately forced to retire from the engagement due to the unexpected appearance of two other steamships on the horizon—one believed to have been an auxiliary cruiser and the other a destroyer. Despite the weather being clear, with high visibility, the *Messina* saw neither of these ships and believed that her German attacker had simply given up due to the increasing range between the two vessels. She also did not hear any additional shots being fired or depth charge explosions in the distance.

This is curious because Franz recorded that the larger steamer, with two masts, one thick stack, and a tall, central superstructure, which gave him "the impression of a well-armed auxiliary cruiser and actually had the English war ensign on the gaff,"[45] "made circles [around *U-152*], fired with broadside guns[,] and then aimed at *U-152* with high speed."⁴⁶ This forced *U-152* into an evasive crash dive. In anticipation of the imminent depth charge bombardment from the destroyer, *U-152*

> immediately went to a considerable depth, occasionally . . . sinking to 66 m below the water's surface. Apparently, the depth charges were not absent either. In any case, the feelings we had down there with the rattling, shooting, and the detonations above and around us were not pleasant.⁴⁷

This depth charge attack was confirmed by the American prisoners on board *U-152*, who recounted nine explosions, all of which shook the U-boat but didn't result in any damage. They also reported being surprised that *U-152* submerged to a depth below the shipyard-tested limit of 50 m indicated on the depth gauge—being told by the German crew that this was nothing to be concerned about and that they should get worried only if the lights went out.

Adding to the mystery of the bout, Franz repeatedly logged that the "auxiliary cruiser" was identifying herself as the *U.S.A.* in wireless transmissions sent to Arlington. The problem with this is that there were no vessels, either in American or Royal Navy service, that bore that name. It is unclear what could have led Franz to make such an error in transcribing the signals, but what appears to be certain is that he was attacked by some warship in one form or another, apparently completely unobserved by the *Messina*.

As *U-152* continued on her easterly course toward the Azores, on October 17 she would make her final attempt at attacking a vessel about 950 mi. / 1,529 km east-northeast of Bermuda. This involved another British steamship, the 5,822-ton tanker *Briarleaf*, en route to Sabine, Texas, in ballast. Once again, there is a disparity as to what actually occurred. According to Kapitänleutnant Franz,

> On October 17th we had bad luck in the form of a double failure. In what should have been a textbook underwater attack against a large tanker, the first torpedo we fired, equipped with a special pistol, exploded with a violent detonation between us and the steamer, while the second torpedo, due to a ridiculous mistake on the part of the torpedoman, did not launch but instead got stuck in the tube. The steamer turned away from us and immediately opened fire; we surfaced and were able to pursue the ship at a range of about 60 hm. The opponent shot excellently and at times covered us with his salvoes in such a way that we had to steer zigzag to avoid them. After a large consumption of ammunition, we had to give up the pursuit again as hopeless. The "Briarleaf" calling for help simply ran away from us thanks to her considerably superior speed.⁴⁸

This stands in stark contrast to what the *Briarleaf*'s captain, G. E. Patterson, recollected.

According to his version of the event, he neither heard an explosion nor initiated the attack on the U-boat. In fact, he claimed that he had no idea about *U-152*'s presence in the area until she surfaced and began lobbing high-explosive shells at the *Briarleaf*, with all falling short. Patterson noted that *U-152* fired about 150 shells, with the tanker being able to return only thirty-nine,[48] and felt that one of his shots must have struck the U-boat, since he could find no other reason for her giving up the fight.

Much of Patterson's account is supported by the two American captives on board *U-152*, who recalled that a torpedo had been fired at the *Briarleaf* but was not heard to have exploded and thus probably missed. They estimated the German artillery expenditure at eighty-three shots (fewer than 150 but still excessive) and the *Briarleaf*'s at a more precise forty. They, however, concurred with Franz's rationale for abandoning the fight, agreeing that the steamship was simply too fast for the U-cruiser to pursue.

The following day, with no vessels in sight, Franz took advantage of the "glorious weather" (another "flying weather day") by having his crew put a new coat of paint on *U-152*. He claimed that paint cans salvaged from the wreckage of USS *Ticonderoga* were utilized and that he desired the submarine to have colors more "adapted to the deep blue-gray of the ocean." Even Muller and Fulcher were alleged to have helped complete the job. While the task had a logical foundation, reading between the lines it was obvious that Franz was trying to keep his crew distracted from the greater events of the war. Over the course of the week, numerous radio transmissions were being intercepted advising of the collapse of the western front and, even more troubling, the abandoning of the vital Flanders U-boat bases in Zeebrugge, Ostend, and Bruges. As historian Mark Karau noted,

> On 14 October von Schröder [Adm. Ludwig von Schröder, chief of the Marinekorps Flandern] received orders to fall back as far as Ostend. He was also ordered to prepare for the blocking of Zeebrugge and Antwerp. That evening the remaining minelayers laid a new minefield before the entrances to Zeebrugge[,] after which they were scuttled. On the 15th the lock gates at Zeebrugge were destroyed. On the 16th the order came in to abandon Bruges and it was duly evacuated two days later. The British had moved into Ostend on the 17th and they re-entered Zeebrugge on the 19th.[49]

Although Flanders was still hundreds of miles from Kiel, the base of the U-Kreuzer Flotilla, these disasters were now hitting very close to home and were clearly spelling the imminent German defeat. Adding to the impending doom, the additional German minelaying missions made it apparent that, on top of the Northern Barrage, Franz would have even more obstacles getting in the way of him and his crew reaching home safely. The situation only continued to worsen as the days went on.

At 0630 on October 22, which Franz (ever loyal to the Kaiserreich) later remembered as being the birthday of the empress, *U-152* received a message directed at all U-boats, advising them to return to base immediately and to abandon the *Handelskrieg* on merchant shipping—instructing them that only belligerent vessels could be engaged from that point on. Even more devastatingly, on the twenty-sixth Franz also began receiving the same contradictory radio transmissions from Nauen that *U-139* had, indicating that revolution had taken hold in Kiel and that the officers of the Kaiserliche Marine were no longer in charge. He chose to impart that last bit of information solely to his officers immediately before entering the Northern Barrage and withheld it from the greater part of the crew—planning on disclosing it only after *U-152* had successfully passed through the Allied minefields.

This was not out of a sense of elitism or spite, but instead because he wanted them to remain focused on the task at hand—essentially forbidding such a distraction from affecting their performance and standing in the way of their survival. For the time being, life aboard the U-boat was going to be business as usual. Unfortunately, their focused efforts would not result in any additional victories. Despite observing a three-funneled cruiser on the twenty-eighth, and a large cruiser with a "lattice mast" on the thirty-first, poor positioning and bad weather ruled out any potential attacks on their homeward journey.

Little else was encountered until 1600 on November 11, Armistice Day, when *U-152* approached the upper periphery of the Northern Barrage. Despite the war having effectively come to an end at 1100 that day, the Allies were unconcerned about the fate of the U-boat crews returning to Germany, and no attempt was made at marking the passages through the minefields. Rather than hug the Scandinavian coast or utilize any visual cues (à la Kophamel and Dröscher) to navigate the barrage, Muller and Fulcher recalled that Franz "proceeded at full speed on the surface, through its center,"[50] emerging on the other side successfully twelve hours later. After doing so, he decided to finally break the bad news to his crew. In his words,

> I informed the crew of the events at home that came to my knowledge through the radio, which I had only told my officers before passing the minefield. These men . . . which, for years, and now for months, had voluntarily risked their lives on the front lines every day[,] did not believe the words I had to say to them. Shaken and torn in the depths of their souls, each of them hung on to their own thoughts![51]

The sense of disillusionment was further amplified as *U-152* entered the Skagerrak and encountered SM *U-53* (now under the command of Kapitänleutnant Otto von Schrader) heading in the opposite direction.

After tying off to the smaller U-boat, Franz conferred with his colleague and learned of the true situation he would be encountering at Kiel. Besides the worker and soldier councils and red flags, there were still the expected German minefields to cross, albeit without any minesweepers or torpedo boats present to escort him through. While the U-boat men had been out doing all the fighting for the Kaiserliche Marine on the open seas, the rebellious sailors in the harbor had long since abandoned their posts. Von Schrader, disgusted with this revolutionary atmosphere, informed Franz of his plans to go to Sweden and intern *U-53*, since he and his crew still aligned themselves with the kaiser, not the socialists. First, however, he would help Franz make it home, guiding *U-152* through the mines.

Before taking von Schrader up on his offer and proceeding back to port under the escort of *U-53*, Franz let *U-152*'s fate rest in the hands of his officers and crew—putting the final decision on whether to return to Kiel or intern themselves up to a vote. Distinguishing themselves from the men of *U-53*, nearly 90 percent voted in favor of going home, even if the world they had known their entire lives had been turned completely upside down. As Muller and Fulcher later reported, the men of *U-152* were tired of war at this point and simply wanted to get home to begin rebuilding their collapsed empire.

U-152 would ultimately reach Kiel on November 15, with Franz immediately releasing his prisoners to the care of the barracks ship SMS *Prinz Heinrich*. Here they were provided with their own personal rooms, new undergarments, and hot baths. Despite being given the option to go their separate ways without any delay, the Americans decided to temporarily remain with the men of *U-152*. Although they would make a few trips into the harbor over the course of the following week, they would continue to take their meals with the German crew aboard the U-cruiser—returning to their own forces only when *U-152* was transferred to Harwich as war booty on the twenty-fourth.

Not surprisingly, Franz (and a large complement of his officers) opted to stay behind for this final cruise to Britain. He would be replaced by *U-152*'s boarding officer, Oberleutnant Wille, whose only mission in command of a U-boat was the humiliating final task of surrendering the last of the U-cruisers to the Allies. In fact, *U-152* and *U-155* would lead the procession of German U-boats into Harwich. It was an inglorious end for a campaign that promised so much.

Indeed, by the time *U-139* and *U-152* returned home, their combined efforts resulted in six vessels being sunk, accounting for a paltry 13,663 tons of lost shipping. This, however, was more reflective of their patrols being significantly cut short, not necessarily through a fault of their commanders or from any large-scale tactical blunders. Certainly, any efforts on the part of the Kaiserliche Marine (as a whole) in September and October 1918 could be considered nothing more than a last-gasp effort. The war had already been effectively lost with the German navy's inability to disrupt the Allied blockade and the failure of the German army's spring offensive months prior, which had already begun petering out just as von Nostitz arrived off Chesapeake Bay during his first cruise. One could only speculate how the two U-boats, along with *U-151* and *U-153*, would have performed if the war lasted another three months.

Still, the failure of the North American U-boat campaign to have a meaningful effect on the outcome of the war should not imply it wasn't fruitful in and of itself. The fact that just six German U-boats succeeded in sinking or damaging nearly 200,000 tons of shipping (excluding *U-139* or vessels lost due to accidents) and were directly responsible for more than three hundred deaths almost completely unhindered is proof of this. Regardless of how Adm. Sims and Secretary Daniels wanted to spin the narrative, these numbers were far from being insignificant—particularly when considering that the totals comprised mostly numerous small steamers and sailing vessels instead of just a handful of large troopships or liners.

Even more weight can be ascribed to the campaign when one considers the lessons learned by the German U-boat force, not necessarily for their immediate use during the Great War, but instead for the future. In the decades leading up to the Second World War, the experiences and tactics of the U-cruisers, both their pitfalls and triumphs, were reevaluated and built on. While the Germans recognized the vulnerabilities of North America's sparsely defended coastline from their earlier endeavors, tragically the Americans did not.

Inflated by their victory, and apparently completely ignorant of the actual German objectives, the US Navy dismissed the entire German campaign as a flop and, even worse, actively sold this theory to the public in the immediate postwar years. When the Germans would return to North American waters decades later, they were ready to strike without mercy—the Allies were once again forced to play catch-up.

CHAPTER 13
The End of the Beginning

RAdm. William Sowden Sims, in the preface to his Pulitzer Prize–winning book *The Victory at Sea*, wrote that his work was "not in any sense a history of the operations of our [the US] naval forces in Europe during the Great War, much less a history of the naval operations as a whole."[1] Instead, he claimed it was specifically written as a "response" to any misunderstandings regarding how the US Navy conducted itself during the German submarine campaign. This was a good way to describe the book, since it very explicitly divorced it from any objectivity. Sims, in many ways, was just one of many Allied commanders to, as historians Richard Guilliatt and Peter Hohnen put it, "tailor the historical record to their own self-image."[2]

While Guilliatt and Hohnen were critical of the Allied historical assessments of the German surface raiders, the parallels to Sims and the North American U-boat war are unmistakable. One particular example they cited was from *Naval History of the Great War: Volumes IV–V*, by Sir Henry Newbolt (himself involved in the British War Propaganda Bureau), which professed,

> The interference which they [the German surface raiders] had aimed at was presumably such as raiders may effect by setting up a panic, or at least the feeling of uncertainty, in great ports of shipment, so that masters refuse to sail, bankers withhold trade credits, wharves, warehouses and railway sidings become congested with goods which cannot be transported; and as the result of all this economic and strategic arrangements are broken down or dangerously delayed. No such dislocation was affected even to the smallest degree by the German raiders, and the steadily progressive nature of their failure would seem to indicate either that the effort was ill-timed, or that it was ill-designed.[3]

All Newbolt had to do was substitute the word "raider" for "U-boat" and he could have easily ghostwritten many of Sims's chapters. Indeed, this was exactly how the US Navy interpreted the German submarine war off North America, despite the U-boats actually succeeding in many of the aforementioned endeavors.

When Sims weighed the effect of the U-Kreuzers, which he claimed "proved to be the least harmful of any of the German types,"[4] he was selling a version of history that bore little resemblance to reality, asserting, much like Newbolt, that from the end of May until October, there was nearly always one submarine operating off our coast. . . . These submarines, however, attacked almost exclusively sailing vessels and small coastwise steamers, rarely, if ever, using torpedoes. A number of mines were laid at different points off our ports, on what the Germans believed to be traffic routes; but the information which we had concerning them made it possible to counter successfully their efforts and, from a military point of view, the whole of the submarine operations off our coast can be dismissed as one of the minor incidents of the war, as the Secretary of the Navy described in his Annual Report. The five submarines sunk in all approximately 110,000 tons of shipping, but the vessels were, for the most part, small and of no great military importance. The only real victory was the destruction of the cruiser *San Diego*, which was sunk by a mine . . . off Fire Island.[5]

Missing from *The Victory at Sea* was any mention of USS *Ticonderoga*, the *Frederic R. Kellogg*, or the *Dwinsk*—the latter two being sunk by torpedoes, with a substantial loss of life. Sims also failed to recognize USS *Saetia*, which struck a mine in the same vicinity as USS *Minnesota* due to the Navy's failure to sweep the area until January 1919.

The ships lost during accidents within domestic waters were other obvious omissions—the indirect American losses to the German U-boats (*SC-209* being the worst of these cases). Using William Clark's figures, such vessels would account for an additional eleven (six cargo ships and five warships) vessels being sunk, for 30,655 tons, and bringing the North American U-boat campaign's death toll up to 435 lives lost—another overlooked statistic.[6] Considering that the U-cruisers were the "least harmful" of the U-boat types, one can only wonder why Sims nearly halved the estimated tonnage lost, which excluded vessels that were damaged and temporarily removed from service, and diminished their overall impact on the war.

This may have been due to the fact that he didn't consider the vessels being attacked as being the primary targets for the U-Kreuzers, and thus placed little emphasis on them or their crews. Like Secretary Daniels, his laser focus on the protection of troopships forced him to see the campaign through a distorted lens. This was clearly evidenced in correspondence with Capt. William Pratt, then the assistant CNO, on August 13.

Despite August being the month with the peak U-boat attacks off the United States, Sims lamented that

> when the history of this war comes to be written there will be a number of features that will not be very creditable to the United States Navy. If hearings are held on the conduct of the war, a number of rather

disagreeable facts must inevitably be brought out. Without going into details, I may say that as far as the Navy is concerned we will have fought this war with the bulk of our experienced personnel of the Navy on the side of the ocean where there is no war. We will have to be able to show that it was necessary that we should have had to fight the war over here with a very large proportion of reserve officers who did not have the necessary experience.[7]

Considering that nearly all the newest and best destroyers, battleships, and cruisers had been dispatched to Europe or put into convoy service in 1917, leaving major American ports on the side of the ocean where there was "no war" under the protection of SP boats, wooden sub chasers, and other antiquated warships manned by reservists, Sims's statement is puzzling to say the least. It does, however, support his stance of considering the losses on the American side of the Atlantic negligible.

Given that both Sims and Daniels were exonerated during the 1919 congressional investigation into the conduct of the Navy Department during the war (which Sims himself initiated),[8] it seemed Congress was also willing to accept Sims's position. Additionally, the fact that *The Victory at Sea* was "published with the full approval of the Navy Department" ensured that Sims's interpretation of the campaign would be cemented both in naval circles and the wider American public. The Germans, however, saw the matter quite differently.

As mentioned by von Nostitz in his postmission report, American coastal shipping had increased exponentially as the railways became tied up with war materiel and the movement of personnel. He noted that "everything else . . . has to be transported by water if possible," and understood that the interruption of these supplies would, much like the British blockade's effect on the German populace, "mean a radical disruption of American economic life."[9] While Sims noted that the vessels being sunk by U-cruisers were small steamers and sailing ships, von Nostitz pointed out that the latter were being utilized almost exclusively for the transport of coal, the fuel for railways, big liners, and troop transports, and that the former were responsible for carrying other vital resources such as copper and rubber. These were precisely the types of vessels that the Germans considered worth sinking.

Given that the German U-cruiser command never deviated from the objectives originally assigned to *U-151* on the campaign's onset, through the nearly seven months that elapsed until the Armistice, it was apparent that they believed their strategy was effective. Despite *U-140* and *U-117* sinking only a combined twenty-nine vessels, for an average tonnage of 2,248 tons each (a figure brought down by the high volume of fishing vessels sunk by *U-117*), the BdU still "generally approved" of their patrols, feeling that they were "worth undertaking, particularly along the American coastline." In fact, the only thing that troubled the U-cruiser command was that those patrols had to be cut short due to the dramatic fuel losses. As seen later, *U-155*, *U-152*, *U-139*, *U-151*, and *U-153*, all departing months after *U-151*'s and *U-156*'s initial patrols, were given nearly identical orders, which, despite their cruises being drastically shorter in length, were on track to yield similar results.

This was particularly frightening to American industry, which, recognizing that the effectiveness of the U-cruisers couldn't be measured solely by the number of troopships sunk, interpreted the North American U-boat campaign much like the Germans did. In fact, the economic impact of the U-cruisers was realized in the very initial stages of the campaign, when *U-151*'s arrival prompted insurance rates to skyrocket, ports to close, and cargoes to be transferred from marine vessels to railways—creating logistical bottlenecks that impeded the movement of war materiel. Although these were only temporary measures, the lack of an adequate defensive effort on the part of the US Navy forced some industries to take more-extreme, more-permanent, and more-costly measures to safeguard their goods. One such example occurred on August 1, 1918, after *U-151* had already sunk more than 50,000 tons of shipping unmolested and while *U-156* was in the midst of her onslaught off New England.

In what was borderline clairvoyant knowledge of von Nostitz's report about the vulnerable coal supply being shipped along the coast, the US Railroad Administration redirected its Allegheny Region's coal fleets from Philadelphia to Port Reading, New Jersey. Instead of sailing on the open Atlantic, the coal-laden vessels would now avoid the ocean entirely, essentially taking back channels to reach the New York and New England markets. Unfortunately, this change necessitated tying up the already busy rail lines with coal shipments (90 tons per car) that would then terminate at a single McMyler coal dumper in Port Reading for transit along the Arthur Kill—a narrow, 10-mile waterway between New Jersey and Staten Island. The process was slower, but much safer. Following this change, only three vessels carrying coal would be sunk, with only one of those (the *Dorothy B. Barrett*) sinking in the affected geographic area, ironically being sunk just prior to the arrival of the Navy's hyped sub chasers, which successfully thwarted *U-117*'s further attacks that day.

Indeed, the presence of the three sub chasers in Delaware Bay that morning, as well as the arrival of USS *Hull* on June 4 and USS *Stringham* on August 10, exhibited what could have been accomplished had the United States placed more of an emphasis on the defense of the home front. Sims, in his justification for not keeping any modern warships "on the American side of the Atlantic for 'home defense,'" claimed that American "destroyers and anti-submarine craft" would be able to easily cross the Atlantic in ten days and refuel in home ports . . . as soon as the Germans started for America. . . . These agile vessels would reach home waters about three weeks before the submarines arrived; they would thus have plenty of time to refit and welcome the uninvited guests.[10]

Sims, neglecting to mention why this never occurred, or the true losses incurred during the campaign, then went on to elucidate on his theory, later echoed by ambassador to Germany James Gerard, that the U-boats should have come to America in 1917 to prevent the vast resources of the US from being deployed to Europe. Again, this is a case of confirmation bias based on what the US Navy believed the ultimate goals of the Kaiserliche Marine actually were. A partiality, unfortunately resonating to this day.

The Canadian historians Michael Hadley and Roger Sarty, in their well-researched chronicle of the Canadian Naval Forces, *Tin-Pots and Pirate Ships*, arrived at a similar conclusion regarding the goals of the U-cruisers, noting,

What mattered was that over five hundred vessels had sailed for the war fronts from Canadian ports—on schedule and without loss—since *U-156*'s first appearance off Nova Scotia in early August [this discounts the loss of the troopship *City of Vienna*, which beached herself on July 2, attempting to hug the coastline too closely]. What was more, not one major anti-submarine vessel had to be dispatched from European waters to achieve this result.[11]

The legitimacy of this interpretation, however, rests on its ambiguity. As they noted in the preceding paragraph of their book, "Canadian patrol vessels had had but one encounter with U-boats—and that with rather embarrassing results."[12] They justified this by noting that the "better-equipped American ships had also come up empty-handed," but this is a bit of a cop-out and evokes the biggest issue with the entire campaign. Regardless of what was actually being sunk, whether it be a small fishing boat or a large tanker, the U-boats were able to engage these vessels almost completely unopposed.

Had the Germans arrived in the spring of 1917 as Sims suggested, their campaign may have succeeded in keeping the bulk of the US destroyer forces in American waters. However, in doing so it would likely have made their patrols far less fruitful. Instead of facing a sparsely defended coastline patrolled by, as von Nostitz reported, "only a few and older vehicles with untrained personnel available for them," they would have borne the brunt of the US Navy's destroyer fleets in concentrations similar to what Hans Rose and *U-53* observed off Rhode Island back in 1916.

By contrast, with the majority of US naval forces overseas in late 1918, the Germans were rarely prevented from attacking targets in the busy North American coastal shipping lanes. In fact, the poor performance and slow speeds of the U-cruisers were more often than not responsible for them having to break off attacks—not because of Allied patrols. This is particularly true of Studt's cruise with *U-155*, which operated primarily in the area described by Hadley and Sarty. Although he was able to sink only eight vessels, he had observed thirty. The story was much the same for the other U-cruiser commanders, who failed to add to their tonnage tallies not because of Allied warships, but because of poor weather, slow speeds, or malfunctions of one kind or another. It was just plain luck that more vessels weren't sunk during the period, not because the Allied strategy was actually working.

Adm. Mayo, the commander in chief of the Atlantic Fleet, realized this fact fairly quickly into the U-cruiser campaign. In his "Estimate of the Situation in the Atlantic Ocean," sent to Secretary Daniels on August 10, he noted that

> the development of the cruiser submarine has so increased the area of the submarine operations that destroyer escort for troops convoys throughout the entire trans-Atlantic voyage is desirable. Destroyer escort for merchant convoys throughout the entire voyage is also desirable but on account of the number of destroyers required, not, as yet, practicable.[13]

Mayo, apparently reeling from the loss of the transport *Dwinsk* and the potential sinking of the *Von Steuben* at the hands of *U-151*, was well aware of the vulnerabilities of his troopships when they traveled beyond the range of Allied escorts. He also recognized that their losses, even if they were on return voyages and thus empty, were still substantial. While destroyers were ultimately not pulled from European service in any significant numbers, Mayo understood the deadly potential of the U-cruisers, which, had they been more numerous, could have had a more devastating effect on cross-Atlantic shipping—particularly if it were unprotected.

So did historian Henry James, a firsthand witness to *U-156*'s attack in Provincetown. Not only was he cognizant of the actual toll of the U-cruiser campaign, but also its possible impact in a later war—a war, for instance, like the one that had broken out just a year prior to his book *German Subs in Yankee Waters* being published. Writing in 1940, he noted,

> From a military standpoint American authorities are unanimous in their assertions that the U-boat raids were last[-]minute futile efforts to divert attention from the center of military activity. . . . If America did not learn its lesson of unpreparedness from its experience with the U-boat

raiders, there is none to blame but its military advisors. If a half[-]dozen submarines could wreak havoc under such unfavorable conditions as the U-boats operated in 1918, what might be the result should a foreign power send its entire fleet of super-submarines to our shores at the outbreak of war? Those who cry for peace when there is no peace and bemoan the enormous expenditures for capital ships to be used offensively could have little grievance toward a naval program that provided for the construction of fleets of destroyers, subchasers, patrol boats, and mine-sweepers, which could be used solely for defensive purposes.[14]

James wouldn't have to wait very long to observe the consequences of the naive, interwar American naval policy.

The Germans, having gained valuable experience in the First World War by testing the limits of their operational ranges, developing rudimentary wolf-pack tactics, learning how to engage convoys, and observing what was to be expected along the shipping lanes in the open Atlantic instead of merely the waters immediately off continental Europe, were far more prepared for their second go at the American Eastern Seaboard than the Americans were to defend it. As Oberleutnant Körner of *U-151* ominously told Lowell Thomas in 1918,

> To those who can see into the future, surely this is a warning of what later wars may bring. For the day will come when submarines will think no more of a voyage across the Atlantic than they do now of a raid across the North Sea. . . . America's isolation is now a thing of the past.[15]

Indeed, many of the U-boat commanders who had continued to serve with the German navy following World War I, most notably Karl Dönitz (commander of *UC-25* and later *UB-68*), had been anticipating such an operation since 1918. The substantial German victories during the "American shooting season" or "Second Happy Time," during Operation Paukenschlag from January through August 1942 were clear evidence of this fact.

In this period, the US Navy, yet again, was faced with a shortage of escort and antisubmarine vessels and required a massive naval spending and expansion program to catch up. As a result, initial coastal defense on the Eastern Seaboard (from New England to Hatteras) was left up to seven Coast Guard cutters, four converted yachts, three 1919-vintage patrol boats, two gunboats dating back to 1905, and four wooden submarine chasers.[16] These were far fewer vessels than were available during World War I for the same purpose and were woefully inadequate to mount any effectual counterattack on any modern U-boat raiders. Additionally, while some destroyers were recalled for the purpose of protecting shipping along the East Coast, US naval tactics favored using them offensively (in the vein of hunter squadrons) instead of concentrating them on the defense of convoys, which, despite proving their worth in World War I, were only belatedly reintroduced in May 1942. The experiences from the previous war had obviously been long forgotten.

This is all the more disappointing because the US Navy had seemed to finally hit its stride in antisubmarine warfare by the end of the First World War. In the case of the wooden sub chasers, their crews were becoming adept at utilizing their listening devices, as well as tracking and engaging enemy U-boats—proving their worth, if not by sinking enemy submarines, then by forcing them to abandon their attacks. The destroyers, most of which had been stationed abroad, had likewise gained valuable experience escorting convoys on the final legs of their journeys into Britain and France, both hunting and depth-charging U-boats in cooperation with their counterparts in the Royal Navy in the process.

Naval seaplanes likewise showed promise, even if the bombs equipped to them often failed to explode. As Kophamel and Dröscher continually noted in their logs, just the presence of an aircraft was enough to force them to submerge to avoid being detected or bombed. Just how effective

U-117 being destroyed by aerial bombs off the Virginia coast. *NH 43927, courtesy of the Naval History & Heritage Command*

they could be when their munitions actually worked was proven in 1921, when *U-117* (awarded to the US as war booty following her surrender at Harwich) was sunk by three Navy Felixstowe F5L flying boats off the Virginia coast. Unfortunately, this lesson was disregarded as well, and by 1941 the Navy was equipped only with small seaplanes incapable of mounting long-distance, antisubmarine patrols. The larger planes were in the hands of the US Army Air Force, which had no interest in antisubmarine warfare whatsoever. Still, the US Navy was not completely ignorant to the lessons of the U-boat war off North America.

At the end of the war, when the surrendered German submarines were divvied up among the Allies, the United States took ownership of *U-117*, *U-140*, *UC-97*, *UB-88*, *UB-148*, and *U-111*[17] from the Royal Navy under the condition that they be destroyed within a year. Their immediate purpose was to be used in Victory Bond drives, touring the ports of the American East Coast. In the case of *U-117* and *U-140*, upon completion of the drive they were sent to the Philadelphia Navy Yard, where they were disassembled and evaluated in detail before eventually being sunk (*U-117* by aerial bombs, as mentioned before, and *U-140* by gunfire from USS *Dickerson*).

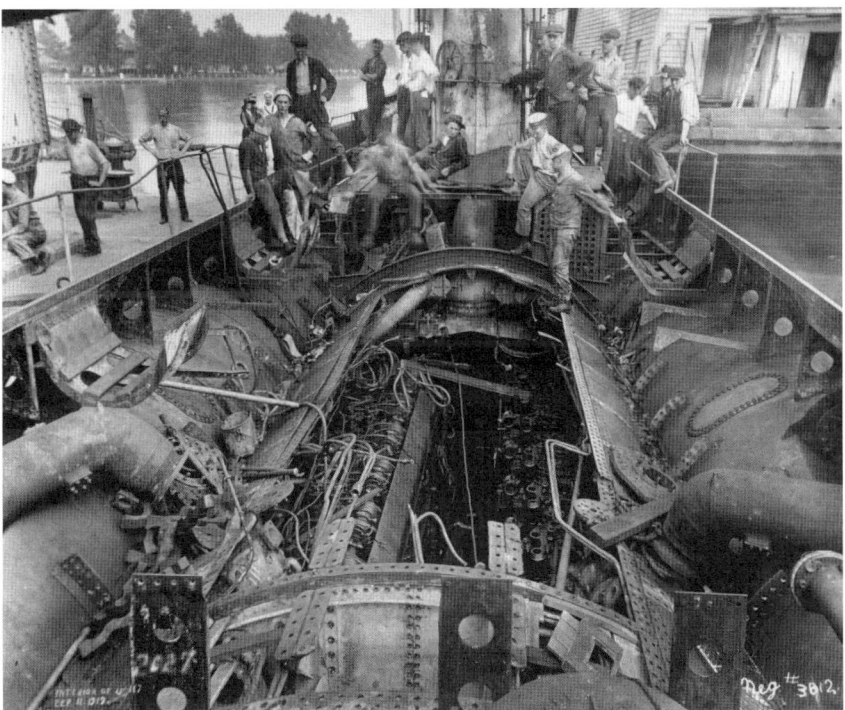

U-117 being dismantled and evaluated at the Philadelphia Navy Yard. *19-N-3612, courtesy of the National Archives*

Despite Sims's insistence that they were the most innocuous type of U-boat, they would serve as the foundation for the American *V-4*, *V-5*, and *V-6* submarines—with the *V-4 Argonaut* being a minelayer more closely resembling *U-117*, and the *V-5 Narwhal* and *V-6 Nautilus* being akin to a U-139-class submarine. Their shared genes are superficially very obvious, even to an untrained eye, though the American versions were 14 m longer and displaced nearly 44 percent more tonnage than their German ancestors. Submarines *V-5* and *V-6* even utilized German-designed ten-cylinder diesel engines ultimately built by the Bureau of Steam Engineering, with the *V-4* receiving genuine MAN six-cylinder engines. All would go on to serve in the Pacific (with *Nautilus* having the most illustrious tour of duty), where their superior range could best be put to use, and never got the opportunity to battle with their German cousins in the Atlantic. Paradoxically, when the Germans came around to conceiving their equivalents to the U-cruisers of the First World War in 1935, they opted for a much-smaller design.

The conning tower of *U-140* while in US possession as a war prize. *19-N-98575, courtesy of the National Archives*

The type IXB U-boats, which would be sent across the Atlantic to attack North America, displaced 46 percent fewer tons than the U-139 class, were 15.5 m and 2.36 m shorter in length and beam, respectively, and instead of being armed with twin 15 cm deck guns carried just a single 10.5 cm gun (indicative of the way the submarine war would now be waged). Even with the reduction in dimensions, these U-boats still had six 21-inch torpedo tubes (four forward and two aft, just like *U-139*) and a respectable range of 13,450 nautical miles. This maximum range, while just 1,200 nm less than the U-117-class minelayers, was still 4,300 less than the U-139 class and an incredible 13,000 nm less than the converted merchant submarines, meaning that the length of the patrols would, in theory, be considerably shorter. To maximize their effectiveness, Dönitz would dispatch five type IXB U-boats to the United States simultaneously. They would operate within varying zones along the North American coast, in waters that would have been very familiar to the U-cruiser commanders of the First World War.

In fact, Reinhard Hardegan, the commander of *U-123* (the most successful of the initial five U-boats sent to North America), was directed on a course nearly identical to that of *U-117*—first approaching New York City and then proceeding southward to Cape Hatteras. This wasn't the only parallel to the previous war. Like von Nostitz, he reported that almost nothing existed in the way of resistance from the US Navy (or the US Army Air Force) when he arrived. Additionally, when he entered New York Harbor on January 15, 1942, he was bearing witness to yet another example of American First World War hubris prevailing into the modern era—the city was lit up as if it were peacetime.

While Sims ridiculed the police commissioner of New York for enforcing blackout restrictions following *U-151*'s foray back in 1918, Hardegan would illustrate the dangers of failing to do so in 1942. Using the backlit horizon, he was able to spot the silhouettes of vessels traveling along the coast at night, not only in New York City but off the resort cities of Asbury Park and Atlantic City in New Jersey. In the case of the latter two, they refused to ever fully implement blackout protective measures, out of fears of losing out on tourist revenue. Unfortunately, the escapism achieved through the brightly lit nighttime amusements often yielded a very sobering scene in the morning, with beachgoers being presented with "a beach covered not with clamshells and seaweed but with burned wood, pools of fuel, and twisted metal—the grim debris of a ship that had been . . . sunk."[18] Owing to the complete lack of response either from the Navy or the civilian populace during this period, by the end of the "first wave" of Operation Paukenschlag, Hardegan had sunk seven vessels for a total of 46,744 tons, retiring only because he ran out of torpedoes.

His colleagues in the other four U-boats would fare very much the same in the two-month period: Zapp (*U-66*) would sink five ships for 33,456 tons; Bleichrodt (*U-109*), four for 27,651 tons; Folkers (*U-125*), just one for 6,666 tons; and Kals (*U-130*), six for 36,988 tons. Together they inflicted a material loss of 151,505 tons on the Allies and a death toll of nearly nine hundred lives lost, with Dönitz later remarking that the opportunities to sink vessels grossly exceeded the means of the U-boats to sink them.

Comparatively, the five U-cruisers that actually reached North America in 1918 had sunk ninety-two vessels (granted, most were small sailing ships) for a loss of 174,539 tons of shipping and 133 lives. It was only because the war ended that their campaign ended, not because Allied naval doctrine successfully adapted to their patrols or because the Germans considered it a failure. Despite this, their cruises were written off by the Allies as fools' errands, mere distractions to the greater war in Europe and to be ignored. Operation Paukenschlag, on the other hand, was understood to be a tragedy, with historian Michael Gannon going as far as calling it "America's Second Pearl Harbor." It prompted an immediate response from the United States and resulted in significant changes to American naval policy.

Had the US spent the interwar years properly analyzing the U-boat war off North America rather than immediately downplaying its effects as soon as hostilities ended, the "American shooting season" may have alternately been two months of depth-charging "German fish in a barrel." Instead, just as the *Kölnische Volkszeitung* noted about *U-151*'s patrol back in 1918, the Americans, no longer safe from the storm on the other side of the "great herring pond," would once again have to feel the "fist of the warlord." They had sown the wind and would once again be forced to reap the whirlwind.

Appendixes

APPENDIX A
German Naval Ranks and Their Equivalents in the US and Royal Navies

Kaiserliche Marine	US Navy	Royal Navy
Großadmiral	N/A[1]	Admiral of the fleet
Admiral	Admiral	Admiral
Vizeadmiral	Vice admiral	Vice admiral
Konteradmiral	Rear admiral	Rear admiral
Kommodore	N/A[2]	Commodore
Kapitän zur See	Captain	Captain
Fregattenkapitän	Commander	Captain
Korvettenkapitän	Lieutenant commander	Commander
Kapitänleutnant	Lieutenant	Lieutenant commander
Oberleutnant zur See	Lieutenant, jr. grade	Jr. lieutenant
Leutnant zur See	Ensign	Sublieutenant

APPENDIX B
Lists of Sunken or Damaged Vessels

Vessels Sunk or Damaged by *U-151* (April 18, 1918–July 20, 1918)

Date	Location	Name of Vessel	GRT	Type of Vessel	Nationality	Cargo	Method of Attack	Result
May 25, 1918	37°24'N 67°05'W	Hattie Dunn	435	3-masted schooner	American	Ballast	2 explosive charges	Sunk
–	37°27'N 75°09'W	Hauppauge	1,446	4-masted schooner	American	Ballast	2 explosive charges, 3 shots from the 15 cm deck gun	Damaged
–	37°30'N 74°52'W	Edna	325	3-masted schooner	American	6,000 cases of motor oil, 4,000 cases of gasoline	2 explosive charges	Damaged
June 2, 1918	39°20'N 73°14'W	Winneconne	1,869	Steamship	American	Coal	3 explosive charges	Sunk
–	39°20'N 73°13'W	Isabel B. Wiley	776	3-masted schooner	American	Unknown	2 explosive charges	Sunk
–	39°07'N 73°04'W	Jacob M. Haskell	1,778	4-masted schooner	American	Coal	2 explosive charges	Sunk
–	38°58'N 73°12'W	Edward H. Cole	1,791	4-masted schooner	American	Coal	3 explosive charges	Sunk
–	38°55'N 73°23'W	Texel	3,210	Steamship	American	Sugar	3 explosive charges	Sunk
–	38°51'N 73°16'W	Carolina	5,093	Steamship	American	Passengers, sugar	1 torpedo (dud), 8 shots from 15 cm deck gun	Sunk
June 3, 1918	Approx. 37°47'N 75°05'W	Herbert L. Pratt	7,145	Tanker	American	Crude oil	Mine	Damaged
–	38°02'N 73°23'W	Sam C. Mengel	915	4-masted schooner	American	Palm kernels	2 explosive charges	Sunk

Date	Location	Name of Vessel	GRT	Type of Vessel	Nationality	Cargo	Method of Attack	Result
June 4, 1918	37°25'N 73°44'W	Edward R. Baird	279	3-masted schooner	American	Lumber	2 explosive charges	Damaged
–	36°56'N 73°47'W	Eidsvold	1,570	Steamship	Norwegian	Sugar	7 shots from 15 cm deck gun	Sunk
June 5, 1918	36°39'N 74°03'W	Harpathian	4,588	Steamship	British	Ballast	1 torpedo	Sunk
–	36°35'N 73°58'W	Vinland	1,144	Steamship	Norwegian	Sugar	2 explosive charges	Sunk
June 8, 1918	36°15'N 74°55'W	Pinar Del Rio	2,504	Steamship	American	Sugar	2 shots from 15 cm deck gun	Sunk
June 10, 1918	36°21'N 71°25'W	Vindeggen	3,179	Steamship	Norwegian	2,100 tons of copper, 1,000 balls of wool	3 explosive charges	Sunk
–	36°07'N 72°20'W	Henrik-Lund	4,322	Steamship	Norwegian	Coal, copper, engine parts	3 explosive charges	Sunk
June 14, 1918	37°29'N 71°53'W	Samoa	1,138	3-masted barque	Norwegian	Copper, wool	3 shots from 15 cm deck gun	Sunk
–	38°02'N 71°40'W	Kringsjaa	1,750	4-masted barque	Norwegian	Linseed oil	6 shots from 15 cm deck gun	Sunk
June 18, 1918	38°39'N 61°25'W	Dwinsk	8,173	Steamship	British	Empty troopship	1 torpedo, 6 shots from 15 cm deck gun	Sunk
June 19, 1918	39°13'N 53°31'W	Chilier	2,965	Steamship	Belgian	Ballast	1 torpedo (dud), 6 shots from 15 cm deck gun	Sunk
June 23, 1918	39°03'N 52°47'W	Augvald	3,406	Steamship	Norwegian	Ballast	15 shots from 15 cm deck gun	Sunk
June 28, 1918	42°25'N 40°08'W	Dictator	124	2-masted schooner	Canadian	148 tons of salt	2 explosive charges	Sunk

Vessels Sunk or Damaged by *U-156* (June 26, 1918–August 26, 1918)

Date	Location	Name of Vessel	GRT	Type of Vessel	Nationality	Cargo	Method of Attack	Result
June 26, 1918	55°50'N 15°30'W	Tortuguero	4,175	Steamship	British	Ballast	1 torpedo	Sunk
July 7, 1918	40°0'N 50°35'W	Marosa	1,987	Barque	Norwegian	Coal	Explosive charges	Sunk
July 8, 1918	40°0'N 52°0'W	Manx King	1,729	Tall ship	Norwegian	Oil, cotton, barbed wire, iron, shoes	Explosive charges	Sunk
July 19, 1918	40°30'N 73°0'W	USS *San Diego*	13,680	Armored cruiser	American	N/A	Teka mine	Sunk
July 21, 1918	41°46.5'N 69°53'W (approx.)	Perth Amboy	435	Tugboat	American	N/A	Shots from 15 cm deck gun	Damaged
–	–	Lansford	830	Barge	American	Ballast	Shots from 15 cm deck gun	Sunk (later salvaged)
–	–	No. 403	422	Barge	American	Ballast	Shots from 15 cm deck gun	Sunk
–	–	No. 740	680	Barge	American	Ballast	Shots from 15 cm deck gun	Sunk
–	–	No. 766	527	Barge	American	Granite	Shots from 15 cm deck gun	Sunk
July 22, 1918	42°42'N 68°23'W	Robert and Richard	140	Fishing schooner	American	30,000 lbs. of halibut and 7,000 lbs. of assorted fish	Explosive charge	Sunk
August 2, 1918	44°17'N 67°W	Dornfontein	766	Motorized schooner	Canadian	Lumber	Set afire	Damaged and towed to port, claimed as a total loss
August 3, 1918	43°29'N 66°53.5'W (approx.)	Muriel	120	Fishing schooner	American	Ballast	Explosive charge	Sunk
–	43°25'N 66°44'W (approx.)	Sydney B. Atwood	100	Fishing schooner	American	Ballast	Explosive charge	Sunk
–	–	Annie Perry	116	Fishing schooner	American	Ballast	Explosive charge	Sunk
–	43°22.5'N 66°34'W (approx.)	Rob Roy	112	Motorized schooner	American	Ballast	Explosive charge	Sunk
August 4, 1918	–	Nelson A.	72	Fishing schooner	Canadian	Fish	Explosive charge	Sunk
August 5, 1918	42°59'N 65°43'W (approx.)	Agnes B. Holland	100	Fishing schooner	Canadian	Ballast	Explosive charge	Sunk

Date	Location	Name of Vessel	GRT	Type of Vessel	Nationality	Cargo	Method of Attack	Result
–	–	Gladys Hollett	203	3-masted schooner	Canadian	Salt herring	Explosive charge	Damaged
–	43°48'N 63°40'W	Luz Blanca	4,868	Tanker	Canadian	Ballast	Shots from 15 cm deck guns	Sunk
August 8, 1918	41°30'N 65°22'W	Sydland	3,031	Steamship	Swedish	Ballast	3 explosive charges	Sunk
August 11, 1918	39°50'N 67°25'W	Penistone	4,139	Steamship	British	General cargo	1 torpedo, 2 explosive charges	Sunk
August 17, 1918	42°10'N 64°42'W	San Jose	1,586	Steamship	Norwegian	Ballast	Explosive charges	Sunk
August 20, 1918	44°30'N 61°29'W (approx.)	Triumph	239	Steam trawler	Canadian	Ballast	Explosive charges	Captured (later scuttled on 22 Aug.)
–	44°21'N 61°28'W (approx.)	A. Piatt Andrew	141	Fishing schooner	American	Ballast	Explosive charges	Sunk by the Triumph
–	–	Francis J. O'Hara, Jr.	117	Fishing schooner	American	Ballast	Explosive charges	Sunk by the Triumph
–	–	Uda A. Saunders	124	Fishing schooner	Canadian	77 tons of fish, 7 casks of oil	Explosive charges	Sunk
–	–	Lucille M. Schnare	121	Fishing schooner	Canadian	Ballast	Explosive charges	Sunk by the Triumph
–	–	Pasadena	119	Fishing schooner	Canadian	Ballast	Explosive charges	Sunk by the Triumph
August 21, 1918	45°32'N 58°57'W	Notre Dame de le Garde	145	Fishing schooner	French	320 tons of fish	Explosive charges	Sunk by the Triumph
–	–	Sylvania	136	Fishing schooner	American	Ballast	Explosive charges	Sunk by the Triumph
August 25, 1918	47°4'N 57°36'W (approx.)	Erik	583	Whaler (steam powered)	British	Ballast	Explosive charges	Sunk
–	46°33'N 57°33'W	E.B Walters	126	Fishing schooner	Canadian	Ballast	Explosive charges	Sunk
–	–	C.M Walters	107	Fishing schooner	Canadian	Ballast	Explosive charges	Sunk
–	–	Verna D. Adams	132	Fishing schooner	Canadian	Ballast	Explosive charges	Sunk
–	–	J.J Flaherty	162	Fishing schooner	American	Ballast	Explosive charges	Sunk
–	–	Clayton W. Walters	116	Fishing ship	Canadian	Ballast	Explosive charges	Sunk
–	–	Marion Adams	99	Fishing ship	Canadian	Ballast	Explosive charges	Sunk
August 26, 1918	46°02'N 57°35'W	Gloaming	130	Fishing schooner	Canadian	Unknown	Explosive charges	Sunk

Vessels Sunk or Damaged by *U-140* (July 2, 1918–September 20, 1918)

Date	Location	Name of Vessel	GRT	Type of Vessel	Nationality	Cargo	Method of Attack	Result
July 27, 1918	39°18'N 60°40'W	Porto	1,079	3-masted barque	Portuguese	600 bales of cotton and barrel staves	2 explosive charges	Sunk
August 2, 1918	39°3'N 70°26'W	Tokuyama Maru	7,029	Steamship	Japanese	1,300 tons of chalk	1 torpedo, 3 shots from 15 cm deck gun	Sunk
August 4, 1918	36°36'N 74°20'W	O.B Jennings	10,289	Tanker	American	Ballast	10 shots from 15cm deck gun	Sunk
August 5, 1918	35°2'N 73°20'W	Stanley M. Seaman	1,060	4-masted schooner	American	1,414 tons of coal	1 explosive charge	Sunk
August 6, 1918	35°5'N 75°19'W	Merak	3,024	Steamship	American	5,600 tons of coal	1 torpedo	Sunk
–	–	Diamond Shoals Lightship (LV-71)	590	Lightship	American	N/A	3 shots from 15 cm deck gun	Sunk
August 21, 1918	40°39'N 65°21'W	Diomed	7,523	Steamship	British	Ballast	4 shots from 15 cm deck gun	Sunk

Vessels Sunk or Damaged by *U-117* (July 11, 1918–September 22, 1918)

Date	Location	Name of Vessel	GRT	Type of Vessel	Nationality	Cargo	Method of Attack	Result
August 10, 1918	10nm radius of 39°18'N 60°40'W	Aleda May	31	Fishing schooner w/ auxiliary motor	American	Ballast	1 explosive charge	Sunk
–	–	William H. Starbuck	53	–	American	Ballast	Shots from 15 cm deck gun	Sunk
–	–	Progress	34	–	American	Ballast	1 explosive charge	Sunk
–	–	Reliance	19	–	American	Ballast	1 explosive charge	Sunk
–	–	Earl & Nettie	24	–	American	Ballast	Shots from 15 cm deck gun	Sunk
–	–	Cruiser	28	–	American	Ballast	Shots from 15 cm deck gun	Sunk
–	–	Old Time	18	–	American	Ballast	Shots from 15 cm deck gun	Sunk

Date	Location	Name of Vessel	GRT	Type of Vessel	Nationality	Cargo	Method of Attack	Result
–	–	Mary E. Sennett	27	–	American	Ballast	Shots from 15 cm deck gun	Sunk
–	–	Katie L. Palmer	21	–	American	Ballast	1 explosive charge	Sunk
August 12, 1918	40°10'N 72°45'W	Sommerstad	3,875	Steamship	Norwegian	Ballast	1 torpedo	Sunk
August 13, 1918	39°55'N 73°54'W	Frederic R. Kellogg	7,127	Tanker	American	Oil	1 torpedo	Sunk (later salvaged)
August 14, 1918	38°43'N 74°28'W	Dorothy B. Barrett	2,088	5-masted schooner	American	Coal	1 torpedo (missed), shots from 15 cm deck gun	Sunk
August 15, 1918	37°30'N 74°38'W	Madrugada	1,613	4-masted schooner	American	1,000 tons of cement	10 shots from 15 cm deck gun	Sunk
August 16, 1918	35°35'N 75°21'W	Mirlo	6,978	Tanker	British	12 holds of gasoline, 2 of kerosene	1 torpedo	Sunk
August 17, 1918	36°20'N 73°36'W	Nordhav	2,846	4-masted barque	Norwegian	Flaxseed	2 explosive charges	Sunk
August 20, 1918	38°18'N 71°16'W	Ansaldo III	5,310	Steamship	Italian	Unknown	Approx. 100 shots from 15 cm gun	Damaged
August 24, 1918	42°54'N 61°40'W	Bianca	408	Schooner	Canadian	Tobacco	1 explosive charge	Damaged
August 26, 1918	44°39'N 57°52'W	Rush	162	Steam trawler	American	Ballast	1 explosive charge	Sunk
August 27, 1918	45°14'N 55°12'W	Bergsdalen	2,555	Steamship	Norwegian	Ballast	1 torpedo	Sunk
August 30, 1918	47°30'N 50°2'W	Elsie Porter	136	Fishing schooner	Canadian	190,400 lbs. of fish	1 explosive charge	Sunk
–	–	Potentate	136	Fishing schooner	Canadian	179,200 lbs. of fish	1 explosive charge	Sunk
September 29, 1918	38°11'N 74°41'W	USS Minnesota	17,949	Battleship	American	N/A	1 UC 200 mine	Damaged
October 4, 1918	39°40'N 73°55'W	San Saba	2,458	Steamship	American	General cargo	1 UC 200 mine	Sunk
October 27, 1918	39°45'N 73°50'W	Chaparra	1,510	Steamship	Cuban	14,000 bags of sugar	1 UC 200 mine	Sunk
November 9, 1918	38°19'N 74°56'W (approx.)	USS Saetia	2,873	Steamship	American	Ballast	1 UC 200 mine	Sunk

Vessels Sunk or Damaged by *U-155* (August 11, 1918–November 11, 1918)

Date	Location	Name of Vessel	GRT	Type of Vessel	Nationality	Cargo	Method of Attack	Result
August 31, 1918	46°10'N 32°0'W	Gamo	315	Fishing schooner	Portuguese	Fish	2 explosive charges	Sunk
September 2, 1918	44°18'N 35°3'W	Stortind	2,560	Steamship	Norwegian	Railroad ties and wire	Shots from 15 cm deck gun	Sunk
September 7, 1918	43°20'N 46°8'W	Sophia	162	Fishing schooner	Portuguese	Codfish	1 explosive charge	Sunk
September 12, 1918	42°12'N 57°23'W	Leixões	3,245	Steamship	Portuguese	Ballast	1 torpedo	Sunk
September 20, 1918	43°58'N 62°12'W	Kingfisher	353	Trawler	American	Ballast	3 explosive charges	Sunk
October 3, 1918	38°24'N 67°2'W	Alberto Treves	3,883	Steamship	Italian	Unknown	1 torpedo	Sunk
October 4, 1918	37°58'N 66°40'W	Industrial	330	Schooner	Canadian	Salt	2 explosive charges	Sunk
October 12, 1918	36°6'N 62°59'W	Amphion	7,410	Steamship	American	Ballast	Approx. 200 shots from 15 cm deck guns	Damaged
October 17, 1918	38°4'N 50°50'W	Lucia	6,744	Steamship	American	Automobiles and general equipment	1 torpedo	Sunk

Vessels Sunk or Damaged by *U-152* (September 5, 1918–November 11, 1918)

Date	Location	Name of Vessel	GRT	Type of Vessel	Nationality	Cargo	Method of Attack	Result
September 11, 1918	62°30'N 0°35'W	Constance	199	Schooner	Denmark	Lumber	3 explosive charges and 50 shots from 15 cm deck	Damaged
September 29, 1918	43°40'N 37°42'W	USS George G. Henry	6936	Tanker	American	Ballast	116 shots from 15 cm deck guns	Damaged
September 30, 1918	44°7'N 37°25'W	USS Ticonderoga	5130	Steamship	American	Railroad ties, 115 Army soldiers	83 shots from 15 cm deck guns	Sunk
October 13, 1918	37°25'N 53°40'W	Stifinder	1745	3-masted barque	Norwegian	Light petroleum incl. naphtha and turpentine	3 explosive charges	Sunk
October 15, 1918	37°20'N 52°30'W	Messina	4271	Steamship	British	Ballast	Shots from 15cm deck guns	Damaged

Vessels Sunk or Damaged by *U-139* (September 11, 1918–November 11, 1918)

Date	Location	Name of Vessel	GRT	Type of Vessel	Nationality	Cargo	Method of Attack	Result
October 1, 1918	45°12'N 11°24'W (approx.)	Bylands	3309	Steamship	British	Phosphate	Shots from 15 cm deck guns	Sunk
–	–	HMS Perth	2502	Auxiliary cruiser	British	N/A	Shots from 15 cm deck guns	Damaged
–	–	Manin	2691	Steamship	Italian	Unknown	Torpedo	Sunk
October 2, 1918	46°49'N 13°16'W (approx.)	Rio Cavado	301	3-masted Lugger	Portuguese	Port wine	Shots from 15 cm deck gun	Sunk
October 14, 1918	36°37'N 21°7'W (approx.)	Augusto De Castilho	487	Trawler / auxiliary minelayer	Portuguese	Cement	Shots from 15 cm deck guns	Sunk

APPENDIX C
The Sinking of USS *Ticonderoga* from a German Perspective

A translated excerpt from Adolf Franz's *Zum zehnjährigen Gedenktag des Artillerie-Kampfes der deutschen Untersee-Kreuzers U 152 mit dem Amerikanischen Hilfskreuzer und Truppentransport-Dampfers Ticonderoga an atlantisches Ozean am 30 September 1918.*

September 30, 1918, at 5.50 a.m. The arrival of a very cloudy dawn was announced, and the officer on watch was just about to wake up the commander so that I would be present on the tower as usual during these most critical minutes of the day, so I was unexpectedly torn out of sleep by the sharp command "Rudder hard to port." The officer on watch had shouted this order to the helmsman in the tower, and its repetition had also echoed down through the control room and the gangway of the boat into my open cabin. In a fraction of a minute, I was on the tower, and my brave second, who was sleeping in his hammock in front of the commander's cabin, hurried after me, as usual, with jacket, scarf, and gloves and binoculars. What was going on!? My eyes, blinded by the albeit dimmed electric light inside the boat, tried desperately to grasp the situation in the glassy and early gray and yet almost dark dawn of the day.

In the otherwise hazy weather, the officer on watch had spotted a steamer going in the opposite direction about 7 points to port at a distance of about 2,500 to 3,000 m during a momentary clearing on a course of 285°. The steamer was similar to yesterday's; that is, painted in completely mixed-up patterns, chessboard shaped and stripes, so that in the brightness of the day the bow and stern were difficult to distinguish, and thus the direction of its course was difficult to determine. The officer on watch might have turned toward the steamer a little too eagerly and bravely, and as a result of a misunderstanding, I took the bow of the steamer for its stern for a short time and wanted to continue turning to port, first bringing the stern of the steamer to the starboard side of my cruiser and following in the steamer's wake. This error (i.e., the mix-up of bow and stern) was recognized immediately, but it was no longer possible to stop the cruiser's strong turn once it had been initiated. At the same time, however, we also noticed that the steamer also turned to port toward us, in order, after it had probably sighted us, to turn its broadside away from a possible launched torpedo or to ram us. With my appearance on the tower, the entire crew of the cruiser was alerted and immediately manned the guns to begin the artillery attack. A quick dive and an attempt at a submerged attack did not come into my consideration for a second in the situation that suddenly stood in front of us, and we had to continue turning extremely quickly. An attempt to dive, to dive away, would have been our undoing. With the water as smooth as glass, *U-152* had been able to submerge in about forty to sixty seconds several times. In normal weather and a wind force of 3 to 4, depending on the sea and swell, you could expect two, three, four, or more minutes until you had the tower under water, so there was enough time for the steamer, in the given situation and weather, to run over the heap of us.

The crew was as nimble as ever. With unbelievable speed the gun operators and the ammunition transport people appeared from their deep sleep through the front, aft, and tower hatches on the upper deck; had loosened the lashed guns; removed the muzzle and locks of the barrels; and torn the ready ammunition from the so-called asparagus beds on the upper deck from their packing containers, the guns loaded and aimed at the commanded target. It was still so dark that the scaled sights on the gun attachments could not be seen; a ban on the use of torches for adjusting the sight attachment was yelled from the turret on deck by the commander and artillery officer. Answer: "I can't see anything on the guns!" Command: "Night distance (12 hm) and aim toward the top edge of the smoke stacks!" According to our artillerists instincts, that had to "stain" [USS *Ticonderoga*] and it did!

While *U-152* was passing across the bow of the steamer with the utmost power of both engines ahead, we opened fire with both 15 cm guns aimed starboard abeam (this time without a warning shot!) because the steamer was visibly pushing toward us with the undoubted intention of ramming us.

Both initial shots were hits, one on the bridge of the steamer, which immediately caused a great fire effect. The steamer continued to turn to port, and *U-152* also slowly turned slightly to port, keeping the enemy under fire with consistent hits. The enemy shot at us with about two to four salvos; his shots were wide and short but still very close to us. A fire on the steamer, especially on the command bridge, began to burn brightly. As the steamer continued to turn to port, a so-called ongoing artillery battle developed on parallel though somewhat divergent courses. We had to struggle to dodge the enemy's volleys of shells, because the enemy fired well with guns fore and aft.

Suddenly flashes of fire were sighted at a greater distance from the direction in front of the bow of the steamer, and then shortly afterward in the same direction a vessel with two to three smokestacks, which was identified as a cruiser, began roaring toward it with large zigzag course changes and high speed.

In view of the cruiser and the steamer that was about 25 meters away and still burning and firing at us, we broke off the artillery battle and submerged. The lashing down of the guns, the stowage of the remains of ammunition in the ship so that they could not float up after diving and give us away, the disappearance of the crews from the upper deck, the closing of the hatches, and the diving maneuvers of the cruiser were a great pleasure for the commander to observe. The crew was inspired by an admirable will and a brilliant heroic spirit. The wind and swells had meanwhile increased while the cruiser was steered underwater, whereby depth control was initially quite difficult due to the ammunition consumption that had occurred and the lightened ammunition stowage. With increasing daylight, only the still-burning and heavily smoking steamer could be seen through the periscope, which, however, was not yet sinking. Unfortunately, my efforts to shoot an underwater torpedo at the steamer, which was always turning in large circles to port, were unsuccessful. After my earlier months of experience as a teacher of numerous U-boat commander students, such a task was a "trick" in terms of U-boat technology. After my two unsuccessful attempts, the steamer gradually took a straight course, about 270°, and steamed away while *U-152* remained astern of her. It was now 7:05 a.m. In order not to let the steamer escape, I surfaced, blowing out all the diving tanks by using compressed air. The cruiser shot out of the water with the tower, bow, and upper deck, and the compressed air throwing up welling eddies on both sides of the ship. The tower hatch flew open due to the overpressurization within the boat, which threatened to break your eardrums, and climbing out of the tower first, I could not see anything around except the steamer sailing in front of us. Like the Heinzelmanns,[1] the awaiting gun crews were back at their guns through the open hatches. As soon as our tower emerged from the water, the steamer immediately opened fire on us again with its stern gun. At a distance of 25 to 35 hm we returned fire, using the so-called high-explosive shells and shrapnel shells that, depending on the setting of their fuses, burst in midair before hitting the ground. I could decide on this ammunition only with a heavy heart, since I knew how devastating it would be if the detonation point was in the right position. Our high-explosive projectiles were loaded as one could only ever have wished for as an artilleryman in a well-guided peacetime firing exercise. As before, the ship began smoking, and we also observed numerous hits in the ship's side and in the deck structures of the steamer. But the enemy also shot excellently with his 15.2 cm guns, but without hitting us, with the fragments of his shells that burst in our vicinity whizzing around our ears. A piece of shrapnel wounded our excellent gunner at the front gun, not insignificantly, in the knee, and another smashed into the inner protective wall of the turret right next to my arm. At a distance of about 25 hm I had bypassed the stern of the steamer being pursued in favor of its starboard and windward side in order to facilitate our gunners' task, which had been made more difficult by the smoke from the steamer drifting toward us. When we were able to take a bearing on the steamer exactly from astern, it was found that there were no longer any lifeboats hanging in the boat davits on the ship's sides.

At about 7:45 a.m., with the sharpest observation through our binoculars, we could make out people with raised arms on the superstructure decks of the steamer. After the enemy apparently stopped firing, I also stopped firing. The stern of the steamer sank visibly lower. In order to question survivors and possibly take them on board, I had the cruiser steered toward the shot-up life rafts and wreckage floating nearby. The steamer gradually sank farther and finally over its stern into the depths, after it had raised its bow almost bolt upright out of the water toward the sky. A horrible sight! Our ammunition consumption was thirty-five rounds before and forty-eight after diving, in total eighty-three rounds!

The steamer crew had fought bravely, heroically, and with admirable tenacity to the end.

The nature of the fire raid at dawn and the artillery battle that followed required a total engagement of the U-cruiser. There was no question that we would have to open fire at the last moment of danger—without a warning shot—if we didn't want to endanger our lives and the existence of the U-cruiser even further, leading to our eventual undoing. In such moments, the submarine commander does not have a second to think about it, but decisions have to be made and implemented in a flash and instinctively. To this end, the commander and the entire crew must undergo extremely thorough training through maneuver exercises that have been increased to the maximum or through experiences of war. And we had experienced this training partly in months of warlike exercises and partly at the front.

The complete utilization of the cruiser had led to success. The surface-maneuvering characteristics of this restrained U-cruiser type were, however, even at the highest cruising speed with both machines full speed ahead and the assist of the electric motors, once again shown to be exceptionally poor. Even when the sea was still relatively favorable, this vessel turned worse than a capital ship. And when it finally started to turn, it could be stopped only with a "hard rudder against." I knew the maneuverability of a large battleship through my own six years of experience.

The crew of the U-cruiser had done their duty in an excellent manner throughout the battle. With such a crew, one could confidently go into battle, relying on each and every one! The artillery crews deserve special mention with their excellent gunners, the ammunition crews, who jumped around with their shells like dolls, and the entire machine and ship's central personnel, who waited under unbearable heavy oil smoke in the engine and control rooms, worked and had fought.

The fight was over. The commander was faced with what was perhaps the most difficult decision of his life. We found ourselves in the midst of a debris field of surviving people, some of whom were seriously wounded and half or completely swimming in the water, and the remains of ships and boats. At the same time expecting a reappearance of enemy forces on each side. The cries for help of the agonizing people hanging on life belts, beams, and other debris went to our bones. The full horror of war was before our eyes now that the fighting was over. While we were still contemplating what nationality our heroic and now-defeated enemies might belong to, who had defended their lives on a cow-ferry steamer up to the last moment and had tried to destroy us, we saw to our greatest astonishment that all the survivors were dressed in uniforms, American uniforms, and hearing these people begging us for help and rescue, some in our own native language. German Americans! How terrible and cruel is this war; it pierced our hearts! What to do and where to start with this pitiful and wretched remnant of partly shredded human remains that were swimming in the water (make a hospital ship out of our warship)? How many could there be, whose fate now stirred our hearts violently? Was it even possible to help many of them with their torn limbs and open wounds that turned the water around them red!? Wouldn't taking all the survivors and wounded on board endanger the health of my own crew!? Was it at all possible to take everyone on board and accommodate them without seriously endangering our boat ourselves?

We were supposed to take care of, bandage, and heal those who were to be taken on board, but how should they be able to stand or lie in a boat with a crew of seventy-seven, for which every little corner, nook, and cranny was completely taken up and used? Our own crew lived and slept for weeks on end between ammunition stacks, torpedoes, and mines; when the weather was bad, the air inside the boat was often almost unbearable for healthy people. Which survivor should be turned away from boarding? At five, ten, twenty, thirty, forty, fifty, or were there even more of them!?

War, war, and still war, four years of war and no end in sight! This thought and that of my own homeland, people, and fatherland finally made me decide to make the most-extreme restrictions in the rescue of the survivors. We were out here in the middle of the ocean to wage war, on our own. Concern for my own crew was the first priority for me as commander; our goal was to carry out my operational task. Millions of people had lost their lives in the war, and the longer the war lasted, the harder the struggle of a whole world of enemies against us became. Humanity has its limits in war! Just as we would probably have had to sail around the ocean for days and weeks with several dozen survivors on board, hampered in the conduct of the war, it was to be expected, on the other hand, that that American escort cruiser, which had disappeared from the scene so remarkably quickly, would reappear any minute and take up the fight against us for the survivors who had been left behind, forcing our boat, which was overcrowded by the rescued people, to dive without us having the probability that such a maneuver could even take place, given the unusual burden and inhibition caused by the wounded and those unaccustomed to submarines, for any success. In the event of such an unsuccessful attempt to dive, would the enemy not suspect anything and not shoot at us and his own fellow countrymen or try to run over us? Or should we set the white flag when the enemy appears in order to hand over the rescued? A few months earlier, a German U-cruiser commander had dropped off a large number of prisoners, I think there was also a young mother with a baby, on the American East Coast. The result of this humanity was an immediately far-ranging ambush by American naval forces from all ports on the East Coast on this German U-cruiser, which then made life damn difficult for him.[2]

By questioning the shipwrecked, the two most senior surviving officers of the steamer were identified and taken on board from the wreckage of the boat, which had been shot up, flooded, and overflowing with wounded people; they were sparsely clad, one of them barefoot, in a nightgown, trousers, and a uniform jacket. The takeover could be accomplished only through the use of volunteers from the U-cruiser, who were tied to lines, and then after jumping overboard into the water in their full clothing and swimming carefully were they able to bring the two officers, who came gladly and happily, over to us to put them on board. They immediately lost consciousness and were carefully carried through the front hatch into the interior of the boat. One of the two, the 2nd machinist of the steamer, named "Fulscher" or Mueller,[3] who was considerably wounded by shrapnel in his legs, was given his room by our chief engineer of his own free will, where the wounded man was immediately put to bed and operated on by our efficient ship's doctor with great success. The other 1st officer of the steamer was also undressed, toweled, and wrapped in warm woolen blankets and received a very strong sip of rum and, as a bed, the sofa in our officers' mess, which had previously served the mess steward as a place to sleep due to lack of space.

With clenched teeth and after the hardest internal struggle, I gave the order at 9.45 a.m.: "Both machines full speed ahead; march on to continue our operational task!"

Toward evening the interrogation of the two rescued prisoners, who remained separated for the first three days and knew nothing of each other and who were now linked for better or worse with our fate, could begin by our English-speaking prize officer. He found the following:

The steamer that we sunk and destroyed in artillery combat was called "Ticonderoga" and was the former German steamer "Camilla Rickmers" of 5,130 GRT. The steamer belonged to a convoy of eighteen ships, which left New York on September 22 (i.e., eight days before) under the escort of a cruiser and consisted only of American and English ships. The steamer itself came from Norfolk, Virginia, and was carrying troops and war material of all kinds as general cargo for the western front. It was owned by the American government—that is, as an auxiliary warship; the entire crew was in the service of the state and wore uniforms. According to the chief officer's statement, the crew, including troops, numbered 231 people. The old convoy steamers also had troops on board. The prisoners did not know where the path of Ticonderoga led, probably via Marseille in France.

The artillery of our U-cruiser had worked horribly and gruesomely, so a total of over 190 dead, wounded, and drowned remained. The shrapnel, which would have been very effective, had had an almost devastating effect. Our first two shots, fired from the front of the steamer, rushed the steamer's bridge, shot off a leg; the bridge crew were killed instantly, the ship's rudder jammed to port, and the wireless failed due to damage.

Ticonderoga had left the convoy at a speed of 8 knots during the night in hazy weather and was trying to catch up again at dawn. The convoy or escort cruiser had been close to the battlefield, as indicated by the flashes of foreign gunfire during the first leg of the battle. The escort cruiser was the only vehicle in the convoy with two funnels. The captain and 1st machinist of *Ticonderoga* had fallen in battle or drowned.

Early in the morning of September 30, *U-152* was standing at the point aimed for the evening before; namely, west of 44°7' north latitude and 37°25' west longitude. Here, numerous American soldiers lost their lives in the heaviest battle of the war in the course of a short four-hour episode, which was certainly peculiar and perhaps unique due to the type and location of the battle: "In the middle of the ocean, almost equidistant from the western European and eastern American coasts."

To honor the fighters and to commemorate the Americans who died on this battlefield, let us commemorate the tenth anniversary of that day, September 30, 1918!

Not to whip up passions for war and not to reopen and dig into the wounds that war inflicted on all the peoples of the earth, but now that the war is ten years behind us, both parties in this struggle can also be allowed to receive their full justice!

If ever a battle at sea was "fair," it was between those two vessels of war. The prerequisite for the battle in the middle of the ocean was undoubtedly the diving ability of the German cruiser and the possibility this gave her of evading superior enemy countermeasures when approaching and fighting. In the battle itself, this time the U-boat as such—namely, in the submerged attack—was denied success. However, the temporary disappearance of the U-cruiser as an initial defensive measure against the escort cruiser that appeared had perhaps in turn prompted the latter to evacuate the battlefield in order not to run the risk of becoming a victim of the submarine in a submerged attack.

The enemy, who was attacked by artillery and in self-defense, which apart from its bright paintwork had the appearance of a peaceful merchant ship, had turned out to be a warship with the bravest war crew and an equal opponent.

There were numerous reproaches and accusations against the commander of the German U-cruiser for his behavior after the end of the battle for his cruelty and inhumanity. Yes, even bestiality has been spoken of.

I ask whether an American submarine commander in the same or a similar situation acted or is acting differently then or now.

The cries of the American press and radio stations that abused us at the time about the inhumanity, bestial cruelty, and barbarism of the German submarine commander, which we caught on the day immediately following the annihilation of *Ticonderoga* and on later days with tendentious descriptions of the process, they are now a decade ago and behind us.

But now the opponent, whether he wins or loses, should be treated with justice. War is a cruel handicraft and will remain so for all time.

ENDNOTES

Introduction

1. *Seiner Majestät Unterseeboot* (His Majesty's Submarine). The technical way to identify U-boats of this period would be to precede the numeric identity with SM, such as SM *U-117*. This practice, for obvious reasons, did not continue into the Second World War, and those U-boats were simply identified with a U followed by a number. Throughout this book, the SM is often excluded for the sake of brevity. When World War II U-boats will be mentioned, they will be clearly identified as such.
2. U-boats.
3. Alexander Watson, *Ring of Steel: Germany and Austria-Hungary in World War I* (New York: Basic Books, 2014), 444.
4. Lowell Thomas, *Raiders of the Deep* (Garden City, NY: Doubleday, Doran, 1928), 48–49.

Chapter 1: America, Meet Deutschland

1. The German equivalent to a lieutenant commander in the US Navy.
2. German Imperial Navy.
3. Eliza von Moltke, ed. *Generaloberst Helmuth von Moltke. Erinnerungen, Briefe, Dokumente, 1877–1916. Ein Bild vom Kriegsausbruch, erster Kriegführung und Persönlichkeit des ersten militärischen Führers des Krieges* (Stuttgart: Der Kommende Tag, 1922), 308.
4. Alfred Carpenter, *The Blocking of Zeebrugge* (London: Herbert Jenkins, 1922), 276.
5. Robert Massie, *Castles of Steel* (New York: Ballantine Books, 2003), 696.
6. German Ocean Shipping Company.
7. Friedrich Krupp Germania Shipyard. The shipyard was also responsible for the construction of prewar German Imperial Navy battleships.
8. Mark Jefferson, "Our Trade in the Great War," *Geographical Review* 3, no. 6 (June 1917), 479.
9. Dwight Messimer, *The Merchant U-boat: Adventures of the Deutschland 1916–1918* (Annapolis, MD: Naval Institute Press, 1988), 3.
10. Jefferson, "Our Trade in the Great War," 479.
11. Cecil Spring-Rice, *Letters and Friendships*, vol. 2 (Boston: Houghton Mifflin, 1929), 343.
12. US Navy equivalent of an ensign.

13. "World War I U-boat Commanders: Paul König," https://uboat.net/wwi/men/commanders/423.html, accessed December 13, 2020.
14. Paul König, *Voyage of the Deutschland* (New York: Hearst's International Library, 1916), 6–7.
15. Erich Gröner, *German Warships, 1815–1945*, vol. 2, *U-boats and Mine Warfare Vessels* (Annapolis, MD: Naval Institute Press, 1991), 20.
16. Ibid., 13.
17. Jamie Bisher, *The Intelligence War in Latin America, 1914–1922* (Jefferson, NC: McFarland, 2016), 142.
18. United States Office of Naval Records and Library, *German Submarine Activities on the Atlantic Coast of the United States and Canada*, Publication 1 (Washington, DC: US Government Printing Office, 1920), 17.
19. Gröner, *German Warships, 1815–1945*, 2:20.
20. *Papers Relating to the Foreign Relations of the United States, Supplement, the World War*, Document 1001 (Washington, DC: US Government Printing Office, 1916), file no. 763.72111/3847, pp. 765–66, https://history.state.gov/historicaldocuments/frus1916Supp/d1001, accessed November 9, 2020.
21. *Baltimore Sun* (morning edition), July 10, 1916, 1.
22. König, *Voyage of the Deutschland*, 129.
23. Ibid., 145.
24. "Preserving a Part of the City's German Past," *Baltimore Sun*, July 14, 2014, https://www.baltimoresun.com/maryland/bs-xpm-2010-01-24-bal-md-backstory24jan24-story.html, accessed 9 Dec. 2020.
25. It is unclear if König was aware how deeply involved Frederick Hinsch was in German intelligence, but he certainly must have had an inkling. Besides the plans for a wireless station to be built in Mexico, it has been alleged that part of the gold bullion transported by the *Deutschland* was utilized by German agents to fund a biological warfare lab in Chevy Chase, Maryland ("Tony's Lab"). This lab was responsible for incubating anthrax and glanders cells, which were later injected into livestock being shipped over to Europe for the Allied war effort. Even more disconcerting, Hinsch was later identified as being the mastermind of the Black Tom Explosion and other acts of sabotage on the Continent. Ultimately (according to the *New York Times* on July 18, 1917) he would escape back to Bremen after boarding a schooner leaving South Amboy, New Jersey, and was never convicted of any crimes.
26. König, *Voyage of the Deutschland*, 153.
27. *Washington Times* (Washington, DC, evening edition), July 9, 1916, 9.

28. *Papers Relating to the Foreign Relations of the United States, Supplement, the World War*, Document 1005 (Washington, DC: US Government Printing Office, 1916), file no. 763.72111D48/14b, https://history.state.gov/historicaldocuments/frus1916Supp/d1005, accessed November 9, 2020.

29. *Papers Relating to the Foreign Relations of the United States, Supplement, the World War*, Document 1006 (Washington, DC: US Government Printing Office, 1916), file no. 763.72111D48/26, https://history.state.gov/historicaldocuments/frus1916Supp/d1006, accessed November 9, 2020.

30. Ibid.

31. United States Office of Naval Records and Library, *German Submarine Activities*, 17.

32. König, *Voyage of the Deutschland*, 160.

33. Messimer, *The Merchant U-boat*, 108.

34. *New York Times*, July 11, 1916, 2.

35. German Imperial Admiralty Staff.

Chapter 2: A Series of Unfortunate Events

1. Submarine school.

2. Markus Robinson and Gertrude Robinson, *Der Kapitän: U-boat Ace Hans Rose* (Gloucestershire, UK: Amberley, 2018), 118.

3. "Ships Hit by Hans Rose," https://uboat.net/wwi/men/commanders/273.html, accessed January 1, 2021.

4. Robinson and Robinson, *Der Kapitän*, 126.

5. Edwyn Gray, *A Damned Un-English Weapon: The Story of British Submarine Warfare, 1914–1918* (London: Seeley, Service, 1971), 200–202. Varley was nearly court-martialed for his victory, since he ignored his original patrol orders and went off hunting on his own. Although he escaped serious discipline, he was denied any recognition for his feat for a year. Having done his penance, he was belatedly rewarded for his daring with the Distinguished Service Order.

6. Four crew members would survive the attack, escaping through various hatches. A detailed account of this incident is recalled in Robinson and Robinson, *Der Kapitän*, 127–29.

7. Hans Rose, *Auftauchen! Kriegsfahrten von U-53* (Essen, Germany: Essener Verlagsanstalt, 1939), 42.

8. Douglas Robinson, *The Zeppelin in Combat: A History of the German Naval Airship Division, 1912–1918* (Sun Valley, CA: John W. Caler, 1971), 162.

9. Commander of the U-boats, Frigate Capt. Hermann Bauer (1875–1958). He held this position until June 1917, when he took command of the battleship SMS *Westfalen*. Although he declared himself available for military service during the Second World War, he was never recalled. His book *Das Unterseeboot* was translated into English by US admiral Hyman Rickover and would become a standard text for the US submarine service.
10. Reinhard Scheer, *Germany's High Seas Fleet in the Great War* (New York: Peter Smith, 1934), 263.
11. The *Hamburg* was a light cruiser of the prewar Bremen class. Following the Battle of Jutland, its obsolescence ever more apparent, it became a floating headquarters and barracks ship in Wilhelmshaven.
12. Werner von Langsdorff, *U-Boote am Feind: 45 Deutsche U-Boot-Fahrer Erzählen* (Gütersloh, Germany: Verlag C. Bertelsmann, 1937), 158.
13. Gröner, *German Warships, 1815–1945*, 2:8.
14. Robinson and Robinson, *Der Kapitän*, 135.
15. *Kriegstagebuch SM U-53 für die Zeit der Fernunternehmen von 15 September 1916–28 Oktober 1916* (Cuxhaven-Altenbruch, Germany: Freundeskreis Traditionsarchiv Unterseeboote e.V), 1–2.
16. Gröner, *German Warships, 1815–1945*, 2:8.
17. Wellington Long, "The Cruise of the U-53," *United States Naval Institute Proceedings* 92, no. 764 (October 1966): 88.
18. Robinson and Robinson, *Der Kapitän*, 27.
19. Scheer, *Germany's High Seas Fleet in the Great War*, 264.
20. Rose, *Auftauchen! Kriegfahrten von U-53*, 58.
21. Messimer, *The Merchant U-boat*, 60.
22. *Aberdeen Press and Journal* (Aberdeenshire, Scotland), November 4, 1916, 4.
23. *Liverpool Daily Post*, October 2, 1916, 8.
24. R. H. Gibson and Maurice Prendergast, *The German Submarine War, 1914–1918* (Uckfield, UK: Naval and Military Press, 2003), 103.
25. Gray, *A Damned Un-English Weapon*, 218.
26. "Pre-WWII Torpedoes of the United Kingdom / Britain," http://www.navweaps.com/Weapons/WTBR_PreWWII.php, accessed January 2, 2021.
27. Gray, *A Damned Un-English Weapon*, 218.
28. *Kriegstagebuch SM U-53*, October 3, 1916.
29. Bodo Herzog and Günter Schomäkers, *Ritter der Graue Wölfe: Die Erfolgreichsten U-Boot-Kommandanten der Welt* (Munich: Verlag Welsermühl, 1976), 161.

30. This event further illustrates the disparity between the treatment of *U-53*'s mission compared to that of the commercial submarines; had the same consideration been given to the *U-Bremen* weeks prior, her sinking may have not been so mysterious, if not avoided altogether.
31. Robinson and Robinson, *Der Kapitän*, 30–31.
32. *Kriegstagebuch SM U-53*, 1000, September 23, 1916.
33. Robinson and Robinson, *Der Kapitän*, 35.
34. Langsdorff, *U-Boote am Feind*, 166.

Chapter 3: The Empire Strikes Back

1. This, of course, excludes the two American submarines in service during the Civil War, the Union *Alligator* and the Confederate *Hunley*, which technically did not battle with "foreign" navies.
2. Paul Silverstone, *US Warships of World War I* (Garden City, NY: Doubleday, 1970), 134. SM *U-53*, in contrast, had two 2,400 hp diesel engines for surface travel, a total displacement of 1,060 tons, and four 50 cm (19.7") torpedo tubes.
3. James Connolly, *The U-boat Hunters* (New York: Charles Scribner's Sons, 1918), 10.
4. Long, "The Cruise of the U-53," 90.
5. Herzog and Schomäkers, *Ritter der Graue Wölfe*, 164.
6. Ibid.
7. Ibid.
8. Lawrence Perry, *Our Navy in the War* (New York: Charles Scribner's Sons, 1918), 30.
9. United States Office of Naval Records and Library, *German Submarine Activities*, 22.
10. Robinson and Robinson, *Der Kapitän*, 46.
11. Gröner, *German Warships, 1815–1945*, 8.
12. *Papers Relating to the Foreign Relations of the United States, Supplement, the World War*, Document 1011 (Washington, DC: US Government Printing Office, 1916), file no. 763.72/2926a, https://history.state.gov/historical-documents/frus1916Supp/d1011, accessed November 9, 2020.
13. Perry, *Our Navy in the War*, 31.
14. *Kriegstagebuch SM U-53*, 0535, October 8, 1916.
15. Langsdorff, *U-Boote am Feind*, 171.
16. Rose, *Auftauchen!*, 101.
17. Robinson and Robinson, *Der Kapitän*, 48.

18. Perry, *Our Navy in the War*, 31.
19. SS *Strathdene*, Wreck Site, https://www.wrecksite.eu/wreck.aspx?18406, accessed January 30, 2021.
20. Langsdorff, *U-Boote am Feind*, 172.
21. SS *Christian Knudsen*, Wreck Site, https://www.wrecksite.eu/wreck.aspx?145580, accessed January 30, 2021.
22. *Kriegstagebuch SM U-53*, 0803, October 8, 1916.
23. Ibid., 0952, October 8, 1916.
24. Ibid., 1140, October 8, 1916.
25. Ibid., 1235, October 8, 1916.
26. RAdm. Albert Gleaves, commander, Destroyer Force, to RAdm. Henry T. Mayo, commander, Atlantic Fleet, November 2, 1916, Naval History and Heritage Command, https://www.history.navy.mil/research/publications/documentary-histories/wwi/1916/rear-admiral-albert/_jcr_content.html, accessed December 31, 2020. Concerning the destroyers being dispatched, the destroyer USS *Balch* was already at sea and was the first American ship to begin taking on survivors. The first destroyer to depart Rhode Island was USS *Jervis*, commanded by Lt. Davis, and was followed by USS *Drayton*, Lt. Bagley; USS *Ericsson*, Lt. Cmdr. Miller; USS *O'Brien*, Lt. Cmdr. Courtney; USS *Benham*, Lt. Cmdr. Gay; USS *Cassin*, Lt. Cmdr. Vernou; USS *McCall*, Lt. Stewart; USS *Porter*, Lt. Cmdr. Wortman; USS *Fanning*, Lt. Austin; USS *Paulding*, Lt. Howard; USS *Winslow*, Lt. Cmdr. Nichols; USS *Aylwyn*, Lt. Cmdr. Fremont; USS *Cushing*, Lt. Kettinger; USS *Cummings*, Lt. Cmdr. Neal; USS *Conyngham*, Lt. Cmdr. Johnson; and USS *Melville*, Cmdr. Price. Adm. Gleaves remained at port on USS *Birmingham* coordinating the rescue efforts via the wireless.
27. *Kriegstagebuch SM U-53*, 1505, October 8, 1916.
28. Ibid., 1540, October 8, 1916.
29. SS *Blommersdijk*, Wreck Site, https://www.wrecksite.eu/wreck.aspx?139190, accessed February 3, 2021.
30. *Kriegstagebuch SM U-53*, 1730, October 8, 1916.
31. Robinson and Robinson, *Der Kapitän*, 50.
32. *Kriegstagebuch SM U-53*, 1740, October 8, 1916.
33. Ibid., 1740, October 8, 1916.
34. RAdm. Gleaves, https://www.history.navy.mil/research/publications/documentary-histories/wwi/1916/rear-admiral-albert/_jcr_content.html, accessed December 31, 2020.
35. *Kriegstagebuch SM U-53*, 1740, October 8, 1916.
36. Ibid., 1740, October 8, 1916.

37. Ibid., 1740, October 8, 1916.
38. SS *Stephano*, Wreck Site, https://www.wrecksite.eu/wreck.aspx?18424, accessed February 8, 2021.
39. *Liverpool Daily Post*, October 11, 1916.
40. Robinson and Robinson, *Der Kapitän*, 51.
41. Peter Ericson, *The Kaiser Strikes America: The U-boat Campaign off America's Coast in WWI* (Morrisville, NC: Lulu, 2008), 45.
42. United States Office of Naval Records and Library, *German Submarine Activities*, 23.
43. *Kriegstagebuch SM U-53*, 2230, October 8, 1916. Interestingly, the captain of an Italian steamer, the *Dante Alighieri*, reported that he had intercepted this message on October 9 and claimed that it read, "Have sunk several ships, but am after nine. Signed: Rose." (*New York Tribune*, November 22, 1916, 2). This story does not resemble anything mentioned in Rose's war diary, to say nothing of the fact that the message was encoded and it is unlikely that the Italian captain had the cipher. Further evidence against this claim can be found in *U-53*'s log for the ninth, with Rose writing, "Due to the increasing swell of the sea, the antenna was removed to protect it from tearing apart" his other antenna on the net deflector, which had "no reception due to isolating errors."
44. Robinson and Robinson, *Der Kapitän*, 53.

Chapter 4: Changing Tides

1. *Papers Relating to the Foreign Relations of the United States, Supplement, the World War*, Document 1011.
2. "*Tribune* Graphic," *New York Tribune*, October 15, 1916, section 2, p. 1.
3. *Papers Relating to the Foreign Relations of the United States, Supplement, the World War*, Document 1023 (Washington, DC: US Government Printing Office, 1916), file no. 763.72/2958, https://history.state.gov/historicaldocuments/frus1916Supp/d1023, accessed November 9, 2020.
4. Ibid.
5. Ibid.
6. *Papers Relating to the Foreign Relations of the United States, Supplement, the World War*, Document 1025 (Washington, DC: US Government Printing Office, 1916), https://history.state.gov/historicaldocuments/frus1916Supp/d1025, accessed November 9, 2020.
7. Ibid.
8. *Washington Herald* (Washington, DC), December 2, 1916, 6.

9. James Gerard, *My Four Years in Germany* (New York: Grosset & Dunlap, 1917), 248.
10. *New York Tribune*, November 11, 1916, 4.
11. *Washington Herald*, December 2, 1916, 6.
12. Arthur Link, "President Woodrow Wilson's Plan to Resign in 1916." *Princeton University Library Chronicle* 23, no. 4 (1962): 171–72.
13. Inauguration Day was held on March 4, beginning immediately after George Washington's first inauguration in 1789. In the case of Inauguration Day in 1917, it was March 5, since the fourth fell on a Sunday. The change to being on January 20 didn't occur until 1937. This is why Wilson was concerned about a "four-month" lame-duck period instead of the two-month period modern readers would expect.
14. Messimer, *The Merchant U-boat*, 112.
15. Ibid., 123.
16. Ibid., 124.
17. König, *Voyage of the Deutschland*, 155.
18. Messimer, *The Merchant U-boat*, 127.
19. *New York Tribune*, November 11, 1916, 4.
20. United States Office of Naval Records and Library, *German Submarine Activities*, 17. Pertaining to the nickel loaded onto the *Deutschland*, it consisted of 360 tons that was actually purchased from Canada in 1914 before the war broke out.
21. Messimer, *The Merchant U-boat*, 136.
22. *New York Tribune*, November 18, 1916, 1.
23. Ibid.
24. *New York Times*, November 18, 1916, 1.
25. The four members of the crew who died on the *T. A. Scott Jr.* were William Caton (engineer), Edward Stone (fireman), Eugene Durant (deckhand), and Clarence Davison (the cook).
26. *New York Tribune*, November 21, 1916, 3.
27. *New York Tribune,* November 22, 1916, 3.
28. Scheer, *Germany's High Seas Fleet in the Great War*, 245.
29. Massie, *Castles of Steel*, 704.
30. Chief of the admiralty staff, Adm. Henning von Holtzendorff, German Imperial Marine Service, to chief of the Army General Staff, General Paul von Hindenburg, December 22, 1916, https://www.history.navy.mil/research/publications/documentary-histories/wwi/1916/chief-of-the-admiral/_jcr_content.html, accessed February 9, 2021.

31. Herbert Bayard Swope, *Inside the German Empire in the Third Year of the War* (New York: Century, 1917), 97.
32. Watson, *Ring of Steel*, 443.
33. Gerard, *My Four Years in Germany*, 189.
34. Swope, *Inside the German Empire in the Third Year of the War*, 70.

Chapter 5: Si Vis Pacem, Para Bellum
1. Gerard, *My Four Years in Germany*, 261.
2. Ibid., 250.
3. Ibid., 263.
4. Ibid., 262.
5. "Memoranda Enclosed in the Bernstorff Note to Secretary Lansing," in *Source Records of the Great War*, vol. 5, *1917*, ed. Charles Horne and Walter Austin (New York: National Alumni, 1923), 7.
6. Bradley Fiske, *From Midshipman to Rear-Admiral* (New York: Century, 1919), 550.
7. Thomas Hone and Curtis Utz, *History of the Office of the Chief of Naval Operations, 1915–2015* (Washington, DC: Department of the Navy Naval History and Heritage Command, 2020), 31.
8. George W. Baer, *One Hundred Years of Sea Power: The US Navy, 1890–1990* (Stanford, CA: Stanford University Press, 1996), 59.
9. Hone and Utz, *History of the Office of the Chief of Naval Operations, 1915–2015*, 31–32.
10. Ibid., 32.
11. The Neff system was an experimental propulsion system that did away with the use of battery-powered electric motors for submerged travel and instead relied on the same diesel engines used for surface travel. It used compressed air to provide oxygen for the engine intakes and used a collector for the exhaust gases. The submarine was planned to be designated SS-108, but the plans were canceled and the submarine was never actually built.
12. Archibald Oden Jr., ed., *Navy Yearbook 1917 and 1918* (Washington, DC: US Government Printing Office, 1919), 463–65.
13. Ibid., 439.
14. Secretary Josephus Daniels to President Woodrow Wilson, March 23, 1917, https://www.history.navy.mil/research/publications/documentary-histories/wwi/march-1917/secretary-of-the-nav-2.html, accessed March 31, 2021.
15. *New York Tribune*, November 18, 1916, 1.
16. William Sowden Sims, *The Victory at Sea* (New York: Doubleday, Page, 1920), 375.

17. Ibid.
18. Mary Klachko, *Admiral William Shepherd Benson: First Chief of Naval Operations* (Annapolis, MD: Naval Institute Press, 1987), 84.
19. Ibid., 69.
20. Ibid., 108.
21. William Bell Clark, *When the U-boats Came to America* (Boston: Little, Brown, 1929), 12.
22. Alexander Moffat, *Maverick Navy* (Middletown, CT: Wesleyan University Press, 1976), 12.
23. Ibid., 13.
24. William Washburn Nutting, *The Cinderellas of the Fleet* (Jersey City, NJ: Standard Motor Construction, 1920), 57.
25. Dwight Messimer, *Find and Destroy: Antisubmarine Warfare in World War I* (Annapolis, MD: Naval Institute Press, 2001), 124.
26. Nutting, *The Cinderellas of the Fleet*, 59.
27. Messimer, *Find and Destroy*, 125.
28. Nutting, *The Cinderellas of the Fleet*, 73.
29. Baer, *One Hundred Years of Sea Power*, 73.
30. Sims, *The Victory at Sea*, 395.
31. The "L" designation meant that the plane was equipped with a twelve-cylinder, 27-liter, 400 hp Liberty engine, as opposed to the underpowered eight-cylinder, 18-liter, 180 hp Curtiss V-X engine.
32. Ibid., 396–97.
33. *Unterseekreuzer*, or simply U-Kreuzer, translates to submarine cruiser. Essentially a large submarine with a greatly expanded range of operations and improved armament.
34. Eberhard Rössler, *Die Deutschen U-Kreuzer und Transport U-Boote* (Bonn, Germany: Bernard & Graefe Verlag, 2003), 61.
35. Ibid., 63.
36. The G6AV* torpedoes were 50 cm in diameter and 6 m in length and contained a warhead consisting of 200 kg of TNT and hexanitrodiphenylamine. Concerning the name of the torpedoes, the *G* stood for the series of torpedo, 6 was for the length in meters, AV was for the German word *Anwärmvorrichtung* (heating device, since it was a dry-heater type and did not utilize steam power), and the asterisk indicated it was a higher-pressure type and had a 500 m longer range than the G6AV type.
37. Rössler, *Die Deutschen U-Kreuzer und Transport U-Boote*, 65.
38. Gröner, *German Warships, 1815–1945*, 17.

39. These submarines were built by two different firms, with *U-117–121* being built by Vulkan AG and *U-122–126* being constructed at Blohm & Voss. The B&V types were somewhat smaller, carried fewer torpedoes, and had a shorter overall range of operations than the Vulkan types. Since *U-117* was the only UE II type submarine to operate off the American East Coast, only the Vulkan-built U-boat specifications will be mentioned in this book.
40. Gröner, *German Warships, 1815–1945*, 15.
41. Rössler, *Die Deutschen U-Kreuzer und Transport U-Boote*, 74.
42. Messimer, *The Merchant U-boat*, 165.
43. Gröner, *German Warships, 1815–1945*, 21.

Chapter 6: They Came to Casablanca for the Waters

1. Messimer, *The Merchant U-boat*, 159.
2. Ibid., 167.
3. *Kriegstagebuch SM U-155 Bd. 1: 23 Mai 1917–5 August 1917* (Cuxhaven-Altenbruch, Germany: Freundeskreis Traditionsarchiv Unterseeboote e.V), 1200, July 26, 1917.
4. Ibid., July 31, 1917.
5. As an interesting aside, this patrol also marked the first time a U-Kreuzer would engage an American naval vessel—occurring when *U-155* shelled the port of Porta Delgada in the Azores, where the collier USS *Orion* (AC-11) happened to be undergoing repairs. Although a brief artillery duel between the two vessels ensued, neither was damaged and only four people were killed within the city. This, however, was enough to scare the US Navy into establishing a base at Porta Delgada, fearing further U-boat attacks on the defenseless island. It also made the Americans question what a similar U-boat could do to ports within US waters. The Portuguese government would later honor the crew of *Orion* with the Order of the Tower and Sword, attributing *U-155* breaking off the raid as a result of the engagement with the collier.
6. Rössler, *Die Deutschen U-Kreuzer und Transport U-Boote*, 80.
7. *Kriegstagebuch SM U-151 Bd. 1: 21 Juli 1917–26 Dezember 1917* (Cuxhaven-Altenbruch, Germany: Freundeskreis Traditionsarchiv Unterseeboote e.V), 3–4.
8. Ibid., 1715, September 17, 1917.
9. Capt. Maurice Blackwood's report was published in the September 1966 edition of the *Naval Historical Review*. It can be read online at https://www.navyhistory.org.au/q-ship-sinks-U-boat-hms-stonecrop-1917/.
10. E. Keble Chatterton, *Q-Ships and Their Story* (Annapolis, MD: Naval Institute Press, 1972), 243.

11. Ibid., 244.
12. *Kriegstagebuch SM U-151 Bd. 1: 21 Juli 1917–26 Dezember 1917*, time illegible, September 18, 1917.
13. Ibid., 0600, October 12, 1917.
14. Ibid., 0745, October 12, 1917.
15. The actual identity of the British ship remains debated to this day. The predominant theory is that this was the HMS *Begonia*, a minesweeping sloop later converted to a Q-ship, which sunk as a result of the collision. Other sources claim that the ship really was a destroyer, the HMS *Parthian*, which was damaged and fled. The critical review by the chief U-boat inspector on February 12, 1918, lends credence to the former theory, believing that since no surface vessels were present on the horizon (not even smoke visible in the distance) just a half hour after the collision, the "destroyer" must have been sunk.
16. *Kriegstagebuch SM U-151 Bd. 1: 21 Juli 1917–26 Dezember 1917*, 11–12.
17. Ibid., 21–22.

Chapter 7: My Needle . . . Always Settles between West and South-Southwest

1. VAdm. William S. Sims, commander, United States Naval Forces Operating in European Waters, to Capt. William V. Pratt, assistant chief of naval operations, April 29, 1918, https://www.history.navy.mil/research/publications/documentary-histories/wwi/april-1918/vice-admiral-william-76.html, accessed May 19, 2021.
2. VAdm. William S. Sims, commander, United States Naval Forces Operating in European Waters, to secretary of the Navy Josephus Daniels, April 30, 1918, https://www.history.navy.mil/research/publications/documentary-histories/wwi/april-1918/vice-admiral-william-78.html, accessed May 19, 2021.
3. Ibid.
4. Patrick Beesly, *Room 40: British Naval Intelligence, 1914–1918* (Oxford: Oxford University Press, 1984), 38.
5. Sims to Daniels, April 30, 1918.
6. VAdm. William S. Sims, commander, United States Naval Forces Operating in European Waters, to Adm. William S. Benson, chief of naval operations, May 1, 1918, https://www.history.navy.mil/research/publications/documentary-histories/wwi/may-1918/vice-admiral-william.html, accessed February 9, 2021.
7. *Kriegstagebuch SM U-151: 27 Dezember 1917–18 April 1918* (Cuxhaven-Altenbruch, Germany: Freundeskreis Traditionsarchiv Unterseeboote e.V), 9.
8. Thomas, *Raiders of the Deep*, 287.
9. United States Office of Naval Records and Library, *German Submarine Activities*, 23.

10. *Kriegstagebuch SM U-151: 18 April 1918–20 Juli 1918* (Cuxhaven-Altenbruch, Germany: Freundeskreis Traditionsarchiv Unterseeboote e.V), 1200, May 2, 1918.

11. Thomas, *Raiders of the Deep*, 289.

12. *Kriegstagebuch SM U-151: 18 April 1918–20 Juli 1918*, time illegible, May 15, 1918.

13. United States Office of Naval Records and Library, *German Submarine Activities*, 23.

14. Von Nostitz wrote in his war diary that a four-stacked, armored cruiser, with simple pole masts, of the Charleston class was recognized, leading him to dive. This is unlikely, since the Charleston-class protected cruiser (C-2) had a single stack and was lost in 1899. In actuality, he likely spotted USS *Charleston* (C-22), which was actually a St. Louis–class protected cruiser. There were only three ships in this class, and USS *Charleston* is the only one that would have been sailing in the area of Newport News, Virginia, at the time. USS *St. Louis* (C-20) was escorting convoys originating in New York City bound for British and French ports, and USS *Milwaukee* (C-21) was lost attempting to refloat the American submarine *H-2* in 1917. Körner repeats the same mistake when recounting the incident during his postwar interview, but he later describes a cruiser of the St. Louis class in the area, towing a target; it was likely the same ship, the C-22.

15. Office of the chief of naval operations, Memorandum to Forces in American Coastal Waters, May 17, 1918, https://www.history.navy.mil/research/publications/documentary-histories/wwi/may-1918/office-of-the-chief-3.html, accessed May 24, 2021.

16. Thomas, *Raiders of the Deep*, 290.

17. RAdm. Edwin A. Anderson, commander, Squadron One, Patrol Force, Atlantic Fleet, Plan for the Protection of Shipping in the Florida Straits, May 25, 1918, https://www.history.navy.mil/research/publications/documentary-histories/wwi/may-1918/rear-admiral-edwin-a.html, accessed May 24, 2021].

18. Ibid. The systems were the zone, lane, and convoy systems. He defined them as (1) zone—the entire straits would be patrolled, and all sea traffic would be singly directed through the area, (2) lane—establish a shipping lane 10–15 miles wide that all shipping would be directed to, and (3) convoy—all vessels would be collected and then escorted to their destination. He goes on to list the advantages and disadvantages of each, concluding that the "convoy system" in generally the best strategy for daylight operations, and the "zone system" is the most efficient for operating in the darkness, noting that a combination of both would logically be ideal.

19. *Kriegstagebuch SM U-151: 18 April 1918–20 Juli 1918*, 1200, May 24, 1918.

20. Ibid.
21. Ibid., 1923, May 24, 1918.
22. Ibid., 69.
23. Rössler, *Die Deutschen U-Kreuzer und Transport U-Boote*, 105.
24. Ibid., 106.
25. *New York Times*, June 6, 1918, 12.
26. *New York Times*, June 9, 1918, 4.
27. United States Office of Naval Records and Library, *German Submarine Activities*, 26.
28. *Kriegstagebuch SM U-151: 18 April 1918–20 Juli 1918*, 1130, May 25, 1918.
29. Thomas, *Raiders of the Deep*, 296–97.
30. *Kriegstagebuch SM U-151: 18 April 1918–20 Juli 1918*, 1400, May 25, 1918.
31. United States Office of Naval Records and Library, *German Submarine Activities*, 28.
32. Thomas, *Raiders of the Deep*, 298–99.
33. *Kriegstagebuch SM U-151: 18 April 1918–20 Juli 1918*, 2110, May 25, 1918.
34. United States Office of Naval Records and Library, *German Submarine Activities*, 28.
35. Clark, *When the U-boats Came to America*, 38.
36. *Kriegstagebuch SM U-151: 18 April 1918–20 Juli 1918*, 2302, May 25, 1918.
37. Ibid., 0050–1210, May 27, 1918.
38. Thomas, *Raiders of the Deep*, 304.
39. *Kriegstagebuch SM U-151: 18 April 1918–20 Juli 1918*, 1015–2204, May 28, 1918. No further specifics are given about the "southern German cable," but it can be assumed that this was likely the line going from New York to Panama. On May 29, von Nostitz refers to another "northern German cable" being cut, but again goes no further in describing it, and no American sources allude to any more of their lines going "dead."
40. Clark, *When the U-boats Came to America*, 40.
41. *Kriegstagebuch SM U-151: 18 April 1918–20 Juli 1918*, 1200, June 1, 1918.
42. United States Office of Naval Records and Library, *German Submarine Activities*, 31–32.
43. Ibid., 33.
44. Thomas, *Raiders of the Deep*, 311.
45. United States Office of Naval Records and Library, *German Submarine Activities*, 34.
46. Clark, *When the U-boats Came to America*, 47.

47. United States Office of Naval Records and Library, *German Submarine Activities*, 34.
48. *Kriegstagebuch SM U-151: 18 April 1918–20 Juli 1918*, 1620, June 2, 1918.
49. Clark, *When the U-boats Came to America*, 51.
50. *Kriegstagebuch SM U-151: 18 April 1918–20 Juli 1918*, 1845, June 2, 1918.
51. Clark, *When the U-boats Came to America*, 52.
52. *Kriegstagebuch SM U-151: 18 April 1918–20 Juli 1918*, 1920, June 2, 1918.
53. *New York Tribune*, June 5, 1918, 1–2.
54. Ibid., 2.
55. Ibid., 4.
56. *Kriegstagebuch SM U-151: 18 April 1918–20 Juli 1918*, 1530–1935, June 3, 1918.
57. *New York Tribune*, June 5, 1918, 4.
58. Ibid.
59. Rössler, *Die Deutschen U-Kreuzer und Transport U-Boote*, 106.
60. *New York Tribune*, June 4, 1918, 1.
61. Ibid., 5.
62. Ibid., 1.
63. *New York Tribune*, June 6, 1918, 4.
64. *Washington Times*, June 4, 1918, 1.
65. *Washington Times*, June 5, 1918, 1.
66. *Kriegstagebuch SM U-151: 18 April 1918–20 Juli 1918*, time illegible, June 4, 1918.
67. United States Office of Naval Records and Library, *German Submarine Activities*, 43.
68. Ibid., 43.
69. *Kriegstagebuch SM U-151: 18 April 1918–20 Juli 1918*, time illegible, June 4, 1918.
70. Thomas, *Raiders of the Deep*, 316–17.
71. *Kriegstagebuch SM U-151: 18 April 1918–20 Juli 1918*, time illegible, June 5, 1918.
72. Ibid., time illegible, June 5, 1918.
73. *Evening Star* (Washington, DC), June 7, 1918.
74. *New York Tribune*, June 6, 1918, 4.
75. United States Office of Naval Records and Library, *German Submarine Activities*, 44.
76. *Kriegstagebuch SM U-151: 18 April 1918–20 Juli 1918*, noon, June 5, 1918.

77. Thomas, *Raiders of the Deep*, 319.
78. *Kriegstagebuch SM U-151: 18 April 1918–20 Juli 1918*, p.m. hour, time illegible, June 5, 1918.
79. Ibid., June 6, 1918.
80. United States Office of Naval Records and Library, *German Submarine Activities*, 45.
81. *Kriegstagebuch SM U-151: 18 April 1918–20 Juli 1918*, time illegible, June 8, 1918.
82. Clark, *When the U-boats Came to America*, 88.
83. SS *Pinar del Rio*, Wreck Site, https://www.wrecksite.eu/wreck.aspx?22478, accessed July 5, 2021.
84. *Kriegstagebuch SM U-151: 18 April 1918–20 Juli 1918*, time illegible, June 9, 1918.
85. Ibid., time illegible, June 10, 1918. The term von Nostitz uses in his log concerning the patrols is *Bewachern*, which literally translates to guards. He is likely referring to the private craft leased by the Navy for coastal-defense purposes and intraharbor patrols. Capt. Kaltenborn, being so close to Norfolk at the time of the sinking, had probably encountered them at port and received the warning as he left the harbor.
86. Thomas, *Raiders of the Deep*, 324.
87. *Kriegstagebuch SM U-151: 18 April 1918–20 Juli 1918*, time illegible, June 10, 1918.
88. United States Office of Naval Records and Library, *German Submarine Activities*, 46.
89. *Kriegstagebuch SM U-151: 18 April 1918–20 Juli 1918*, 1715–1850, June 13, 1918. Von Nostitz's statement regarding the "bright paint" that was easy to see indicates that German commanders were still confused as to the true purpose of the dazzle camouflage; namely, that it was not intended to conceal the ship but instead to make the ship's range, speed, and course more difficult to discern.
90. Ibid., 0500, June 14, 1918.
91. Thomas, *Raiders of the Deep*, 327.
92. *Kriegstagebuch SM U-151: 18 April 1918–20 Juli 1918*, 0750, June 14, 1918.
93. Ibid., 1615, June 14, 1918.
94. Ibid., 0820–1050, June 18, 1918.
95. USS *Von Steuben* was originally the Norddeutscher Lloyd Liner *Kronprinz Wilhelm*, which, upon the outbreak of World War I, was then commissioned into the Kaiserliche Marine as an auxiliary cruiser—the SMS *Kronprinz*

Wilhelm. Her life as a cruiser was relatively successful, capturing sixteen Allied ships, until widespread sickness among the crew and short supplies of coal forced her to the nearest port, Newport News—becoming interned since April 1915. Following the American declaration of war against Germany, the US Navy seized the ship, repaired her, and once again put her back into service as an auxiliary cruiser / troop carrier.

96. *Kriegstagebuch SM U-151: 18 April 1918–20 Juli 1918*, 1301–1600, June 18, 1918.
97. Ibid., June 22, 1918.
98. Ibid., time illegible, June 23, 1918.
99. Ibid., time illegible, June 25, 1918.
100. Ibid.
101. Ibid., 0600, June 27, 1918.
102. *Evening Telegram*, January 31, 1919, 8.
103. *Kriegstagebuch SM U-151: 18 April 1918–20 Juli 1918*, 95.
104. Ibid., 1840, July 13, 1918.
105. Clark, *When the U-boats Came to America*, 124.
106. VAdm. William S. Sims, commander, United States Naval Forces Operating in European Waters, to the secretary of the British Admiralty, Sir Oswyn A. R. Murray, June 11, 1918, https://www.history.navy.mil/research/publications/documentary-histories/wwi/june-1918/vice-admiral-william-38.html, accessed August 21, 2021.
107. Adm. William S. Benson, chief of naval operations, to VAdm. William S. Sims, commander, United States Naval Forces Operating in European Waters, June 12, 1918, https://www.history.navy.mil/research/publications/documentary-histories/wwi/june-1918/admiral-william-s-be-11.html, accessed August 21, 2021.
108. *Kriegstagebuch SM U-151: 18 April 1918–20 Juli 1918*, von Nostitz's report to U-boat command, 64–65.
109. Clark, *When the U-boats Came to America*, 107.

Chapter 8: A Fisher of Men

1. Jake Klim, *Attack on Orleans: The World War I Submarine Raid on Cape Cod* (Charleston, SC: History Press, 2014), 24.
2. The US Navy publication *German Submarine Activities on the Atlantic Coast of the United States and Canada* erroneously identifies the commander as Kapitänleutnant von Oldenburg. This mistake would be repeated in subsequent American publications, including both *When the U-boats Came to America* and *German Subs in Yankee Waters*.

3. Clark, *When the U-boats Came to America*, 131.
4. Office of the Chief of Naval Operations to Naval District Commandants, June 24, 1918, https://www.history.navy.mil/research/publications/documentary-histories/wwi/june-1918/office-of-the-chief-13.html, accessed August 12, 2021.
5. The blame for the incident would be placed on the captain of USS *Florida* by the Naval Court of Investigation, which found that incorrect navigation on the part of the merchant captain led to the collision instead of any wrongdoing by Navy men ("ex-USS *Schurz*," Monitor National Marine Sanctuary, National Oceanic and Atmospheric Administration, https://monitor.noaa.gov/shipwrecks/schurz.html), accessed August 18, 2021.
6. Clark, *When the U-boats Came to America*, 130.
7. Civilian Identification Numbered Ships Photo Archive, NavSource Naval History Online, http://www.navsource.org/archives/12/172990.htm, accessed August 18, 2021.
8. USS *Lake Bridge* was armed both with 5-inch/51-caliber and 3-inch/50-caliber deck guns. The designation of 5"/51 caliber meant that the gun fired a 5-inch projectile fired from a barrel of a length of 51 calibers (255 in. / 6,500 mm). This would have been the only deck gun capable of reaching *U-156* during the engagement, since the 3-inch gun's range was only up to 7,000 yards.
9. United States Office of Naval Records and Library, *German Submarine Activities*, 51.
10. Ibid., 53.
11. *New York Times*, July 13, 1918, 5.
12. Rössler, *Die Deutschen U-Kreuzer und Transport U-Boote*, 107.
13. USS *San Diego* had originally been named USS *California*, since all cruisers in this class originally were named after states. With the arrival of the Tennessee-class battleships in 1914, the cruisers were renamed after cities located in their previously christened state (USS *Maryland* becoming USS *Frederick* and so on).
14. Alexis Catsambis and Chris Martin, *USS San Diego 2017 Survey: Field Report* (Washington, DC: Naval History and Heritage Command, 2018), 2.
15. Gary Gentile, *USS San Diego: The Last Armored Cruiser* (Philadelphia: Gary Gentile, 1989), 41–42.
16. Catsambis and Martin, *USS San Diego 2017 Survey*, 5.
17. Messimer, *Find and Destroy*, 76.
18. Report telephoned at 8:30 a.m., July 20, Captain Blamer to Duty Officer, in *Special Subject Notebook No. 50: USS San Diego, 2 Volumes* (Beach Haven: New Jersey Maritime Museum), 1.
19. Catsambis and Martin, *USS San Diego 2017 Survey*, 5.

20. United States Office of Naval Records and Library, *German Submarine Activities*, 127.
21. Report telephoned at 8:30 a.m., July 20, in *Special Subject Notebook No. 50: USS San Diego, 2 Volumes*, 2.
22. *New York Tribune*, July 20, 1918, 1.
23. Henry J. James, *German Subs in Yankee Waters* (New York: Gotham House, 1940), 77.
24. Report telephoned at 8:30 a.m., July 20, in *Special Subject Notebook No. 50: USS San Diego, 2 Volumes*, 2.
25. *New York Times*, July 21, 1918, 7.
26. Clark, *When the U-boats Came to America*, 145.
27. Ibid.
28. Alvin B. Feuer, *The US Navy in World War I: Combat at Sea and in the Air* (Westport, CT: Praeger, 1999), 105.
29. Albert Gleaves Report to the Navy Department, July 19, 1918, in *Special Subject Notebook No. 50: USS San Diego, 2 Volumes*.
30. Report Made to the Navy Department, Washington, re Sinking of the USS *San Diego*, by Telephone, July 20, 1918, in *Special Subject Notebook No. 50: USS San Diego, 2 Volumes*.
31. United States Office of Naval Records and Library, *German Submarine Activities*, 137.
32. *New York Times*, July 21, 1918, 7.
33. Ibid.
34. Klim, *Attack on Orleans*, 47.
35. Gibson and Prendergast, *The German Submarine War, 1914–1918*, 219.
36. Ibid., 134.
37. Klim, *Attack on Orleans*, 100.
38. Ibid., 49.
39. James, *German Subs in Yankee Waters*, 81.
40. Klim, *Attack on Orleans*, 56.
41. James, *German Subs in Yankee Waters*, 86.
42. Ibid., 88.
43. Klim, *Attack on Orleans*, 100.
44. Office of Naval Intelligence to VAdm. William S. Sims, commander, United States Naval Forces Operating in European Waters, September 30, 1918, https://www.history.navy.mil/research/publications/documentary-histories/wwi/september-1918/office-of-naval-inte.html, accessed August 21, 2021.
45. Messimer, *Find and Destroy*, 135.

46. James, *German Subs in Yankee Waters*, 82–83.
47. Clark, *When the U-boats Came to America*, 168.
48. United States Office of Naval Records and Library, *German Submarine Activities*, 56.
49. *New York Tribune,* July 26, 1918, 4.
50. "Old News: U-boat Sinks Schooner off Cape Porpoise," *Seacoast Online*, https://www.seacoastonline.com/article/20081218/LIFE/812180356, accessed September 12, 2021.
51. *New York Times*, July 25, 1918, 22.
52. United States Office of Naval Records and Library, *German Submarine Activities*, 11.
53. Ibid.
54. *Kriegstagebuch SM U-140 Bd. 2: 2 Juli 1918–20 September 1918* (Cuxhaven-Altenbruch, Germany: Freundeskreis Traditionsarchiv Unterseeboote e.V), 1200, July 27, 1918.
55. Clark, *When the U-boats Came to America*, 193.
56. United States Office of Naval Records and Library, *German Submarine Activities*, 57.
57. Navy Department to commandants, Naval Districts One through Eight (Radiogram), August 2, 1918, https://www.history.navy.mil/research/publications/documentary-histories/wwi/august-1918/navy-department-to-c.html, accessed September 19, 2021.
58. United States Office of Naval Records and Library, *German Submarine Activities*, 58.
59. Ibid., 138.
60. *New York Tribune*, August 6, 1918, 1.
61. United States Office of Naval Records and Library, *German Submarine Activities*, 59.
62. Ibid., 61.
63. Cablegram from Adm. William S. Benson, chief of naval operations, to VAdm. William S. Sims, commander, United States Naval Forces Operating in European Waters, August 7, 1918, https://www.history.navy.mil/research/publications/documentary-histories/wwi/august-1918/admiral-william-s-be-1.html, accessed September 19, 2021.
64. Radiogram from the Office of the Chief of Naval Operations to Adm. Henry T. Mayo, commander in chief, United States Atlantic Fleet, and naval district commanders, August 8, 1918, https://www.history.navy.mil/research/publications/documentary-histories/wwi/august-1918/office-of-the-chief-15.html, accessed September 19, 2021.

65. James, *German Subs in Yankee Waters*, 101.
66. *New York Times*, August 18, 1918, 1.
67. United States Office of Naval Records and Library, *German Submarine Activities*, 64.
68. James, *German Subs in Yankee Waters*, 102.
69. United States Office of Naval Records and Library, *German Submarine Activities*, 65.
70. Ibid., 66.
71. Bisher, *The Intelligence War in Latin America, 1914–1922*, 216.
72. Clark, *When the U-boats Came to America*, 234.
73. United States Office of Naval Records and Library, *German Submarine Activities*, 66.
74. Clark, *When the U-boats Came to America*, 259.
75. United States Office of Naval Records and Library, *German Submarine Activities*, 68.
76. Ibid., 69.
77. "QF" meaning quick firing, 12-pounder meaning the rounded weight of the 3-inch projectile, and 12 cwt meaning 12-hundred weight, which was the weight of the barrel and breech. This gun had been in service on naval vessels from as early as 1894 and as late as 1945.
78. Keith Calow, "Rough Justice: The Court Martial of Lieutenant Robert Douglas Legate," *Northern Mariner / Le marin du nord* 15, no. 4 (October 2005): 9.
79. Ibid., 11.
80. United States Office of Naval Records and Library, *The Northern Barrage and Other Mining Activities*, Publication 2 (Washington, DC: US Government Printing Office, 1920), 12.
81. Ibid., 123–24.
82. Bradley Sheard, *Lost Voyages: Two Centuries of Shipwrecks in the Approaches to New York* (New York: Aqua Quest, 1998), 122.
83. Ibid., 124–25.
84. United States Office of Naval Records and Library, *The Northern Barrage and Other Mining Activities*, 125.

Chapter 9: A Tale of Two Cruisers

1. It seems like a cliché having a parrot on board a ship that both is named Polly and can speak, but this, whether it is true or not, was reported by the *New York Times* on August 15, 1918. Allegedly, after the *Frederic R. Kellogg* had been struck by a torpedo and her crew was hurriedly evacuating the ship,

the tanker's cook abandoned his pet parrot, Polly, "who spoke good English and called out 'Don't forget poor Polly' when he left the bird hanging in the cage outside the galley." *New York Times*, August 15, 1918, 11.

2. Most of the U-139-class U-cruisers (even the ones that weren't finished by the war's end) were commissioned using the names of famous U-boat aces instead of identification numbers. *U-139* was commissioned as "*Kapitänleutnant Schwieger*" (Walther Schwieger), *U-140* as "*Kapitänleutnant Weddigen*" (Otto Weddigen), *U-145* as "*Kapitänleutnant Wegener*" (Bernhard Wegener), *U-146* as "*Oberleutnant zur See Saltzwedel*" (Reinhold Saltzwedel), *U-147* as "*Kapitänleutnant Hansen*" (Klaus Hansen), *U-148* as "*Oberleutnant zur See Pustkuchen*" (Herbert Pustkuchen), *U-149* as "*Kapitänleutnant Freiherr von Berkheim*" (Egenolf von Berkheim), and *U-150* as "*Kapitänleutnant Schneider*" (Rudolf Schneider). For brevity's sake, the numeric identifier will be utilized throughout the chapter.

3. *Kriegstagebuch SM U-140 Bd. 1: 28 Marz 1918–1 Juli 1918* (Cuxhaven-Altenbruch, Germany: Freundeskreis Traditionsarchiv Unterseeboote e.V), April 26, 1918, 0020. The modifications mentioned by Kophamel included some simple changes, such as removing the net saw from the bow and re-locating torpedoes and ammunition, to more-extreme design changes. The latter included adding a 15-ton wooden belt to improve stability, and removing armor plating from the conning tower and periscope.

4. Ibid., May 17, 1918.

5. Ibid., May 25–June 29, 1918.

6. *Kriegstagebuch SM U-140 Bd. 2: 2 Juli 1918–20 September 1918*, July 8, 1918, 0500.

7. *Kriegstagebuch SM U-140 Bd. 1*, "Stellungnahme des Verbandskommandos," July 1, 1918.

8. Adolf Beckmann, *U-Boote vor New York: Die Kriegsfahrt eines deutschen Unterseebootes nach Amerika* (Stuttgart: Franckh'sche Verlagshandlung, 1931), 7.

9. *Kriegstagebuch SM U-117 Bd. 1: 11 Juli 1918–22 September 1918* (Cuxhaven-Altenbruch, Germany: Freundeskreis Traditionsarchiv Unterseeboote e.V), August 3, 1918.

10. Ibid., July 23, 1918, 1200.

11. *Kriegstagebuch SM U-140 SM U-140 Bd. 1*, "Stellungnahme des Verbandskommandos," July 1, 1918.

12. *Kriegstagebuch SM U-140 Bd. 2*, July 11, 1918, 1200. In actuality this was likely HMS *Duke of Edinburgh*, of the eponymous cruiser class. All vessels in the Bacchante class had already been sunk or were on patrols far from this location in late 1918.

13. Ibid., July 15, 1918, 0730.
14. Ibid., July 19, 1918, time not recorded.
15. *Kriegstagebuch SM U-117 Bd. 1*, July 26, 1918, 0330.
16. This quantity of shells was the figure noted in SM *U-140*'s *Artillerie-Munitionsnachweisung*. The officers aboard the *British Major* tallied 203 shots.
17. *Kriegstagebuch SM U-140 Bd. 2*, July 26, 1918, 2030.
18. United States Office of Naval Records and Library, *German Submarine Activities*, 71.
19. Clark, *When the U-boats Came to America*, 177.
20. The *Osterley* indicated that she was being chased by a U-boat, but no German submarines were operating in the area at the time. Her signal was uncannily similar to the ones sent by the *Florence Olson* (off Barnegat Light, New Jersey) and USS *Colhoun* (in Delaware Bay) when they both believed they were being attacked by *U-156* on July 27.
21. *Kriegstagebuch SM U-140 Bd. 2*, July 29, 1918, 1600.
22. Ibid., July 30, 1918, 1050.
23. United States Office of Naval Records and Library, *German Submarine Activities*, 72.
24. *Kriegstagebuch SM U-117 Bd. 1*, August 1, 1918, 0100.
25. All the other three-stacked Paulding-class destroyers were sent over to Queensland, Ireland, for escort and antisubmarine duties off the British and French coasts. Concerning the flush-decked destroyers, USS *Conner* was only one of two three-stacked Caldwell variants actually commissioned by August 1918, and the only one still in service. The second destroyer, USS *Stockton* (DD-73), had been in Liverpool for repairs after colliding with British cargo ship *Slieve Bloom* on March 30, 1918.
26. *Kriegstagebuch SM U-117 Bd. 1*, August 2, 1918, 1500–1530.
27. Aluminum oxide is the cargo noted by Kophamel in his log. Other sources claim that the cargo was chalk.
28. *Kriegstagebuch SM U-140 Bd. 2*, August 2, 1918, 1600.
29. Ibid.
30. Ibid., August 4, 1918, 1018.
31. United States Office of Naval Records and Library, *German Submarine Activities*, 73.
32. Ibid., 74.
33. Clark, *When the U-boats Came to America*, 180–81.
34. *Kriegstagebuch SM U-140 Bd. 2*, August 4, 1918, 1200.
35. Clark, *When the U-boats Came to America*, 181.

36. Todd Woofenden, "The Newsletter of the Subchaser Archives," *Subchaser Archives* 12, no. 10 (October 2016), https://www.subchaser.org/SAN-Vol-12-No-10.
37. United States Office of Naval Records and Library, *American Ship Casualties of the World War Including Naval Vessels, Merchant Ships, Sailing Vessels, and Fishing Craft* (Washington, DC: US Government Printing Office, 1923), 6.
38. *Kriegstagebuch SM U-140 Bd. 2*, August 6, 1918, 1320–1820.
39. *New York Tribune*, August 10, 1918, 1.
40. Clark, *When the U-boats Came to America*, 185.
41. *New York Tribune*, August 13, 1918, 1.
42. Ibid.
43. David A. Norris, "The War at Home," *Our State: Down Home in North Carolina* 75, no. 1 (June 2007): 28.
44. *Kriegstagebuch SM U-140 Bd. 2*, August 7, 1918, 0855–1200.
45. *Hearing before a Subcommittee on Naval Affairs, United States Senate, Sixty-Sixth Congress, Second Session on Senate Resolution 285, "Awarding of Medals in the Naval Service"* (Washington, DC: US Government Printing Office, 1920), 68.
46. *Kriegstagebuch SM U-140 Bd. 2*, August 10, 1918, hour not noted.
47. Following the sinking of the *O. B. Jennings* on August 4, *U-140* was found to be leaking fuel as badly as *U-117* and shared the same accompanying oil trail in her travels.
48. American navy records indicate that fifteen depth charges were actually dropped.
49. *Kriegstagebuch SM U-140 Bd. 2*, August 10, 1918.
50. Clark, *When the U-boats Came to America*, 189.
51. *Kriegstagebuch SM U-140 Bd. 2*, August 10, 1918, 1200.
52. Ibid., 1400.
53. Deck Log, USS *Stringham* / DD-83: July 2, 1918–June 2, 1922 (National Archives, Washington, DC), August 10, 1918, 1000–1200.
54. *Kriegstagebuch SM U-140 Bd. 2*, August 11, 1918, 0200.

Chapter 10: An Unending Trail of Destruction, and Oil . . .

1. VAdm. William S. Sims, commander, United States Naval Forces Operating in European Waters, to the office of the chief of naval operations, August 7, 1918, https://www.history.navy.mil/research/publications/documentary-histories/wwi/august-1918/vice-admiral-william-104.html, accessed September 19, 2021.

2. Clark, *When the U-boats Came to America*, 207.
3. Beckmann, *U-Boote vor New York*, 27.
4. Ibid.
5. United States Office of Naval Records and Library, *German Submarine Activities*, 83.
6. *New York Tribune*, August 14, 1918, 12.
7. United States Office of Naval Records and Library, *German Submarine Activities*, 87.
8. "Plan for Defense against a Submarine Attack in Home Waters," submitted to CNO Benson, February 6, 1918, in United States Office of Naval Records and Library, *German Submarine Activities*, 143–51. This plan was later amended to clarify that mines may be legitimately used for defensive purposes in the harbors of New York, the capes of the Chesapeake, and the entrance to the Long Island Sound as long as ample space was left for the transit of shipping. These planned minefields, however, never materialized.
9. *New York Tribune*, August 8, 1918, 1.
10. *New York Tribune*, August 14, 1918, 12.
11. Beckmann, *U-Boote vor New York*, 28.
12. United States Office of Naval Records and Library, *German Submarine Activities*, 90.
13. Ibid., 91.
14. Joseph Bilby and Harry Ziegler, *A History of Submarine Warfare along the Jersey Shore* (Charleston, SC: History Press, 2016), 31.
15. *Kriegstagebuch SM U-117 Bd. 1*, August 12, 1918.
16. *New York Times*, August 14, 1918, 4.
17. Beckmann, *U-Boote vor New York*, 33.
18. *New York Tribune*, August 15, 1918, 3.
19. *Kriegstagebuch SM U-140 Bd. 2*, August 15, 1918, 1200.
20. *Kriegstagebuch SM U-117 Bd. 1*, August 13, 1918.
21. The first three crew members killed in the engine room were Samuel L. Johnson (second assistant engineer), Alex A. Jorgensen (fireman), and John M. Carlsen (oiler). The four who died in their quarters were Chester C. Cubberley (USNRF, quartermaster 3rd class), William T. Stillman (USNRF, quartermaster 3rd class), James Kramer (third assistant engineer), and Francisco de Souza (mess boy).
22. United States Office of Naval Records and Library, *German Submarine Activities*, 92–93.
23. *Kriegstagebuch SM U-117 Bd. 1, Minenskizze*.
24. *Asbury Park Press*, August 14, 1918, 1.

25. *Asbury Park Press*, November 18, 1918, 1.
26. Edwin C. Bearss, *Historic Resource Study: Fort Hancock, 1895–1948; Gateway National Recreation Area, New York / New Jersey* (Denver, CO: US Department of the Interior, National Park Service Historic Preservation Division, Denver Service Center, 1981), 383–84.
27. Ibid., 384.
28. The Wilhelm being referred to is Wilhelm Vogel (perhaps a pseudonym), a stoker aboard *U-117* who acted as Beckmann's assistant. Being the youngest man aboard the U-boat, Beckmann repeatedly makes reference to him for comic relief or when something of questionable moral standing is introduced.
29. Literally translating to "hammer uncocked." It is a German term used to signify the end of a hunt.
30. Beckmann, *U-Boote vor New York*, 37.
31. United States Office of Naval Records and Library, *German Submarine Activities*, 79.
32. *Kriegstagebuch SM U-140 Bd. 2*, August 13, 1918.
33. Ibid., August 17, 1918, 1200.
34. *Kriegstagebuch SM U-117 Bd. 1*, August 14, 1918.
35. United States Office of Naval Records and Library, *German Submarine Activities*, 93.
36. *Kriegstagebuch SM U-117 Bd. 1*, August 14, 1918.
37. United States Office of Naval Records and Library, *German Submarine Activities*, 94.
38. Deck Log, *SC-144*: April 1, 1918–March 31, 1919 (National Archives, Washington, DC), August 14, 1918.
39. *Kriegstagebuch SM U-117 Bd. 1*, August 14, 1918.
40. Deck Log, *SC-73*: March 20, 1918–December 31, 1918, Log 1 (National Archives, Washington, DC), August 14, 1918, 1419.
41. *Kriegstagebuch SM U-117 Bd. 1*, August 14, 1918, 1312.
42. Ibid., August 11, 1918.
43. Adm. William S. Benson, CNO to various officers in the United States' Waters, August 16, 1918, https://www.history.navy.mil/research/publications/documentary-histories/wwi/august-1918/admiral-william-s-be-7.html, accessed September 19, 2021.
44. Ibid.
45. Beckmann, *U-Boote vor New York*, 34–35.
46. *Kriegstagebuch SM U-117 Bd. 1*, August 16, 1918, 1330–1730.

47. Some sources claim that ten sailors died in the sinking; however, the website Wreck Site, using the Commonwealth War Graves Commission as a source, confirms only nine. This is later reinforced by interviews with the Coast Guard crew who rescued the stricken sailors. Given that this is the only source that goes as far as naming the victims of the sinking, this book will use nine dead as the final figure.
48. Taped interviews, Leroy Midgett with historians Fred Roush and William Harris, March 26, 1959, and March 21 and April 15, 1963, as quoted in the article "Story of the Mirlo Rescue," US Life-Saving Station Chicamacomico Historic Site, https://chicamacomico.org/mirlo-rescue/, accessed December 22, 2021.
49. *Kriegstagebuch SM U-117 Bd. 1*, August 16, 1918, 1930.
50. Ibid., August 17, 1918, 0700.
51. Beckmann, *U-Boote vor New York*, 39–40.
52. *Kriegstagebuch SM U-117 Bd. 1*, August 17, 1918.
53. Deck Log, USS *Helvetia* / SP-3096: July 18, 1918–March 1, 1919 (National Archives, Washington, DC), August 17, 1918, 1255.
54. *Kriegstagebuch SM U-117 Bd. 1*, August 20, 1918.
55. *New York Tribune*, August 23, 1918, 3.
56. According to period photographs, "Algeria–Sverige" was written in a bold font just below the deck in the center of the vessel, clearly indicating her as a neutral vessel in the event her flag could not be observed.
57. United States Office of Naval Records and Library, *German Submarine Activities*, 97.
58. Ibid.
59. *New York Tribune*, August 24, 1918, 4.
60. Ibid.
61. Clark, *When the U-boats Came to America*, 230.
62. *Kriegstagebuch SM U-140 Bd. 2*, August 21, 1918, 0850.
63. Ibid., August 21, 1918, 1057.
64. *St. John's Daily Star*, September 12, 1918, 1.
65. *Kriegstagebuch SM U-140 Bd. 2*, August 24, 1918, 0240–0343.
66. Ibid., August 27, 1918, 1200.
67. Ibid., August 28, 1918, 0000.
68. Beckmann, *U-Boote vor New York*, 40–41.
69. *Kriegstagebuch SM U-117 Bd. 1*, August 25, 1918.
70. United States Office of Naval Records and Library, *German Submarine Activities*, 97.

71. *Kriegstagebuch SM U-117 Bd. 1*, August 30, 1918.
72. "The Sinking of Elsie Porter," *South Shore Breaker*, November 10, 2021.
73. *St. John's Daily Star*, September 3, 1918, 4.
74. Beckmann, *U-Boote vor New York*, 41.
75. *Kriegstagebuch SM U-117 Bd. 1*, September 2, 1918.
76. Ibid., September 5, 1918, 1000.
77. Beckmann, *U-Boote vor New York*, 47.
78. A French term meaning "run for your lives" or "every man for himself."
79. Beckmann, *U-Boote vor New York*, 48.
80. *Kriegstagebuch SM U-117 Bd. 1*, September 6, 1918.
81. *Kriegstagebuch SM U-140 Bd. 2*, September 17, 1918, 1200.
82. United States Office of Naval Records and Library, *The Northern Barrage and Other Mining Activities*, 106.
83. *Kriegstagebuch SM U-140 Bd. 2*, September 20, 1918, 1200.
84. United States Office of Naval Records and Library, *German Submarine Activities*, 130.
85. *U-117* traveled 9,136 nm on the surface and 90 nm submerged, and *U-140* traveled 10,708 nm on the surface and 97 nm submerged.
86. "Stellungnahme des U-Kreuzerverbands zum Kriegstagebuch 'U 140–Kapitänleutnant Weddigen' Kommandant Korvettenkapitän Kophamel für die Zeit vom 2. Juli bis 20, September 1918," in *Kriegstagebuch SM U-140 Bd. 2*.
87. Ibid.
88. "Stellungnahme des B.d.U zum Kriegstagebuch U 117–Kommandant Kapitänleutnant Dröscher–für die Zeit vom 11. Juli bis 22, September 1918," in *Kriegstagebuch SM U-117 Bd. 1*.
89. Clark, *When the U-boats Came to America*, 258.
90. Lt. Cmdr. Guy E. Davis, commander, Submarine Division Seven, to the office of the chief of naval operations, September 11, 1918, https://www.history.navy.mil/research/publications/documentary-histories/wwi/september-1918/lieutenant-commander.html, accessed February 12, 2022.
91. "N-5," in *Dictionary of American Naval Fighting Ships*, https://www.history.navy.mil/content/history/nhhc/research/histories/ship-histories/danfs/n/n-5.html, accessed February 12, 2022.

Chapter 11: The Final Voyage of the *U-Deutschland*

1. *Kriegstagebuch SM U-155 Bd. 3: 11 August 1918–14 November 1918* (Cuxhaven-Altenbruch, Germany: Freundeskreis Traditionsarchiv Unterseeboote e.V), 6.

2. Ibid.
3. It should be remembered that the old guns from SMS *Zähringen* consistently broke their mounts and had to be shimmed, with Meusel concluding that they were essentially worthless. Despite also firing 15 cm shells, the newly installed L/45 C/16 guns were considerably lighter, had better mounts, and had a lower muzzle velocity, allowing for easier firing and less wear.
4. Rössler, *Die Deutschen U-Kreuzer und Transport U-Boote*, 80.
5. Messimer, *The Merchant U-boat*, 187.
6. *Kriegstagebuch SM U-155 Bd. 3*, August 11, 1918, 0030.
7. Rössler, *Die Deutschen U-Kreuzer und Transport U-Boote*, 108.
8. United States Office of Naval Records and Library, *German Submarine Activities*, 101.
9. Michael L. Hadley and Roger Sarty, *Tin-Pots and Pirate Ships: Canadian Naval Forces and German Sea Raiders, 1880–1918* (Montreal: McGill-Queen's University Press, 1991), 284. The authors credit a Dr. Günther Reibhorn for "deciphering" essential parts of *U-155*'s *Kriegstagebuch*, which is, just as they described, very poorly handwritten and often completely illegible. In instances where I have been unable to transcribe the log myself, I have directly cited the transcriptions as published in Hadley and Sarty's book. In all other cases, citations will refer to my translations of the actual log.
10. Ronald Jack, "McAvity's Munition Girls–St. John in 1918," The Lost Valley—an Internet History of St. John, N.B., http://thelostvalley.blogspot.com/2014/08/mcavitys-munitions-girls-saint-john-in.html, accessed February 22, 2022.
11. USS *Mount Vernon* would actually be torpedoed, although not sunk, by *U-82* on her return leg back to the United States on September 5, 1918. This was confirmed in a cable: Vice Admiral William S. Sims, commander, United States Naval Forces Operating in European Waters, to Secretary of the Navy Josephus Daniels, September 19, 1918, Naval History and Heritage Command, https://www.history.navy.mil/research/publications/documentary-histories/wwi/september-1918/vice-admiral-william-74.html, accessed February 14, 2022.
12. *Kriegstagebuch SM U-155 Bd. 3*, September 2, 1918, 1710. Although Studt's log notes the use of *Granaten* to sink the steamer, the literal translation to "grenades" should not imply that *Sprengpatronen* were used. It instead referred to the high-explosive shells fired from the 15 cm guns.
13. Ibid., September 7, 1918, 1900.
14. *New York Tribune*, September 17, 1918, 3.
15. United States Office of Naval Records and Library, *German Submarine Activities*, 102.

16. One of the four lifeboats, being commanded by the third officer with ten crew on board, would never be rescued. According to the *New York Tribune* on September 24, "A battered lifeboat and the body of a negro sailor floated ashore" on the twenty-third (eleven days after the sinking) and was believed to be the missing launch from the *Leixões*.
17. United States Office of Naval Records and Library, *German Submarine Activities*, 102.
18. *Kriegstagebuch SM U-155 Bd. 3*, September 13, 1918, 1020.
19. United States Office of Naval Records and Library, *German Submarine Activities*, 103.
20. Hadley and Sarty, *Tin-Pots and Pirate Ships*, 286.
21. Intelligence section, staff of VAdm. William S. Sims, commander, United States Naval Forces Operating in European Waters, Information Bulletin Number 219, https://www.history.navy.mil/research/publications/documentary-histories/wwi/september-1918/intelligence-section-0.html, accessed September 20, 2021.
22. *Kriegstagebuch SM U-155 Bd. 3*, September 17, 1918, 0900.
23. Ibid., September 18, 1918, 0100–0255.
24. Hadley and Sarty, *Tin-Pots and Pirate Ships*, 287.
25. *Kriegstagebuch SM U-155 Bd. 3*, September 19, 1918, 0049.
26. FV *Kingfisher*, Wreck Site, https://www.wrecksite.eu/wreck.aspx?154909, accessed February 22, 2022.
27. Clark, *When the U-boats Came to America*, 269.
28. Office of the Chief of Naval Operations to commandants of Third, Fourth, Fifth Naval Districts, and Lt. Cmdr. Warren C. Nixon, commander in chief, USS *Patterson*, September 29, 1918, https://www.history.navy.mil/research/publications/documentary-histories/wwi/september-1918/office-of-the-chief-14.html, accessed February 22, 2022.
29. RAdm. Sir W. Reginald Hall, R.N., Naval Intelligence Division, British Admiralty, to VAdm. William S. Sims, commander, United States Naval Forces Operating in European Waters, September 25, 1918, https://www.history.navy.mil/research/publications/documentary-histories/wwi/september-1918/rear-admiral-sir-w-r.html, accessed February 22, 2022.
30. James, *German Subs in Yankee Waters*, 158.
31. *Kriegstagebuch SM U-155 Bd. 3*, October 3, 1918, 0700.
32. United States Office of Naval Records and Library, *German Submarine Activities*, 104.
33. Clark, *When the U-boats Came to America*, 273.
34. *Kriegstagebuch SM U-155 Bd. 3*, October 17, 1918, 1740.

35. United States Office of Naval Records and Library, *German Submarine Activities*, 105.
36. Ibid.
37. Ibid.
38. Rössler, *Die Deutschen U-Kreuzer und Transport U-Boote*, 109.
39. Hadley and Sarty, *Tin-Pots and Pirate Ships*, 285.

Chapter 12: The Howling Wolves Fell Silent
1. Often shortened to "K.u.K," this term referred to the imperial and royal nature of the Dual Monarchy of Austria-Hungary, wherein the emperor of Austria was also referred to as the king of Hungary.
2. Georg von Trapp, *To The Last Salute* (Lincoln: University of Nebraska Press, 2007), 32.
3. Ibid.
4. Ibid., 177.
5. Rössler, *Die Deutschen U-Kreuzer und Transport U-Boote*, 109.
6. *O-Befehl für "U-151" und "U-153,"* October 1, 1918 (Cuxhaven-Altenbruch, Germany: Freundeskreis Traditionsarchiv Unterseeboote e.V).
7. Ibid.
8. Ibid.
9. Rössler, *Die Deutschen U-Kreuzer und Transport U-Boote*, 125.
10. Ibid., 126.
11. Thomas, *Raiders of the Deep*, 336.
12. The damage incurred on the *Perth* consisted of the "port fore bridge deck awning" being destroyed and a shell hole on the port side forward. The two casualties were RNR sublieutenant Frederick Stevenson (died instantly at 1320) and RNR assistant paymaster Charles Maile (succumbed to his injuries at 1740). Royal Navy Log Book: HMS *Perth*—October 1915 to November 1918, October 1, 1918, 1320, https://naval-history.net/OWShips-WW1-09-HMS_Perth.htm, accessed December 6, 2021.
13. Thomas, *Raiders of the Deep*, 337–38.
14. Royal Navy Log Book: HMS *Perth*, October 1, 1918, 1600.
15. Rössler, *Die Deutschen U-Kreuzer und Transport U-Boote*, 127.
16. Thomas, *Raiders of the Deep*, 341.
17. VAdm. William S. Sims, commander, United States Naval Forces Operating in European Waters, to Adm. William S. Benson, chief of naval operations, September 10, 1918, https://www.history.navy.mil/research/publications/documentary-histories/wwi/september-1918/vice-admiral-william-17.html, accessed February 22, 2022.

18. Rössler, *Die Deutschen U-Kreuzer und Transport U-Boote*, 128.
19. Thomas, *Raiders of the Deep*, 340.
20. Rössler, *Die Deutschen U-Kreuzer und Transport U-Boote*, 129.
21. Radio message from Rügen to all U-boats, September 9, 1918, 0900.
22. VAdm. William S. Sims, commander, United States Naval Forces Operating in European Waters, to Secretary of the Navy Josephus Daniels, September 27, 1918, https://www.history.navy.mil/research/publications/documentary-histories/wwi/september-1918/vice-admiral-william-42.html, accessed February 14, 2022.
23. *Kriegstagebuch SM U-152 Bd. 2: 9 September 1918–15 November 1918* (Cuxhaven-Altenbruch, Germany: Freundeskreis Traditionsarchiv Unterseeboote e.V), September 11, 1918, 1330.
24. Ibid., September 11, 1918, 1650.
25. Ibid., September 14, 1918, 1615.
26. Ibid., September 15, 1918, 0800.
27. Ibid., September 18, 1918, 1615.
28. Adolf Franz, *Zum zehnjährigen Gedenktag des Artillerie-Kampfes der deutschen Untersee-Kreuzers U 152 mit dem Amerikanischen Hilfskreuzer und Truppentransport-Dampfers Ticonderoga an atlantisches Ozean am 30 September 1918* (Cuxhaven-Altenbruch, Germany: Freundeskreis Traditionsarchiv Unterseeboote e.V, 1928), 6.
29. Ibid., 7–8.
30. Clark, *When the U-boats Came to America*, 277.
31. Feuer, *The US Navy in World War I*, 75.
32. Franz, *Zum zehnjährigen Gedenktag des Artillerie-Kampfes der deutschen Untersee-Kreuzers U 152*, 8.
33. Ibid., 9.
34. Ibid., 9–10.
35. United States Office of Naval Records and Library, *German Submarine Activities*, 106.
36. Ibid. 107.
37. Clark, *When the U-boats Came to America*, 280.
38. Franz, *Zum zehnjährigen Gedenktag des Artillerie-Kampfes der deutschen Untersee-Kreuzers U 152*, 12–13.
39. Ibid., 15–16.
40. Ibid., 16.
41. United States Office of Naval Records and Library, *German Submarine Activities*, 111.

42. Specifically, 213 lives were lost, consisting of 10 naval officers, 102 sailors, 2 Army officers, and 99 soldiers. Muller and Fulcher would survive the war after being taken back to Kiel upon the Armistice.
43. Clark, *When the U-boats Came to America*, 290.
44. United States Office of Naval Records and Library, *German Submarine Activities*, 117.
45. *Kriegstagebuch SM U-152 Bd. 2*, October 15, 1918, 1745.
46. Franz, *Zum zehnjährigen Gedenktag des Artillerie-Kampfes der deutschen Untersee-Kreuzers U 152*, 24.
47. Ibid.
48. Ibid., 25.
49. Mark Karau, *The Naval Flank of the Western Front: The German Marinekorps Flandern, 1914–1918* (Barnsley, UK: Seaforth, 2003), 222.
50. United States Office of Naval Records and Library, *German Submarine Activities*, 113.
51. Franz, *Zum zehnjährigen Gedenktag des Artillerie-Kampfes der deutschen Untersee-Kreuzers U 152*, 27.

Chapter 13: The End of the Beginning

1. Sims, *The Victory at Sea*, IX
2. Richard Guilliatt and Peter Hohnen, *The Wolf: The Mystery Raider That Terrorized the Seas during World War I* (New York: Free Press, 2010), 294.
3. Ibid.
4. Sims, *The Victory at Sea*, 283.
5. Ibid., 319.
6. Clark, *When the U-boats Came to America*, 310.
7. VAdm. William S. Sims, commander, United States Naval Forces Operating in European Waters, to Capt. William V. Pratt, assistant chief of naval operations, August 13, 1918, https://www.history.navy.mil/research/publications/documentary-histories/wwi/august-1918/vice-admiral-william-25.html, accessed November 12, 2020.
8. Both Adm. Sims and Secretary Daniels traded barbs at each other throughout the hearing. Rather cuttingly, Daniels accused Sims of being an Anglophile with little understanding of the greater naval war from his office in London.
9. *Kriegstagebuch SM U-151:18 April 1918–20 Juli 1918*, von Nostitz's report to U-boat command, 64–65.
10. Sims, *The Victory at Sea*, 316.
11. Hadley and Sarty, *Tin-Pots and Pirate Ships*, 289.

12. Ibid., 288.
13. Adm. Henry T. Mayo, commander in chief, Atlantic Fleet, to Secretary of the Navy Josephus Daniels, "An Estimate of the Naval Situation in the Atlantic Ocean," August 10, 1918, https://www.history.navy.mil/research/publications/documentary-histories/wwi/august-1918/admiral-henry-t-mayo.html, accessed September 20, 2021.
14. James, *German Subs in Yankee Waters*, 187.
15. Thomas, *Raiders of the Deep*, 333.
16. Michael Gannon, *Operation Drumbeat: The Dramatic True Story of Germany's First U-boat Attacks along the American Coast in World War II* (New York: HarperCollins, 1990), 182.
17. Concerning the other U-cruisers surrendered to the Allies: Britain would receive *U-155* and *U-152*, which were likewise used on publicity tours. While *U-152* was eventually scuttled, *U-155* was first sold as a tourist attraction and then for scrap. France got *U-139* and *U-151*, with the former entering service in the Marine Nationale as the *Halbronn* (serving until 1935) and the latter being evaluated and then destroyed by artillery.
18. Bilby and Ziegler, *A History of Submarine Warfare along the Jersey Shore*, 90.

Appendix A

1. This would equate to the US Navy's rank of fleet admiral, or five-star admiral; however, this was never a rank during the First World War. It had been created for Adm. Dewey in 1903, following the Spanish-American War, and disappeared upon his death. It wouldn't be reinstated until 1944.
2. The rank of commodore was disestablished in 1899. It would be reestablished during World War II and is currently an honorary title.

Appendix C

1. Heinzelmanns were essentially sprites or elves from North German mythology.
2. He is referring to von Nostitz and *U-151* but is muddling the specifics of what actually transpired.
3. Franz couldn't remember the names of the officers. In this case, he is referring to the first assistant engineer, Lt. J. Fulcher. Lt. F. Muller was the less wounded executive officer.

BIBLIOGRAPHY

Books

Baer, George W. *One Hundred Years of Sea Power: The US Navy, 1890–1990.* Stanford, CA: Stanford University Press, 1996.

Bauer, Hermann. *Das Unterseeboot. Seine Bedeutung als Teil einer Flotte. Seine Stellung im Völkerrecht. Seine Kriegsverwendung. Seine Zukunft.* Berlin: Verlag von E. S. Mittler & Sohn, 1931.

Bearss, Edwin C. *Historic Resource Study: Fort Hancock, 1895–1948; Gateway National Recreation Area, New York / New Jersey.* Denver, CO: US Department of the Interior, National Park Service Historic Preservation Division, Denver Service Center, 1981.

Beckmann, Adolf. *U-Boote vor New York: Die Kriegsfahrt eines deutschen Unterseebootes nach Amerika.* Stuttgart: Franckh'sche Verlagshandlung, 1931.

Beesly, Patrick. *Room 40: British Naval Intelligence, 1914–1918.* Oxford: Oxford University Press, 1984.

Bidwell, R. L. *Currency Conversion Tables: A Hundred Years of Change.* London: Rex Collings, 1970.

Bilby, Joseph, and Harry Ziegler. *A History of Submarine Warfare along the Jersey Shore.* Charleston, SC: History Press, 2016.

Bisher, Jamie. *The Intelligence War in Latin America, 1914–1922.* Jefferson, NC: McFarland, 2016.

Botting, Douglas. *The Seafarers: The U-boats.* Alexandria, VA: Time-Life Books, 1979.

Boyse, Burke, and George Zimmer. *K-7: Spies at War.* New York: D. Appleton Century, 1934.

Carpenter, Alfred. *The Blocking of Zeebrugge.* London: Herbert Jenkins, 1922.

Catsambis, Alexis, and Chris Martin. *USS San Diego 2017 Survey: Field Report.* Washington, DC: Naval History and Heritage Command, 2018.

Chatterton, E. Keble. *Q-Ships and Their Story.* Annapolis, MD: Naval Institute Press, 1972.

Clark, William Bell. *When the U-boats Came to America.* Boston: Little, Brown, 1929.

Clephane, Lewis. *History of the Naval Overseas Transport Service in World War I.* Washington, DC: US Government Printing Office, 1969.

Coletta, Paolo E. *Admiral Bradley A. Fiske and the American Navy.* Lawrence: University Press of Kansas, 1979.

Colledge, J. J., and Ben Warlow. *Ships of the Royal Navy: The Complete Record of All Fighting Ships from the 15th Century to the Present.* London: Chatham, 2006.

Connolly, James. *The U-boat Hunters.* New York: Charles Scribner's Sons, 1918.

Cronon, David, ed. *The Cabinet Diaries of Josephus Daniels, 1913–1921*. Lincoln: University of Nebraska Press, 1963.

Dickey, John L. *A Family Saga: Flush-Deck Destroyers, 1917–1955*. Boothbay, ME: Prints Charming, 2000.

Ericson, Peter. *The Kaiser Strikes America: The U-boat Campaign off America's Coast in WWI*. Morrisville, NC: Lulu, 2008.

Feuer, Alvin B. *The US Navy in World War I: Combat at Sea and in the Air*. Westport, CT: Praeger, 1999.

Fiske, Bradley. *From Midshipman to Rear-Admiral*. New York: Century, 1919.

Friedman, Norman. *Naval Weapons of World War One*. Barnsley, UK: Seaforth, 2011.

Friedman, Norman. *US Submarines through 1945: An Illustrated Design History*. Annapolis, MD: Naval Institute Press, 1995.

Fürbringer, Werner. *FIPS: Legendary U-boat Commander*. Translated by Geoffrey Brooks. Barnsley, UK: Leo Cooper, 1999.

Gannon, Michael. *Operation Drumbeat: The Dramatic True Story of Germany's First U-boat Attacks along the American Coast in World War II*. New York: HarperCollins, 1990.

Gayer, Albert. *Die Deutschen U-Boote in Ihrer Kriegsführung, 1914–1918*. 4 vols. Berlin: Verlag E. S. Mittler & Sohn, 1920–1930.

Gentile, Gary. *USS San Diego: The Last Armored Cruiser*. Philadelphia: Gary Gentile, 1989.

Gerard, James. *My Four Years in Germany*. New York: Grosset & Dunlap, 1917.

Gibson, R. H., and Maurice Prendergast. *The German Submarine War, 1914–1918*. Uckfield, UK: Naval and Military Press, 2003.

Gimblett, Richard H., ed. *The Naval Service of Canada, 1910–2010: The Centennial Story*. Toronto: Dundurn, 2009.

Gleaves, Albert. *A History of the Transport Service: Adventures and Experiences of United States Transports and Cruisers in the World War*. New York: George H. Doran, 1921.

Gray, Edwyn. *A Damned Un-English Weapon: The Story of British Submarine Warfare, 1914–1918*. London: Seeley, Service, 1971.

Gröner, Erich. *German Warships, 1815–1945*. Vol. 2, *U-boats and Mine Warfare Vessels*. Annapolis, MD: Naval Institute Press, 1991.

Guilliatt, Richard, and Peter Hohnen. *The Wolf: The Mystery Raider That Terrorized the Seas during World War I*. New York: Free Press, 2010.

Hadley, Michael L., and Roger Sarty. *Tin-Pots and Pirate Ships: Canadian Naval Forces and German Sea Raiders, 1880–1918*. Montreal: McGill-Queen's University Press, 1991.

Halpern, Paul. *A Naval History of World War I*. Annapolis, MD: Naval Institute Press, 2012.

Hashagen, Ernst. *U-boats Westward!* Translated by Vesey Ross. New York: G. P. Putnam's Sons, 1931.

Heinrich, Thomas. *Ships for the Seven Seas*. Baltimore: Johns Hopkins University Press, 1997.

Herzog, Bodo, and Günter Schomäkers. *Ritter der Graue Wölfe: Die Erfolgreichsten U-Boot-Kommandanten der Welt*. Munich: Verlag Welsermühl, 1976.

Hone, Thomas, and Curtis Utz. *History of the Office of the Chief of Naval Operations, 1915–2015*. Washington, DC: Department of the Navy, Naval History and Heritage Command, 2020.

James, Henry J. *German Subs in Yankee Waters*. New York: Gotham House, 1940.

Karau, Mark. *The Naval Flank of the Western Front: The German Marinekorps Flandern, 1914–1918*. Barnsley, UK: Seaforth, 2003.

Klachko, Mary. *Admiral William Shepherd Benson: First Chief of Naval Operations*. Annapolis, MD: Naval Institute Press, 1987.

Klim, Jake. *Attack on Orleans: The World War I Submarine Raid on Cape Cod*. Charleston, SC: History Press, 2014.

König, Paul. *Voyage of the Deutschland*. New York: Hearst's International Library, 1916.

Langsdorff, Werner von. *U-Boote am Feind: 45 Deutsche U-Boot-Fahrer Erzählen*. Gütersloh, Germany: Verlag C. Bertelsmann, 1937.

Lochner, R. K. *The Last Gentleman of War: The Raider Exploits of the Cruiser Emden*. Annapolis, MD: Naval Institute Press, 1988.

Luebke, Frederick C. *Bonds of Loyalty: German-Americans and World War I*. DeKalb: Northern Illinois University Press, 1974.

Massie, Robert. *Castles of Steel*. New York: Ballantine Books, 2003.

McCartney, Innes. *British Submarines of World War I*. New York: Osprey, 2008.

Messimer, Dwight. *Find and Destroy: Antisubmarine Warfare in World War I*. Annapolis, MD: Naval Institute Press, 2001.

Messimer, Dwight. *The Merchant U-boat: Adventures of the Deutschland, 1916–1918*. Annapolis, MD: Naval Institute Press, 1988.

Moffat, Alexander. *Maverick Navy*. Middletown, CT: Wesleyan University Press, 1976.

Moltke, Eliza von, ed. *Generaloberst Helmuth von Moltke. Erinnerungen, Briefe, Dokumente, 1877–1916: Ein Bild vom Kriegsausbruch, erster Kriegsführung und Persönlichkeit des ersten militärischen Führers des Krieges*. Stuttgart: Der Kommende Tag, 1922.

Nagiewicz, Stephen. *Hidden History of Maritime New Jersey*. Charleston, SC: History Press, 2016.

Neureuther, Karl, and Claus Bergen, eds. *U-boat Stories*. Translated by Eric Sutton. Uckfield, UK: Naval Military Press, 2005.

Nutting, William Washburn. *The Cinderellas of the Fleet*. Jersey City, NJ: Standard Motor Construction, 1920.

Packard, Wyman H. *A Century of US Naval Intelligence*. Washington, DC: US Government Printing Office, 1996.

Perry, Lawrence. *Our Navy in the War*. New York: Charles Scribner's Sons, 1918.

Polmar, Norman, and Kenneth Moore. *Cold War Submarines: The Design and Construction of US and Soviet Submarines, 1945–2001*. Dulles, VA: Potomac Books, 2004.

Rintelen, Franz von. *The Dark Invader: Wartime Reminiscences of a German Naval Intelligence Officer*. New York: Macmillan, 1933.

Robinson, Douglas. *The Zeppelin in Combat: A History of the German Naval Airship Division, 1912–1918*. Sun Valley, CA: John W. Caler, 1971.

Robinson, Markus, and Gertrude Robinson. *Der Kapitän: U-boat Ace Hans Rose*. Gloucestershire, UK: Amberly, 2018.

Rose, Hans. *Auftauchen! Kriegsfahrten von U-53*. Essen, Germany: Essener Verlagsanstalt, 1939.

Rössler, Eberhard. *Die Deutschen U-Kreuzer und Transport U-Boote*. Bonn, Germany: Bernard & Graefe Verlag, 2003.

Rössler, Eberhard. *Die Unterseeboote der Kaiserliche Marine*. Bonn, Germany: Bernard & Graefe Verlag, 1997.

Scheer, Reinhard. *Germany's High Seas Fleet in the Great War*. New York: Peter Smith, 1934.

Schröder, Joachim. *Die U-Boote des Kaisers*. Bonn, Germany: Bernard & Graefe Verlag, 2003.

Sheard, Bradley. *Lost Voyages: Two Centuries of Shipwrecks in the Approaches to New York*. New York: Aqua Quest, 1998.

Silverstone, Paul. *US Warships of World War I*. Garden City, NY: Doubleday, 1970.

Sims, William Sowden. *The Victory at Sea*. New York: Doubleday, Page, 1920.

Spiegel, Edgar von und zu Peckelsheim. *The Adventures of the U-202: An Actual Narrative*. New York: Century, 1917.

Spindler, Arno. *Der Krieg zur See, 1914–1918—Der Handelskrieg mit U-Booten—1 Band*. Berlin: Mittler & Sohn Verlag, 1932.

Spring-Rice, Cecil. *Letters and Friendships*. Vol. 2. Boston: Houghton Mifflin, 1929.

Swope, Herbert Bayard. *Inside the German Empire in the Third Year of the War*. New York: Century, 1917.

Thomas, Lowell. *Raiders of the Deep*. Garden City, NY: Doubleday, Doran, 1928.

Tirpitz, Alfred von. *My Memoirs*. 2 vols. New York: Dodd, Mead, 1919.

Trapp, Georg von. *To the Last Salute*. Lincoln: University of Nebraska Press, 2007.

United States Office of Naval Records and Library. *American Ship Casualties of the World War Including Naval Vessels, Merchant Ships, Sailing Vessels, and Fishing Craft*. Washington, DC: US Government Printing Office, 1923.

United States Office of Naval Records and Library. *Antisubmarine Tactics*. Washington, DC: US Government Printing Office, 1918.

United States Office of Naval Records and Library. *German Submarine Activities on the Atlantic Coast of the United States and Canada*. Publication 1. Washington, DC: US Government Printing Office, 1920.

United States Office of Naval Records and Library. *The Northern Barrage and Other Mining Activities*. Publication 2. Washington, DC: US Government Printing Office, 1920.

Watson, Alexander. *Ring of Steel: Germany and Austria-Hungary in World War I*. New York: Basic Books, 2014.

Weigley, Russell. *The American Way of War: A History of United States Military Strategy and Policy*. Bloomington: Indiana University Press, 1973.

Woofenden, Todd. *Hunters of the Steel Sharks: The Submarine Chasers of WWI*. Bowdoinham, ME: Signal Light Books, 2006.

Deck Logs, War Diaries, and Other Primary Sources

Carnegie Endowment for International Peace Division of International Law, ed. *Official German Documents Relating to the World War*. 2 vols. New York: Oxford University Press, 1923.

Cubberley, Chester, M. A. Cubberley, A. Duncombe, and Earl Reed Silvers. Chester Cubberley Correspondence of the Rutgers College War Service Bureau, 1917–1918. Rutgers University Library, Special Collections and University Archives, New Brunswick, NJ. https://doi.org/doi:10.7282/T3JD50HT.

Deck Log, *SC-71*: March 28, 1918–April 30, 1919. National Archives, Washington, DC.

Deck Log, *SC-73*: March 20, 1918–December 31, 1918, Log 1. National Archives, Washington, DC.

Deck Log, *SC-144*: April 1, 1918–March 31, 1919. National Archives, Washington, DC.

Deck Log, USS *Helvetia* / SP-3096: July 18, 1918–March 1, 1919. National Archives, Washington, DC.

Deck Log, USS *San Diego*: Partial Copy, July 17, 1918. National Archives, Washington, DC.

Deck Log, USS *Stringham* / DD-83: July 2, 1918–June 2, 1922. National Archives, Washington, DC.

Franz, Adolf. *Zum zehnjährigen Gedenktag des Artillerie-Kampfes der deutschen Untersee-Kreuzers U 152 mit dem Amerikanischen Hilfskreuzer und Truppentransport-Dampfers Ticonderoga an atlantisches Ozean am 30 September 1918*. Cuxhaven-Altenbruch, Germany: Freundeskreis Traditionsarchiv Unterseeboote e.V, 1928.

German Submarines in Question and Answer: Navy Department Office of Naval Intelligence, June 1918. Washington, DC: US Government Printing Office, 1918.

Großer Bilderatlas des Weltkrieges: Seekrieg–Amerika–Ferner Osten. Munich: F. Bruckmann Verlag AG, 1918.

Hearing before a Subcommittee on Naval Affairs, United States Senate, Sixty-Sixth Congress, Second Session on Senate Resolution 285, "Awarding of Medals in the Naval Service." Washington, DC: US Government Printing Office, 1920.

Horne, Charles, and Walter Austin, eds. *Source Records of the Great War*. 7 vols. New York: National Alumni, 1923.

Kriegstagebuch SM U-53 für die Zeit der Fernunternehmen von 15 September 1916–28 Oktober 1916. Cuxhaven-Altenbruch, Germany: Freundeskreis Traditionsarchiv Unterseeboote e.V.

Kriegstagebuch SM U-117 Bd. 1: 11 Juli 1918–22 September 1918. Cuxhaven-Altenbruch, Germany: Freundeskreis Traditionsarchiv Unterseeboote e.V.

Kriegstagebuch SM U-140 Bd. 1: 28 Marz 1918–1 Juli 1918. Cuxhaven-Altenbruch, Germany: Freundeskreis Traditionsarchiv Unterseeboote e.V.

Kriegstagebuch SM U-140 Bd. 2: 2 Juli 1918–20 September 1918. Cuxhaven-Altenbruch, Germany: Freundeskreis Traditionsarchiv Unterseeboote e.V.

Kriegstagebuch SM U-151 Bd. 1: 21 Juli 1917–26 Dezember 1917. Cuxhaven-Altenbruch, Germany: Freundeskreis Traditionsarchiv Unterseeboote e.V.

Kriegstagebuch SM U-151: 27 Dezember 1917–18 April 1918. Cuxhaven-Altenbruch, Germany: Freundeskreis Traditionsarchiv Unterseeboote e.V.

Kriegstagebuch SM U-151: 18 April 1918–20 Juli 1918. Cuxhaven-Altenbruch, Germany: Freundeskreis Traditionsarchiv Unterseeboote e.V.

Kriegstagebuch SM U-151: 21 Juli 1918–17 Oktober 1918. Cuxhaven-Altenbruch, Germany: Freundeskreis Traditionsarchiv Unterseeboote e.V.

Kriegstagebuch SM U-152 Bd. 1: 23 Dezember 1917–19 April 1918. Cuxhaven-Altenbruch, Germany: Freundeskreis Traditionsarchiv Unterseeboote e.V.

Kriegstagebuch SM U-152 Bd. 1: 20 April 1918–5 September 1918. Cuxhaven-Altenbruch, Germany: Freundeskreis Traditionsarchiv Unterseeboote e.V.

Kriegstagebuch SM U-152 Bd. 2: 9 September 1918–15 November 1918. Cuxhaven-Altenbruch, Germany: Freundeskreis Traditionsarchiv Unterseeboote e.V.

Kriegstagebuch SM U-155 Bd. 1: 23 Mai 1917–5 August 1917. Cuxhaven-Altenbruch, Germany: Freundeskreis Traditionsarchiv Unterseeboote e.V.

Kriegstagebuch SM U-155 Bd. 3: 11 August 1918–14 November 1918. Cuxhaven-Altenbruch, Germany: Freundeskreis Traditionsarchiv Unterseeboote e.V.

Lloyd's Register of Shipping from 1st July 1917 to the 30th of June 1918. Vol. 2, *Steamers*. London: Lloyd's Register of Shipping.

Oden, Archibald, Jr., ed. *Navy Yearbook 1917 and 1918*. Washington, DC: US Government Printing Office, 1919.

Special Subject Notebook No. 50: USS San Diego. 2 vols. Beach Haven: New Jersey Maritime Museum.

Newspapers

Aberdeen Press and Journal

Asbury Park Press

Baltimore Sun

Evening Star (Washington, DC)

Evening Telegram (St. John's, Newfoundland)

Liverpool Daily Post

New York Times

New York Tribune

South Shore Breaker (Nova Scotia)

St. John's Daily Star

Washington Herald

Washington Times

Periodicals

Calow, Keith. "Rough Justice: The Court Martial of Lieutenant Robert Douglas Legate." *Northern Mariner / Le marin du nord* 15, no. 4 (October 2005).

Furer, J. A. "The 110-Foot Submarine Chasers and Eagle Boats." *United States Naval Institute Proceedings* 45, no. 195 (May 1919).

Herwig, Holger, and David Trask. "The Failure of Imperial Germany's Undersea Offensive against World Shipping, February 1917–October 1918." *The Historian* 33, no. 4 (August 1971).

Jefferson, Mark. "Our Trade in the Great War." *Geographical Review* 3, no. 6 (June 1917).

Kimball, Carol W. "The Top-Secret Decoy." *Sea Classics* 50, no. 12 (December 2017).

Link, Arthur. "President Woodrow Wilson's Plan to Resign in 1916." *Princeton University Library Chronicle* 23, no. 4 (Summer 1962).

Long, Wellington. "The Cruise of the U-53." *United States Naval Institute Proceedings* 92, no. 764 (October 1966).

Online Sources

Blackwood, Henry. "Q-Ship Sinks U-boat—HMS Stonecrop 1917." *Naval Historical Review*, September 1996. https://www.navyhistory.org.au/q-ship-sinks-U-boat-hms-stonecrop-1917/. Accessed May 8, 2021.

Library of Congress Newspaper Collection. https://www.loc.gov/newspapers/.

Memorial University of Newfoundland. Digital Archives Initiative. https://collections.mun.ca/.

Naval History and Heritage Command. https://www.history.navy.mil.

NavSource Naval History. http://www.navsource.org/.

Papers Relating to the Foreign Relations of the United States, Supplement, the World War. Document 1001. Washington, DC: US Government Printing Office, 1916. File no. 763.72111/3847, pp. 765–66. https://history.state.gov/historical-documents/frus1916Supp. Accessed November 9, 2020.

"Pre-WWII Torpedoes of the United Kingdom / Britain." http://www.navweaps.com/Weapons/WTBR_PreWWII.php. Accessed January 2, 2021.

Royal Navy Logbooks of the WW1 Era. https://naval-history.net/.

The Subchaser Archives. https://www.subchaser.org.

U-boat.net. https://uboat.net/.

Wreck Site. https://www.wrecksite.eu.

INDEX

A

A. Piatt Andrew, 184, 185, 343
Agnes B. Holland, 173, 342
Ainsleigh, Charles, 162, 165
Alban, 310
Alberto Treves, 289, 346
Aleda May, 226, 227, 229, 230, 344
Alert, 62
Algeria, 259, 260
Alicke, Rudolf, 316, 319,
Amirault, Louis, 228, 231
Anderson, Edwin, 103
Annie Perry, 173, 342
Ansaldo III, 257, 345
Arabia, 60
Army Coastal Artillery Corps, 219, 231
Arnauld de la Perière, Friedrich von, 308
Arnauld de la Perière, Lothar von, 298, 300–305, 308
Asbury Park Press, 237
Atlantic Fleet (USN), 44, 58, 72, 100, 103, 180, 221, 332
Atlantic Submarine Flotilla, 69
Augusto de Castilho, 304, 305, 347
Augvald, 142, 143, 341
auxiliary cruisers (refer to specific vessel name)
Azores, 81, 84, 85, 88, 92, 93, 95, 97, 98, 145, 278, 279, 282, 290, 293, 298, 304, 319, 321, 322

B

Bacchante-class cruiser, 202
Baden, Prince Maximilian von, 290
Bainbridge-class destroyer, 71, 72, 122, 221, 248
Baltimore, Maryland, 20, 21, 25, 26, 28, 36, 58–61, 99, 100, 120, 124, 128, 135, 266

Barbour, T. R. D., 115, 116
Barclay, Colville, 22
Barnegat, New Jersey, 118, 127, 172, 235–237, 274
Baron Napier, 205,
Bastin, Rene, 213, 214, 218–220, 222, 223, 235, 261, 270
Batt, Alfred E., 260
battleships (refer to specific vessel name)
Bauer, Hermann, 32, 33, 82
Bay of Fundy, 172, 175, 281, 286
Beckmann, Adolf, 200, 201, 226, 230, 231, 233, 234, 238, 245, 248, 254, 255, 258, 264–268, 270–272, 276, 301
Belgian relief ship, 177, 204
Bencleuch, 217
Benson, William, 67, 69, 71, 72, 94, 95, 119, 147, 148, 178, 180, 225, 246, 247, 255, 276, 304
Bergsdalen, 265, 266, 276, 345
Bernstorff, Johann Heinrich von, 26, 53, 58, 67
Bethlehem Steel, 229
Bethmann-Hollweg, Theobald von, 56, 63–65, 177
Bianca, 264, 265, 345
Bjørnstjerne Bjørnson, 307
Block Island, 118
Blommersdijk, 49–52
Bogota, 60
Bradshaw, George, 37
Briarleaf, 322, 323
British blockade, 10, 13, 16–19, 29, 39, 53, 58, 125, 146, 171, 177, 226, 270, 326, 329
British intelligence (see Room 40)
British Major, 205
Brosund, 133, 134

Bureau of Steam Engineering, 336
Burdigala, 282
Bussan, 160
Bylands, 302, 347

C

C. M. Walters, 188, 343
cable cutting, 97, 110, 111, 162, 279, 280, 283, 286, 287, 299, 300
Cacique, 128
Calypso, 31
Caldwell-class destroyer, 209
Canadian Navy (see Royal Canadian Navy)
Cape Charles, 103, 104, 276
Cape Hatteras, 117, 118, 128, 173, 197, 211, 215, 216, 218, 219, 250, 252, 280, 294, 298, 299, 337
Cape Henlopen, 126
Cape Henry, 127–129, 131, 215
Cape May, 11, 78, 109, 116, 118, 127, 136, 138, 220, 241, 242, 257, 289
Capelle, Eduard von, 80
Capto, 215
Carolina, 115–117, 121, 171, 340
Carpenter, Alfred, 17
Cattaro, 296, 297
Chadwick, Francis L., 204, 315
Chaparra, 274, 286, 345
Chase, Jehu Valentine, 273
Chatham Naval Air Station, 150, 164–167
Cheruskia (see *Leixões*)
Chesapeake Bay, 16, 19, 24, 28, 72, 98, 103–105, 124, 128, 220, 252, 326
chief of naval operations (CNO), 68, 69, 71, 72, 93, 94, 101, 119, 147, 152, 178, 225, 246, 255, 276, 304, 328
Chilier, 141, 142, 341
Christian Knudsen, 48, 112
Christy, Harley Hannibal, 158–161
City of Vienna, 153, 331
Clan MacArthur, 293
Clayton W. Walters, 188, 343
Coast Guard Act of 1915, 68

Coast Guard Station, 129, 134, 160, 162, 164, 166, 219, 237
Coastwise routing office, 120
Coffey, M., 208
Commission for Belgian Relief, 177
Connolly, James, 93
Constance, 306, 307, 347
Cook, Frederick, 249
Crenella, 101, 109
Cruiser, 227, 228, 344
cruisers (refer to specific vessel name)
Cubberley, Chester C., 195, 196
Curtiss Aeroplane and Motor Company, 77, 150, 165, 166, 241, 242

D

Dagwell, Charles E., 172
Daniels, Josephus, 67-69, 71, 73, 77, 78, 94, 95, 119, 120, 143, 146, 152, 161, 326, 328, 329, 332
Delaware Bay, 98, 104, 106, 109, 118, 119, 121, 126, 127, 134, 135, 138, 171, 172, 197, 238, 241, 243, 246, 252, 276, 330
Derbyshire, 183
destroyers (refer to specific vessel name)
Deutsche Ozean-Reederei, 18–20, 81
Diamond Shoals Lightship, 217, 218, 225, 344
Dictator, 8, 145, 341
Diomed, 260–262, 276, 344
Dönitz, Karl, 333, 337, 338
Doon, 123
Dornfontein, 172, 173, 176, 184, 342
Dorothy B. Barrett, 241, 243, 330, 345
Doucette, Fred, 227, 231
Dröscher, Otto, 14, 15, 197, 198, 200–202, 204, 205, 208–211, 217, 225–228, 230, 231, 233-235, 238, 241–246, 248–260, 263–269, 271, 272, 274, 275, 276, 294, 301, 324, 334
Dwinsk, 139–144, 328, 332, 341
dynamometer (for cable cutting), 110, 111, 286

E

E. B. Walters, 188, 343
E. P. Jones, 160
Earl and Nettie, 226, 227, 344
Eastern Forwarding Company, 25, 62
Eaton, Phillip, 150, 166
Eckelmann, Erich, 278–280
Edna, 106, 107, 114, 125, 340
Edward H. Cole, 113, 114, 340
Edward R. Baird, 122, 123, 125, 341
Eidsvold, 123–125, 127, 128, 132, 341
Eisenhauer, Irvin, 231, 266,
ELCO (Electric Launch Company), 74
Elizabeth von Belgie, 177
Ellen Benzo, 307
Elsie Porter, 230, 231, 266, 345
Emergency Naval Fund, 70
Erik, 187, 188, 343
Espagne, 257
Evans, David, 181–183
evaporator (see fresh water generator)

F

Faroe Islands, 34, 269, 307
Fechter, Hans, 300, 301, 303, 305
Feldt, Richard, 151, 153–157, 162–164, 166, 170–178, 180–188, 190, 191, 193, 194, 202, 248, 276
Felix Taussig, 276, 277
Feltore, 314
Fenwick Island, Delaware, 246, 248, 273, 274
First Yale Unit, 160
Fiske, Bradley, 67–69
Flandre, 257
Florence Olson, 172
Florida, 153
Ford Eagle Boat, 76, 180
Fort Hancock, 231–233, 237, 238
Francis J. O'Hara Jr., 185, 343
France, 282, 309
Frank H. Buck, 262
Franz, Adolf, 298, 306–316, 319–325, 348
Frederic R. Kellogg, 195, 196, 235–237, 274, 328, 345

fresh water generator, 83, 201
Fulcher, Junius, 318, 319, 323–325
Fulker, G. C., 41, 42, 44
Funchal, Madeira, 163

G

Gamo, 281, 282, 346
Gansser, Konrad, 151, 163
gas shells (see poison gas)
George W. Truitt, Jr., 137
Gerard, James, 56, 64, 66, 331
Germaniawerft, 18, 20, 80, 82, 86, 200, 276, 279
Gilmore, C. W., 106, 107
Gladys M. Hollett, 173, 343
Gleaves, Albert, 44, 45, 48, 50, 71, 160
Glenlee, 144
Gloaming, 190, 343
Gordon Castle, 138
Greene, C. L., 242, 243
Grey, Edward, 27, 55, 56, 59, 69
Gulf of Suez, 60
Gurney, John, 61-63, 65

H

Halifax, Nova Scotia, 29, 40, 52, 173–176, 264, 265, 280, 284–288, 298
Hall, Reginald, 93, 94, 287
Hardegan, Reinhard, 337
Harpathian, 125, 126, 341
Hattie Dunn, 105, 107, 114, 136, 340
Hattie Gage, 153
Hauppauge, 105–108, 111, 114, 340
Helgoland, 23, 31, 33, 35, 38
Hellferich, Karl, 66
Henrik-Lund, 133, 341
Henry Woermann (see *Uberaba*)
Herbert L. Pratt, 118, 119, 121, 340
Herman Winter, 181
Hersing, Otto, 14, 296
Hertling, Georg von, 289
High Seas Fleet, 31–33, 63, 67
Hindenburg, Paul von, 64, 289
Hinsch, Frederick, 25, 62
HMCS *Cartier*, 189, 190

HMCS *Grilse*, 285, 286
HMCS *Hochelaga*, 189, 190
HMCS *Stadacona*, 189
HMS *Mantua*, 37
HMS *Marksman*, 193
HMS *Perth*, 301, 302, 347
HMS *Tuberose* (see *Mauretania*)
Hohenzollern, Wilhelm II, 33, 65, 66, 93, 290, 325
Hohenzollern, Heinrich, 79–81
Høie, Hans, 143
Holbrook, C. E., 105, 107
Holtzendorff, Henning, von, 34, 64, 92, 121
Holtzendorff Memorandum, 64, 92
House, Edward, 69
Howard, Edward, 165, 166
HS-1L seaplane, 78, 150, 151, 165
HS-2L seaplane, 78, 241, 242, 244
Hughes, Charles Evan, 57
Huntress, 99–102
Huntsend, 129
hydrophones, 75, 244, 285

I

Industrial, 289, 290, 346
Infanta Isabel de Borbon, 100, 184
Isabel B. Wiley, 112, 113, 340

J

J. J. Flaherty, 188, 343
Jacob M. Haskell, 113, 340
James, Henry, 164, 167, 168, 181, 332, 333
Jennings, Allyn, 119
Jenny, Belmont Joseph von, 121
Johansen, Johannes, 123, 132
Jonancy, 101, 109
Joseph Cudahy, 203
Jutland (see Skagerrak)

K

Kaiser Wilhelm II (person, see Hohenzollern)
Kaiser Wilhelm II (vessel, see USS *Agamemnon*)

Kaltenborn, Axel, 133
Kamilla Rickmers (see USS *Ticonderoga*)
Kanguru, 163
Katie L. Palmer, 228–231, 345
Kiel Mutiny, 278, 294, 305, 324, 325
Knight, Austin M., 43–46
Kansan, 47, 48
Keemun, 135, 136
Kermanshah, 207, 208
Kingfisher, 287, 288, 346
Knöckel, Paul Richard, 155, 169, 170, 172, 174, 178, 181, 184, 188
Knudsen, Waldemar, 112
Koch, von (*FdU* U-Cruiser Flotilla), 95, 199, 202
Köln (see USS *Amphion*)
Kölnische Volkszeitung, 149, 338
König, Paul, 16, 18, 19–21, 23–26, 28–30, 33, 36, 37, 58–63, 66, 85, 174, 278
Kophamel, Waldemar, 88-91, 95, 96, 197–199, 202–214, 216–224, 235, 239–241, 246, 252, 253, 257, 260–263, 269–271, 274–276, 279, 294, 300, 301, 312, 324, 334
Körner, Frederick, 16, 96, 98, 99, 101, 102, 105, 107, 109, 110, 113–115, 122, 124, 125, 127, 130, 131, 133, 134, 137, 139–141, 333
Kringsjaa, 136, 138, 341
Kronprinzessin Cecile (see USS *Mount Vernon*)

L

Lackawanna, 182
Lake, Simon, 36, 134
Lansford, 162, 165, 342
Lansing, Robert, 22, 57, 67
Lathigee, Robert, 114
Leary, C. F., 291, 293
Legate, Robert Douglas, 189, 190
Leixões, 283, 287, 346
Lingard, Eric, 150, 151, 165, 166
Llanstephan Castle, 135, 136
Lowry, K.B, 114, 115
Lucia, 291–293, 346
Lucille Schnare, 186, 343

Ludendorff, Eric, 64, 289
Luger pistol, 113
Lusitania, 10, 15, 24, 51, 69, 89
Luz Blanca, 174–176, 343

M

Madison, James J., 314
Madrugada, 249, 250, 253, 345
Malden, 160
Manin, 302, 347
Malte, 91
MAN Diesels, 81, 336
Mantilla, 128
Manx King, 155, 156, 342
Marcussen, Sven, 253–255
Marina, 56, 60
Marinha Portuguesa (Portuguese Navy), 304
Marion Adams, 188, 343
Marinekorps Flandern, 323
Mark IV bomb, 166, 167
Marosa, 155, 156, 342
Marshall, Thomas, 57
Mary E. Sennett, 227, 228, 345
Mauretania, 203, 304, 309
Mayo, Henry T., 180, 332
McAloney, William, 215, 216
McCumber, Porter James, 186
McGuirk, Henry Francis, 190
McKean, Josiah, 71
Melita, 205
Merak, 216–218, 344
Mequita, Joseph P., 185
Merritt, William, 241–244
Messina, 321, 322, 347
Meusel, Karl, 85–88, 91, 95, 96, 278, 279
Michelsen, Andreas, 305
Midgett, John Allen, 252
Midgett, Leroy, 252
Milton, J. P., 159
Minenskizze (mine map), 233
Mirlo, 250, 251, 345
ML boats, 74, 301, 302
Moffat, Alexander, 73
Monmouth, 282

Moorish Prince, 319
Muller, Frank, 318, 323–325
Müller, Karl von, 129, 151, 154, 186
Muriel, 173, 342
Murray, Oswyn, 147

N

Nantucket Lightship, 46–49, 66, 197, 211, 224, 240
Naval Act of 1916, 69, 70, 77
Naval Appropriations Act, 70, 73
Naval Bureau of Construction and Repair, 74
Naval Coastal Defense Reserve, 70
naval district:
    1st, 100, 167, 171, 173, 176, 246
    2nd, 100, 173, 246, 256
    3rd, 100, 160, 161, 173, 204, 235, 246, 237
    4th, 100, 118, 136, 173, 235, 237, 242, 244, 246, 287
    5th, 100, 102, 120, 131, 137, 152, 173, 180, 215, 221, 246, 287
    6th, 100, 173, 180, 219, 246
    7th, 100, 119, 173, 246
    8th, 100, 173, 284
    9th, 100
    15th, 100
Naval Overseas Transport Service, 144, 274
NDL, 16, 18, 19, 24, 25, 36, 59
Nebel-U-boots-Anlage (N.U.A), 97, 154
Neckar, 25, 61
Nelson, Henry, 139, 141
Nelson A., 173, 342
Nevasa, 145, 288, 289
New York City, 41, 66, 97, 105, 110, 114, 121, 129, 133, 134, 136, 138, 153, 156–158, 175, 180, 197, 205, 210, 211, 231, 233, 249, 253, 260, 276, 284, 286, 289, 319, 321, 337
Newbolt, Henry, 327
Newby Hall, 284
Newcombe, H. G., 114
Newport, Rhode Island, 33, 34, 38–42, 44, 46, 48, 49, 52, 54, 55, 58

Nichols, Neil E., 223
Nicholson, 124, 125, 145
Norddeutscher Lloyd (see NDL)
Nordhav, 253–255, 257, 264, 345
Nordstrom, George W., 212–215
Northern Barrage, 23, 87, 154, 191–193, 199, 270, 281, 293, 300, 306, 324
Nostitz und Jänckendorf, Heinrich von, 16, 92, 96, 98–119, 121–148, 151, 152, 154, 155, 162, 171, 172, 191, 193, 201, 202, 230, 248, 286, 298, 326, 329–331, 337
Notre Dame de la Garde, 186, 187, 343
Nutting, William Washburn, 74
Nyanza, 101, 109

O

O. B. Jennings, 211–215, 218, 344
Olaf Maersk, 204
Old Time, 227, 228, 344
Operation *Paukenschlag*, 333, 337, 338
Orleans, Massachusetts, 151, 162, 164, 166, 167
Ostend, 74, 323
Osterley, 207
Otter Paravanes, 158, 251
Overfalls lightship, 109, 118, 126
Oxfordshire, 293

P

Page, Walter, 54, 55
Pan-American Oil and Transport Company, 195
Pasadena, 186, 343
Pastuszyk, Paul, 298
Patterson, G. E., 323
Paulding-class destroyer, 209
Penistone, 180, 181, 183, 184, 343
Perth Amboy, 162–165, 170, 342
Petersen, Alfred, 143
Philippines, 56, 72
Phillips, William, 27
Pinar del Rio, 130, 131, 133, 341
Pistor, *1st Artillerie-Offizier Korvettenkapitän*, 303

Pleiades, 262
poison gas, 218, 219
Pola Flotilla, 88, 197
Polk, Frank, 26, 27, 54–56
Pomone, 282, 283
Poole gun, 74
Port Said, 98, 99, 101
Porto, 206, 227, 344
Poseidon, 99, 125
Potentate, 266, 345
POW camp, 145, 213
Prize Crew (*Prisenkommando*), 52, 81, 85, 105, 106, 113, 115, 131, 133, 142, 155, 169, 170, 172, 173, 178, 182, 183–186, 188, 307, 320
Progress, 226, 344
Pyrrhus, 235, 237

Q

Q-ships (in general, refer to vessel name for specifics), 22–24, 30, 37, 48, 89, 143, 147, 255,

R

R-9 seaplane, 77, 166
Radeoleine, 122
Reginolite, 288
Reliance, 226, 228, 344
Ringelman, Gustav, 314, 316
Rintelen, Franz von, 57
Rio Cavado, 303, 305, 347
Risberg, Eric, 259, 260
Rob Roy, 173, 342
Robert and Richard, 169, 171, 172, 206, 342
Room 40, 95, 151, 171, 193, 205, 287
Roosevelt, Franklin Delano, 67
Rose, 162, 167
Rose, Hans, 21, 31–35, 37–40, 42–53, 55, 56, 58, 66, 70, 81, 83, 87, 201, 331
Royal Canadian Navy, 11, 176, 189, 190
Royal Navy, 17, 23, 24, 29, 31, 36, 40, 52, 61, 71, 74, 77, 94, 97, 138, 191, 193, 203, 300, 322, 334, 335, 339
Rügen, 99, 146, 300, 305, 306, 309

Rumpel, Walter, 31
Rush, 265, 345

S

Saba (see *Pinar del Rio*)
Sable Island, 175, 206, 280, 283, 286, 288, 300
Samuel C. Mengel, 118, 119, 340
Samoa, 136–138, 341
San Jose, 182, 183, 186, 264, 343
San Miguel, 304
San Saba, 274, 345
Sandy Hook (New Jersey), 141, 184, 232, 233, 236–238, 259, 260, 274
Scheer, Reinhard, 31–35, 63, 64
Schleswig, 16, 19
Schrader, Otto von, 325
Schröder, Ludwig von, 323
Schwab, Charles, 229
Schwartzkopf, Karl, 21, 35
Schwieger, Walther, 14, 89
Seal Island, 173
Second Happy Time (see Operation *Paukenschlag*)
secret U-boat bases, 13, 120, 121
section patrol boats:
 SP-*136*, 153
 SP-*544*, 242
 SP-*590*, 153
 SP-*735*, 168
Seyffertitz, Hugo von, 297
Shaw, C. Raymond, 245
Shields, Edward, 165
Sims, William Sowden, 10, 71, 72, 74, 77, 78, 87, 93, 94, 98, 119, 123, 127, 143, 146, 147, 151, 152, 153, 167, 171, 178, 194, 198, 225, 229, 230, 238, 239, 247, 274, 275, 280, 283, 285, 287, 294, 304, 306, 326, 327–331, 336, 337
Skagerrak (Jutland), 164, 271, 306, 312, 325
Smith, Clifton, 51
Smith, Robert H., 207, 208
Smith Island, North Carolina, 219

SMS Emden, 10, 129, 151, 154
SMS Geier (see *USS Schurz*)
SMS Hamburg, 33
SMS Hannover, 272
SMS Kronprinz Wilhelm (see *USS Von Steuben*)
SMS Prinz Heinrich, 325
SMS Rio Negro, 85
SMS Thüringen, 312
SMS Zähringen, 83
Sommerstad, 234, 235, 237, 345
Sophia, 283, 346
Snowdonian, 87
Spiegel von und zu Peckelsheim, Edgar von, 13
Sprengpatronen, 113, 115, 132, 155, 173, 181, 185, 254, 264, 266, 321
Spring-Rice, Cecil, 18, 27
spy, 121, 213, 214
Standard Motor Company, 74
Standard Oil, 213
Stephano, 51–54
Stillman, William T., 195, 196
Stirling, Yates Jr., 58, 59, 139–141
Stanley M. Seaman, 215, 216, 344
Stonecrop (other aliases *Glenfoyle* and *Winona*), 89
Stortind, 282, 346
Strathdene, 47, 48
Sucena, Joaquim F., 283
Svarfard, 281
Studt, Ferdinand, 278–286, 288–291, 293, 294, 332
submarines, American:
 D-2, 41, 42
 E-2, 255–257
 L-5, 134, 135
 N-5, 276, 277
 O-6, 220, 221
 V-4 Argonaut, 336
 V-5 Narwhal, 336
 V-6 Nautilus, 336
submarines, Austro-Hungarian:
 SM U-14, 296
 SM U-5, 296
 SM U-47, 297

submarines, British:
    G-13, 37
    H-5, 31
    L-8, 193, 194
submarines, German (see U-boats)
submarine chasers:
    SC-71, 241, 242, 244, 245
    SC-73, 244, 245
    SC-77, 73
    SC-132, 126
    SC-144, 244, 245
    SC-187, 215
    SC-209, 276, 277, 328
    SC-210, 245
    SC-234, 131
    SC-294, 321
Surprise, 163
Sussex Pledge, 47, 49, 52, 55, 56, 63, 64
Swasey, Albert Loring, 74
Swope, Herbert Bayard, 66
Sydland, 177-179, 182, 343
Sydney B. Atwood, 173, 342
Sylvania, 186, 343

T

T. McAvity & Son Munition Factory, 281
T. A. Scott Jr., 61–63
Tampico, 157, 174, 195, 235
Tapley, J. P., 163
Texel, 114, 115, 340
Thebaud, Leo, 220
Thespis, 258
Thorbjørnsen, Hans, 182
Tirpitz, Alfred von, 64
Tokuyama Maru, 210, 211, 344
Tortuguero, 151, 342
Trapp, Georg von, 296, 297
Triumph, 183–187, 189, 343
Trotha, Adolf von, 33, 38

U

U-boats (World War I era):
    SM U-12, 308
    SM U-14, 15

SM U-20, 14, 15, 24, 197
SM U-21, 14, 296
SM U-24, 24
SM U-33, 151
SM U-35, 10, 197, 298
SM U-38, 24, 163
SM U-51, 31, 33
SM U-53, 10, 21, 31, 33–40, 42–55, 58, 63, 70, 74, 79, 81, 87, 98, 112, 325, 331
SM U-55, 56
SM U-57, 58, 61
SM U-81, 21
SM U-88, 89
SM U-91, 271
SM U-100, 271
SM U-111, 335
SM U-117, 14, 81, 83, 97, 134, 135, 172, 194, 196–198, 200, 201, 204–206, 208–211, 214, 225–255, 257–260, 263–276, 286, 287, 294, 298, 299, 301, 310, 329, 330, 334–337, 344
SM U-139, 80, 81, 83, 193, 275, 293, 297, 298, 300–306, 309, 324, 326, 330, 336, 337, 347
SM U-140, 80, 81, 134, 135, 172, 173, 178, 180, 194, 196, 198–200, 202-208, 210, 211, 213–219, 221–225, 227, 235, 239, 243, 245, 253, 257, 258, 260–262, 269–271, 275, 276, 279, 287, 294, 298, 300, 301, 310, 329, 335, 336, 344
SM U-151, 15, 16, 84, 88–92, 95–119, 121–128, 130–149, 151, 152, 157, 161, 162, 171, 172, 193, 197, 198, 201, 208, 215, 227, 231, 248, 277–279, 286, 288, 293, 294, 298–300, 306, 308, 326, 329, 330, 332, 333, 337, 338, 340
SM U-152, 15, 84, 92, 280, 298–300, 306–312, 314–316, 318–326, 330, 347

SM U-153, 84, 293, 298–300, 308, 326, 330
SM U-155, 80, 83–88, 262, 278–294, 298, 299, 306, 319, 325, 330, 332, 346
SM U-156, 15, 84, 92, 145, 146, 151–157, 160, 162–166, 168, 169, 171–178, 180–190, 193, 194, 196–198, 202, 206–208, 215, 225, 231, 233, 235, 239, 245, 264, 270, 276, 330–332, 342
SM U-157, 84, 92, 100, 163, 184, 306
SM U-161, 193
U-Bremen, 21, 29, 30, 33, 35–39, 43, 53, 58
U-Deutschland, 10, 20–30, 33, 35, 36, 38, 57–63, 65, 74, 79, 82, 83, 85, 86, 88, 91–93, 95–98, 120, 139, 151, 201, 277, 278, 280, 294
U-Oldenburg, 84, 88, 95
SM UB-68, 333
SM UB-87, 271
SM UB-88, 335
SM UB-148, 335
SM UC-25, 333
SM UC-43, 37
SM UC-97, 335
U-boats (World War II era):
　U-66, 337
　U-109, 337
　U-123, 337
　U-125, 337
　U-130, 338
Uberaba, 221, 223
Uda A. Saunders, 185, 343
Ugland Family, 129, 131
Umbria, 215
unrestricted submarine warfare, 14, 17, 47, 63–67, 217, 231
Unterseekreuzer Flotilla, 95, 199
Uppland, 204
US Army Air Force, 335, 337

US Railroad Administration, 330
USS *Agamemnon*, 202
USS *Albany*, 211
USS *Amphion*, 290, 291, 346
USS *Balch*, 52
USS *Bainbridge*, 71, 72, 122, 221, 248
USS *Cassin*, 70, 71
USS *Charles Whittemore*, 256, 276
USS *Charleston*, 101, 103
USS *Clemson*, 71
USS *Colhoun*, 172
USS *Columbia*, 144
USS *Cyclops*, 319
USS *Dochra*, 144
USS *Ericsson*, 52
USS *Fairfax*, 292, 293
USS *Freehold*, 274
USS *Galveston*, 204, 312, 314, 315
USS *George G. Henry*, 311, 312, 347
USS *George Washington*, 202
USS *Harrisburg*, 156, 157, 180, 202
USS *Hawaiian*, 291–293
USS *Helvetia*, 255–257
USS *Hull*, 122, 123, 215, 221, 330
USS *Israel*, 273
USS *Jouett*, 204
USS *Kearsarge*, 253
USS *Kingfisher*, 242, 243, 245
USS *Lake Bridge*, 154, 193
USS *Lake Forest*, 144, 145
USS *Louisiana*, 111
USS *Maui*, 160
USS *Mayrant*, 209
USS *McClellan*, 145
USS *Minneapolis*, 145
USS *Minnesota*, 11, 272–274, 328, 345
USS *Mount Vernon*, 202, 282
USS *New Hampshire*, 111, 112
USS *New York*, 11
USS *O'Brien*, 70
USS *Ohio*, 111, 112
USS *Pastores*, 239–241
USS *Patterson*, 138, 287, 289
USS *Paul Jones*, 72, 137, 220, 221
USS *Perkins*, 209

USS *Rathburne*, 128
USS *Robert H. McCurdy*, 256
USS *Saetia*, 274, 328, 345
USS *San Diego*, 9, 11, 157–161, 172, 174, 184, 194, 196, 234, 251, 273, 328, 342
USS *Schurz*, 153, 161
USS *South Carolina*, 131
USS *Stringham*, 221–223, 245, 276, 330
USS *Tacoma*, 126
USS *Teal*, 274
USS *Texas*, 11
USS *Ticonderoga*, 11, 281, 312–316, 319, 320, 323, 328, 347, 348, 349, 354, 355
USS *Tingey*, 176
USS *Tucker*, 71
USS *Von Steuben*, 139–141, 145, 208, 332
USS *West Haven*, 190
USS *Wickes*, 71, 221
USS *Winslow*, 51

V

Vail, William, 311
Valentiner, Max, 163
Varley, Cromwell, 31
Verna D. Adams, 188, 343
Villareal (see *Pinar del Rio*)
Vindeggen, 129–133, 139, 201, 341
Vinland, 127, 128, 341
Vitruvia, 207
Vogel, E. W., 115, 116
Vulkan Werke, 200, 271, 276

W

Walter d'Noyes, 134
Waltham, 104
War Plan Black, 67
War Ranee, 267–269
Werner, H. W., 115
West Point, 48, 49
Wharton, Robert, 169–171
White, C. H., 195, 236
Wilhelmshaven, 14, 31–33, 36, 58

Willehad, 61
William H. Starbuck, 226, 227, 344
William Green, 241, 242, 246
Williams, Elijah, 150, 164
Williams, William Roose, 251
Willie G., 188
Wilson, Woodrow, 47, 55, 57, 64–69, 72, 169, 290
Wimble Shoals, 250, 299
Winneconne, 112, 114, 136, 340
Winona (see *Stonecrop*)
Winslow, Stephen McRae, 118
Winter Quarter Lightship, 249, 250
Withey, W. E., 62
Wood, Spencer, 171
Workers and Soldiers' Council, 305
Wright, Carroll, 220

Y

Y-gun, 75, 168

Z

Zeebrugge, 17, 74, 308, 323
zeppelins, 17, 32, 38, 65, 297, 308
  L-13, 32
  L-17, 38
Zimmermann, Arthur, 66
Zimmermann Telegram, 67